IMAGERY AND CREATIVITY

IMAGERY
&
CREATIVITY

Ethnoaesthetics and Art Worlds
in the Americas

edited by

Dorothea S. Whitten and
Norman E. Whitten, Jr.

THE UNIVERSITY OF ARIZONA PRESS
TUCSON & LONDON

The University of Arizona Press
Copyright © 1993
The Arizona Board of Regents
All rights reserved

⊚ This book is printed on acid-free, archival-quality paper.
Manufactured in the United States of America

98 97 96 95 94 93   6 5 4 3 2 1

Library of Congress Cataloging-in-Publication Data

Imagery and creativity : ethnoaesthetics and art worlds in the
   Americas / edited by Dorothea S. Whitten and Norman E. Whitten, Jr.
      p. cm.
    Includes bibliographical references and index.
    ISBN 0-8165-1247-7
    1. Ethnic art — America.   2. Ethnic art — South America.   3. Art,
Primitive — America.   4. Art, Primitive — South America.   I. Whitten,
Dorothea S.,   II. Whitten, Norman E., Jr.
  N6501.I42   1993
  700'.89'97–dc20   92-25853
                                 CIP

British Cataloguing-in-Publication Data
A catalogue record for this book is available from the British Library.

This book is dedicated to all the people of the Americas
whose aesthetic forces inform our museums, videos,
films, magazines, books, and journals, and
whose names and identities more often
than not remain unrecorded.

"The artist touches the eternal infinite and relates it to the
observer, who sees it, touches it himself, discovers himself
in the midst of it."
                                                    Peter Minshall

"Let nothing or nobody interfere with the creative
process."
                                                    Carl Beam

"Yachaj awashca, sumaj"
['knowledgeably made, beautiful']   Clara Santi Simbaña

CONTENTS

1

Introduction

Dorothea S. Whitten and Norman E. Whitten, Jr.

Artistic expressions are embedded in specific cultures and traditions yet possess aesthetic force that is understandable cross-culturally through time and under changing circumstances. One purpose of this book is to illuminate the ways by which various forms of artistic expression reflect universal human imagery and creativity. More specifically, this book focuses on the graphic, narrative, and performance arts of peoples of the Americas. The authors present an array of contemporary and ancient arts within North, Central, and South America and the Caribbean. From the varied backgrounds of contemporary ethnography, ethnohistory, and archaeology, seemingly disparate essays converge on the second purpose of this book: to address the basic problem of understanding culturally patterned creative expressions caught up in art worlds, which are institutionalized patterns among artists, art promoters, and consumers that inevitably involve, to some degree, politico-economic power and control (Becker 1982).

Most of the contributors deal with various contemporary people who share a legacy of formative European mercantilist-capitalist expansion, colonial domination and hegemony, and eventually nation-state domination.[1] Two authors offer the deep time perspective of the cultural heritages of the Central Andes and Mesoamerica, examining artistic traditions that are today part and parcel of both national prehistory and anthropological knowledge. These papers prompt us to think about the icon-making forebears of contemporary New World peoples and to work against the polarity that separates modern ethnography from archaeology.

The people whose creativity and imagery constitute the substance of this book are depicted in four different ways: a general survey of the arts of a region; intensive studies of the aesthetic genres and styles of a culture; examinations of the historical and ethnohistorical features of artistic and cultural hegemony; and reconstructions of life histories in cultural context. The contemporary people portrayed include Native American artists of Canada and the southwestern United States, the Saramaka Maroons of Suriname, Trinidadian carnival designers, and the Canelos Quichua of Amazonian Ecuador. Other essays deal with the relationships of ancient indigenous iconographies and systems of power and with appropriations of indigenous art by Western museums and art markets.

This book grew out of a symposium, Imagery and Creativity, held at the Krannert Art Museum of the University of Illinois, Urbana-Champaign, in the spring of 1988. The symposium was held in conjunction with an art exhibition entitled From Myth to Creation: Art from Amazonian Ecuador. The exhibition was highly specific, focusing from an ethnoaesthetic perspective on one of hundreds of cognate cultures worldwide. It displayed the material culture of a vibrant, dynamic, future-oriented people who possess great consciousness of their indigenous past. The presentation was based on indigenous concepts of beauty, knowledge, power, and value as embodied in the graphic arts, especially ceramics. These concepts were related to salient issues in Western discourse with regard to understanding different and contrasting modalities of thought. A companion book, also entitled *From Myth to Creation* (Whitten and Whitten 1988), illustrates the specific dimensions of imagery and creativity within the rich diversity and complexity of Upper Amazonian Canelos Quichua life and culture. The symposium was designed to highlight the general dimensions and concepts of imagery and creativity portrayed in the exhibition.

The ethnoaesthetic perspective, especially as developed by Sally Price and Richard Price (e.g., 1980) insists on presenting the art and aesthetics of non-Western cultures from the standpoint of the creators themselves (see Dark 1978 and Silver 1979 for reviews of the development of ethnoaesthetics). This perspective follows the definitions given by Hatcher (1985:246), and it can provide information for the comparative studies suggested by Hatcher (1985:2) and Dark (1967:132). Dark (1967:144) stressed the necessity of studying the totality of the context of art to understand its symbolic structure and integration with other domains of culture. The approach that the Prices and we advance also stresses the importance of communicating this knowledge to our own and other cultures if one is to become "a spokesman for people who have not yet had the opportunity to speak directly for themselves" (Price and Price 1980:188). To communicate across cultural boundaries, this perspective promotes the understanding and appreciation of unique aesthetic traditions and art forms in their social and cultural milieus (see Maquet 1979 [1971]; Maquet 1986:151–59; Sieber and Walker 1989:12–27). By using this approach, the exhibition From Myth to Creation (Whitten and Whitten 1988), like that of the Prices' *Afro-American Arts of the Suriname Rain Forest* (Price and Price 1980), was designed to show how art, myth, ritual, and narrative discourse could transcend their specific cultural traditions to communicate with other audiences.[2]

The symposium format was not organized specifically around ethnoaesthetics. Rather, we cast a wide net to find current research dealing with human imagery and creativity. Perhaps unsurprisingly, symposium participants seemed quite divergent, yet they shared nearly consensual interests. It was apparent that all the participants were committed to the idea that aesthetic force transcends time, space, traditions, and cultural boundaries. Human beings create works that have "an affecting presence" (Armstrong 1971:25), an autonomous power to affect, which we take to be aesthetic force. Symposium participants eschewed many prevalent polarities regarding art and instead concentrated on the kaleidoscopic aesthetic force that emerges when "human artistic creation transcends location and time" (Clifford 1988:242).[3]

Prominent among shared interests was the strong desire to communicate to an outside audience the inner meanings generated by creators from diverse cultures. Paralleling this ethnoaesthetic focus was a multifaceted interest in the relations between indigenous arts and nonindigenous worlds: outside influence, direct or incipient, on inner creativity and style, on creation and production, on acquisition and consumption, and on the immediate and ultimate fate of indigenous arts in varied contexts.

This latter mutual concern led to the second grounding concept of this book: art worlds. Developed by Howard Becker in his book *Art Worlds* (1982), this concept refers to the organized sets of relationships existing among artists, their products, promoters, and consumers. Art worlds shift and change but focus primarily on "art utilities," such as aesthetic appreciation, collection, and display, rather than on the creative expression of artists. Becker's exploration of the many dimensions and ramifications of the institutional relations that exist among producers and consumers of art relates directly to an emerging theme of the symposium: appropriation.[4] The appropriation of art and aesthetics refers to processes whereby ideas and artifacts, which were created as part of culturally specific social transactions, are moved to a realm wherein ownership and even the control of skills are determined by people other than the artists or artisans themselves. Such processes appear to be part and parcel of the development of art worlds around any given genre of human creativity.

Although Becker does not include indigenous arts in his examples, he analyzes many problems and topics that were discussed in the symposium. He applies sociological theory to those who control institutions that promote and authenticate "art":

> By shifting the locus of the definitional problem from something inherent in the object to a relation between the object and an entity called an art world, the institutional theory provided a new justification for the activities of contemporary artists, and an answer to the philosophically distressing questions leveled at their work, which asked for a demonstration of skill or beauty, thought or emotion, in the works regarded as excellent, and which wanted to know if the same works could not have been produced by a chimpanzee, child, insane person, or any ordinary member of the society without particular artistic talent. . . .
>
> We see, too, that in principle any object or action can be legitimated as art, but that in practice every art world has procedures and rules governing legitimation which, while not clear-cut or foolproof, nevertheless make the success of some candidates for the status of art very unlikely. Those procedures and rules are contained in the conventions and patterns of cooperation by which art worlds carry on their routine activities. (Becker 1982:162–63)

The contemporary peoples discussed in this book are not all clearly of the "Fourth World" in the strictest sense of Nelson Graburn's definition, but they share the features of being national minorities living in countries that are economically dependent on a world system characterized by Euroamerican hegemony.[5] It seems appropriate, then, to consider Graburn's statement that the study of the art and narrative of Fourth World peoples (and here we include the forebears of the actual Fourth World people) "must take into account more than one symbolic and aesthetic system, and the fact that the arts may be produced by one group for consumption by another . . . is, par excellence, the study of *changing* arts — of emerging ethnicities, modifying identities, and commercial and colonial stimuli and repressive actions" (Graburn 1976:2).

These and related issues and themes are addressed by the various authors who deal with the imagery and creativity of indigenous and Afro-American New World people. By treating common issues ethnographically, ethnohistorically, and archaeologically, these themes may be highlighted in one essay, muted but present in an ensuing essay, and come to the fore again later.

Imagery, Creativity, and Reflexivity

Imagery, creativity, and reflexivity, as we use these terms, constitute a tripartite construct of mental processes that develop in human interaction and that characterize the human psyche. Historically, we prefer to combine Charles Horton Cooley's stress on affectivity with George Herbert Mead's emphasis on cognition to place the processes of imagery, creativity, and reflexivity in a "matrix of social relations and interactions among individuals" (Mead 1974:223n) as this occurs within cultural contexts.

Imagery is, quite simply, the corpus of images — concrete and allusive, stable and changing, patterned and chaotic, mimetic and inventive — developed by individuals from many sources in the course of their interactions. People draw on this corpus to create; creativity is the execution or expression of imagery, the communication of inner imagery to others.[6] Reflexivity is the inward-looking process that involves the incorporation, integration, and interpretation of social interaction experiences (see Babcock 1980,

1987). It is a mediator between inner imagery and the outward expression of creativity, and it is central to the highly complex, continuous feedback that occurs in self-other interactions. As Mead noted long ago, the individual can take the attitude of significant others toward himself (Mead 1959) through reflexivity (our substitution for his "reflexiveness"), which is the turning back of the social experience of others upon oneself.

The fluid interdependence of imagery, reflexivity, and creativity may be seen in a seemingly individual act of personal adornment, as noted by Simmel (Wolff 1950:339), and in complex, culturally patterned expressions of "weeping that moves women to song," and "song that moves men to tears" described by Feld (1982:86–129, 163–216). We hope that these constructs will further the ethnoaesthetic approach, for we agree with the Prices that "learning how to look at, understand, and fully appreciate an artistic creation depends on knowing something of how its creators (and those for whom it was created) *themselves* viewed, understood, and used it" (Price and Price 1980:9).

The contributors to this book present a series of themes embodied in the imagery and creativity of native art, narrative, and performance that reflect something of the interplay between concepts and objects in cultures and in art worlds. They explore ways by which ethnographic, ethnohistoric, and archaeological information contributes to understanding the processes of imagery and creativity in distinct New World cultures. They also explore the ways by which hegemony and appropriation enter these universal processes.

In the opening essay, "Provenances and Pedigrees: The Western Appropriation of Non-Western Art," Sally Price introduces many of the themes presented in subsequent chapters as they are manifest in the late twentieth century. In a penetrating look at the uses and abuses of "primitive" art in the "civilized" world, she explores the processes by which the focus on signatures and provenances — which is standard in the assessment and understanding of Western art — is routinely replaced by a focus on the pedigrees (the record of Western owners and exhibitions, for example) of objects with "primitive" origins. By denying the individuality (and the capacity for artistic intentionality) of artists from other cultures, she argues, Western connoisseurs "see themselves as doing for African sculpture (for example) what Andy Warhol did for Brillo boxes or Marcel Duchamp for urinals."[7]

Susan Gillespie continues the theme of appropriation by taking us back in time to ancient Mesoamerica to look deeply into the portrayed aesthetic contours of key artistic styles there. She convincingly demonstrates that careful ethnoaesthetic readings of the iconography of the Olmec, Maya, and Aztec can show how native people once strove to make their images and creations communicate. By focusing directly on "Power, Pathways, and Appropriations in Mesoamerican Art," Gillespie quite literally reads the ways by which those at the pinnacles of control, or would-be control, appropriated sections of the art and narrative of the cosmos to portray themselves as "visually juxtaposed with a pathway to the other cosmic levels as a didactic device to explicate a more abstract idea: the rulers, by virtue of their qualities or their office, had access to cosmic supernatural forces and qualities."

J. Edson Way's contribution, "The Modern Gallery Exhibition as a Form of Western-Indigenous Discourse," highlights the theme of appropriation by referring to the legacies of the modern museum. He speaks of museum history as a voyage of domination within which "the journey from the indigenous population to the museum gallery was usually greater than can be measured in miles, and any attempt at dialogue between native creators and museum curators usually resulted at best in muffled echoes of Native voices projected through material objects and interpreted by non-Native museum staff members." Rather than preserving the heritage of indigenous imagery and creativity, the modern museum emerged as the interpretive institution of exotic cultures as defined by Western aesthetic values. Prominent anthropologists, too, are chastised for their role in this cultural hegemony. One of the most poignant sections of the chapter deals with Ishi and Alfred L. Kroeber. For the dedication of the Lowie Museum at the University of California at Berkeley, Ishi, the last of the "wild" Yahi Indians of California, was relegated by one of the molders of modern cultural anthropology to a small exhibition room rather than being subjected to hundreds of curious strangers at the "civilized" reception.

No book dedicated to the subjects of imagery and creativity in the Americas could fail to take into account the antiquity of the knowledge involved in producing beauty in the Central Andes of South America. Helaine Silverman addresses this heritage in "Style and State in Ancient Peru." She uses the lens of the modern states' appropriation of ancient indigenous cultural products to examine cognate processes — appropriation and exploitation — of art "of the past *in* the past." Archaeologists must, she argues, recognize and communicate the aesthetic as well as the political (i.e., manipulatable) nature of art. She reassesses scholarly theories and interpretations and their ideological underpinnings in Peruvian prehistory from Tello onward by reexamining numerous examples of ancient art, artists, and artisans as "integral parts of a societal context that was neither static nor monolithic over time but was instead dynamic and heterogeneous."

Nelson H. H. Graburn brings us back to the dynamic present in his comprehensive essay "Ethnic Arts from the Fourth World: The View from Canada." Beginning with the presentation of a striking event of the traditional — and ethnic — art world, the First National Native Indian Artists' Symposium, which brought together artist representatives from all the major Indian communities of Canada, he identifies five genres, ranging from what once would have been called "primitive art" through various resurgent and modern indigenous art movements of self-conscious reflection concerning Indian artists' own styles. He relates these movements to the culturally pluralist ideology of modern Canada and to the various art markets there. Significantly, in Graburn's terms these "artists [were and are] concerned both with the continuity of embedded tradition and the commercial necessities of making a living." He documents the convergence of ethnoaesthetics and art worlds throughout Canada and demonstrates this convergence through a dialogic discourse among native American artists there.

In "Shaping Selves, Reshaping Lives: The Art and Experience of Helen Cordero," which focuses on Cordero's life and her famous pottery Storyteller creations, Barbara Babcock examines how Pueblo culture is transmitted and identity maintained. In doing so, Babcock draws out the personal, cultural, and economic significance of traditional Cochiti pottery making and storytelling. "Like their subjects [stories], Storyteller figurines have themselves become a means of bringing and keeping Pueblo people together, attesting to the power of the hand as well as the word and demonstrating that cultures and the individuals within them constitute, reflect upon, and reconstitute themselves not only through what they say and what they do but also through articulations of the material world." The relationship of art to personal and cultural experience and to systems of signification, she asserts, "is no simple matter of representation and reflection but is instead a complicated relationship of continuity and reciprocity, and of economic and political consequence as well." By exploring the relationships between storytelling and Storytellers, Babcock raises penetrating questions about the construction and presentation of conventional life histories. She again directs our attention to the themes of narrative and performance, the topics of the ensuing chapters.

Richard and Sally Price pursue the theme of narrative and performance style in "Collective Fictions: Performance in Saramaka Folktales." In a village of Afro-American Maroons deep in the rain forest of Suriname, a wake is in progress. "*Mató!*" cries out one of those present, and another replies, "*Tòngôni!*" At this signal, everyone present steps over the invisible barrier into folktale-land. As the Saramaka tellers narrate the night away, their stories evoke the elephants of Africa remembered, the fauna of the rain forest known, and especially the metaphoric juxtaposition of other space-times imagined. By maintaining the multivocalic structure of Saramaka discourse, with all the interruptions, digressions, claims of factuality ("Yes, I was there!") as a response to something impossibly mythic, and the sequencing of music, mime, and drumming, this essay paves the way for a genuine ethnoaesthetic appreciation of the nature of indigenous communication within and across the boundaries of language.

In "Peter Minshall: The Good, Bad and the Old in Trinidad Carnival," John Nunley portrays the artistic creativity of a noted designer of masquerade bands, costumes, and dancing mobiles. Drawing from traditional and contemporary sources, Minshall "demonstrates his talent for synthesizing artistic movements into a unified singular style with a content concerned with the paradox of good and evil." Minshall weaves the imagery of domination — oil pollution, atomic explosion, *Star Wars* — into traditional Carnival themes to creative vibrant, technologically sophisticated costumes and mobiles. Nunley not only takes us farther on the voyage of domination and the creative representation of hegemony of the other but also brings us back to the reality of artists' self-consciousness of their own creations. In Minshall's words, "The artist touches the eternal infinite and relates it to the observer, who sees it, touches it himself, and discovers himself in the midst of it."

The Canelos Quichua of modern Amazonian Ecuador portray vivid imagery in their songs, myths, traditional ceramics, and festival enactment. In "Creativity and Continuity; Communication and Clay," we explore this imagery and the reflexivity that enters the creative process. As Canelos Quichua artists become increasingly involved in art worlds, they communicate to outside audiences through the reflexive explication of the meanings of their deep cultural traditions and knowledge. This final essay reviews themes presented in this book by referring to the cultural consciousness of a contemporary Upper Amazonian people who balance continuity with aesthetic transformations amidst escalating chaos.

The Dialectics of Imagery

The late British structuralist Edmund Leach, ever the skeptic, boldly submitted a universal aesthetic as the genesis of humanity:

> The eighteenth-century philosophers said that true men differed from sub-men because they were rational philosophers rather than poets; the nineteenth-century positivists said that true men differed from sub-men because they were scientists rather than superstitious believers in magic; I am saying that men are men and not non-men because they have created artistic imagination which is bound up with the use of language and other forms of patterned but arbitrary expression, e.g., dancing and music. . . . We are human beings, not because we have souls but because we are able to conceive of the possibility that we might have souls. (Leach 1982:108)

A view like Leach's presupposes a paradigmatic view of culture. "Cultural phenomena," according to Clifford Geertz (1983:3), "should be treated as significative systems posing expositive questions" (with regard to art, see especially Geertz 1983:97, 120; also Leach 1976). Such systems carry meaning and raise questions. They constitute what one needs to know to understand the individual and collective thought of people living a particular way of life. Significative systems that pose expositive questions are fundamentally tropic; they are composed of figures of speech through which humans express themselves aesthetically and unaesthetically in varied contexts of social discourse. The universal human ability to conceptualize known and alien, observed and imagined phenomena through exceedingly varied languages, signs, and symbols does not mean that different peoples conceive of people, places, things, and beings in the same way. The structures of languages, signs, and symbols themselves clearly influence thought and emotions, imagery and creativity.

To understand imagery and creativity cross-culturally (e.g., Boon 1982), and across time and space (e.g., Turner 1985:205–46), we are guided by the premise of psychic unity. This premise, which is based on extensive cross-cultural research and modern theory, holds that aggregates of people everywhere today possess, and have possessed for the past 50,000 years or more, the same capacity to comprehend the observed and imagined universe through their own languages (see, e.g., Geertz 1977 [1964]; for a history of psychic unity, including its racist uses, see Stocking 1968:110–32). The mental qualities called imagery and creativity are universal properties of the human psyche. The overt expression of these abilities separates humans from other primates in a qualitative manner signaling a rapid evolutionary expansion of new relationships between the left and right hemispheres of the brain and the concomitant emergence of culture and rapid diversification of the human species (see, e.g., Hockett 1973:98–121, 362–419; Turner 1985:257–89).[8]

Imagery and creativity are both enriched and constrained by the patterning of symbolic and strategic interactions, taken as cultural traditions through time and as ethnic styles at a given time. "Styles are meaning-bearing sign vehicles, which provide the emblematic templates for social order, and which may be utilized by speakers in establishing and transforming social relationships" (Urban and Sherzer 1988:285). Within traditions and within styles it is also possible to discern patterns of radical change presaged by processes of correspondence structuring and the exaggeration of presumed oppositions.

James Boon (1982:19) discusses the process of "how cultures, perfectly commonsensical from within, nevertheless flirt with their own 'alternities,' gain critical self-distance, formulate complex (rather than simply reactionary) perspectives on others, embrace negativities, confront (even admire) what they themselves are *not*." The antitheses of the acceptable that forever garb intracultural and intercultural discourse with the mantle of real or potential reversal must remain in all frameworks of cross-cultural understanding of patterned interaction (see also, e.g., Babcock 1978; Tedlock 1983).

Processes of imagery and creativity constantly emanate from the human mind, are shaped by the discourses of social interaction, and gain form in and through cultural transmission (see, e.g., Whitten and Whitten 1972; Kapferer 1976). The very process of speaking a language competently is one of reciprocal influence on the imagery and creativity of the mind. Bringing a new trope into discourse, for example, is effective to the degree that its inventiveness is, to some tangible extent, mutually recognized, and that, in turn, is a result of obeying implicit and largely unconscious rules to disobey rules of phonology, grammar, or discourse. Designing and inscribing an icon that is both explicit with regard to the known universe and impelling aesthetically so as to suggest novel realms of imagination is an aesthetic act that crosses or blurs distinctions of power and hegemony. Imagery and creativity spring from the imagination, but they also make people think and reflect, consciously and unconsciously, about and upon reality.

Observations that influenced the development of the concept of psychic unity led Carl Jung to reason that the basis of the structure of mind derives from primordial, universal archetypes; Sigmund Freud to note the universal properties of dreams wherein the ontogeny of the unconscious recapitulates the phylogeny of the human species; and more recently Claude Lévi-Strauss to write of the mythical neurological network of the brain that leads a specific study of culture to contribute to a general study of mind. However, theoreticians who produced major cornerstones of Western thought also warped the conceptual value of psychic unity to bring about a new racism that, ironically, sponsored the field of modern cultural anthropology and associated it intimately with the metaphors drawn from evolutionary biology tied to primitiveness (see Stocking 1968). The tangible imagery and creativity of peoples labeled "tribal" came to be studied in terms of "primitive art," while peoples in sustained relationship with state systems were studied as "peasants" and their "folklore" and "folk art" recorded as though they were static or "cold" (Lévi-Strauss 1966:234; contra this perspective, see Hill 1988:43–45 and T. Turner 1988:235–39). A linear, "evolutionary" track was developed for the transformation from primitive to folk, with "cultural loss" and "production for market" taken to be the markers of the transition from genuine to spurious, from authentic to unauthentic products (e.g., Sapir 1957 [1924]; contra this perspective, see Clifford 1988:215–51; Geertz 1983:120; Kuper 1988; Maquet 1986; Sieber and Walker 1989; V. Turner, ed. 1982).

Master theorists championed this mode of "scientific" thought. Jung, extending Lévy-Bruhl's ideas, regarded "primitive tribal lore" (Staub de Laszlo 1959 [1938]:288) as conscious expressions of the collective unconscious images that have existed universally since earliest human times. Freud, too, thought of myth as "primitive" history that came to be embodied in the dream-work ontology of civilized minds (Freud 1946 [1918]; Ritvo 1990). Frederick V. Engels (1972 [1942]), drawing on the theories and observations of Lewis Henry Morgan, took it to be axiomatic that "primitive man" was communal but that the evolutionary processes of the layered structures of domination moved societies in a dialectical manner from natural, communal tendencies (eventually, with the demise of capitalism and the First World) toward civilized world communism. More recently, anthropological structuralist Lévi-Strauss has produced works of sheer genius by combining the "cognitive" properties of myth with *"savage"* (*sauvage*, wild) thought to understand the universal attributes of *the* (nonliterate, preliterate) mind that exists within the civilized head of rational man, forever generating recombinant binary oppositions.[9] Nowhere is the creativity and imagery of native artists or narrators more conspicuously absent, and nowhere is serious, professional ethnographic fieldwork with the creators of art and narrative less respected, than in Lévi-Strauss's recent ouevres *The Way of the Masks* (1982) and *The Jealous Potter* (1988).

It has been all too common in cultural anthropology, art history, and sociology, as elsewhere, to think in terms of disappearing cultures and lost traditions without adequately recognizing the fact that people keep on interacting and communicating in systems of radical change, just as they do in systems of sustained traditions. Writers as divergent in their professional interests as Bernard Smith (1985), Jacques Maquet (1986), James Clifford (1985, 1988), George Stocking (1985), Ira Jacknis (1985), and Adam Kuper (1988) converge resoundingly on the historical moments in anthropology and art history when, through efforts to collect and salvage the "authentic" before it disappeared, the polar, self-reflecting images of the "modern" and the "primitive" emerged. All of the authors in this work seek to subvert that polarity in their various discussions of imagery and creativity. Ethno-aesthetics counters these polarities, which are themselves the product of peculiar contours of hegemonic Western discourse, while the idea of art worlds maps the very contours of the discourse.

Transformations of Imagery

The ancient proclivity of people to collect almost anything from anybody, anywhere, is well documented. Indeed, collections of "curiosities" formed the basis for early elite or royal private museums and eventually for ethnographic museums (Chávez 1981; Clifford 1985, 1988; Helms 1988; Honour 1975a, 1975b; Kaeppler 1978; Newton 1967, 1978; Rubin 1984; Smith 1985; Stocking 1985; Silverman, this volume; Way, this volume).[10] Writing from what we think are different positions in the same spectrum, Mary Helms (1988) discusses the power that politico-religious elites of traditional societies derived from the possession and knowledge of things distant and exotic, while James Clifford (1988:215) deals with the way "exotic objects have been contextualized and given value" in modern Western society.

Clifford (drawing on the work of Raymond Williams, e.g., 1966) writes that "art and culture emerged after 1800 as mutually reinforcing domains of human *value*, strategies for gathering, marking off, protecting the best and most interesting creations of 'Man'. . . . [In the twentieth century] [t]he plural, anthropological definition of culture emerged as a liberal alternative to racist classifications of human diversity" (Clifford 1988:234). During the twentieth century, attitudes toward "primitive art" underwent revision: "[A]s culture was being extended to all the world's functioning societies, an increasing number of exotic, primitive, or archaic objects came to be seen as 'art' . . . equal in aesthetic and moral value with the greatest Western masterpieces. . . . Art and culture, categories for the best creations of Western humanism, were in principle extended to all the world's peoples" (Clifford 1988:235). The long battle to place objects from other cultures on the altars of modern Western aesthetic values was finally won and celebrated in the contemporary art museum, most conspicuously with the establishment of the Museum of Primitive Art (originally named The Museum of Indigenous Art) in 1957 and the Michael C. Rockefeller Memorial Wing of the Metropolitan Museum of Art in 1982.

It would appear that the West had incorporated traditional societies' "fund of power" (Helms 1988:169) and tamed the mysterious appeal of "primitive otherness" through categorization, appropriation, and approbation (Clifford 1988; S. Price, and Way, this volume). But the issue of "whose arts these are I think I know" was revived by the 1984 exhibition 'Primitivism' in 20th Century Art, at the Museum of Modern Art, and by the accompanying publication (Rubin 1984; see the reviews by Clifford [1985, 1988], and S. Price [1986]). Primitivism, an offspring of Symbolism out of Modernism (e.g., Boon 1972), is used by art historians as a descriptive, classificatory term, just as they use *Gothic*, *Romantic*, or *Pop* to denote certain periods and/or styles of art (see Rubin 1984:5, 74–75). Many writers protest the pejorative implications of the word *primitive* and deny that their works convey standard English meanings given, for example, in *Webster's Ninth New Collegiate Dictionary*: "belonging to or characteristic of an early stage of development: crude, rudimentary." Then, having protected themselves with the blessing of *primitivism* (which *Webster's Ninth* defines as "belief in the superiority of nonindustrial society to that of the present"), they proceed to write about "primitive man," "his" mind, soul, psyche, and even intentions as concrete reality par excellence.

While a conceptual battle had been won in some quarters by the middle of this century, and "primitive art" had been reclassified, revalued, and appropriated by the avant-garde, skirmishes continued among proponents of differing views of what Marshall Sahlins (1976:54) calls "the West and the rest." Writing critically of Rubin's *'Primitivism' in 20th Century Art* (1984), especially about the negative reaction to his repeated assertions concerning the celebration of decontextualization, Sally Price says of this joyful song unto primitivism (our trope) so prevalent among art historians:

> We can be grateful to William Rubin in particular for singing so loudly when he is off-key and for presenting his aria in such a magnificent and centrally located theater. For he has made even potentially sympathetic

members of the audience hear and analyze the tones that do not ring true. Rubin's catalog — together with the rash of responses it has engendered — is reading that no one interested in modern art or views of the Other can afford to neglect. (Price 1986:580)

Many scholars of the "art of others" go about their work apparently with no need to classify people according to the primitive/civilized hegemonic polarity (e.g., Bascom 1973; Fernandez 1973; contributors to Greenhalgh and Megaw 1978; Hatcher 1974 [1967], 1985; Jules-Rosette 1984; Otten 1971; Reichel-Dolmatoff 1971, 1987, 1988; Sturtevant 1986; Witherspoon 1977).[11] However, a brief review of several well-known works (and their bibliographies) of the last three decades shows that the terms *primitive* and *tribal* were used unabashedly by other anthropologists and art historians.[12] When rereading some of these volumes, it occurred to us that whether the term *primitive art* was defended or deplored in the introductions, the various authors sent a clear message: the closer (more involved, knowledgeable) an author was to his or her data, the more s/he spoke of *art*, identified by types (e.g., pottery, masks, baskets) and by names of peoples and places, and analyzed it within cultural contexts. Even Newton (1967) stops using *primitive art* when he gets to the heart of his description of his 1964–65 investigations in the Sepik District of New Guinea, and Bateson's article "Style, Grace, and Information in Primitive Art" (a position paper at the Wenner-Gren Conference mentioned immediately below) makes no further reference to that term. For a more recent example, compare Wade's (1986a:16) opening statement in his introduction to his own chapter in the same book (Wade 1986b:243–54) and to his other informative works (Wade and Strickland 1981, 1985).

At the Wenner-Gren Conference on Primitive Art in 1967, Edmund Leach asked, "How is it that the art of one culture can have meaning or validity for critics raised in a different culture?" and Gregory Bateson answered, "[I]f art is somehow expressive of something like grace or psychic integration, then the *success* of this expression might well be recognizable across cultural barriers. . . . The *code* whereby perceived objects or persons (or supernaturals) are transformed into wood or paint is a source of information about the artist and his culture" (Bateson 1972:129, 130).

Bateson applied his theory of levels of meaning in communication to an analysis of Balinese painting (executed with "skill of a certain elementary but highly disciplined sort"; Bateson 1972:147) and came to the conclusion that the picture "can be seen as an affirmation that to choose either turbulence or serenity [the two outstanding qualities portrayed in this particular painting] as a human purpose would be a vulgar error" (Bateson 1972:151). The conception and creation of this painting was seen as a corrective response to a human dilemma: "The unity and integration of the picture assert that neither of these contrasting poles [turbulence and serenity] can be chosen to the exclusion of the other, because the poles are mutually dependent" (Bateson 1972:152; for additional views of the interdependence of oppositions in aesthetic force, see Freud 1958 [1919]:122–61 and Benjamin 1968 [1955]:217–51).

The aesthetic epoxy that Freud, Benjamin, Bateson and many others have found appears to be what Ellen Dissanayake (1988) seeks. She endeavors to develop an ethological, evolutionary behavioral theory of art by eschewing notions and definitions of it that are prevalent in the Western world and raises the question that titles her book: *What Is Art For?* She searches through numerous forms of artistic expression among many non-Western cultures and finds that life and art are integrated "so that the sacred and profane coexist, the spiritual suffuses the secular"; she characterizes art as "consisting of transformation, 'bracketing,' recognizing and entering an alternative reality," which she terms "making special" (Dissanayake 1988:98). Imbuing things and acts with special meanings that arise out of cultural symbols and values, individual feelings, and shared emotions is akin to our concept of creativity. She negates this process, however, in her own definition of art: "mere making or creating is neither making special nor art" (Dissanayake 1988:99). In positing her theory of art as behavior, Dissanayake sees "making special" as "a fundamental behavioral tendency that I claim lies behind the arts in all their diverse and dissimilar manifestations from their remotest beginnings to the present day" (1988:92). She stresses the "importance of the interaction between the development of the need for culture and the evolution of the brain. . . . In a sense, even a culture's traditions develop through 'natural selection,' but on a psychosocial rather than genetic basis" (1988:120).

Conceptually allied with what art historian Bernard Smith (1985:5) calls "soft primitivism," Dissanayake insists that the term *primitive* is less value-laden than other cognates and that she uses it objectively, although she confesses that her "natural sympathies err on the side of extolling traditional rather than modern peoples, worldviews, and ways of life" (1988: 43–44). Early in the book she claims that "the basic characteristics of the thought of primitive peoples differ in important ways from those of their modern counterparts, reflecting the cognitive demands of a 'man-centered' and opposed to a 'thing-centered' (and recently, 'text-centered') environment" (Dissanayake 1988:42). She is perilously close in her modern ethological behaviorism to rediscovering Lucien Lévy-Bruhl's "law of participation," published in *Les Fonctions mentales dans les sociétés inférieures* (1910) and translated into English rather surprisingly as *How Natives Think* (1966). Although Lévy-Bruhl is not cited, Jung and Lévi-Strauss are.

When she returns to her thesis about the nature of art and its place in modern life, it is clear that the pleasurable, integrated sense of aesthetics and art of "primitive man" has been replaced by "capital-A art" (Dissanayake 1988:168), abstracted from the social milieu and devoid of universal meaning (for a strikingly similar perspective, see Wade 1986a:16). Despairing over the fate of humanity, she sees hope in the " 'new aestheticism' . . . as a means to the satisfaction of fundamental human needs" (Dissanayake 1988:192), and she admonishes isolated, literate moderns to seek fulfillment "in the lives of humans who are closer than we to our original environment of adaptedness" (Dissanayake 1988:196). She concludes "that what the arts *were* for, an embodiment and reinforcement of socially shared significances, is what we crave and are perishing for today" (Dissanayake 1988:200, emphasis added).

The craving for scientific information by Europeans more than two centuries ago contributed to an acceptable scientific theory of organic evolution and perhaps to the rise of the social evolutionary theories exemplified by Lucien Lévy-Bruhl and Dissanayake. Bernard Smith (1985) carefully documents how the quest for objective knowledge from 1768 into the 1850s brought about a fascinating alignment between art and science, a relationship that changed through time according to people's preconceptions, perceptions of the newly acquired knowledge, and the feedback of that knowledge into social processes. When the control of scurvy and the construction of reliable chronometers made long voyages possible, the British Royal Society and the Admiralty launched the scientific expedition of Captain James Cook to the Pacific archipelagos. The practice of recording observations in diaries, maps, and illustrations was well established among many previous explorers. Hugh Honour (1975a:43), for example, emphasizes the aesthetic *and* informative contributions of cartographers, when trained as scientific illustrators, to the earliest visions of America, and he notes the early transformation of natural history into empirical scientific study during the first century of exploration in the Americas (Honour 1975b:34). According to William Sturtevant (1976:444), "it was precisely the new European need to visualize and comprehend the broader world that led, finally in the eighteenth century, to the rise of scientific illustrating." This transition in the presentation of images was solidified in England, where the Royal Society established "a set of 'Directions for Seamen, bound for far voyages' . . . . mainly concerned with the assembling of verbal and numerical data. But one direction involved the graphic arts. . . . Recognition of the usefulness of skill in drawing among seamen was one of the reasons which led to the establishment, on the advice of Sir Christopher Wren, Samuel Pepys, and others, of a Drawing School at Christ's Hospital in 1693" (Smith 1985:8–9).[13]

Smith details how the artists, working with natural scientists on Cook's voyages, became adept at depicting their observations to the point of incorporating the natural observer's role. They soon developed a style of painting "typical landscapes" (1985:4) that were actually ideal types (see, e.g., Weber 1964 and Boon 1982:3–26), constructs of everything that could occur within a particular setting. Their work was informative if at times romanticized. As artists turned their attention to newly found human "types," they portrayed them with "soft primitivism." Classical images of "noble savages," seen as "children of nature," again found prominence in Europe (Smith 1985:5), repeating the sixteenth-century fusion of Golden Age ideology with exotic New World images derived from the exploration of the Americas (Honour 1975a, 1975b; Sturtevant 1976).

Calvinistic reactions to images of and information about Pacific peoples swayed the artists to become more interpretive in their landscapes and to portray humans with "hard primitivism" (Smith 1985:5), as savages to be conquered and converted by evangelism and its handmaiden, colonialism. The Europeans' growing interest in obtaining accurate ethnographic information about native peoples seemed to be accompanied by a growing dislike and distrust (Smith 1985:133–51), while at the same time natural history data provided a scientific basis for the organic theory of evolution. Smith (1985:100) states that

> The steady accumulation of information concerning natural history and man in the Pacific contributed materially to the eventual triumph of the idea of evolution over primitivistic theories during the second half of the nineteenth century. While it may be said that the Pacific contributed much to one of the last chapters of the long history of primitivism, it also began to contribute to theories of evolution from the moment they became influential in eighteenth-century thought.

Evolutionary theory did not displace primitivism, however, and depicting non-European human beings by primitive and primitivistic images continued among ensuing generations of social analysts.[14] George Stocking, Jr., minces no words in dealing with influential sectors of anthropological thought: "In turn-of-the-century evolutionary thinking," he writes, "savagery, dark skin, and a small brain and incoherent mind were, for many, all part of the single evolutionary picture of 'primitive' man, who even yet walked the earth" (Stocking 1968:132).

Nearly twenty years later, Stocking found that classical evolutionary assumptions had been somewhat revised but were still present in the halls of anthropology (Stocking 1987:328–29). Adam Kuper (1988:8) writes that "the theory of primitive society is on a par with the history of the theory of aether. The theory of primitive society is about something which does not and never has existed." Later in the same work he asserts that

> The relativism of the anthropological account also carried the message that social forms were not fixed. Reform was possible, indeed inevitable. . . . The most powerful images of primitive society were produced by very disparate political thinkers — Maine, Engels, Durkheim, and Freud. Yet all were transformations of a single basic model. What each did, in effect, was to use it as a foil. They had particular ideas about modern society and constructed a directly contrary account of primitive society. Primitive society was the mirror image of modern society — or, rather, primitive society as they imagined it inverted the characteristics of modern society as they saw it. (Kuper 1988:240)

Each to each a looking-glass

Reflects the other that doth pass (Cooley 1964 [1902]: 184)

We have met the enemy and he is us (Kelly 1971)

Je est un autre (Rimbaud 1966 [1871]: 304)

Contexts of Imagery

In his review of the exhibition 'Primitivism' in 20th Century Art and five other exhibitions shown in New York City during 1984–85, Clifford (1985, 1988) writes of the overwhelming tendency of the art world to pluck "tribal objects" from their original contexts — social, cultural, historical, and individual in terms of their creators — and to contextualize them according to contemporary ethnographic or aesthetic standards. Exceptions to this were exhibitions of Northwest Coast, Asante, and Igbo arts, which brought in the sense of living history, and in the case of Igbo art, of continuing, dynamic aesthetic traditions. Sally Price also describes the "decontextualization" of art found in the 'Primitivism' exhibition and accompanying books as "the purification of expressive culture from its original intended meaning" (Price 1986:580).

When members of contemporary art worlds strip non-Western objects of their original meanings and reclothe them in their own styles, they essentially place these arts in an ahistorical social vacuum. The processes of decontextualization and recontextualization give no clue that the arts and narratives of others come from people who are interacting to communicate, shape, store, and retrieve knowledge and evocations about imagery and creativity, who construct meanings of the self and the other, who form, continue, and yet alter cultural traditions. Recontextualization ignores the fact that the people who made the objects now displayed in Western aesthetic imagery interact beyond the confines of their primary family, kin, and household groups, and that their interaction is part of overarching politico-economic institutions.

Art worlds are inextricably bound to the upper realms of wealth and power in modern nation-states, just as they were once bound to the same features of inequality in colonial and precolonial societies. Art worlds constitute institutional mechanisms of control that seek hegemony over the perception of aesthetic force as well. But there are other dimensions of power that shape and communicate aesthetic force. W. Arens and Ivan Karp (1989:xii) put it this way: "The concept of 'power' as it is used by all peoples encodes ideas about the nature of the world, social relations, and the effects of actions in and on the world and the entities that inhabit it."

Power, as all analysts discover, ranges from social authority and physical force — the ability to force one's will upon others in spite of their resistance (Weber 1964:152) — to deep moods and motivations derived from cosmogonic, psychic, or aesthetic manifestations (e.g., Geertz 1973 and Turner 1974). Power is a universal property of social transactions; it is prominent in stratified institutional structures and equally prominent in the inner recesses of individual and collective creativity (e.g., Arens and Karp 1989). But hegemony — the ability to make people accept standards, to influence cultural orientations even with respect to individual psyches (e.g., Forgacs and Nowell-Smith [Gramsci] 1985; Taussig 1986) — is far from universal.

The past century has borne witness to the phenomenal growth of nation-states and the globalization of relationships among the powerful, leaving in the wake of this radical change the imagery of domination and its creative reciprocal, resistance, expressed variously by peoples worldwide. Aesthetic force is an important mechanism of politico-economic globalization, and it is an equally important feature of the local or regional expression of acquiescence or resistance. In the interplay of art worlds and ethnoaesthetics, we seek contemporary transformations of ancient forces that can be uncovered historically, revealed through narrative, or even, at times, unearthed archaeologically.

The elements and themes of cultural traditions may come from any source, ranging from the creativity of the individual who goes against the grain of acceptability at a given time and place to forced, appropriated, or expropriated labor to produce standardized artifacts sought by dominant individuals or institutions. Time depth is the basic criterion by which traditions are recognized. Traditions are not static; they may change radically for a variety of reasons (Hobsbawm and Ranger 1983; Shils 1981). Emergent patterns, with very shallow time depths, nonetheless suggest relationships to the past and trajectories toward the future. Both Sahlins (e.g.,

1981:7) and Kuper (1988) correctly locate *transformation* as a means of understanding tradition.

If we consider human beings as interacting in myriad aggregations around the globe, it immediately becomes apparent that the elements, complexes, and themes that compose traditions are spread and sorted variously by continuing transactions within actual groups. Cultures embrace diversities of traditions while at the same time scrutinizing their arbitrary nature (e.g., Babcock 1978:29). Traditional arts exist as objects (sculpture, painting, pottery) or stylistic renditions (folklore, dance, music) that particular people take to be part of their heritage.[15]

Ethnic arts also draw on traditions, but their focal and evocative strengths derive, at least in part, from acceptance by people classed by their producers as the "other." Our use of the terms *traditional arts* and *ethnic arts* in this volume, as elsewhere (Whitten 1985; Whitten and Whitten 1988), is adapted from Graburn's (1976) distinction between inwardly directed arts and those made for consumption by an external, dominating world. We recommend that readers consult his pioneering classification of Fourth World arts and his discussion of many themes dealt with in this book (Graburn 1976:1–32; for an excellent illustration of a cognate perspective on Africa, see Jules-Rosette 1984). Just as the embodiment of history is critical to a working definition of traditional arts, the contrast between the self and the other is basic to the use of the ethnic-arts trope. Graburn (1976:4–5) notes that inwardly directed arts help to maintain ethnic identity while externally directed arts project to an outside world an ethnic image that is part of a boundary-defining system.

Ethnic imagery emerges in sharp relief in nation-states undergoing movements of intense nationalist self-consciousness, where *ethnic* comes to mean something other than what nationalist ideologues proclaim is "traditional" to an "authentic past" of the nation.[16] As nationalism promotes imagery of the nation-state by laying claim to its authentic cultural heritage, it also initiates and promulgates a complex of "tribalization" to limit and subjugate its expanding and increasingly resistant ethnic groups. Jonathan Hill, drawing on the work of ethnohistorian Neil Whitehead (1992) uses the term *tribalization* "to refer to the reduction of complex, regionally interdependent networks of indigenous trade and alliance. ['Tribal'] formations developed in symbiotic, mirror-like fashion with the formation of bounded, colonial states that later gave rise to independent nation-states, each identifying itself with a distinct language and culture" (Hill 1990:xx). We come, then, to the polarity between national and "tribal" authenticity as another worldwide manifestation of the continuity of the dichotomy between the "civilized" and the "primitive." Use of the tropes "traditional arts" and "ethnic arts" avoids both polarities with which anthropology, sociology, history, art history, and other disciplines have been so long associated.

By focusing on illuminations of various forms of artistic expression in the Americas that reflect universal dimensions of human imagery and creativity, the authors in this book seek to combine an ethnoaesthetic respect for the local-level creation and production of art, narrative, and performance with an understanding of macro-level institutional manifestations of art-world domination and hegemony. The task of a combination of ethnoaesthetics and art worlds is to understand the cultural contexts of aesthetic force and to communicate this understanding to others. "The chief problem presented by the sheer phenomenon of aesthetic force, in whatever form and in result of whatever skill it may come, is how to place it within the other modes of social activity, how to incorporate it into the texture of a particular pattern of life" (Geertz 1983:97). Our intent in editing this book is to contribute to the solution of this problem.

ACKNOWLEDGMENTS

The sponsors of the Krannert Art Museum exhibition and the accompanying book and symposium were the following units of the University of Illinois, Urbana-Champaign: the College of Liberal Arts and Sciences (which provided a State-of-the-Art Conference grant), the Krannert Art Museum, the Natural History Museum, the Department of Anthropology, the Center for Latin American and Caribbean Studies, the Laredo Taft Fund of the School of Architecture, and the George A. Miller Endowment. Additional support included the Afro-American Program, the School of Art and Design, the Program on Ancient Technologies and Archaeological Materials, the Department of Geography, the Department of Political Science, the

Program in Religious Studies, the University of Illinois Press, the Department of Sociology, the Department of Spanish, Italian, and Portuguese, the Program of Women in International Development, the School of Humanities, and the Office of the Chancellor. Outside of the University of Illinois, the Sacha Runa Research Foundation in Urbana and the Illinois Humanities Council provided needed assistance.

Funds for research on art and narrative in Ecuador were provided by three Wenner-Gren Foundation for Anthropological Research Grants (nos. 3287, 4405, and 5232), a Fulbright-Hays grant, and funds from the Center for Latin American and Caribbean Studies, the Research Board, and the College of Liberal Arts and Sciences of the University of Illinois, Urbana-Champaign.

We thank Peter Heinreicher, Dewight Middleton, John Nunley, Geoffrey Pope, Sally Price, Richard Price, William Sturtevant, Marta Zambrano, and Jonathan Zilberg for their constructive comments. We are also indebted to Dee Robbins, who coordinated the project that led to the book manuscript while we were in Ecuador in 1986–87, who handled many complex aspects of the symposium at the Krannert Art Museum in 1987–88, and who coordinated our communications between Ecuador and the United States during the summer of 1992. We greatly appreciate the work of Stephen Cox in getting this book on track and in guaranteeing the highest possible quality in illustrations and their integration into the text. We also are indebted to Alan M. Schroder for humane and painstaking labor in seeing the entire manuscript through to publication and in helping each author to bring forth her and his precise intent.

NOTES

1. It is beyond the scope of this chapter to review the histories of the European discovery, exploration, conquest, and colonization of the Americas. We suggest the following resources selected from a steadily rising number of studies. With reference to various interpretations of European-American transactions, see Boon 1982; Boorstin 1985; Campbell 1988; Chiapelli 1976; Crosby 1972, 1986; Flaherty 1992; Hallowell 1976 [1960]; Honour 1975a, 1975b; Leach 1982; Levenson 1991; Morison 1971, 1974; and Sturtevant 1976. With reference to interpretations of black imagery in Europe, the European exploration of Africa, the Euro-American impact on Afro-Americans and current Afro-American studies, see Devisse and

INTRODUCTION

Mollat 1979; Herskovits 1958 [1941]; Honour 1989a, 1989b; Pescatello 1977; Price 1979; Rout 1976; Whitten and Szwed 1970; and Whitten and Torres 1992. For a comparison of changing and contrasting images of Afro-Americans and Native Americans, see Parry 1974.

2. Silver's "Ethnoart " review essay for the *Annual Review of Anthropology* (1979) is required reading for the contexts that established the intellectual bases for the present book. By judicious use of his 105 carefully chosen references spanning such issues as terminology, style, approaches to art, theory, the history of anthropological and psychoanalytical perspectives, aesthetics systems, and radical change, he offers an exceptionally balanced basis for reading about a number of subjects only mentioned or even omitted from this brief Introduction. Because of Silver's article, we will not try to trace either the descent of the Boasians or the varied bases of symbolic or structuralist study here. For an expressly Marxist perspective, see Wolff 1984. Raymond Williams (e.g., 1977) clearly portrays critical dimensions of Marxist cultural theory, including the history, deployment, and utility of such concepts as ideology, domination, hegemony, cultural practice, and aesthetics. Jules-Rosette (1984) offers a splendidly balanced exposition of African tourist arts by combining local-level imagery with art-world incentives and constraints.

3. Discussions of various polarities may be found in Clifford 1988, Maquet 1979 [1971] and 1986, and S. Price 1989.

4. Graburn (1976:29) notes that borrowing the identity of minority peoples (who are often crushed or suppressed) is international and that the United States is perhaps foremost in taking over symbols of its Fourth World indigenous minorities. At the University of Illinois at Urbana-Champaign, founded as a land grant college in 1879, the enduring heritage of bygone indigenous inhabitants is symbolized by all "Illini" athletes and ceremonially enacted by "Chief Illiniwek." Just before the "Fighting Illini" revenue-generating male teams return to the Astroturf or hardboards after halftime, the "Chief" performs a gyrating interpretation of a sacred Plains sun dance, wearing "authentic" dress appropriated from North Dakota Lakota Sioux. Then spectators sway, with linked arms, and sing "Hail Alma Mater, Victory, Illinois Varsity," while the "Chief" stands with arms uplifted. In his off-hours, the "Chief" talks to local organizations about how Plains Indians *lived* and what kind of culture they *had*, as if they no longer existed.

5. The idea of the First World is employed by world-system theory to depict the beginning and continuation of Western European capitalist expansion; the Second World is the socialist alternative to capitalist expansion, which gained momentum with the Russian Revolution. The idea of a Third World emerged after World War II, and it refers, in Peter Worsley's words, "to groups of countries conscious of their common colonial history and its legacy: underdevelopment" (Worsley 1984:

306). Nelson Graburn applied the term *Fourth World* to "all the aboriginal or native peoples whose lands fall within the national boundaries and techno-bureaucratic administrations of the countries of the First, Second, and Third Worlds, . . . peoples who are usually in the minority and without the power to direct the course of their collective lives" (Graburn 1976:1).

6. See Anderson 1989 [1967]:131–32 for a discussion of the role of imagery in the creative process, and Anderson 1989 [1967], Hatcher 1985, and Goodale and Koss 1967 for further discussions of the psychological and cultural conditions of creativity.

7. Clifford's complementary 1988 work analyzes many similar themes, including the appropriation of art, as well as many notable examples of art, including urinals.

8. Laughlin and d'Aquili 1974 is a serious attempt to understand the relationships between modern neuropsychiatric research on the brain and structuralist studies of culture. Subsequently, the authors of the essays in d'Aquili et al. 1979 applied their findings and perspectives to human ritual. Still later, Victor Turner (1985:249–89) presented a provocative review of research and publication with regard to the brain, ritual, structure, and much more. The reader should also see Laughlin, McManus, and d'Aquili 1990 for the most recent examination by these authors of the neurophenomenology of human consciousness. To understand the unique "design features" of language (e.g., displacement, productivity, and the duality of patterning) in the evolutionary and linguistic theory of fully human beings, see Hockett 1973.

9. For a witty and engaging argument that Lévy-Bruhl was obsessed with the properties of the right (symbolic-affective) hemisphere of the brain, while Lévi-Strauss has spent his career working on the left (linguistic-cognitive) hemisphere, see Victor Turner 1985:275–89, esp. 280. Two special issues of the *American Ethnologist* (8 [3] and 9 [4]) deal extensively with the areas of symbolism and cognition in contemporary cultural anthropology. William C. Sturtevant (1972 [1964]) presents a comprehensive review of the historical development of "ethnoscience" in American anthropology from its European and North American origins to the predominance of linguistics in such studies in the early 1960s.

10. Not content with importing only things, Europeans took home living New World people encountered in their earliest explorations. In 1550, to honor a state visit by King Henri II to Rouen, France, a "Brazilian jungle village" was reconstructed on the banks of the Seine. It was populated by about fifty Tupinambá people, whose ranks were swelled with appropriately feather-bedecked and painted Frenchmen (Boorsch 1976:509–10; Honour 1975a:Pl. 8; Honour 1975b:63; Sturtevant 1976:428–29).

INTRODUCTION

11. In 1951 a general stock-taking of the state of professional anthropology was sponsored by the Wenner-Gren Foundation for Anthropological Research. Published as *Anthropology Today* (1953) under the editorship of A. L. Kroeber, the only review not written by an anthropologist was the one on style by the art historian Meyer Shapiro. In this serious and wide-ranging chapter, he states that "Art is now one of the strongest evidences of the basic unity of mankind" (Shapiro 1953:291). This work has influenced many dimensions of anthropology and should be consulted. A significant later inventory was initiated by Sol Tax and resulted in *Horizons of Anthropology* (Tax and Freeman 1977 [1964]), wherein the late ethnomusicologist and anthropologist Alan P. Merriam reviewed the literature in his essay "Anthropology and the Arts" without any need whatsoever to raise the Western notion of the "primitive."

12. See, for example, Biebuyck 1973; Forge 1973; Fraser 1966; Hooper and Burland 1953; Jopling 1971; Layton 1981; and Rockefeller 1978. Anderson 1989 [1967] adopted *small-scale* instead of *primitive* in the title and text of the second edition of his well-known book in order to avoid the negative connotations and denotations of the latter term. By contrast, a defense of the anthropological avowal of the virtues of "primitive life and world view" asserts that "it is possible nowadays as it was in Columbus' time to exaggerate or distort the truth, but it is valid now and was valid then to speak of primitive virtues" (W. Washburn 1976:349).

13. This was the same year that the English king and queen finally chartered the College of William and Mary in the New World colony of Virginia, one of its purposes being to establish an Indian School to teach Indian boys reading, writing, arithmetic, and the principles of Christian religion. This mission was advanced by a bequest in 1692 from the estate of the British scientist Robert Boyle, with an equal amount going to Harvard College to Christianize the local natives (Morpurgo 1976:33–35). Two centuries later, William and Mary's athletic teams appropriated the name "The Indians" and adopted as their mascot a feather-bedecked caricature of a Native American. This specific image has been replaced by a supposedly less offensive name, "The Tribe." For a comprehensive examination of Indian education in colonial America, see Szasz 1988.

14. Although we draw from the works of Cooley (e.g., 1963 [1909], 1964 [1902]) and Mead (e.g., 1959 [1934], 1974 [1934]) and from symbolic interaction theory, which was stimulated in part by them, it is necessary to note that they too were caught up in the social Darwinism of their era and frequently resorted to introspective analyses of "primitive man" in contrast to their own modern selves. For an excellent review of a segment of anthropological individual and institutional history bearing on social Darwinism and related subjects, see Hinsley 1981.

15. Concepts of Fourth World cultures, traditional arts, and ethnic arts are often bundled into the global idea of "popular art" in contrast to "elite art" and "traditional art." See Gans 1974 for an analysis of "popular culture" in American society and for various etymologies of such tropes as taste culture and mass culture. For a review of the popular arts of Africa, see the *African Studies Review* 1987, 30 (3), especially the lead article, by Karin Barber (1987:1–78). In such a tripartite contrast, "traditional" slides over into the "primitive" and the identification of the we/they contrast is lost to an imposed class universality that negatively defines "popular" as "unofficial." "Popular art" is viewed from one polarized perspective as contributing to heightened consciousness, and from the opposite perspective as slavish adherence to common tradition. In New World Spanish, *arte popular* and *arte vernacular* are ubiquitous elite labels for virtually anything that is, from a hegemonic perspective "common or rude" or from a Marxist perspective "grass roots and potentially revolutionary." The "popular arts" trope (and more recent "public culture") is a clear and genuine attempt to acknowledge that people everywhere use whatever aspect of modern technology that may be available to them to create special imagery appropriate to varied cultural foci. At the same time, however, the trope feeds into hegemony and dominance in contemporary nation-states. For a review of these and related concepts from the standpoint of cultural Marxism, see especially Williams 1966, 1977.

16. The term *ethnicity* itself is notoriously difficult to define (see, e.g, Despres 1984). We refer readers who wish to pursue the debates and discussion to Despres 1984, Royce 1982, B. Williams 1989, R. Williams 1975, Yinger 1985, and to the *Encyclopaedia Britannica* entry "Minorities and Ethnic Groups" (*Encyclopaedia Britannica* 1976, 12:260–67).

REFERENCES CITED

Anderson, Richard L.
>   1989   *Art in Small-Scale Societies.* Englewood Cliffs, N.J.: Prentice-Hall. A
>   [1967]   revision of *Art in Primitive Societies.*

Arens, W., and Ivan Karp
>   1989   Introduction to *Creativity of Power: Cosmology and Action in African Societies,* edited by W. Arens and Ivan Karp, xi–xxix. Washington, D.C.: Smithsonian Institution Press.

Armstrong, Robert Plant
>   1971   *The Affecting Presence: An Essay in Humanistic Anthropology.* Urbana: University of Illinois Press.

Babcock, Barbara
  1980   Reflexivity: Definition and Discriminations. Introduction to *Semiotica*
          30 (1/2): 1–14.
  1987   Reflexivity. In *Encyclopaedia of Religion*, 234–38. New York: Mac-
          millan.

Babcock, Barbara, ed.
  1978   *The Reversible World: Symbolic Inversion in Art and Society.* Ithaca,
          N.Y.: Cornell University Press.

Barber, Karin
  1987   Popular Arts in Africa. *African Studies Review* 30 (3): 1–78.

Bascom, William R.
  1973   *African Art in Cultural Perspective: An Introduction.* New York:
          W. W. Norton.

Bateson, Gregory
  1972   *Steps Toward an Ecology of Mind.* New York: Ballantine Books.

Becker, Howard S.
  1982   *Art Worlds.* Berkeley: University of California Press.

Benjamin, Walter
  1968   *Illuminations.* Edited by Hannah Arendt. Translated by Harry John.
  [1955] New York: Schocken Books.

Biebuyck, Daniel
  1973   *Tradition and Creativity in Tribal Art.* Berkeley: University of Califor-
          nia Press.

Boon, James A.
  1972   *From Symbolism to Structuralism: Lévi-Strauss in a Literary Tradi-
          tion.* New York: Harper & Row.
  1982   *Other Tribes, Other Scribes: Symbolic Anthropology in the Compara-
          tive Study of Cultures, Histories, Religions, and Texts.* New York: Cam-
          bridge University Press.

Boorsch, Suzanne
  1976   America in Festival Presentations. In *First Images of America: The Im-
          pact of the New World on the Old,* vol. 1: *First Visual Images,* edited by
          Fredi Chiapelli, 503–15. Berkeley: University of California Press.

Boorstin, Daniel J.
  1985   *The Discoverers.* New York: Vintage Books.

Campbell, Mary B.
1988   *The Witness and the Other World: Exotic European Travel Writing, 400–1600*. Ithaca, N.Y.: Cornell University Press.

Chávez, Sergio J.
1981   History of Andean Archaeology. In *Museums of the Andes*, 162–66. Newsweek Great Museums of the World series; distributed by W. W. Norton.

Chiapelli, Fredi
1976   *First Images of America: The Impact of the New World on the Old*. 2 vols. Berkeley: University of California Press.

Clifford, James
1985   Histories of the Tribal and the Modern. *Art in America*, April, 164–215.
1988   *The Predicament of Culture: Twentieth-Century Ethnography, Literature, and Art*. Cambridge, Mass.: Harvard University Press.

Columbus, Christopher
1960   *The Journal of Christopher Columbus*. Translated by Cecil Jane. New York: Clarkson N. Potter.

Cooley, Charles Horton
1963   *Social Organization*. New York: Schocken Books.
[1909]
1964   *Human Nature and the Social Order*. New York: Schocken Books.
[1902]

Crosby, Alfred W., Jr.
1972   *The Columbian Exchange: Biological and Cultural Consequences of 1492*. Westport, Conn.: Greenwood Press.
1986   *Ecological Imperialism: The Biological Expansion of Europe, 900–1900*. New York: Cambridge University Press.

d'Aquili, Eugene, Charles D. Laughlin, Jr., and John McManus, eds.
1979   *The Spectrum of Ritual*. New York: Columbia University Press.

Dark, Philip J. C.
1967   The Study of Ethno-Aesthetics. In *The Visual Arts: Essays on the Verbal and Visual Arts*, edited by June Helm, 131–48. Seattle: University of Washington Press.
1978   What Is Art for Anthropologists? In *Art in Society: Studies in Style, Culture and Aesthetics*, edited by Michael Greenhalgh and Vincent Megaw, 31–50. London: Gerald Duckworth.

Despres, Leo
1984   Ethnicity: What Data and Theory Portend for Plural Societies. In *The Prospects for Plural Societies*, edited by David Maybury-Lewis, 7–29. Washington, D.C.: American Ethnological Society.

Devisse, Jean
1979   *The Image of the Black in Western Art*. Vol. 2, Pt. 1: *From the Demonic Threat to the Incarnation of Sainthood*. Ladislas Burgner, general editor. Cambridge, Mass.: Harvard University Press.

Devisse, Jean, and Michel Mollat
1979   *The Image of the Black in Western Art*. Vol. 2, Pt. 2: *Africans in the Christian Ordinance of the World (Fourteenth to the Sixteenth Century)*. Ladislas Burgner, general editor. Cambridge, Mass.: Harvard University Press.

Dissanayake, Ellen
1988   *What Is Art For?* Seattle: University of Washington Press.

Engels, Frederick V.
1972   *The Origin of the Family, Private Property and the State*. Edited by
[1942]   Eleanor Burke Leacock. New York: International Publishers.

Feld, Steven
1982   *Sound and Sentiment: Birds, Weeping, Poetics, and Song in Kaluli Expression*. Philadelphia: University of Pennsylvania Press.

Fernandez, James W.
1973   The Exposition and Imposition of Order: Artistic Expression in Fang Culture. In *The Traditional Artist in African Societies*, edited by Warren L. d'Azevedo, 62–78. Bloomington: Indiana University Press.

Flaherty, Gloria
1992   *Shamanism and the Eighteenth Century*. Princeton, N.J.: Princeton University Press.

Forgacs, David, and Geoffrey Nowell-Smith
1985   *Antonio Gramsci: Selections from Cultural Writings*. Cambridge, Mass.: Harvard University Press.

Forge, Anthony, ed.
1973   *Primitive Art and Society*. London: Oxford University Press.

Fraser, Douglas, ed.
1966   *The Many Faces of Primitive Art*. Englewood Cliffs, N.J.: Prentice-Hall.

Freud, Sigmund

1946 *Totem and Taboo.* Translated by A. A. Brill. New York: Random House.
[1918]

1958 The Uncanny. In *On Creativity and the Unconscious,* edited by Benja-
[1919] min Nelson, 122–61. New York: Harper & Brothers.

Gans, Herbert J.

1974 *Popular Culture and High Culture.* New York: Basic Books.

Geertz, Clifford

1973 *The Interpretation of Culture.* New York: Basic Books.

1977 The Transition to Humanity. In *Horizons of Anthropology,* edited by
[1964] Sol Tax and Leslie G. Freeman, 21–32. Chicago: Aldine.

1983 *Local Knowledge: Further Essays in Interpretive Anthropology.* New
York: Basic Books.

George, Wilma

1969 *Animals and Maps.* Berkeley: University of California Press.

Goodale, Jane, and Joan D. Koss

1967 The Cultural Context of Creativity Among Tiwi. In *Essays on the Verbal and Visual Arts,* edited by June Helm, 175–91. Seattle: University
of Washington Press.

Graburn, Nelson H. H., ed.

1976 *Ethnic and Tourist Arts: Cultural Expressions from the Fourth World.*
Berkeley: University of California Press.

Greenhalgh, Michael, and Vincent Megaw, eds.

1978 *Art in Society: Studies in Style, Culture and Aesthetics.* London:
Gerald Duckworth.

Hallowell, A. Irving

1976 The Beginnings of Anthropology in America. In *Selected Papers from
[1960] the* American Anthropologist, *1888–1920,* edited by Frederica de La-
guna, 1–90. Washington, D.C.: American Anthropological Association.

Hatcher, Evelyn Payne

1974 *Visual Metaphors: A Formal Analysis of Navajo Art.* St. Paul: West
[1967] Publishing Co.

1985 *Art as Culture: An Introduction to the Anthropology of Art.* Lanham,
Md.: University Press of America.

Helms, Mary W.

1988 *Ulysses' Sail: An Ethnographic Odyssey of Power, Knowledge, and
Geographic Distance.* Princeton, N.J.: Princeton University Press.

Herskovits, Melville
1958   *The Myth of the Negro Past.* Boston: Beacon.
[1941]

Hill, Jonathan D.
1990   Demystifying Structural Violence. *Society for Latin American Anthropology Journal* 1 (2): 42–48.

Hill, Jonathan D., ed.
1988   *Rethinking History and Myth: Indigenous South American Perspectives on the Past.* Urbana: University of Illinois Press.

Hinsley, Curtis M., Jr.
1981   *Savages and Scientists: The Smithsonian Institution and the Development of American Anthropology, 1846–1910.* Washington, D.C.: Smithsonian Institution Press.

Hobsbawm, Eric, and Terence Ranger, eds.
1983   *The Invention of Tradition.* New York: Cambridge University Press.

Hockett, Charles F.
1973   *Man's Place in Nature.* New York: McGraw-Hill.

Honour, Hugh
1975a   *The European Vision of America.* Cleveland: Cleveland Museum of Art.
1975b   *The New Golden Land: European Images of America from the Discoveries to the Present Time.* New York: Pantheon.
1989a   *The Image of the Black in Western Art.* Vol. 4, Pt. 1: *Slaves and Liberators.* Ladislas Burgner, general editor. Cambridge, Mass.: Harvard University Press.
1989b   *The Image of the Black in Western Art.* Vol. 4, Pt. 2: *Black Models and White Myths.* Ladislas Burgner, general editor. Cambridge, Mass.: Harvard University Press.

Hooper, J. T., and C. A. Burland
1953   *The Art of Primitive Peoples.* London: Fountain Press.

Jacknis, Ira
1985   Franz Boas and Exhibits: On the Limitations of the Museum Method of Anthropology. In *Objects and Others: Essays on Museums and Material Culture,* edited by George W. Stocking, Jr., 75–111. Madison: University of Wisconsin Press.

Jopling, Carol F.
1971   *Art and Aesthetics in Primitive Societies: A Critical Anthology.* New York: E. P. Dutton.

Jules-Rosette, Bennetta
1984   *The Message of Tourist Art: An African Semiotic System in Comparative Perspective.* New York: Plenum Press.

Jung, Carl G.
1959   Archetypes of the Collective Unconscious. In *The Basic Writings of*
[1934] *C. G. Jung,* edited by Violet Staub de Laszlo, 286–326. New York: Modern Library.

Kaeppler, Adrienne L.
1978   *Cook Voyage Artifacts in Leningrad, Berne, and Florence Museums.* Honolulu: Bishop Museum Press.

Kapferer, Bruce
1976   Transactional Models Reconsidered. Introduction to *Transaction and Meaning: Directions in the Anthropology of Exchange and Symbolic Behavior,* edited by Bruce Kapferer, 1–22. Philadelphia: Institute for the Study of Human Issues (ISHI).
1979   Mind, Self, and Other in Demonic Illness: The Negation and Reconstruction of Self. *American Ethnologist* 6 (1): 110–33.

Kelly, Walt
1971   *Pogo Poster for Earth Day.*

Kroeber, Alfred L.
1953   *Anthropology Today.* Chicago: University of Chicago Press.

Kuper, Adam
1988   *The Invention of Primitive Society: Transformations of an Illusion.* London: Routledge.

Kupler, George
1991   *Esthetic Recognition of Ancient Amerindian Art.* New Haven, Conn.: Yale University Press.

Laughlin, Charles D., Jr., and Eugene G. d'Aquili
1974   *Biogenetic Structuralism.* New York: Columbia University Press.

Laughlin, Charles D., Jr., John McManus, and Eugene G. d'Aquili
1990   *Brain, Symbol and Experience: Toward a Neurophenomenology of Human Consciousness.* Boston: Shambhala Publications.

Layton, Robert
1981   *The Anthropology of Art.* New York: Columbia University Press.

Leach, Edmund
1976   *Culture and Communication: The Logic by Which Symbols Are Connected.* New York: Cambridge University Press.

1982   *Social Anthropology.* New York: Oxford University Press.

Levenson, Jay A., ed.

1991   *Circa 1492: Art in the Age of Discovery.* New Haven, Conn.: Yale University Press.

Lévi-Strauss, Claude

1966   *The Savage Mind.* Chicago: University of Chicago Press.

1982   *The Way of the Masks.* Seattle: University of Washington Press.

1988   *The Jealous Potter.* Chicago: University of Chicago Press.

Lévy-Bruhl, Lucien

1910   *Les fonctions mentales dans les sociétés inférieures.* Paris: Payot.

1966   *How Natives Think.* Translation by Lilian A. Clare of Lévy-Bruhl 1910.

[1910]   New York: Washington Square Press.

Maquet, Jacques

1979   *Introduction to Aesthetic Anthropology.* Malibu, Calif.: Undana Pub-

[1971]   lications.

1986   *The Aesthetic Experience: An Anthropologist Looks at the Visual Arts.* New Haven, Conn.: Yale University Press.

Mead, George Herbert

1959   *The Social Psychology of George Herbert Mead.* Edited by Anselm

[1934]   Strauss. Chicago: University of Chicago Press.

1974   *Mind, Self, and Society.* Edited by Charles W. Morris. Chicago: Univer-

[1934]   sity of Chicago Press.

Morison, Samuel Eliot

1971   *The European Discovery of America: The Northern Voyages,* A.D. *500–1600.* New York: Oxford University Press.

1974   *The European Discovery of America: The Southern Voyages, 1592–1616.* New York: Oxford University Press.

Morpurgo, J. E.

1976   *Their Majesties' Royall Colledge: William and Mary in the Seventeenth and Eighteenth Centuries.* Williamsburg, Va.: The Endowment Association of the College of William and Mary in Virginia.

Newton, Douglas

1967   Oral Tradition and Art History in the Sepik District, New Guinea. In *Essays on the Verbal and Visual Arts,* edited by June Helm, 200–215. Seattle: University of Washington Press.

1978   Primitive Art: A Perspective. In *Masterpieces of Primitive Art: The Nelson A. Rockefeller Collection,* 27–47. New York: Alfred A. Knopf.

Nunley, John W.
1988   *Caribbean Festival Arts.* Seattle and St. Louis: University of Washington Press and the St. Louis Art Museum.

Otten, Charlotte M., ed.
1971   *Anthropology and Art: Readings in Cross-Cultural Aesthetics.* Garden City, N.J.: Natural History Press.

Parry, Ellwood
1974   *The Image of the Indian and the Black Man in American Art, 1590–1900.* New York: George Braziller.

Pescatello, Ann M., ed.
1977   *New Roots in Old Lands: Historical and Anthropological Perspectives on Black Experiences in the Americas.* Westport, Conn.: Greenwood Press.

Price, Richard, ed.
1979   *Maroon Societies: Rebel Slave Communities in the Americas.* Baltimore: Johns Hopkins University Press.

Price, Sally
1986   Review of *'Primitivism' in 20th Century Art,* edited by William Rubin. *American Ethnologist* 13 (3): 578–80.
1989   *Primitive Art in Civilized Places.* Chicago: University of Chicago Press.

Price, Sally, and Richard Price
1980   *Afro-American Arts of the Suriname Rain Forest.* Los Angeles: Museum of Cultural History, University of California, and the University of California Press.

Reichel-Dolmatoff, Gerardo
1971   *Amazonian Cosmos: The Sexual and Religious Symbolism of the Tukano Indians.* Chicago: University of Chicago Press.
1987   *Iconography of Religions.* Vol. 9, Pt. 1: *Shamanism and Art of the Eastern Tukanoan Indians.* Institute Of Religious Iconography, State University of Groningen. Leiden: E. J. Brill.
1988   *Goldwork and Shamanism.* Medellín, Colombia: Editorial Colina.

Rimbaud, Arthur
1966   *Rimbaud: Complete Works, Selected Letters.* Edited and translated by Wallace Fowlie. Chicago: University of Chicago Press.

Ritvo, Lucille B.
1990   *Darwin's Influence on Freud: A Tale of Two Sciences.* New Haven: Yale University Press.

Rockefeller, Nelson A.
1978   Introduction to *Masterpieces of Primitive Art: The Nelson A. Rockefeller Collection*, 27–47. New York: Alfred A. Knopf.

Rout, Leslie J.
1976   *The African Experience in Spanish America, 1502 to the Present Day.* New York: Cambridge University Press.

Royce, Anya Peterson
1982   *Ethnic Identity: Strategies of Diversity.* Bloomington: Indiana University Press.

Rubin, William, ed.
1984   *'Primitivism' in 20th Century Art.* 2 vols. New York: Museum of Modern Art.

Sahlins, Marshall
1976   *Culture and Practical Reason.* Chicago: University of Chicago Press.
1981   *Historical Metaphors and Mythical Realities: Structure in the Early History of the Sandwich Islands Kingdom.* Ann Arbor: University of Michigan Press.

Sapir, Edward
1957   Culture: Genuine and Spurious. In *Culture, Language and Personal-*
[1924] *ity: Selected Essays*, edited by David G. Mandelbaum, 78–119. Berkeley: University of California Press.

Shapiro, Meyer
1953   Style. In *Anthropology Today*, edited by A. L. Kroeber, 287–312. Chicago: University of Chicago Press.

Shils, Edward
1981   *Tradition.* Chicago: University of Chicago Press.

Sieber, Roy, and Roslyn Adele Walker
1989   *African Art in the Cycle of Life.* Washington, D.C.: Smithsonian Institution Press for the National Museum of African Art.

Silver, Harry R.
1979   Ethnoart. *Annual Review of Anthropology*, 8:267–307. Palo Alto, Calif.: Annual Reviews, Inc.

Smith, Bernard
1985   *European Vision and the South Pacific.* New Haven, Conn.: Yale University Press.

Staub de Laszlo, Violet, ed.

1959 *The Basic Writings of C. G. Jung.* New York: Modern Library.
[1938]

Stocking, George

1985 Philanthropoids and Vanishing Cultures: Rockefeller Funding and the End of the Museum Era in Anglo-American Anthropology. In *Objects and Others: Essays on Museums and Material Culture*, edited by George W. Stocking, Jr., 112–45. Madison: University of Wisconsin Press.

1987 *Victorian Anthropology.* New York: Free Press.

Stocking, George, ed.

1968 *Race, Culture, and Evolution: Essays in the History of Anthropology.* New York: Free Press.

1989 *Romantic Motives: Essays on Anthropological Sensitivity.* Madison: University of Wisconsin Press.

Sturtevant, William C.

1972 Studies in Ethnoscience. In *Culture and Cognition: Rules, Maps, and*
[1964] *Plans,* edited by James P. Spradley, 129–67. San Francisco: Chandler.

1976 First Visual Images. In *First Images of America: The Impact of the New World on the Old.* Vol. 1: *First Visual Images,* edited by Fredi Chiapelli, 417–54. Berkeley: University of California Press.

1986 The Meanings of Native American Art. In *The Arts of the North American Indian: Native Traditions in Evolution,* edited by Edwin L. Wade, 23–44. New York: Hudson Hills Press.

Szasz, Margaret Connell

1988 *Indian Education in the American Colonies, 1607–1788.* Albuquerque: University of New Mexico Press.

Taussig, Michael

1986 *Shamanism, Colonialism, and the Wild Man: A Study in Terror and Healing.* Chicago: University of Chicago Press.

Tax, Sol, and Leslie G. Freeman, eds.

1977 *Horizons of Anthropology.* Chicago: Aldine.
[1964]

Tedlock, Dennis

1983 *The Spoken Word and the Work of Interpretation.* Philadelphia: University of Pennsylvania Press.

Turner, Terrence
  1988   Ethno-Ethnohistory: Myth and History in Native South American Rep-
          resentations of Contact with Western Society. In *Rethinking History
          and Myth: Indigenous South American Perspectives on the Past*, edited
          by Jonathan D. Hill, 235–81. Urbana: University of Illinois Press.

Turner, Victor
  1974   *Dramas, Fields, and Metaphors: Symbolic Action in Human Societies.*
          Ithaca, N.Y.: Cornell University Press.
  1985   *On the Edge of the Bush: Anthropology as Experience.* Edited by Edith
          L. B. Turner. Tucson: University of Arizona Press.

Turner, Victor, ed.
  1982   *Celebration: Studies in Festivity and Ritual.* Washington, D.C.: Smith-
          sonian Institution Press.

Urban, Greg, and Joel Sherzer
  1988   The Linguistic Anthropology of Native South America. *Annual Review
          of Anthropology,* 17:283–307. Palo Alto, Calif.: Annual Reviews, Inc.

Wade, Edwin L.
  1985   The Ethnic Art Market in the American Southwest, 1880–1980. In *Ob-
          jects and Others: Essays on Museums and Material Culture*, edited by
          George W. Stocking, Jr., 167–91. Madison: University of Wisconsin
          Press.
  1986a   What is Native American Art? Introduction to *The Arts of the North
          American Indian: Native Traditions in Evolution*, edited by Edwin L.
          Wade, 15–20. New York: Hudson Hills Press in association with the
          Philbrook Art Center, Tulsa, Okla.
  1986b   Straddling the Cultural Fence: The Conflict for Ethnic Artists Within
          Pueblo Societies. In *The Arts of the North American Indian: Native
          Traditions in Evolution*, edited by Edwin L. Wade, 243–54. New York:
          Hudson Hills Press in association with the Philbrook Art Center, Tulsa,
          Okla.

Wade, Edwin L., and Rennard Strickland
  1981   *Magic Images: Contemporary Native American Art.* Norman: Univer-
          sity of Oklahoma Press and the Philbrook Art Center, Tulsa, Okla.

Warren, D. M., and J. Kweku Andrews
  1977   *An Ethnoscientific Approach to Akan Arts and Aesthetics.* Working
          Papers in Traditional Arts, no. 3. Philadelphia: Institute for the Study
          of Human Issues (ISHI).

Washburn, Wilcomb E.
1976   The Clash of Morality in the American Forest. In *First Images of America: The Impact of the New World on the Old*, vol. 1: *First Visual Images*, edited by Fredi Chiapelli, 335–50. Berkeley: University of California Press.

Weber, Max
1964   *The Theory of Social and Economic Organization*. Edited by Talcott Parsons. New York: Free Press.

Whitehead, Neil L.
1992   Tribes Make States and States Make Tribes: Warfare and the Creation of Colonial Tribes and States in Northeastern South America, 1492–1820. In *Expanding States and Tribal Warfare: A Global Perspective*, edited by R. Brian Ferguson and Neil L. Whitehead, 127–50. Santa Fe, N.Mex.: School of American Research Press.

Whitten, Dorothea S., and Norman E. Whitten, Jr.
1988   *From Myth to Creation: Art from Amazonian Ecuador*. Urbana: University of Illinois Press.

Whitten, Norman E., Jr.
1985   *Sicuanga Runa: The Other Side of Development in Amazonian Ecuador*. Urbana: University of Illinois Press.

Whitten, Norman E., Jr., and John F. Szwed, eds.
1970   *Afro-American Anthropology: Contemporary Perspectives*. New York: Free Press.

Whitten, Norman E., Jr., and Arlene Torres
1992   The Black Americas and the African Diaspora in the Late Twentieth Century: An Introduction. In *Blackness in Latin America and the Caribbean: Social Dynamics and Cultural Transformations*. New York: Carlson Publishing.

Whitten, Norman E., Jr., and Dorothea S. Whitten
1972   Social Strategies and Social Relationships. *Annual Review of Anthropology*, 1:247–70. Palo Alto, Calif.: Annual Reviews, Inc.

Williams, Brackette F.
1989   A Class Act: Anthropology and the Race to Nation Across Ethnic Terrain. *Annual Review of Anthropology*, 18:401–44. Palo Alto, Calif.: Annual Reviews, Inc.

Williams, Elizabeth A.
1985   Art and Artifact at the Trocadero: Ars Americana and the Primitivist

Revolution. In *Objects and Others: Essays on Museums and Material Culture*, edited by George W. Stocking, Jr., 146–66. Madison: University of Wisconsin Press.

Williams, Raymond

    1966   *Culture and Society, 1780–1950.* New York: Harper & Row.

    1977   *Marxism and Literature.* New York: Oxford University Press.

Williams, Robin M., Jr.

    1975   Race and Ethnic Relations. *Annual Review of Sociology,* 1:125–64. Palo Alto, Calif.: Annual Reviews, Inc.

Witherspoon, Gary

    1977   *Language and Art in the Navajo Universe.* Ann Arbor: University of Michigan Press.

Wolff, Janet

    1984   *The Social Production of Art.* New York: New York University Press.

Wolff, Kurt H.

    1950   *The Sociology of Georg Simmel.* Glencoe: Free Press.

Worsley, Peter

    1984   *The Three Worlds: Culture and World Development.* Chicago: University of Chicago Press.

Yinger, Milton J.

    1985   Ethnicity. *Annual Review of Sociology,* 2:151–80. Palo Alto, Calif.: Annual Reviews, Inc.

2

Provenances and Pedigrees

The Western Appropriation of Non-Western Art

Sally Price

Toni Morrison's novel *Beloved* describes a confrontation between a white man and a slave who has taken the liberty of killing, butchering, cooking, and eating a hog that belonged to the estate. The white man, known as "schoolteacher," tries to make the slave admit that what he had done was theft, but the slave presents a perfectly reasonable alternative, suggesting that because the hog served as nourishment for him, and because he belonged to the master, what he had done should rather be viewed as a helpful attempt to "improve master's property." Morrison ends the scene by moving it out of the abstract realm of semantics and into the real world of power relations: "Clever, but schoolteacher beat him anyway to show him that definitions belong to the definers — not to the defined" (Morrison 1987:190).

What I have to offer here is in a sense just an elaboration of the observation that definitions have traditionally belonged to the definers, not to the defined — though I am shifting the scenery from a nineteenth-century American plantation to twentieth-century European and American art galleries. Essentially, I am proposing that the motivated denial of individual identities and individual aesthetic visions to so-called primitive artists has allowed their art to be seen as the product not of their own aesthetic sensibilities but rather as those of Western connoisseurs. The fieldwork I conducted from 1985 to 1987 among "primitive art" collectors exposed a strong and widely shared perception that the aesthetic quality of the objects on their coffee tables and display shelves derives from their discerning "eye" rather than from the aesthetic vision of the people who carved, constructed, or painted these objects. Many collectors see themselves and their colleagues as doing for African sculpture (for example) what Andy Warhol did for Brillo boxes or Marcel Duchamp for urinals.

Since the early years of this century, the Western world has rather triumphantly "discovered" the artistic riches of other societies, as recent comparative research on "primitive" and "modern" art repeatedly reminds us. Less prominent in contemporary scholarship is a recognition that the Western world has at the same time shouldered responsibility for the selective preservation, promotion, distribution, interpretation, and — ultimately — definition of these arts. The situation supports Pierre Bourdieu's observation (regarding the social context of art more generally) that "The games artists and aesthetes play and their struggles for a monopoly over artistic legitimacy are less innocent than they might seem" (Bourdieu 1979:60), but there are also some important differences between "primitive" and Western art in the way these games are played.

Let me begin by making just a few background remarks about the academic study of art. It would probably not raise many eyebrows if I were to characterize the discipline of art history as focusing on the lives and works of named individuals and on the historical succession of distinctive artistic movements. Like music, literature, and drama, the story of the visual arts is presented as a mosaic of contributions by creative individuals whose names are remembered, whose works are distinguished, and whose personal lives and relation to a particular historical period merit our attention. But there is one exception that is rather consistently made to this general focus on individual creativity and historical chronology. In the mainstream Western understanding of things, a work originating outside of the Great Traditions is more often than not viewed as having been produced by an unnamed figure who represents his community and whose craftsmanship respects the dictates of that community's age-old traditions. Before examining this composite fellow more closely, I would like to offer a few observations about the role of individual creativity in the context of communal cultural tradition and the ways in which the interaction between creativity and tradition has been handled in the anthropological record.

On the one hand, the fact that many descriptions of "primitive" societies are written in what is known as the "ethnographic present" serves to abstract cultural expression from the flow of historical time and hence to collapse individuals and whole generations into a single (male) figure who is alleged to represent his fellows, past and present. Malinowski's "Trobriand native" and Evans-Pritchard's "Nuer herdsman" were constructed more to tell us about cultural norms and generalized patterns of behavior than to explore the nature of individual differences or diachronic developments in their respective societies. This mode of description, which is not limited to anthropological monographs, survives today only slightly bruised and selectively discredited by a growing debate about the role of history in the lives of nonliterate peoples.

On the other hand, there have always been anthropologists advocating greater attention to creativity, innovation, and historical change. Franz Boas, even while stressing the conservatism of "primitive art" and the heavy weight of tradition on its makers, radically rephrased the task of understanding such art by placing the artist, rather than the object, at center stage. In both his writing and his teaching, Boas insisted on thorough, firsthand field research, on the elicitation of native explanations, on attention to the "play of the imagination" (Boas 1940 [1908]:589) and the role of virtuosity, and on consideration of the artistic process as well as the finished form. His students carried on these concerns through research that treated the interplay of tradition and creativity as a matter for careful empirical investigation rather than logical deduction. Their efforts began to put on record the degree to which individual non-Western artists could implement conscious, and sometimes innovative, aesthetic choices within the broad outlines of the artistic traditions in which they were trained. As a result, readers of Ruth Bunzel's (1972 [1929]) study of Pueblo pottery become familiar not only with the characteristics of Zuni, Acoma, Hopi, and San Ildefonso styles but also with the more individualized attributes of the work of potters such as Maria Martinez and Nampeyo.

At the same time in England, Raymond Firth, whose approach to the study of social life stressed the freedom of individuals within the normative systems that circumscribe acceptable behavior, focused attention on "the position of the creative faculty of the native artist in relation to his conformity to the local style" (Firth 1979 [1936]:28). Firth also pioneered the use of personal names, portraying in his work the specific individuals whose lives contributed to his ethnographic understanding.

Turning now to writing in art history, the arts of "primitive societies" have often played the role of a "control case" that highlights the uniqueness of the role of artists in Western society. In this comparative context, the artists of Africa, Oceania, and Native America have often been cast as the servants of communal tradition, fashioning objects according to prescriptive rules inherited from past generations. But here, too, new approaches have begun to be explored, especially over the past decade or two. Growing (if not overwhelming) numbers of researchers are applying an art history background to the study of "primitive art," most notably in Africa, and these people are adding significant nuances to our understanding as they chronicle individual artists' lives, document developments in art through time, and refine the stylistic distinctions that identify the provenances of particular pieces. Scholars such as Roy Sieber and Robert Farris Thompson have been particularly vigorous in pioneering a recognition of the dynamism of African artistic traditions and the creativity of particular artists, and other art historians are also attempting to differentiate the work of individual "primitive" artists much as they would that of their European or American counterparts.

The innovative methods of these commentators are beginning to influence their more Western-oriented colleagues as well. William Rubin, former director of the Museum of Modern Art, who approaches primitive art from the perspective of his research on twentieth-century Western painting, is not atypical of his contemporaries in asserting both that "Tribal art expresses a collective rather than individual sentiment" (Rubin 1984: 36) and that "individual carvers had far more freedom . . . than many commentators have assumed" (1984:11). For contemporary historians of art as well as for anthropologists, then, there is a growing recognition of the need for subtlety and caution in describing the delicate interaction between individual creativity and the dictates of tradition.

But in spite of these new trends, and contemporaneous with them, many accounts of "primitive art" (both popular and scholarly) continue to insist that aesthetic choices are governed exclusively by the tyrannical power of custom. Herschel B. Chipp, for example, a distinguished scholar of modern art who has also written on "the art styles of primitive cultures," characterized Maori art as being circumscribed by "a drastic limitation upon the field within which the artist's own personal inventiveness had to be confined. . . . The commission of a technical error—a mistake by . . . a sculptor in observing traditional procedures of work—might interrupt or destroy the customary channels of communication with the spirit world, and might be atoned for with penalties as severe as death" (Chipp 1971: 168). The denial of individual creativity is often proclaimed in rather sweeping generalizations. Henri Kamer, for example, has asserted that "In Africa there is no creative artist, as such. . . . [The African artist] produces the masks and fetishes according to the needs of the moment, always on order of the dignitaries of the tribe and never following his inspiration of the moment" (Kamer 1974:33). From this perspective, individual identity loses its importance, since the artist is participating in aesthetic production much as a factory worker would contribute labor to an assembly line. A conceptual jump is then made from the artist's lack of individual creativity to the artist's lack of individual identity. The artist becomes "anonymous."

Collectors of African and Oceanic art often assert that the "anonymity" of the artist contributes importantly to their enthusiasm. One collector I talked to in Paris became very animated about this component of his passion: "I am completely enchanted by the artist's anonymity. Not knowing the artist is something that causes me enormous pleasure. Once you learn who made an object, it ceases to be primitive art." Similarly, Vincent Price (who, in addition to being an actor, is an avid collector of African art) put it this way: "the anonymity of the creator actually enhances a work of art. . . . [I]t is our very ignorance of the men which supplies some part of the mystery of [its] creation" (*African Arts* 1972:22–23). Another writer, Dennis Duerden, commented: "The identity of the individual African sculptor has tended to become obscured, because he is manipulating forces which exist outside himself, so that once he has caused those forces to enter into the sculpture, he sinks into anonymity" (Duerden 1968:16).

Writing about "primitive artists" in the singular is a popular convention that has the effect of implying their interchangeability, not only within each of their respective societies but even in the larger context of their colleagues throughout the world. Even their personal feelings toward their work may be depicted as common property. To cite one of my favorite images of this generalized fellow, Douglas Newton has written that "The primitive artist moves from naturalism to abstraction without embarrassment" (Newton 1981:53).

Finally, an editorial in *African Arts* treated anonymity as a given and went on to discuss its implications for the recognition of individual artists. "With the artist himself thus reduced to anonymity there cannot develop that cult of the individual that can surround the works of a single European or even Japanese master carver or painter" (*African Arts* 1971:7).

One question that is rarely asked about the anonymity of tribal artists is to whom it belongs. After all, as Nelson Graburn has pointed out, "just because collectors or museum audiences do not know who made something does not mean that the artist's village mates did not" (Graburn 1976:21). But this distinction is not always drawn very clearly. A *New York Times* critic remarked a few years ago in a review of the Center for African Art: "In our name-oriented Western culture, it boggles the mind that such works as these are anonymous" (Glueck 1984). It is not totally inconceivable that this critic intended to point out our own ignorance of the artists' names. Yet I strongly suspect that for her readers, and perhaps for her as well, the anonymity of African artists is understood not as a mind-boggling lapse in the Western preoccupation with names but rather as a feature of tribal art that inheres in its native context.

Some commentators rather easily accept Western ignorance of artists' identities as grounds for dismissing their individuality and assuming that art is produced by the community as a whole. One contributor to *African Arts* remarked nonchalantly, "As little is known of the names of individual African artists, a work is generally considered to be the product of a culture" (Sigel 1971:52). And others who are in fact acutely aware of the individualized role of particular artists sometimes express themselves rather loosely about the concept of anonymity, failing to clarify that they are referring to the *Western* reception of non-Western arts and thus contributing inadvertently to a popular vision of "primitive" artists as undifferentiated producers of cultural artifacts. When Paul Wingert listed "the anonymity of the artist" as one of the "features common to the arts of all primitive areas" (Wingert 1962:377), he volunteered no suggestion that he was discussing anything but the realities of life in "primitive areas." And when Georges

Rodrigues characterized African art as being "with only very rare exceptions anonymous" (Rodrigues 1981:23), he left the same distinction undrawn. But whatever its origin, "anonymity" contributes importantly to the image of "primitive art" in the Western world. As one Paris dealer remarked to me, "If the artist isn't anonymous, the art isn't primitive."

The portrayal of "primitive" artists as the unthinking and undifferentiated tools of their respective traditions — as people who are essentially denied the privilege of technical or conceptual creativity — raises interesting questions about the ways in which "exotic" peoples are used to legitimize Western society and culture. Labeling such portrayals racist or patronizing would perhaps be an oversimplification, but I believe a case can be made that the "anonymity" (and its corollary, the "timelessness") of "primitive art" owes much to the need of Western observers to feel that their society represents a uniquely superior achievement in the history of humanity, a more sophisticated cultural level in the evolutionary scheme.

An article in the popular French magazine *Réalités* argued that the suppression of individuality in favor of a homogenized communal ideology is a fully generalizable characteristic of African and Oceanic societies and that it is expressed through art forms in which personal identities are collapsed into abstract schemata.

> The art of Africa is anonymous. . . . The reason for this lies in the nature of the civilizations that create them. They reflect communal societies, where the individual exists only as a part of the group. . . . In Africa and Oceania, art . . . has to offer the community mirror images in which it can recognize itself. . . . [A]rt is the cement that holds the community together; but for it the tribe would die. (Darriulat 1973:42, 45)

Later in the same issue of the magazine, René Huyghe, a distinguished member of the Académie Française, picked up on the theme, explaining the absence of individuality through an explicitly evolutionary scheme whose suggestions of racism were only poorly concealed by his disclaimer that "African and Oceanic art is in no way inferior to Western art" (Huyghe 1973:67). He argued that in Africa and Oceania "little value is set on individuality, which in more developed societies plays an increasingly important role," and this phenomenon cannot be properly understood without distinguishing the language of words ("connected to thought-processes which take place in the upper brain") from the language of images (which "originate in those areas of the brain where the drives, instincts and emotions are based"). Associating this latter language with the "less developed societies . . . where words are less closely bound to the intellectual process than to the imagination," Huyghe explained that "in these societies art is a complete communal language in itself." He then goes on to say:

> There is no room for individual expression in art of this kind. Forms can be reduced to their primary geometric state, because they are governed by a psychological law, which is itself the reflection of the universal biological principle of the conservation of energy.
>
> Straight lines involve the least expenditure of energy, and the easiest way to remember any given feature of the real world is to reduce it to geometric shapes, which are basic and universal. African and Oceanic art is geometric because its creators are instinctively imitating the ways of nature. It is not in any way the result of sophisticated and concerted research, as modern Western art is, but of an innate way of looking at the world. (Huyghe 1973:67)

Once having determined that the arts of Africa and Oceania are produced by anonymous artists who are expressing communal concerns through instinctual processes based in the lower part of the brain, it is but a quick step to the assertion that they are characterized by an absence of historical change. Even some of the most well-meaning correctives to the misapprehension that "primitives" have no sense of history have a hard time completely abandoning this bit of received wisdom. Claude Roy begins his book *The Art of Savages* by pointing out that some "primitives" do have writing and histories, but he adds a clarification to this statement that completely undermines its initial message: "These are not people without memory; they are simply people with bad memory" (Roy 1957:7). But a categorical denial of the historical dimension is more common in the literature on "primitive art." A statement by Oto Bihalji-Merin in a 1972 essay entitled "Art as a Universal Phenomenon" is relatively typical: "The primitive artists . . . are rooted in religious, mythical conceptions. These anonymous artists feel they are a link in an unending chain of generations" (Bihalji-Merin 1972:7).

An Australian story that came to my attention several years ago provides one illustration of the way in which inadvertent cultural assumptions contribute to the ongoing dehumanization of "primitive art." David Bennett has chronicled the experience of Malangi, an artist from Arnhem Land, under the epithet "the man who was forgotten before he was remembered" (1980). It all began in 1963 when a Hungarian art collector, struck by the "astonishing personal style" of Malangi's bark paintings, took one of them back to Paris and donated it to the Musée des Arts Africains et Océaniens. During the course of the same year, photographs of several bark paintings (including Malangi's) were passed on to a government official who was involved in the conversion of Australia's currency to a decimal system. He in turn passed them on to designers working on the new banknotes. Through this route, Malangi's painting eventually made its way onto the Australian one-dollar bill, but his identity had been lost in the shuffle. Thanks to the combined intervention of a journalist and a schoolteacher who recognized Malangi's design and mentioned the possibility of a lawsuit, the oversight was caught and Malangi received both financial compensation and an inscribed medal in recognition of his work (though on the bill itself credit still appears in the form of the Western designer's initials). When the governor of the Reserve Bank was questioned about how all this had come about, his answer was revealing. He said that everyone involved had simply assumed "that the designs were the work of some traditional Aboriginal artist long dead" (Bennett 1980:45). The conceptual distancing of "primitive art" into a remote and anonymous past — which many people consider to be almost a matter of common sense — is clearly of more than abstract importance in the lives of those who create it. Malangi's story is better documented than most, but it is far from unique.

Putting on hold for a moment the popular image of the "primitive artist" working within an age-old tradition governed by communal custom, let us consider the alternatives. To do this, it will be necessary to shift our attention from a prototypical world citizen known as "the primitive artist" to the actual individuals who are responsible for producing objects of "primitive art."

Bill Holm has commented sensitively on the nature of tribal anonymity in an article devoted to the work of the Kwakiutl artist Willie Seaweed.

> Northwest Coast Indian artists, like "primitive artists" of other cultures, have been largely anonymous in our time. Moreover, when modern man, a product of a society which puts great emphasis on names, fame,

and individual accomplishment, looks at a collection of masks or other works of art from such exotic cultures, he is unlikely to visualize an individual human creator behind each piece. Seldom will he be helped toward personalizing the faceless "primitive artist" by the labels he might read. Work might be identified as "Northwest Coast," "Alaska," or "British Columbia Coast." At best a tribal identification might be made, although the likelihood of its being inaccurate is considerable. The idea that each object represents the creative activity of a specific human personality who lived and worked at a particular time and place, whose artistic career had a beginning, a development, and an end, and whose work influenced and was influenced by the work of other artists is not at all likely to come to mind. (Holm 1974:60)

Other scholars have also been exploring the possibility of illuminating the darkness in which Northwest Coast artists' identities have been shrouded. Robin K. Wright describes progress that has been made in de-anonymizing Haida artists such as Charles Edenshaw, John Robson, John Cross, Tom Price, Gwaitehl, and others. Even for objects crafted in the early or mid nineteenth century, she has demonstrated the potential of careful stylistic analysis for delineating the work of particular individuals. In cases in which a style can be identified but the artist's name is no longer retrievable, she simply creates an epithet such as "Master of the Long Fingers" (Wright 1983).

Researchers have been making progress in other parts of the world as well. In their study of Igbo arts in Nigeria, Herbert M. Cole and Chike C. Aniakor note that "[i]ndividual hands are recognizable in Igbo sculpture, as they are in most African art, and artists were and are well-known locally" (Cole and Aniakor 1984:24). In spite of the fact that a majority of the pieces illustrated in their catalogue were loaned by collectors unable to supply artists' names, the authors' documentation of those identities that were available supports their generalization and communicates their appreciation of Igbo carvers as artistic individuals rather than as interchangeable technicians for some mythical communal spirit. For a few objects in the Cole and Aniakor volume, the indication of authorship was altogether unavoidable (e.g., a mask bearing large black letters on a white background that announced: BY ODOIMILIKE). For many other objects, a relatively straightforward inquiry seems to have been all that was necessary, and one suspects that further attributions might be made through an even more persistent application in Nigeria of the methods of art history and ethnography. In short, although much more can be done to recognize non-Western artists as real people, a start has certainly been made.

Similarly, recent research that applies sophisticated historical and anthropological approaches to the study of the past in Africa, Oceania, and the Americas is building a persuasive case that the nonhistorical reputation of "primitive" societies is a construction of Western cultural biases and the limitations of traditional Western modes of scholarship (e.g., Cohen 1977; Dening 1980; R. Price 1983, 1990; and Rosaldo 1980). This effort is beginning to show that if we do not require our knowledge of the past to come to us in black-and-white pages of date-sprinkled text, the historical dynamism of other peoples, as well as their memory of their own history and their interest in it, are much greater than Western commentators have traditionally imagined.

But the study of *art* in these societies has some serious catching up to do before it fully reflects this increased awareness of historicity. In general, scholars have failed to recognize that the materials necessary to implement the art history of nonliterate peoples are still available, at least for those who are willing to tolerate long hours in dusty museum storerooms and colonial archives and to engage in the challenging enterprise of field research. The overwhelming sense one gets upon reading any large body of popular or scholarly commentary on so-called "primitive art" is that the identity of the makers, and their moment in historical time — in short, the provenances of particular pieces — is, regrettably, lost forever.

What happens, then, when these unprovenanced arts meet up with collectors, museum curators, tourists, and other enthusiasts of exotic artistry whose vision of the world is structured to a significant degree by names and dates? Well-intended but often misdirected attempts to bring disparate art worlds into meaningful contact can sometimes further muddy the already murky channel through which objects pass on their way from tribal obscurity to Western authentication as art — with profound and occasionally farcical consequences for transcultural artistic encounters. Barbara Babcock has provided a particularly poignant example:

> While superintending Pueblo pottery revivals, Kenneth Chapman of the
> Museum of New Mexico insisted that Maria Martinez authenticate and
> increase the value of her pottery by signing it — something that Pueblo
> potters had never done. When the other potters in the village realized
> that pots with Maria's signature commanded higher prices, they asked
> her to sign their pots as well and she freely did so until the Santa Fe
> authorities realized what was happening and put an end to this semiotic
> riot. (Babcock 1987:394–95; see also Bunzel 1972 [1929]:66)

But even under less obviously comical circumstances, the unthinking adjustments that are made to fit non-Western art objects into Western visions of artistic authorship are not brought about without cost.

Let's think for a moment about what happens when an object passes into the hands of a Western collector. There is a subtle but crucial difference between the perspectives of art lovers who satisfy their passion in museums, books, and magazines and those who go on to possess the art itself. Of course, these two populations exhibit a substantial overlap, but for analytical purposes let us consider the limiting cases of, on the one hand, people who attend exhibits regularly and absorb the texts and images of books and magazines but do not often consider buying original works of art and, on the other, those who go beyond reading and attending exhibits to participate regularly in auctions, collectors' events, and gallery openings.

The common ground of noncollectors and collectors is extensive: a responsiveness to line, form, visual balance, and texture; an interest in different styles and media; the development of particular preferences and areas of specialization; a subtle interweaving of spontaneous reactions and acquired knowledge; and an enjoyment of the kinds of discussions that transform a personal passion into a social pleasure. But at least two interrelated considerations distinguish collectors from other art lovers: possession of the art itself and substantial financial commitment. With the personal ownership of a work of art narrowly restricted in its availability (compared, on the one hand, with art museum visits, reproductions, books, and magazines, and, on the other, with consumer goods such as cars, televisions, and clothing), collectors and dealers are operating in a system strongly characterized by the image of limited good. Pieces therefore change hands through auctions, and individual sales can instantly redefine the financial range of the market. The law of supply and demand is king, with the supply being small and the demand malleable. The social world of those who collect original works of art is an exclusive one, simply because relatively few people have the resources to engage in it. Further, because its members are united by their shared goal of expanding personal ownership in a limited pool of objects, their relationships are characterized by a mixture of collegiality and rivalry.

While the central interest of both noncollectors and collectors is the work of art itself, their secondary interest in its history is somewhat differently defined in the two groups. Overstating the case slightly in order to introduce my point, I would propose that collectors sometimes allow a work's artist to be upstaged by its owner. Still generalizing broadly, I would argue that while many noncollectors focus their attention on the object itself and the circumstances of its original creation, collectors more frequently focus theirs on the object itself and the history of its subsequent reception. This is hardly surprising, since collectors — in addition to indulging all the aesthetic enjoyment that forms the raison d'être of their passion — are committing personal resources to playing a game whose stakes are defined by an exceptionally precarious structure of personal judgments that must be seen as ultimately unverifiable by anything other than a general consensus among the players.

This game of competitive acquisition produces a special exhilaration that is unknown among noncollectors. The metaphors that collectors call on to evoke the emotions of collecting vary from game hunting to drug addiction to sexual conquest. Some people have described the thrill of collecting as being like that of stalking wild animals, others have referred to their obsession as a toxicomania, and others have spoken of their desire for possession as "Don Juanism." One dealer told me that he placed noncollectors in the same category as men whose only knowledge of women derives from reading pornographic magazines. He went on to clarify the meaning of his metaphor by confirming it with an anthropological example: just as primitive headhunters have always understood, he proposed, "knowledge is founded upon possession."

Viewing the phenomenon of connoisseurship within the special context of serious collecting, we see that aesthetic considerations lose none of their relevance but that several new elements come into play as well. The additional factors reflect the identity of a given work of art not in terms of its physical form or original creation but in terms of its subsequent history of ownership. Collectively, they define what is commonly referred to as the object's "pedigree."

The pedigree of a work of art, like that of a dog, constitutes an authenticated line of descent, providing for the potential buyer a guarantee of the value of the purchase. In this sense, it is not unlike the deed for an historical landmark or the yellowing bookplates in a rare volume; it specifies the company one will be keeping, in retrospect, by assuming ownership. The pedigree for a work of art lists not only its previous owners but also the exhibits and publications in which it has appeared, the sales at which it has changed hands, and the prices that have been paid at each transfer.

Pedigrees can be negative as well as positive, and they sometimes require laundering. A highly unpopular collector and dealer who put his African sculpture up for sale through a Sotheby's auction with great publicity received scarcely a bid, and those few pieces that were sold fetched prices far below the market value they would have had without his name; I have been told that remarking that a particular object looks like a piece from that collection is taken as a put-down. Or again: some acquisitions conducted under the protection of Nazi uniforms have been laundered by stories that assert that their original collectors were German hobbyists. But let us home in on the case of "primitive art," for collecting in this area involves some special considerations that do not characterize the collecting of other types of art.

After an ethnographic artifact has been removed from "the field" (whether by sale, theft, or some other form of transfer to Western ownership), it is customarily issued a new passport. The pedigree of such an object does not normally provide detailed information on its maker or its original owner; rather, it counts only the Western hands through which the object has passed. An African sculpture that was once owned by Jacob Epstein, Charles Ratton, or Nelson Rockefeller is unrelated, in this system, to a sculpture by the same artist that was not.

The anonymization of "primitive art" is essential to this specialized identity, for by glossing over both the artist and the non-Western owners, people who deal in "primitive art" free themselves to concentrate on a pedigree of more readily recognizable distinction. Edmund Carpenter has pointed out that American Indian artifacts are routinely named after famous previous owners, and of course one of the conventions in museum labeling is to accept the anonymity of "primitive" artists but to show less indifference (and more gratitude) toward the people who have taken possession of the objects once they reach the "civilized world."

If we imagine the identity of an object to be built out of its known history, it is clear that the identity of a European painting, for example, begins at the moment of its creation, within a specific context of artistic movements, interacting schools and personal relationships, innovative responses to a known past, and perhaps the patronage of a historically documented figure. In addition — but always in addition — the identity of a particular piece depends on its subsequent life history. For an Ashanti gold weight or a Xingú feathered headdress, this is not normally the case. The fact of its "anonymity" effectively reduces its documented history to Western collectors, museums, auctions, and catalogues.

In discussions with "primitive art" dealers, I have several times brought up the lost artists and raised the possibility of their relevance. Two kinds of response have been given. One is that it is the gifted or trained connoisseur (by definition a member of Western civilization) who first "sees" the artistic quality of a piece. One dealer was willing to talk to me at length about his understanding of connoisseurship, sensitively analyzing his own "eye" for quality — what aesthetic elements were decisive, what role was played by subjective emotion, how he evaluated closely comparable pieces, and through what kind of discourse he was able to persuade other collectors of the beauty that he had identified. At the end of this rather detailed discussion, I asked whether he thought any of what he saw in a given object would have been recognized or perhaps even intended by the artist who made it. His answer was immediate and emphatic: "Certainly not!" The artist of such an object, he explained, was at most interested in crafting it well, according to the technical and other nonaesthetic standards of the community; he had no appreciation of its artistic qualities, which depended on the European's gaze to be discovered. According to this line of reasoning, responsibility for perceiving objects *as works of art* resides with Western connoisseurs. As one French dealer put it, "The *object* made in Africa . . . became an *art object* upon its arrival in Europe" (Kamer 1974: 33). From this perspective, there is really no point in fussing over the exact identity of those who happened to produce the objects, for these people are both interchangeable as artists with others in the community and insensitive to the aesthetic value of what they have created.

The second argument makes no reference to artistic intent or the locus of connoisseurship but asserts instead that information concerning the identity of artists is, lamentably, not available. According to this view, the practice of documenting a collector's name but not that of the artist (both on museum labels and in dealers' dossiers) results simply from the untraceability of personal identities, which have been lost through a combination of native inattention to named artists (since the intent of the art is purely communal), the absence of written documentation, and the unfortunate but now irremediable insouciance of early collectors. To consider the implications of this claim, let us make a brief detour into the realm of classical art history.

It is true that a great many pieces of Western art bear a "signature" of a sort that is lacking on objects from, say, Native America, Africa, or Oceania. However, even a cursory brush with art history scholarship suffices to abolish the dream that these signatures neatly match objects to makers in any incontestable manner. Rather, a significant number of them serve as a point of departure for a complex ongoing discussion that calls on (and sometimes even exceeds) the considerable erudition of the most specialized devotees, not to mention the most advanced techniques of visual and chemical analysis in the laboratory. To make my point, I would like to draw on an article that Joseph Alsop wrote for the *New York Review* (1986). In summarizing the art history research on what was once known as the Cellini Cup, Alsop offers a brief overview of the devoted attention that Dr. Yvonne Hackenbroch lavished on this object. His story focuses on her conversion from the position she assumed on the basis of her analyses of it in the 1960s — that it was stylistically too late to be the work of Benvenuto Cellini and was instead the creation of a sixteenth-century Delft goldsmith named Jacopo Bilivert or Biliverti — to the stance that she finally adopted a full decade and a half later and supported in her "sober one-hundred-plus [-page] copiously illustrated" contribution to the *Metropolitan Museum Journal* — that it was a "fake," probably crafted in the nineteenth century by a German locksmith's son, the notorious Reinhold Vasters.

The conclusions that both Hackenbroch and Alsop draw from the story are fascinating in their own right, but there is an additional lesson to be gleaned from them when we set them side by side with the widespread anonymity of "primitive" artifacts in Western settings. Scholars of the Fine Arts spare no effort in their search for the true origin of masterpieces (and even lesser pieces). They learn many languages, they fly around the world, they hire technicians to peer through microscopes, they sit for endless hours in libraries, they undertake immensely tedious research in archives and museum storerooms, and they engage in countless learned discussions and published debates with their equally intense and well-versed colleagues on the probability of alternative attributions. The process often consumes the researchers' working hours for a period of many years, not to mention, as one scholar did in his reply to Alsop's commentary on the "Cellini Cup" (Lee 1986:76), the many sleepless nights. Partly because of the traditional segregation of art history and anthropology as disciplines, it is rarely suggested that the same kind of energy might be devoted to establishing the identity of the person responsible for, say, a piece of statuary from Nigeria. Given that a relatively small proportion of such objects predate the nineteenth century, there is a good chance for most that their authorship is as ascertainable as that of Reinhold Vaster's gold cup. In the case of early-twentieth-century art from the rain forest of Suriname, for example, Richard Price and I have found the making of specific attributions to be a challenging task (one that requires language learning, methodological skills, and a theoretical background), but it is certainly no more impossible than most research on provenances as described in traditional art historical scholarship.

What are we to conclude from this differential attention span in the investigation of the original provenances of Western and non-Western art? I believe it is time to acknowledge that it represents a motivated choice. If the Western world substitutes, as it does, the names of collectors for the names of artists, it is not because the artists are anonymous. Nor is it because the people who crafted the objects were not artists in terms of their vision, their intent, or their aesthetic awareness. If provenances are abandoned in favor of pedigrees, it is as part of the appropriation of other cultures that goes on at many levels and in many contexts. The *physical* possession of art objects from other peoples' worlds is complemented by the *conceptual* possession of their artistic intent. The appropriation of non-Western art becomes complete.

Vincent Price once remarked that in "primitive societies" the artist chooses to "write himself out of his creation" (*African Arts* 1972:22), and certainly it would be hard to disagree with the idea that "primitive man" has been removed from the world of recognized artistic creativity. But we should not forget that one of the most time-honored criteria used to distinguish "civilized" and "primitive" societies is the presence or absence of literacy. In this light, it may be appropriate to ask—in thinking about the idea that the "primitive artist" chooses to "write himself out of his creation"—whether he is in fact the one who has taken pen in hand.

NOTE

The ideas presented in this chapter are discussed more extensively in my book *Primitive Art in Civilized Places* (1989).

REFERENCES CITED

African Arts
    1971   First Word. *African Arts* 4 (2): 1–7, 73.
    1972   The Vincent Price Collection. *African Arts* 5 (2): 20–27.
Alsop, Joseph
    1986   The Faker's Art. *New York Review*, October 23, pp. 25–26, 28–31.
Babcock, Barbara A.
    1987   Taking Liberties, Writing from the Margins, and Doing It with a Difference. *Journal of American Folklore* 100:390–411.
Bennett, David H.
    1980   Malangi: The Man Who Was Forgotten Before He Was Remembered. *Aboriginal History* 4 (1): 42–47.
Bihalji-Merin, Oto
    1972   Art as a Universal Phenomenon. In *World Cultures and Modern Art*, edited by Siegfried Wichmann, 2–11. Munich: Bruckmann Publishers.
Boas, Franz
    1940   Decorative Designs of Alaskan Needlecases: A Study in the History of
    [1908] Conventional Designs, Based on Materials in the U.S. National Museum. In *Race, Language and Culture*, by Franz Boas, 564–92. New York: Free Press.

Bourdieu, Pierre
1979   *La Distinction: Critique sociale du jugement.* Paris: Les Editions du Minuit.

Bunzel, Ruth
1972   *The Pueblo Potter: A Study of Creative Imagination in Primitive Art.*
[1929]   New York: Dover.

Chipp, Herschel B.
1971   Formal and Symbolic Factors in the Art Styles of Primitive Cultures. In *Art and Aesthetics in Primitive Societies: A Critical Anthology,* edited by Carol F. Jopling, 146–70. New York: E. P. Dutton.

Cohen, David William
1977   *Womunafu's Bunafu: A Study of Authority in a Nineteenth-Century African Community.* Princeton, N.J.: Princeton University Press.

Cole, Herbert M., and Chike C. Aniakor
1984   *Igbo Arts: Community and Cosmos.* Los Angeles: Museum of Cultural History.

Darriulat, Jacques
1973   African Art and Its Impact on the Western World. *Réalités* (English edition) no. 273:41–50.

Dening, Greg
1980   *Islands and Beaches: Discourse on a Silent Land: Marquesas, 1774–1880.* Honolulu: University Press of Hawaii.

Duerden, Dennis
1968   *African Art.* Feltham, Middlesex: Paul Hamlyn.

Firth, Raymond
1979   *Art and Life in New Guinea.* New York: AMS Press.
[1936]

Glueck, Grace
1984   Show from France Opens New Center for African Art. *New York Times,* September 21, pp. C1, C28.

Graburn, Nelson H. H., ed.
1976   *Ethnic and Tourist Arts: Cultural Expressions from the Fourth World.* Berkeley: University of California Press.

Holm, Bill
1974   The Art of Willie Seaweed: A Kwakiutl Master. In *The Human Mirror,* edited by Miles Richardson, 59–90. Baton Rouge: Louisiana State University Press.

Huyghe, René
    1973   African and Oceanic Art: How It Looks from the West. *Réalités* (English edition) no. 273:66–67.

Kamer, Henri
    1974   De l'Authenticité des sculptures africaines / The authenticity of African sculptures. *Arts d'Afrique Noire* 12:17–40.

Lee, Sherman E.
    1986   Reply to Alsop 1986. *New York Review,* December 18, p. 76.

Morrison, Toni
    1987   *Beloved.* New York: Knopf.

Newton, Douglas
    1981   *The Art of Africa, the Pacific Islands, and the Americas.* New York: Metropolitan Museum of Art.

Price, Richard
    1983   *First-Time: The Historical Vision of an Afro-American People.* Baltimore: Johns Hopkins University Press.
    1990   *Alabi's World.* Baltimore: Johns Hopkins University Press.

Price, Sally
    1989   *Primitive Art in Civilized Places.* Chicago: University of Chicago Press.

Rodrigues, Georges
    1981   Evolution et psychologie des collectionneurs d'art africain. *Antologia di Bella Arte* 17/18:18–24.

Rosaldo, Renato
    1980   *Ilongot Headhunting, 1883–1974.* Stanford, Calif.: Stanford University Press.

Roy, Claude
    1957   *Arts sauvages.* Paris: R. Delpire. Translated as *The Art of Savages.* Sheldon, N.Y.: Golden Griffin Books, 1958.

Rubin, William, ed.
    1984   *'Primitivism' in 20th Century Art: Affinity of the Tribal and the Modern.* New York: Museum of Modern Art.

Sigel, Linda
    1971   A Private Collection at the Art Institute of Chicago. *African Arts* 5 (1): 50–53.

Wingert, Paul
    1962   *Primitive Art: Its Traditions and Styles.* New York: Oxford University Press.

Wright, Robin K.

1983   Anonymous Attributions: A Tribute to a Mid-19th Century Haida Argillite Pipe Carver; The Master of the Long Fingers. In *The Box of Daylight,* edited by Bill Holm, 139–42. Seattle: Seattle Art Museum, and the University of Washington Press.

3

Power, Pathways, and Appropriations in Mesoamerican Art

Susan D. Gillespie

Analyzing the iconography of ancient art as a means of acquiring a more profound understanding of extinct cultural systems has proved to be particularly appropriate for the pre-Columbian peoples of Mesoamerica. Several civilizations once flourished in this culture area, which extends from central Mexico into the northern half of Central America (Fig. 3.1). While some of them developed written record-keeping systems, all of them placed far more emphasis on decorated objects — which we call art — than on writing as a means of communication (Miller 1986:71). These peoples clearly understood the utility of images for creating, disseminating, and even manipulating cultural constructs, and also for their emotive power, which transcends mere communication.

The cultural information to be gained from the study of this art goes far beyond aesthetic notions or religious beliefs to include economic and sociopolitical systems as well. In the holistic perspective of anthropology, all facets of culture are patterned, such that art must reflect society. Since the ancient peoples of Mesoamerica consciously used their decorated objects to communicate messages grounded in shared understandings, embedded within these objects are "the taxonomic and structural bases of the cosmos" (López Austin 1987:259), which oriented not simply the design of artifacts but all aspects of cultural life.

The information symbolically encoded in these artworks can be revealed, at least on a general level, through iconographic analysis despite the absence of exegesis. Indeed, such analysis, whose goal is meaning rather than form or style, is equally productive for cultures that are literate or that have living representatives. This is because "iconography offers precious insight into modes of thinking that words often mask or ignore" (Gould 1988:14). Furthermore, imagery is not restricted to the linear syntax of speech or text (see Freidel and Schele 1988a:550) but instead allows for the simultaneous existence of many multiple, even contradictory, meanings (for a discussion of text versus image as a medium of communication, see, e.g., Berlo 1983 and Miller 1989). The Mesoamerican peoples "used the image as the specific mode of expression of their thought," and their own verbal interpretations of it were insufficient and incomplete (Gruzinski 1987:47). The intended messages also became operational in the context and use of these objects as they functioned in society.

Certain characteristics of the Mesoamerican culture area render it amenable to iconographic interpretation of its ancient artworks. Modern indigenous peoples continue cultural traditions and beliefs that have deep pre-Hispanic roots despite the overlay of five hundred years of Western hegemony. There are numerous ethnohistoric references to pre-Columbian practices and beliefs, including explanations of symbolic images, from the very first years after the Spanish conquest. Archaeological excavations have provided many of the artworks with interpretable cultural contexts. Several of these civilizations left writing systems that can be deciphered, providing insights into the mental worlds of a people long gone.

Most important to this endeavor is the conviction among scholars with long experience in the area that these cultures shared a "unified ideological system," that is, that "all Mesoamerican pre-Columbian cultures, from about 2000 B.C. until the Spanish Conquest, were interlinked in time and space in a single huge cultural system" (Willey 1973:154). Although at the formal level symbolic meanings of specific images necessarily varied over time and space, at the structural level of iconography — which deals with the ordering of symbolic elements as a reflection of the other domains of culture (Lathrap 1977:337–38) — some continuity is ex-

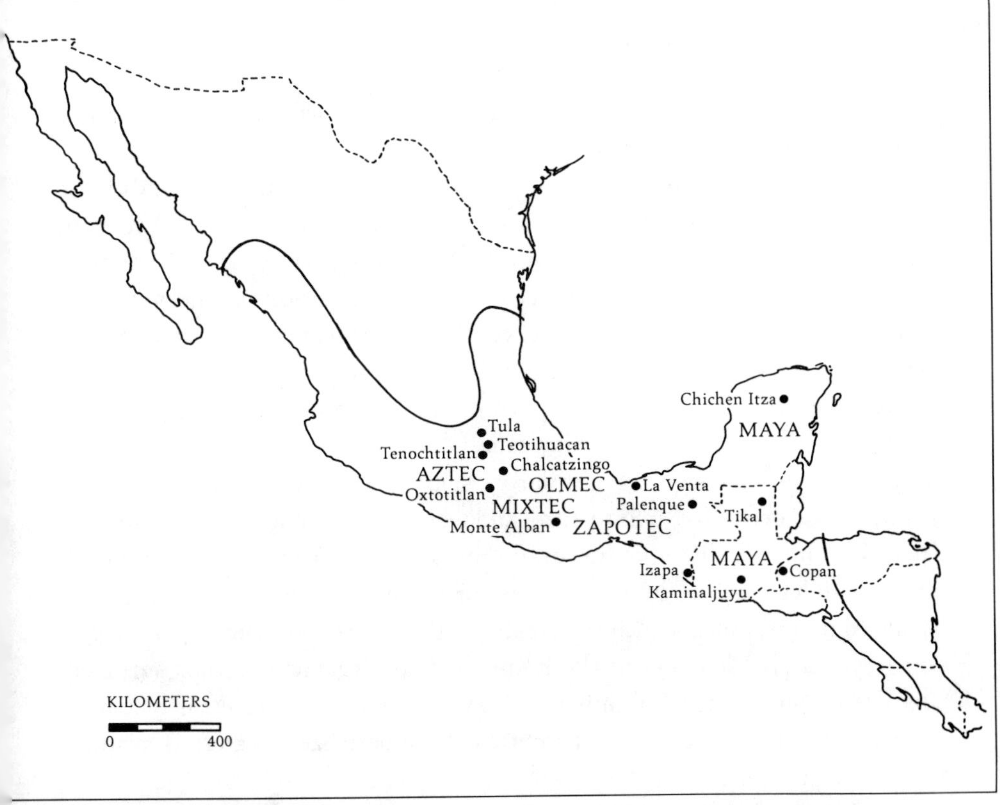

Figure 3.1. The Mesoamerican culture area (bounded by solid lines).

pected, given the unity of Mesoamerican ideology. It is at this level that the ethnographic, ethnohistorical, epigraphic, and archaeological evidence and techniques available to the analyst become most usable so that we can begin to decipher the messages encoded in the art for what they reveal about ancient society.

The surviving artworks of the pre-Columbian Mesoamerican cultures were produced over a period of three millennia, beginning with the Formative or Preclassic period (ca. 1500 B.C.–A.D. 300). This era witnessed the gradual rise of complex cultures based on maize horticulture, such as that of the Olmecs on the Gulf coast at about 1200 B.C. and later the peoples of

Izapa on the southern Pacific coast. The Classic period, from A.D. 300 to 900, was characterized by the rise of urbanism and the state, as occurred at Teotihuacan in central Mexico, the Zapotec capital of Monte Albán in Oaxaca, and the various city-states of the Maya civilization in the lowlands of Guatemala, Yucatan, and adjacent areas. Finally, the Postclassic period rise of empires began at around 900 and lasted until the coming of the Spanish in 1519. Postclassic cultures include the Mixtecs and Aztecs of highland central Mexico, with Tenochtitlan as the premier Aztec capital.

Studies of the communicative role of Mesoamerican imagery usually focus on what can be called public or elite art, in contrast to domestic art produced by or for individual households.[1] Beginning with the development of complex society in the Formative period, the emerging elite group directed the production of artworks especially for their and the community's use. Some of these objects are large, such as stone monuments, painted murals, and decorated architecture, and were located in public or ceremonial places in order to disseminate certain messages to society at large. Elite art also includes smaller, luxury objects, often made of exotic materials, and painted manuscripts, which were usually the property of the upper level in society. Rarely have any of the items made of organic materials survived, so the corpus of pre-Columbian Mesoamerican art is necessarily biased toward objects and decorated structures of nonperishable materials, primarily stone and ceramic artifacts.

The elite artworks functioned at least partly to elucidate aspects of the state and cosmos that were based on a knowledge system, shared by the Mesoamerican peoples, about how their world was constituted. For this reason, the art is not merely representational but incorporates cultural constructs: "the Pre-Columbian artist did not generally represent what he saw, but rather what he knew to be true" (Quirarte 1977:54). Certain themes are manifest in the artworks of all these cultures, and in fact the commonality of these themes helps to define Mesoamerica as a culture area distinct from northern Mexico and southern Central America (Willey 1973:159). Thus their thematic similarities, which can be traced across time and space, do not necessarily suggest direct historical continuities but instead may locate their origins in a shared ideology.

One point of commonality in much of the elite-commissioned art is an emphasis on explaining the nature of rulership — the source or charter of the ruler's power, his qualities as ruler, his relationship to the community he ruled, and his links to the cosmos. As outlined here, the ruling groups appropriated for depiction in the public/elite artworks certain natural features that both ancient and modern Mesoamerican peoples associate with access to supernatural power. That is, rather than introduce radical new images of power, the elite manipulated presumably preexisting symbols for their own purposes. Icons of these natural features, strategically positioned in the ritual landscape of ceremonial centers, thereby linked the power of the ruler with the powers of the cosmos in order to reinforce and even transform concepts concerning the right to rule. These artworks functioned to place the ruling hierarchy visually within the structure of the cosmos as the Mesoamerican peoples conceived it to be.

The Mesoamerican Cosmos

To comprehend Mesoamerican elite art as part of the visual charter for rulership, one must first understand the Mesoamerican view of the cosmos, for it was cosmic power upon which the rulers drew, and society and the cosmos were seen as parallel in structure and operation (excellent descriptions of the Mesoamerican cosmos are provided in Hunt 1977; León-Portilla 1963, 1988; Soustelle 1959; and Thompson 1970). The peoples of Mesoamerica understood the cosmos as being composed of discrete elements organized horizontally in segments oriented to the directions as defined by the daily movement of the sun from east to west and its annual alternation between north and south, and vertically into the upperworld, the middle world (the earth's surface), and the underworld. The upperworld and the underworld are equivalent in the sense of being the "otherworld," the world beyond daily experience and thus a realm of supernatural forces.

These spatial elements were also equated with temporal units such that periods of time were linked to the segments of space in endless cycles. For example, each day was associated with a different direction, time "moving" in a counterclockwise circle from east to north to west to south. Each such spatio-temporal segment was associated with specific qualities and symbolic markers. In addition, the future and the past were linked to the otherworld in opposition to the everyday world of the present on the earth's surface. For this reason, ancestors were often depicted in an otherworldly location in the artworks. In summary, a key characteristic of the ancient (and modern) Mesoamerican view of the cosmos was its division into space-time segments defined by the movement of the sun and linked to one another in a dynamic way, which was the source of cosmic order as opposed to chaos.

The center of the cosmos was the place where all the different elements were conjoined — the horizontal divisions and the three vertical levels. It functioned as a place of balance among all the forces represented by these segments. Balance, and hence stability, was also achieved in a dynamic way by the alternation of the various directions around the center as a pivot or hub, as time rotated through the segments of space. Nevertheless, the center was also a place where opposites conjoined, where time and space were essentially unsegmented and unordered, and as such it was a place of ambiguity, instability, danger, and anomaly (Elzey 1976:324).

In keeping with these qualities, the center was a powerful place. In Mesoamerican thought, power (cognized as movement or force, and hence breath and life [Marcus 1978]) was generated here from the combination of opposites (León-Portilla 1974). Furthermore, it was the place where access was possible to the supernatural influences of the other vertical levels — the "point of encounter with foreign worlds" (Elzey 1976:327). As the sum of all these characteristics, the cosmic center was the quintessential focal point in both religious and political life. It was defined and redefined by each of the Mesoamerican cultures with the help of its art and architecture.

In addition to the center itself, certain transformational or mediating agents were considered to be capable of transcending the boundaries between the discrete cosmic segments and thus capable of uniting their opposed qualities. Some of these agents were gods, culture heroes, and kings, associated with the moving sun, but this category also includes geographic features and natural elements within the world, particularly those that appeared to link the vertical levels of the cosmos. These things were conceived of as mediating pathways whereby the people of the middle world could have access to the supernatural influences of the otherworld.

As shown in the pre-Columbian elite art and architecture, the important pathways are the *cave*, as an entrance into the underworld, the sacred *mountain*, which links the earth's surface and the heavens, and the world *tree*, with its roots underground and its branches in the sky. All three pathways continue to be part of the "sacred geography" of Mesoamerica — among modern Highland Maya peoples, for example (Vogt 1981:119–20) — and they are still a focus of community ritual and folklore at the non-elite level of contemporary society (which one suspects reflects an original, very ancient situation). In addition to these three "static" pathways, certain zoomorphs were thought to be capable of moving between the vertical levels of the cosmos as "dynamic" mediators. This category includes jaguars, birds, crocodilians, and serpents, especially feathered serpents, mythical creatures that combined features of both earth- and sky-dwellers.

These pathways and cosmic connectors can be rather easily depicted because they represent natural elements rather than vague abstractions. Significantly, from the earliest appearance of public monuments in Mesoamerica, among the Gulf coast Olmecs, the elite were already appropriating these mediating pathways to communicate something about themselves, and this perhaps was a rationale for much of Olmec monumental art. The rulers had themselves visually juxtaposed with a pathway to the other cosmic levels as a didactic device to explicate a more abstract idea: the rulers, by virtue of their qualities or their office, had access to cosmic supernatural forces. Furthermore, because the elite are the focus of this imagery, such access was either unique to them or of a highly special nature.

Using the medium of art to communicate these ideas allowed the elite groups in Mesoamerica to manipulate the concepts of their access to power by manipulating the images. Concentrating on the pathways as mediators in a survey of Mesoamerican elite artworks helps to reveal the divergent political ideologies they served. Although all of these pathways were utilized for similar purposes in the art of the various societies, they did not receive the same emphasis and were handled quite differently. These distinctions can be correlated in part with a variation in the constructs concerning the nature of rulership, seen at the most basic level in the contrast between personified and anonymous rulership as it was represented in artistic media. This difference is especially apparent when comparing the portrait art of the lowland Olmec and Maya peoples (in the Formative and Classic periods) with the more depersonalized artworks of some central highland societies, such as Classic period Teotihuacan and the Postclassic Aztecs.

While this dichotomy must be presented here much more simplistically than was the case in reality, this difference in the use of the images among the Mesoamerican cultures is a clue to both regional and chronological variations in the conceptions of rulership that they held. The variation concerning how rulership was believed to be constituted should ultimately be related to the differences in the other aspects of these cultures, to the nature of the interactions that existed among them, and to the processes that resulted in the evolution of the state.

The Cave as Earth Entrance

Caves have been and still are viewed by Mesoamerican peoples as an entrance into places of wealth, abundance, and fertility (e.g., Brady 1988; Grigsby 1986). Rituals were carried out in caves, and it was widely believed that the water for rain was stored there, a critical necessity for an agricultural people. Since the earth was viewed as a source of life and fertility, the cave was like the birth canal leading into the earth as womb. To enter a cave was to return to the past, the place of origin, the time and space of the original cosmogony and the gods (Heyden 1981; Taube 1986).

Another metaphor for the cave as an entrance into the earth, as represented in art, was based on a different body opening: the mouth of a zoomorphic "earth monster." In Aztec pictographic manuscripts, the mouth is the image frequently used to depict the emergence of the original humans from out of the earth via a cave (e.g., Durán 1967: Vol. 2, Fig. 3). The incurving fangs of the earth monster carved above the doorway of many Zapotec tombs in the Valley of Oaxaca connote a similar meaning: a return into the mouth of the earth at death to join the ancestors. Similar representations of a monster's mouth were also placed around or above the doorways of temples or other sanctums of supernatural and royal space (Schávelzon 1980). As used in rituals, this imagery marked the threshold whereby officiants could travel to the othertime, the otherworld, to mediate with the cosmic forces there.

The complexity of meaning of this icon, even at an early date, is seen in an Olmec-influenced "portable doorway" from Formative period Chalcatzingo (Fig. 3.2; Grove 1984).[2] This monument was made from a stone slab pierced with a cruciform opening, which formed the mouth of a face carved in bas-relief. The quatrefoil design around the opening refers not just to the mouth of the earth monster but also to the center of the earth,

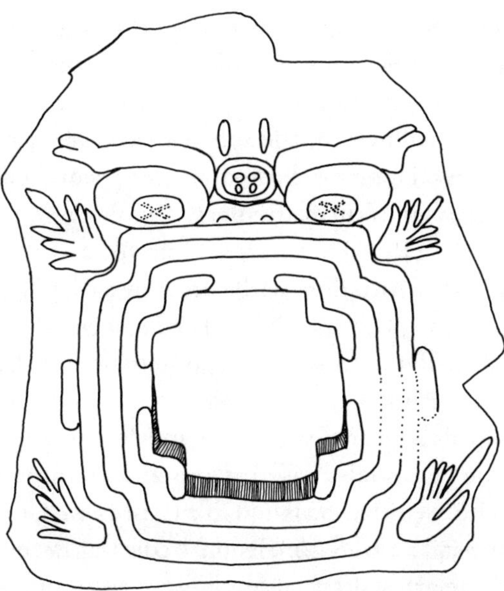

Figure 3.2. This bas-relief carving on Monument 9 from Formative period Chalcat-zingo indicates that the opening through the free-standing stone slab is the cruciform mouth of an earth-monster (height: 1.8 m; width: 1.5 m). (Drawn from Grove 1984:Pl. 8)

since the four segments form a cosmogram, a model of the four directions (Schele 1987b:3). To go through this doorway was to enter the supernatural world at the cosmic center and to have access to the power and agricultural fertility that exist there (the latter quality apparently marked by the plants emerging from the four corners of the mouth).

The juxtaposition of a cave with a quadripartite diagram to mark a cosmic center may explain the location of another great architectural "path-way": the Classic period Pyramid of the Sun at Teotihuacan in central Mexico. Tunneling under this huge pyramid revealed a natural cave with four chambers arranged in the quatrefoil fashion. Archaeological evidence indicates that rituals were held in this cave, and it apparently once con-tained water, matching the Mesoamerican belief that water was stored in the underworld (Heyden 1981:1–4). In these architectural examples — the cave/monster-mouth as the entrance to temples, and the siting of a pyramid as coincident with the cosmic center — the emphasis is on using imagery to denote specific sacred places where access to supernatural power was possible.

Examples from Olmec and Maya art, however, while incorporating the general idea, reveal a major difference: underworld entrances were juxtaposed with particular identified rulers. By showing themselves in the elite art at this cosmic threshold, rulers indicated a source of their right to rule: their physical association with supernatural powers and with the realm of their deified ancestors. They also displayed their personal ability to mediate between the natural and supernatural worlds, a prime characteristic of sacred kingship.

Such portrayals appeared very early in Mesoamerica and were coincident with the rise of complex culture and an elite group. The Formative period Olmec culture of the lowland Gulf coast is well known for its stone monuments, especially three-dimensional colossal heads, statues, and altars. Many of these artworks incorporate true portraits, as determined by the depiction of individual physiognomy and the use of identifying or "naming" motifs in the headdress (Grove 1981:65). It is for this reason that the portrait is presumed to be that of the ruler (rather than a supernatural being or a generic human), and furthermore that these monuments are concerned with him personally, not just his office or position.

Some of the large altars show the ruler seated in a shallow niche, which represents the cave as earth entrance (Fig. 3.3; Grove 1973). On these, he is always shown seated halfway in and halfway out of the niche, indicating that he belongs to both the secular and the sacred worlds and that he can physically transcend and mediate between them. The ruler is an ambiguous being with both mortal and divine qualities, and thus incarnates great power. His ambiguity and power associate him personally with the qualities of the cosmic center.

These carved monuments must also be considered in their cultural contexts as functioning artifacts in Olmec society. As David Grove has shown, the "altars" actually served as thrones or seats of power of the ruler, equivalent in this sense to a South American "shaman's stool" by which shamans and other individuals make contact with underworld forces (Grove 1973; Grove 1981:61–62). The ledge at the top of the La Venta Monument 4 altar carries bas-relief motifs, including the jaw row of the

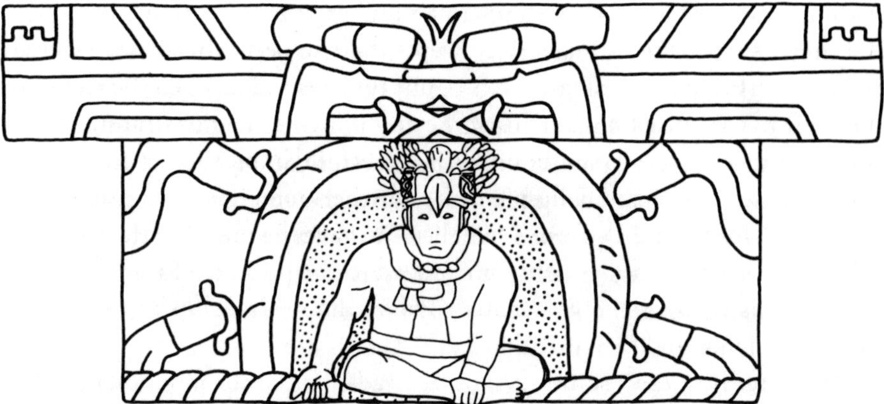

Figure 3.3. This reconstructed front view of Altar 4 at La Venta, a Gulf coast Olmec center, portrays in three-dimensional sculpture a ruler sitting in a niche underneath motifs that represent the earth's surface, the jaw of a crocodilian. Named by his headdress motif, he holds a rope that leads to the portrait of another individual carved in relief on the side (height: 1.6 m). (Drawn from Grove 1973:Fig. 5)

crocodilian earth monster and a zoomorphic head, indicating that it represents the earth's surface. The ruler is shown below the ledge, in an underworld location. Thus, when the living ruler sat on top of the throne, on the surface of the earth, he not only made physical contact with the underworld, he again showed his dual qualities, for his "double" was sitting just below him, just below the surface of the earth (this being his own portrait or possibly that of an ancestor). The "twinning" of the mortal/supernatural aspects of the ruler repeats, in another form, the message of sitting halfway in and halfway out of the niche. In other words, this monument allowed for a certain redundancy of meaning by incorporating various images that all convey essentially the same concept.

The information communicated by these altars and other stone monuments is more complex than the simple commemoration of a particular ruler in an act of ritualistic mediation. The Olmec elite chose to portray themselves in ceremonial centers with the use of huge basalt boulders that had to have been hauled — by strictly human labor — to most of these sites from many miles away. The use of stone artworks is meaningful to the consolidation of Olmec elite status in a number of permutations. Not only did they usurp for their imagery concepts their subjects already considered to be powerful in an ideological sense, but they also supervised the tremendous efforts required to construct the monuments, demonstrating more literal political authority (although it is doubtful that physical coercion was involved; see Grove and Gillespie n.d.). Furthermore, it is conceivable that the use of stone acquired from some distance gave the raw material itself an inherent "otherworldly" quality and added to the prestige of the elite who directed this work (see, e.g., Helms 1979 on the relationship between geographic distance and sacred authority).

While the altars, statues, colossal heads, and other monuments presumably depict only the rulers, it is likely that the ideological messages these artworks were meant to communicate served to benefit all the elite. Indeed, the ruler himself may have become a focus for the appropriation of power by an entire group. The elite used his image in legitimating their de facto position in society, and they continued to manipulate it after his demise.

Like a shaman's instruments of power, the altars and other portraits and objects associated with a ruler were often ritually mutilated and buried, actions which indicate that in one sense the medium was the message. Altars were frequently defaced by knocking off their corners; bas-relief and three-dimensional portraits, by obliterating the face and headdress, by decapitation, or by removal of the power objects held by the rulers; and altars and colossal heads, by carving small depressions in them (Grove 1981). Archaeological evidence indicates that this mutilation occurred continuously, and Grove (1981) has hypothesized that it was an aspect of sacred rulership performed in order to "terminate" these objects, to neutralize the supernatural power they were believed to contain. He has shown that the destruction concentrated on the significata of the ruler — his face and his naming motifs — which identified him and hence made reference to his unique persona.

These acts may have occurred with the death of the ruler, although his successors may have chosen to use their predecessor's monuments, at least temporarily, in order to transfer his power to themselves. This second scenario — in which the right to rule is tied in part to descent from a previous ruler, whose portrait is still required — may reflect the emergence of succession to office via lineal relationships, an evolutionary development that was communicated via the monuments. Some evidence for the reuse of certain monuments, including the recarving of some altars into colossal heads (Porter 1989), as well as the usurpation of a probable ancestor's naming motif juxtaposed with that of the current ruler's name on his portrait (La Venta Stela 2; Grove 1981:67), could indicate a similar motivation.

An Olmec-style carving at Chalcatzingo in central Mexico (Chalcatzingo Monument 1; Grove 1984:Pl. 5) probably portrays such a deified named ancestor seated fully (rather than halfway) within a more explicit profile monster mouth as cave. Billowing clouds and raindrops above the cave show the control over rain and agricultural fertility associated with this figure. The bas-relief depiction, carved high on a hillside, literally places the royal ancestor in a combination underworld/upperworld setting (cave/mountain), reflecting the dualism of the otherworld as well as locating this ancestor at the cosmic center.

More than a millennium later, the Classic period lowland Maya also used the earth monster mouth to indicate the apotheosis of named kings, for whom the mouth served as a threshold to the supernatural otherworld. A well-known example is the sarcophagus of Pakal, a Late Classic ruler of Palenque who was depicted in bas-relief on his sarcophagus lid according to Maya conceptions of his status at the moment of death (Fig. 3.4). He is shown poised just above the partly skeletonized mouth of the monster into which he is falling, indicating his transition from life and the natural world into death and the supernatural world (Robertson 1983:57). Rising more literally above him was an artificial mountain—the pyramid known as the Temple of the Inscriptions, which housed his tomb—indicating that this image, like Chalcatzingo's Monument 1 and the Pyramid of the Sun at Teotihuacan, is located at the juxtaposition of the upperworld and the underworld, the cosmic center, and that Pakal was placed forever precisely at that point.

The World Tree as Axis Mundi

Tropical trees can be very tall, massive, and impressive. Some trees have an extensive network of roots on the ground, while their branches form an umbrellalike canopy that blocks the sunlight. Yucatec Maya still believe

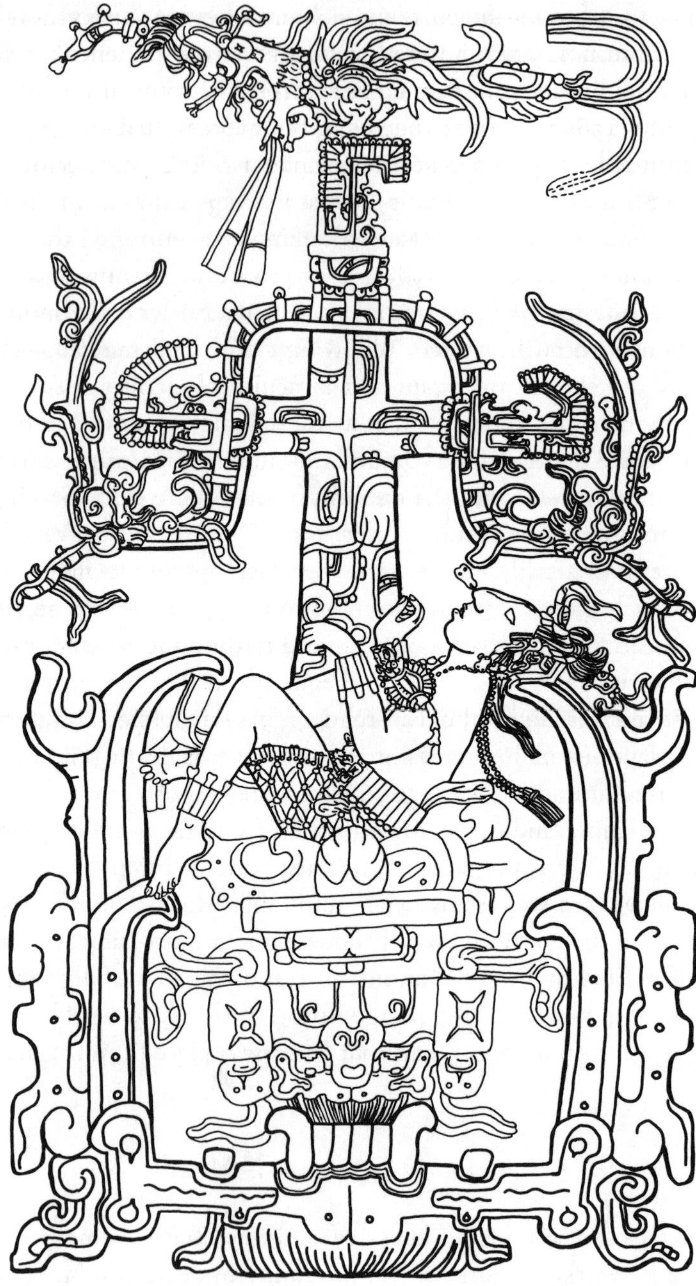

that the huge ceiba tree supports the sky and serves as the pathway used by souls of the dead to reach heaven, while a seventeenth-century Maya text states that the lineage founders emerged from the roots of the ceiba (León-Portilla 1988:136–39). Thus the ceiba, the cypress, and other great trees were perceived by the Mesoamerican peoples as vertical connectors between the upperworld, the middle world, and the underworld (Kolata 1984).

As such, great trees were the metaphorical *axis mundi*, the world axis separating the earth and the sky and thereby maintaining cosmic order. The complex design on an Aztec shield (Kolata 1984:12; Townsend 1979: 38–39) locates the world tree at the center of the horizontal segments of the cosmos, for the solar disk appears in its middle section, with rays pointing to the four world-directions. In fact, four such trees, each with its own symbolic insignia, were thought to be located at each of the world quadrants, with a fifth tree at the cosmic center (see, e.g., central Mexican representations in the *Codex Borgia* 1963:Pls. 49–53; Maya beliefs are described in León-Portilla 1988). Trees were not merely supports, however. Located at the cosmic center, they were conduits by which supernatural powers and influences could be channeled from the otherworld to this world.

As a connector of the vertical levels, a channeler of supernatural power, and the support maintaining cosmic separations and hence world order, the *axis mundi* is a very powerful image. It, too, was appropriated by the state. For example, Aztec rulers were compared in formal speeches with the great trees, for the burden of the kings was the maintenance of social order and stability, while the function of the tree was the maintenance of cosmic order: "The ruler occupied the central position in the social structure, in the same way the ceiba or silk-cotton tree, it was believed, stood at

Figure 3.4. Pakal (died A.D. 683), ruler of Palenque, is shown here at the moment of his death in bas-relief on the lid of his limestone sarcophagus, placed in a tomb beneath the Temple of the Inscriptions. His ornaments are askew as he falls into the maw of a great monster. Above him rises a world tree with a supernatural bird on top and a double-headed serpent in the branches (3.72 m × 2.17 m). (Drawn from Robertson 1983:Fig. 99; surrounding motifs deleted)

the center of the universe" (Heyden 1986:40). In other words, the king was to the state as the tree was to the cosmos (Kolata 1984:14).

The icon of the world tree at the cosmic center is recognizable in Mesoamerican art as a tree or other plant with a bird in the branches representing the celestial sphere and a chthonic zoomorph or other representation of the earth at its base. A common variant was of the world tree as an upturned crocodilian with its head on the earth and its tail in the sky. One example comes from Late Formative Izapa, whose Stela 25 portrays an upended saurian with a bird in the "branches" formed from its tail (Fig. 3.5; Norman 1973). The crocodilian, a symbol of cosmic power in the Americas (Lathrap 1985), also represented the surface of the earth itself and so must be figuratively tilted 90 degrees upward to form the tree. This imagery thereby mimics the unfolding of the cosmos, the original cosmogonic separation between earth and sky that was effected in Aztec belief by gods who separated the crocodilian earth monster into two parts and lifted one part up to form the sky (see, e.g., *Historia de los Mexicanos por sus Pinturas* 1941:210–11; *Histoyre du Mechique* 1905:29).

Moreover, the body of the crocodilian (as the earth) becomes the trunk of the world tree, meaning that the tree is like the earth's interior as the place of origin of peoples (Helms 1977:64). This meaning is apparent in Postclassic period Mixtec manuscript paintings and incised bones that depict the origin of human beings, especially of the ancestors of the rulers, as an emergence out of the trunk of the world tree (Fig. 3.6; Furst 1977; Kolata 1984; compare to Aztec mythology of the emergence of the peoples out of the earth via the earth-monster-mouth/cave). This imagery matches colonial and modern myths from the Mixtec region of a symbolically female "birth tree" (Furst 1977:198).

In contrast to the Mixtec birth tree as the origin place of the ruler's ancestors, their Aztec contemporaries used their own world tree symbol, an eagle perched on a prickly pear cactus growing out of a stone, to mark the location of the most powerful city, Tenochtitlan, at its founding in the past (Fig. 3.7).[3] Thus there is an association between the cosmic center as a tree and the city of Tenochtitlan itself, whose location was divinely marked by the world tree.

Maya rulers, however, showed themselves more individually associated with the world tree, just as the earlier Olmec chiefs and they were

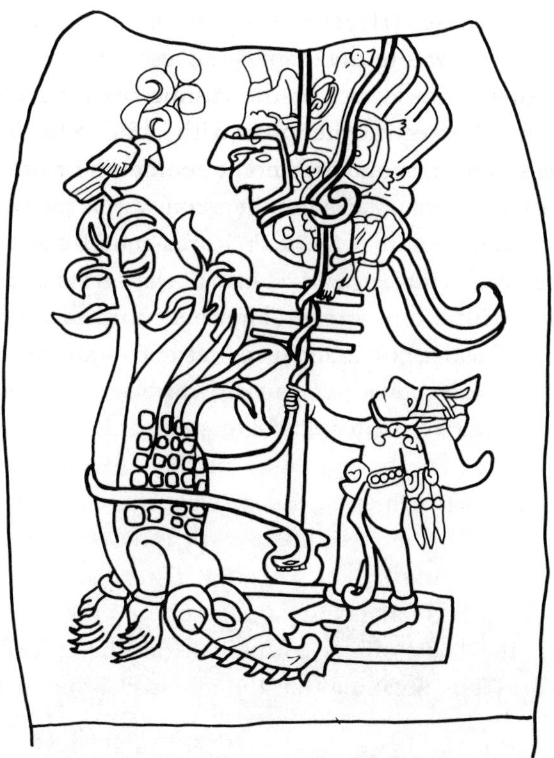

Figure 3.5. Stela 25 from Late Formative Izapa, a Pacific coast lowland site, depicts in low relief an upturned crocodilian transformed into a tree. In its leafy, branching tail sits a bird. A snake's head lies in a vessel, while the snake's body wraps around the crocodile tree, curls around a staff held by a human, and then loops around another, larger bird perched on a staff (height: 1.28 m). (Drawn from Norman 1973:Pl. 42)

portrayed in the cave-like entrance to the underworld. The sarcophagus lid from Pakal's tomb at Palenque (Fig. 3.4) shows the dead king juxtaposed against the world tree, which has the celestial bird at the top and a monster head at the base within the chthonic realm. His successor had himself depicted standing next to similar images of trees on monuments relating his accession as king to the raising of the world tree (Schele and Miller 1986: Figs. II.6, IV.4).

Other Maya artworks reveal that the king himself could take the place of the world tree (see especially Schele and Miller 1986; Freidel and Schele 1988a). Stelae and sumptuary objects were created which depict the ruler wearing a headdress with branching vegetation, such that he took on the characteristics, and hence the qualities, of the tree. This imagery begins early; it appears, for example, in the Late Formative period on Stela 11 from Kaminaljuyu, a highland Maya settlement (Parsons 1986:Pl. 169). On this upright stone the ruler is shown in bas-relief standing on an earth register represented by the incurving fangs of the earth monster. His body is like the trunk of the tree, his headdress has a polymorphic head with leafy branches, and above him is a stylized celestial bird. Late Classic period Maya kings often were shown wearing the abbreviated world tree on their aprons (Schele 1987a:2; Schele and Miller 1986:77).

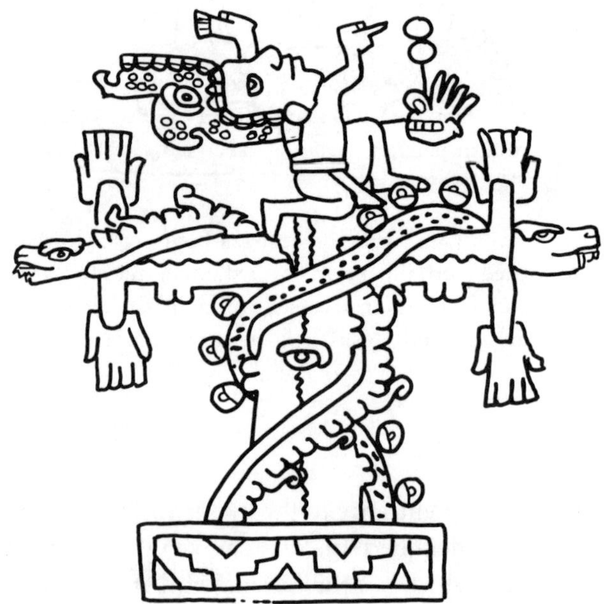

Figure 3.6. A Postclassic Mixtec painted manuscript, the *Codex Selden* (1964 p. 2, position 1), shows the origin of humans as an emergence from a "birth tree." The man coming out of the tree is still tied to it by an umbilical cord. Two snakes, one marked with spots and eyelike stars and the other marked with curls, are entwined around the tree.

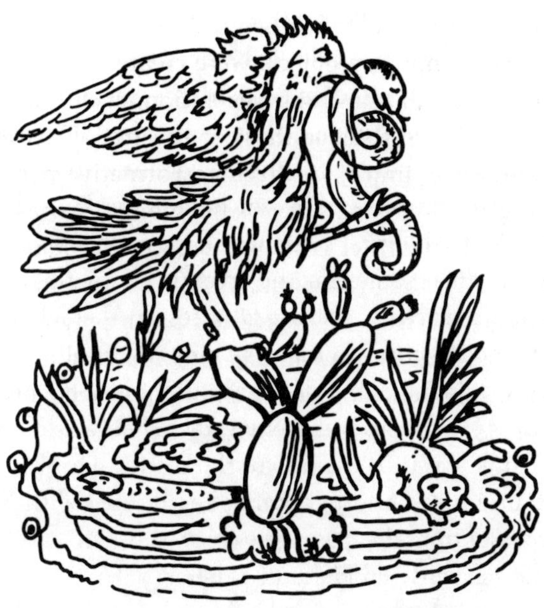

Figure 3.7. This painted illustration of the founding of the city of Tenochtitlan, to accompany Diego Durán's sixteenth-century history of the Aztecs, shows the eagle with a snake in its mouth perched atop a prickly pear cactus, which grows from a rock in the midst of Lake Texcoco. (Drawn from Durán 1967:Vol. 2:Fig. 6)

Thus, whereas the Aztecs related the ruler to a tree by the use of simile—the king, by nature of his position as imposer of state order, is like the great tree—the Maya rulers had themselves individually depicted visually, and even directly referred to, as trees (see Freidel and Schele 1988a). Hieroglyphic texts indicate that Maya stone stelae, on which the rulers were portrayed, were called "tree-stone" (*te-tun*), an image of the ruler as a tree fixed for all time in stone (Schele and Stuart 1986). The artworks suggest that the king himself actually personified the world tree and that his body became a conduit for supernatural forces such that he could temporarily be possessed by them during rituals (Schele and Miller 1986:183). This supposition fits well with a general model of the charismatic quality of Lowland Maya rulership, in which a key feature was "the ability of the king to confront personally the supernatural as a sorcerer, curer, and prophet on behalf of his people" (Freidel and Schele 1988a:559).

The notion that the Maya ruler did indeed become a living world pivot and cosmic center is supported as well in the sacralization of space accomplished by the patterned layout of decorated buildings and plaza areas. From the Late Formative period on, there is architectural information concerning a modeling of the universe in which the Maya king played a dynamic and critical role. Archaeological evidence suggests that some early temple-pyramids served as great stages for the erection of four-part designs, often represented by huge stucco supernatural faces on the side of the pyramid or by four great wooden posts on top. The king, by standing in the fifth and central position, would have completed the design by his presence (Freidel and Schele 1988a:552, 561) and thereby established world order.

The Maya king was thus the hub of the cosmic wheel, and the sun and stars rotated around him. Another symbol associated with Maya kingship is a scepter representing the passageway of the sun and other celestial bodies across the heavens (Freidel and Schele 1988b:73). By holding this scepter, the king not only supported the heavens, like a world tree, but also maintained the cosmic spatio-temporal order established preeminently by the movement of these bodies across the sky.

The use of a tree image to depict the king as an animate mediating pathway can be related to the political situation of the Classic period Lowland Maya. The Maya were divided politically into numerous small rival territories, most of which were headed by independent rulers. Ideologically, these polities competed with each other for the claim of possessing *the* cosmic center in the person of their king. Especially in the Late Classic period, Maya warfare imagery emphasizes the capture of rulers and elite groups from other cities (Schele and Miller 1986:209ff). In the case of the capture and sacrifice of a king, it is as if one could thereby take away the *axis mundi*, the access to supernatural power, of one's rivals, and hence the symbol par excellence of their legitimacy as an independent polity.

The Mountain as Access to the Heavens

Mountains were, and continue to be, the focus of ritual activity in Mesoamerica as the dwelling places of gods and ancestors (Tedlock 1986:128). The pre-Columbian peoples also built artificial mountains, pyramids of stone and earth with buildings on top (called temples), reached by stairways. Photographs of the now jungle-covered Classic Maya city of Tikal indicate an important feature of the five great temple-pyramids there: the bases of the temples lie approximately at the tops of the modern trees. Those temples are literally in the heavens, above the trees. The pyramid, like the Tower of Babel, connects earth and sky and links people to the gods and ancestors in the upperworld.

As a conjunction of upperworld/underworld pathways already described, several of the Maya pyramids are funerary monuments, particularly those with nine architectural levels, possibly symbolizing the layers of the underworld in Mesoamerican thought. They were built over the underground tombs holding the earthly remains of individual named kings (such as the Temple of the Inscriptions overlying Pakal's tomb at Palenque), who were believed to reside in immortal form within the temples at the summit (Miller 1986:56–57).

The use of a pyramid as a stairway to the upperworld and a stage for the rituals performed by charismatic kings began in the Lowland Maya area in the Formative period (Freidel and Schele 1988b:45). Some of these early pyramids are distinguished by the embellishment of giant stucco heads of supernaturals on their façades. The insignia of these heads were later directly appropriated by kings, who not only substituted their own faces for those of the supernaturals but also adorned themselves with the accoutrements of those earlier heads as part of their royal costume (1988b:55, 62). Thus the king was figuratively "wearing" — and hence becoming one with — the pyramid, taking for himself the markers associated with that sacred pathway to the upperworld (just as he also claimed to be the living world tree).

In other parts of Mesoamerica, however, pyramids are associated less with individual kings as sacred persons, who literally embody the power of the state, than with the mapping of sacred places. This contrast is apparent in the Classic period, seen in the very different media and messages in Maya art and in that of the great central Mexican city-state, Teotihuacan, best known for its massive Pyramid of the Sun and Pyramid of the Moon (these are later appellations).[4] Whereas the Maya elite art portrays named kings acting as cosmic pivots and world trees or directly contacting deified ancestors and gods via their sacrificial bloodletting, the art of Teotihuacan lacks such portraiture, emphasizing animals, abstract symbols, supernaturals, and anonymous humans, some distinguished by insignia indicating an office or grouping not yet fully understood. These images are most apparent in the polychrome painted murals that are still preserved in several of the building interiors, as well as on architectural embellishments and portable decorated objects, but there are very few freestanding stone monuments.

The Tepantitla mural at Teotihuacan (Pasztory 1976) portrays what appear to be anonymous priests in the act of "addressing" a central image, interpreted as the cosmic center because a great tree grows out of it. This central image (e.g., Heyden 1981:Fig. 3) may actually represent an anthropomorphized mountain or pyramid (Schele n.d.) drawn with human arms and hands. The size and number of pyramids at this great city are such that the buildings themselves should have been a major focus of Teotihuacan ideology, and their sacred qualities may have been shown in this nonrepresentational and anthropomorphized form.

The lower part of this image is a "cave-like" inverted U from which liquid flows, and liquid also drips from the image's hands. Depicted immediately below this icon, and separated from it by a register marking, is a mountain made of water, which flows off to irrigate agricultural fields. In Mesoamerican belief, as noted above, water was stored in the underworld and the Pyramid of the Sun was erected over a cave that once held water, so this mural may represent the same relationship of a pyramid over a "cave" in terms of its association with access to the water and other sacred qualities of the underworld (Heyden 1981:3, 5). If so, it juxtaposes the pathways of the pyramid-mountain and the world tree, which connect to the upperworld, with an underworld (lower register) scene of watery abundance and agricultural fertility in the context of some ritual performed at that cosmic center by persons who remain anonymous.

The lower part of the Tepantitla mural thereby literally depicts a "water hill," an image that may represent an underworld-upperworld conjunction. In the Nahuatl language of the Aztecs, *altepetl* (Karttunen 1983: 9), meaning "it is water, it is a hill," was the major word for "city" and also referred to the territory ruled by that city and to its king (Marcus 1983a: 207). Other iconographic evidence indicates that mountain or hill symbols were used to represent particular towns or polities—such that this pathway to power connoted an entire community—as early as the Late Formative

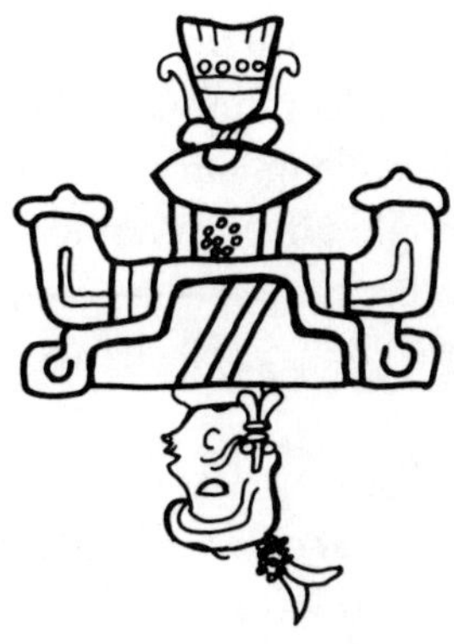 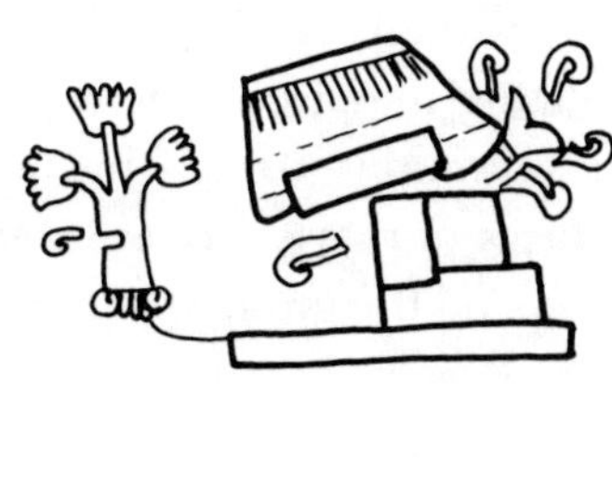

Figure 3.8. Two representations of conquest. On the left is the principal motif from a Late Formative low relief stone slab set into the wall of Building J at the Zapotec center of Monte Albán (drawn from Marcus 1983b:Fig. 4.14). The upside-down head under the stepped mountain glyph indicates conquest of a polity which is named by the glyph on top. The icon on the right, of a burning temple atop a pyramid, is from the sixteenth-century Aztec painted manuscript the *Codex Mendoza* (1980: fol. 6r). The "speaking tree" beside it is the glyph for the town of Quauhnahuac (modern Cuernavaca).

Zapotec culture in the Valley of Oaxaca. At their paramount city, Monte Albán, flat stone slabs were carved in low relief for architectural placement within the ceremonial center. The monuments presumably communicate the "conquest" of other communities. The central message of these monuments is composed of an inverted stepped **U** motif — a mountain — representing a polity, with a glyph on top naming the community conquered and an inverted head below to indicate conquest (Fig. 3.8; see other examples in Caso 1965 and Marcus 1976).

The use of mountain glyphs to represent named towns continued to the time of the Spanish conquest in Mixtec and Aztec painted art. In Postclassic Mixtec painting, the act of conquest was indicated by an arrow piercing the mountain glyph naming a place, or flames emerging from that glyph (Smith 1973:33). In some of the pictographic Aztec manuscript paintings, the conquest of a town was shown by a picture of a burning temple atop the pyramid as an artificial mountain and next to a glyph that represents that town (see *Codex Mendoza* 1980 and Fig. 3.8). These latter depictions reflect the reality of warfare, in which the attacking side attempted to destroy the main temple-pyramid of a community, thereby neutralizing the place of access to its patron gods and signaling the defeat of the community itself. This means that the temple on its pyramid — the ritual focus of that polity as its access to supernatural power — represented the town and the group that lived there (Townsend 1979:54) in actual practice as well as in the art.

Thus, whereas the representations of Late Classic Maya warfare emphasized the capture of named rulers and nobles of rival cities, as if to represent those polities as deprived of their conduits to supernatural power, in highland central Mexico an image of the destruction of the temple-pyramid of a named community was used to communicate this same feat. Here again the contrast is present between the sacred person of the king and the sacred place associated with the community as the focus for both ritual and art.

While the sacred-mountain/temple-pyramid was an important concept and icon among the Late Postclassic Aztecs in highland Mexico, as it was for the earlier Classic Period Teotihuacanos, the Aztec kings are not entirely absent from this imagery. Very late in the pre-Hispanic period, named kings appear in the art, although they are more frequently shown dressed as priests rather than as kings (Klein 1987), making sacrifices and interceding with supernaturals on behalf of their people, as was the function of the separate priesthood. Unlike their earlier Teotihuacan counterparts (who may also have dressed as the priests depicted in the art), we know these individuals are kings of Tenochtitlan because name glyphs were added to their depictions. One example is the low-relief greenstone slab called the Dedication Stone, which portrays the kings Tizoc and Ahuitzotl (Pasztory 1983:150–51, Pl. 95). Dressed as priests, they are engaged in autosacrifice, drawing blood from their ears and legs. Their blood flows into the stylized maw of a great earth monster.

The detailed Aztec ethnohistorical documentation indicates why the kings are shown as priests — rather than in kingly regalia — when performing sacrifices, in contrast to Classic Maya ideology as known from their hieroglyphic writing. The Maya kings used their writing system and art to reiterate their contention that the living kings imitated the acts of the creator gods and thus became one with them. Because of this continuity in ritual action, the kings could contact the gods, often through autosacrifice.

Bloodletting rituals and paraphernalia were an integral part of the imagery of kingship (see especially Schele and Miller 1986). The king's role as the personified conduit to the otherworld is further revealed in Maya art and architecture, indicating that he was the living world tree, the living cosmic pivot.

In contrast, the kings of Tenochtitlan, the most powerful Aztec city, were said to have received the right to rule by being members of a particular ethnic group that acquired hegemony from its tutelary god following a long migration from the place of origin (a cave). In Tenochtitlan state history, elaborated in both ritual and art, the tutelary god, Huitzilopochtli, did not choose the king, nor was the king his lineal descendant. Instead, the god pointed out the sacred place where his chosen people were to build their temple-pyramid, the Templo Mayor (Great Temple), and thus have access to him through the intermediary of a priestly bureaucracy.

This place was marked by a world tree with a celestial bird on top, an eagle that was Huitzilopochtli himself in his solar aspect (see Fig. 3.7). The world tree, shown as a cactus growing from a stone, is actually the place glyph of Tenochtitlan in the pictographic writing system, meaning that this city, and more particularly the temple to its patron god, was the cosmic center. That this pyramid was to be used to contact the god is revealed elsewhere in the Aztec histories, for Huitzilopochtli was said to have been born on top of such a sacred mountain (e.g., *Codex Azcatitlan* 1949; see Fig. 3.9); that is, he originally traveled from the upperworld of gods to the world of mankind via this pathway.

The function of the Templo Mayor as a pivot for the celestial movements that defined spatio-temporal order is seen in its position and orientation in relation to the annual movement of the sun, especially for sighting the sun at equinox (Aveni et al. 1988). As the pivot and access point at the cosmic center, the Templo Mayor, a sacred mountain whose location was marked by the world tree, should metaphorically coincide with the cave-like entrance to the underworld. This may explain why the Dedication Stone described above, a monument thought to have been created to commemorate a major rebuilding of the Templo Mayor in 1487 (Townsend 1979:40), does not depict the pyramid itself but instead shows two kings as priests sacrificing their blood to feed the earth-monster mouth, indicating that the earth-entrance meaning was also associated with the pyramid.

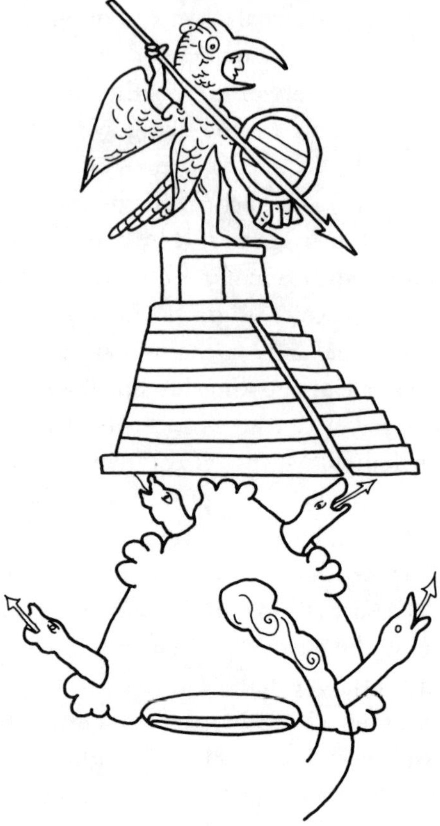

Figure 3.9. A postconquest Aztec painted manuscript, the *Codex Azcatitlan* (1949), shows the "birth" of Tenochtitlan's patron god, Huitzilopochtli, in his hummingbird guise. He stands on a temple-pyramid that sits atop the mountain glyph adorned with serpents, naming this place as Coatepec, the "Serpent-Hill."

All three mediating pathways, but now with the addition of the identified king, coincide in a Late Aztec monolithic sculpture known as the Temple of Sacred War (Fig. 3.10; Townsend 1979:49–62). This sculpture demonstrates the conjunction of the concept of the sacred place with the personalized role of the king in Aztec art during the last few years before the Spanish conquest. It is a three-dimensional model of a temple-pyramid, carved in bas-relief on every surface but its base. It is marked on the back

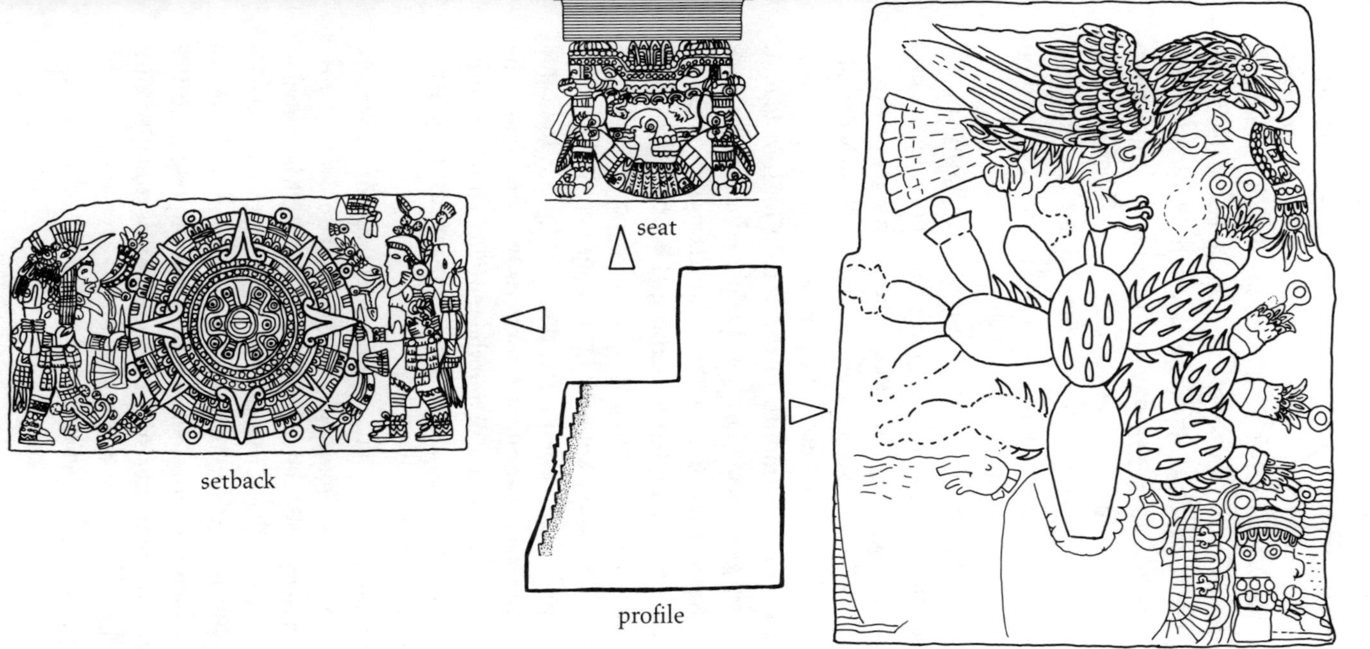

Figure 3.10. This three-dimensional Aztec stone model of a temple-pyramid, called the Temple of Sacred War, combines all three pathways to power, together with a king identified by a name glyph. Besides representing a sacred mountain, this monument is also a throne, as the side-view (lower center) shows. The stippled area indicates the approximate location of the thirteen nonfunctional steps on the front. When the ruler Motecuhzoma II sat on his throne, he leaned back against the solar disk (left), representing the sun and the world directions, on the right side of which he had himself portrayed. He sat down on the mouth of an earth monster (upper center), and behind him, on the eroded back side (right), is the world tree, the symbol of the city of Tenochtitlan at its founding (height 1.2 m). (Drawn from Townsend 1979:50–51 and Pasztory 1983:165–69; other designs omitted)

with the Tenochtitlan place glyph, the prickly pear cactus as world tree, which grows out of an earth monster, indicating that the pyramid represents the community of Tenochtitlan as well as the Templo Mayor at the cosmic center. The front shows the sun disk, its rays forming a cosmogram that also locates the cosmic center. Flanking the disk are two personages. The one on the left has the accoutrements of the patron deity of Tenochtitlan, Huitzilopochtli (Townsend 1979:55), and the one on the right has a name glyph identifying him as Motecuhzoma II, the last pre-Hispanic king of Tenochtitlan (Umberger 1984:73–78). A top view shows that below the solar disk and above the nonfunctional stairway on the pyramid front is an earth monster with a wide-open zoomorphic mouth.

These combined images become more meaningful in terms of the association of this sacred mountain model with kingship when the function of the monolith is considered. Its shape and size indicate that it is a throne (Umberger 1984), so it functioned like the Olmec altars. When Motecuhzoma sat upon it (it was found in the area of his palace [Umberger 1984: 64]), he was literally sitting on the mouth of the earth monster, like an Olmec ruler in his niche or Pakal on his sarcophagus poised above the maw of the earth. When he leaned back against the solar disk, he juxtaposed himself with the moving sun, its rays representing the world directions emerging from the cosmic center. Furthermore, he aligned himself with the world tree (on the back), as Maya kings had centuries before. However, he was sitting on the symbol of his community, the sacred place, indicated by both the temple-pyramid/sacred-mountain form of the throne and the world tree denoting the city of Tenochtitlan and the temple that represented it. Thus his charter of rulership ultimately derived from his association with his people, his city, and their tutelary god.

The conjunction revealed in this late monumental work of what were elsewhere apparently two contrasting ideologies of rulership may reflect the growing interaction between the central highlands and the Maya area — the "grand Mesoamerican synthesis that was effected in the Postclassic period" (Willey 1973:158). It may also represent an evolution in the ideology of Aztec kingship, which was originally based on an impersonal office but which was acquiring the characteristics of a nascent personality cult, aided by the manipulation of imagery in state art.

The Serpent as Mediator

The artworks described in this brief survey include certain animals that in the Mesoamerican worldview were thought of as cosmic connectors: the crocodilian as the world tree; the celestial bird, which links the upperworld and the earth's surface; and the jaguar, often associated with the underworld but which travels on the ground and sleeps in trees (Helms 1977:55). Nevertheless, among all the animals that appear as cosmic agents in the art of Mesoamerica, one stands out because it appears prominently with the imagery of all three mediating pathways: the serpent.

The nonhuman "monster" whose mouth serves as the cave-like entrance to the otherworld is sometimes identifiable as a serpent. An example dating back to the Formative period is a painting of a man in a bird costume seated on a great open-mouthed serpent head. The painting was placed on a hillside above an actual cave entrance at Oxtotitlan in western Mexico (Grove n.d.). The similarities this animal exhibits with the zoomorphic head above the niche on Olmec La Venta Altar 4 (Fig. 3.3) led to the identification of that animal as a serpent also (David Grove, personal communication, 1991). A serpent's mouth is painted around the doorway in which Classic period Maya kings sat at Palenque (House E; Robertson 1985:Fig. 432), placing them in the same setting as an Olmec ruler in his altar niche. The semiskeletonized maw receiving the Maya king Pakal at his death, carved on the lid of his sarcophagus, belongs to a serpent (Fig. 3.4). Many of the temple entrances that were marked as mouths, indicating that their interiors were the sacred space of the otherworld, can also be recognized as serpents (e.g., *Codex Borgia* 1963:Pl. 14; for other examples, see Schávelzon 1980).

As for the world tree, numerous depictions include a serpent or a doubled serpent wrapped around its trunk. For example, a serpent appears in doubled form on a Mixtec "birth tree" (Fig. 3.6). On Izapa Stela 25, with the "crocodilian-tree" (Fig. 3.5), there is a snake wrapped around the body of the saurian, rising from below the earth and wrapping around the celestial bird, linking these motifs to a staff held by a person who mimics the tree. Double-headed serpents loll in the branches of the world tree in some of the Maya artworks, such as on Pakal's sarcophagus lid (Fig. 3.4). On the

Aztec "cactus tree," which serves as the Tenochtitlan place glyph, the eagle on top is sometimes shown grasping a snake in its mouth (Fig. 3.7).

The third pathway, the pyramid as sacred mountain connecting the earth with the sky, sometimes has preserved serpent markings — especially in central Mexican cultures, but there are also some Maya examples. For example, Tenochtitlan's Templo Mayor and a Postclassic pyramid at nearby Tenayuca are decorated with three-dimensional serpent heads and full-figure serpents. Tenochtitlan histories and manuscript paintings collected after the conquest explain one particular relationship between snakes and pyramids in that the sacred mountain where the tutelary god, Huitzilopochtli, was born — that is, where he left the realm of the gods and entered the realm of mankind — is called "Serpent-Hill," the serpent again marking this cosmic pathway (Fig. 3.9).

This imagery appeared much earlier in central Mexico at Teotihuacan, where three-dimensional stone serpent heads with bas-relief bodies decorated the entire outer surface of a major Early Classic pyramid and serpent heads were placed at the tops and bases of many stairway balustrades. Similar serpent icons embellished some Maya pyramids in the Late and Terminal Classic periods, perhaps due to known interregional contact between central Mexico and the Maya area but also resulting from the shared pan-Mesoamerican cosmology. For example, the Terminal Classic Maya site of Chichen Itza in Yucatan has serpent balustrades very similar to those at the later central Mexican Aztec Templo Mayor (Molina Montes 1987:102).

The serpent-marked balustrades give the impression that the stairways that conveyed elite personages to the structures on top of the pyramids were akin to the body of a serpent. More literally, the Hieroglyphic Stairway at the Late Classic Maya site of Copan has been described as the body of a great serpent (Gordon 1902:10). Because the hieroglyphic text carved on its steps names the predecessors of a king, he could go back into the past as he went up the stairs into the upperworld. This serpent stairway was his personal conduit — via his royal predecessors — to other-worldly powers.

One reason why the serpent was linked with these other icons representing the transcendence of cosmic categories in Mesoamerican thought may be its natural characteristics, as these were observed. Different species of snakes live on land, underground, in water, and in trees, and hence seem to link the vertical dimensions of the cosmos. Furthermore, they neither walk nor fly like other creatures of these realms and are ambiguous in this respect (see discussion in Hunt 1977:74–80). Some are poisonous and cause death, but their shape resembles the phallus, umbilical cord, and lightning, referring to fertility, birth, and rain — life-giving imagery. Thus serpents can also indicate a duality of life and death, or death and rebirth when they shed their skins. Most important, however, was the explicit belief that serpents were conceived to be "roads" (Sullivan 1986:14).

The Mesoamerican peoples developed variations on this theme of the transcendence of the serpent as a combined terrestrial and celestial phenomenon, frequently by juxtaposing a snake with a bird. For example, a bird-man sits on a serpent head in the Oxtotitlan painting described above. Other combinations include a winged or feathered serpent, a bird with a "serpent-wing," as occurs on the Celestial Bird on Pakal's sarcophagus (Fig. 3.4; Robertson 1983:60), and a culture hero or deity named Feathered Serpent. Some pyramids at Chichen Itza and also at Tula, its counterpart site in central Mexico, are topped by three-dimensional feathered-serpent columns with their heads on the platform and their tails in the air. These columns served as the doorway into the temple on top so that the serpent is simultaneously the threshold into sacred space (the temple) and the earth-sky connector atop the pyramid.

In all of these cultures, serpents — as cosmic links and power channelers — came to be associated with rulership in the elite artworks, which served to encapsulate and convey messages about the constructed reality. Objects decorated with serpents or made to look like snakes became instruments to denote the qualities of rulership, and as such they again reveal a difference between the more charismatic personified rulers of the Olmecs and Classic Mayas and the anonymous leaders whose status was tied to their office or to a sacred place rather than to personal qualities. In Olmec and Maya artworks, the rulers hold a serpent image to denote their position. For example, a small Olmec greenstone celt is incised with a design showing a man holding a serpent like a ceremonial bar (Joralemon 1976: Fig. 11b), analogous to Late Classic Maya kingship symbols, the double-headed serpent bar and the serpent-footed manikin scepter (Schele and Miller 1986:49).

The Maya kings, who performed blood sacrifice in order to contact the otherworldly realm, expressed this ritualistic threshold status in their art with a giant snake whose body served as the conduit through which supernatural beings could travel to the world of mankind, emerging from the serpent's mouth (Schele and Miller 1986:46–47). The kings had themselves depicted holding these serpent icons to communicate their ability to transcend and connect the different spatio-temporal segments of the cosmos as a world pivot and support for the entire cosmic order. This use of serpents contrasts with the serpent-shaped handles of Postclassic Aztec and Mixtec incense burners. These objects had a similar function as instruments of supernatural contact but were held by anonymous priests (or by kings acting as priests), mediators on behalf of their community as part of an established state hierarchy of positions and functions.

The sacred histories preserved in Aztec exegetical texts of the Postclassic period, collected after the Spanish conquest, help to explain this nonpersonalized relationship between serpents and kings, a concept also found among the Postclassic (as opposed to Classic) Maya, perhaps as a result of interaction with highland Mexico. According to these documents, the founder of the office of kingship itself, from whence later kings derived their power, was a culture hero named Feathered Serpent. Feathered Serpent was both a man and a god, a duality that is reflected as well in his combined terrestrial-celestial name and in his establishment of kingship at the sacred locality that was conceived of as the threshold between the otherworld and this world. Ethnic groups competing for hegemony included in their own histories the story of a migration to the sacred place from which the right to rulership was derived (Gillespie 1989). Thus the serpent as a pathway to cosmic power in these late cultures was associated with the office of kingship, at the top of an impersonal state hierarchy, and not with the persona and ritual actions of individual charismatic kings.

To summarize, among the Mesoamerican cultures certain shared images were used to construct and communicate complex ideas about the state and the cosmos, especially ideas dealing with the nature of a king as a powerful being who transcended cultural categories, for "sovereign power itself partakes of the nature of the opposition, combines in itself the elementary antithesis" (Sahlins 1985:90–91). The decorated objects and architecture, the material manifestation of these ideas, took on a sacred quality, as demonstrated by the "termination" of some artworks and buildings, particularly those of the Olmecs and Mayas that were personally associated with individual kings (Grove 1981; Schele and Miller 1986:43–44). The manipulation of these icons facilitated the reworking of the concepts that shaped their creation. In this way the elite could expand their political power within society in part by modifying the visual expression of their charter of rulership, which was ultimately based on their access to supernatural power, by using these images in public ritual.

Examining the similarity and variety in the manifestation of the different mediating pathways to cosmic power in Mesoamerican art — the cave, the tree, the mountain, and the serpent — has demonstrated, first, that these high cultures did share a unified ideological base, as seen in their adherence to common themes, and second, that major differences in the nature of rulership and the construction of state authority are revealed in the contexts of these images. These differences can be reduced to a dichotomy, which has been simplified here as a contrast between highland (central Mexico and Oaxaca) and lowland (Olmec and Maya) peoples. This dichotomy apparently dissolved at the end of the Classic period, when interregional interactions became more intense and more powerful state organizations extended their hegemonies.

By studying these images from an iconographic perspective, in the totality of their cultural contexts as we understand them, we begin to explore the operation and evolution of society in pre-Columbian Mesoamerica. While we cannot fully decode the messages of these artworks, nor faithfully reconstruct the nature of the experience of creating and using them, we can at least appreciate the significance of art as a highly creative and meaningful medium for human communication, one that still speaks to us today.

ACKNOWLEDGMENTS

My thanks go to David C. Grove, Rosemary A. Joyce, Helaine Silverman, Scott O'Mack, and Alma Gottlieb for their useful information and comments on earlier versions of this paper. I am grateful to Norman and Sibby Whitten for the opportunity to introduce these ideas in the environment of supportive interaction provided by their symposium.

NOTES

1. This usage approximates the distinction Silverman makes in Chapter 5 between "sacred" and "popular" art (following Kubler), although I do not see these two terms as opposed to one another and prefer the more general contrast — elite and non-elite artworks — based on the group in society which archaeologists presume directed its production or for whose use it was intended. Elite artworks are identified by their material, craftsmanship, and spatial context.

2. The figures in this chapter were drawn by the author, based on published versions of varying quality. Several of the stone monuments contain eroded or broken areas. In some cases, surrounding motifs have been eliminated to focus the reader's attention on the major icon under discussion.

3. This symbol has since been appropriated as the central element on the national flag of Mexico.

4. Recent evidence indicates that there were human burials under an early pyramid, the Pyramid of the Feathered Serpent, at Teotihuacan (Sugiyama 1989). These may be part of a complex that marked that pyramid as having some funerary aspects.

REFERENCES CITED

Aveni, Anthony F., Edward E. Calnek, and Horst Hartung
    1988   Myth, Environment, and the Orientation of the Templo Mayor of Tenochtitlan. *American Antiquity* 53:287–309.

Berlo, Janet Catherine, ed.
    1983   *Text and Image in Pre-Columbian Art: Essays on the Interrelationship of the Verbal and Visual Arts.* British Archaeological Reports, International Series, n. 180. Oxford.

Brady, James E.
    1988   The Sexual Connotation of Caves in Mesoamerican Ideology. *Mexicon* 10:51–55.

Caso, Alfonso
    1965   Zapotec Writing and Calendar. In *Handbook of Middle American Indians*, vol. 3: *Archaeology of Southern Mesoamerica*, pt. 2, edited by Gordon R. Willey, 931–47. Austin: University of Texas Press.

Codex Azcatitlan
    1949   Commentary by Robert Barlow. *Journal de la Société des Américanistes de Paris* 38:101–35.

Codex Borgia
1963   Commentaries by Eduard Seler. Mexico City: Fondo de Cultura Económica.

Codex Mendoza
1980   *Códice Mendocino: Documento Mexicano del Siglo XVI.* Commentaries by Jesús Galindo y Villa. Mexico City: Editorial Innovación.

Codex Selden
1964   Commentaries by Alfonso Caso. Mexico City: Sociedad Mexicana de Antropología.

Durán, Diego
1967   *Historia de las Indias de Nueva España e Islas de la Tierra Firme.* 2 vols. Edited by Angel Ma. Garibay K. Mexico City: Editorial Porrua.

Elzey, Wayne
1976   Some Remarks on the Space and Time of the "Center" in Aztec Religion. *Estudios de Cultura Náhuatl* 12:315–34.

Freidel, David A., and Linda Schele
1988a   Kingship in the Late Preclassic Maya Lowlands: The Instruments and Places of Ritual Power. *American Anthropologist* 90:547–67.
1988b   Symbol and Power: A History of the Lowland Maya Cosmogram. In *Maya Iconography*, edited by Elizabeth P. Benson and Gillett G. Griffin, 44–93. Princeton, N.J.: Princeton University Press.

Furst, Jill Leslie
1977   The Tree Birth Tradition in the Mixteca, Mexico. *Journal of Latin American Lore* 3:183–226.

Gillespie, Susan D.
1989   *The Aztec Kings: The Construction of Rulership in Mexica History.* Tucson: University of Arizona Press.

Gordon, George Byron
1902   *The Hieroglyphic Stairway, Ruins of Copan.* Memoirs of the Peabody Museum of American Archaeology and Ethnology, vol. 1, no. 6. Cambridge, Mass.: Peabody Museum.

Gould, Steven Jay
1988   A Tale of Three Pictures. *Natural History* 97 (5): 14–21.

Grigsby, Thomas L.
1986   In the Stone Warehouse: The Survival of a Cave Cult in Central Mexico. *Journal of Latin American Lore* 12:161–79.

Grove, David C.

1973   Olmec Altars and Myths. *Archaeology* 26 (2): 128–35.

1981   Olmec Monuments: Mutilation as a Clue to Meaning. In *The Olmec and Their Neighbors*, edited by Elizabeth P. Benson, 48–68. Washington, D.C.: Dumbarton Oaks.

1984   *Chalcatzingo: Excavations on the Olmec Frontier*. London: Thames and Hudson.

n.d.   Olmec Serpents and Symbols of Rulership. Paper presented at the 86th Annual Meeting of the American Anthropological Association, Chicago, 1987.

Grove, David C., and Susan D. Gillespie

n.d.   Ideology and Evolution at the Pre-State Level: Formative Period Mesoamerica. Paper presented at the School of American Research Advanced Seminar "Ideology and the Cultural Evolution of Civilizations." Santa Fe, 1987.

Gruzinski, Serge

1987   Colonial Indian Maps in Sixteenth-Century Mexico. *Res: Anthropology and Aesthetics* 13:46–61.

Helms, Mary W.

1977   Iguanas and Crocodilians in Tropical American Mythology and Iconography with Special Reference to Panama. *Journal of Latin American Lore* 3:51–132.

1979   *Ancient Panama: Chiefs in Search of Power*. Austin: University of Texas Press.

Heyden, Doris

1981   Caves, Gods, and Myths: World-View and Planning in Teotihuacan. In *Mesoamerican Sites and World-Views*, edited by Elizabeth P. Benson, 1–35. Washington, D.C.: Dumbarton Oaks.

1986   Metaphors, Nahualtocaitl, and Other "Disguised" Terms Among the Aztecs. In *Symbol and Meaning Beyond the Closed Community: Essays in Mesoamerican Ideas*, edited by Gary H. Gossen, 35–42. Studies on Culture and Society, vol. 1. Albany, N.Y.: Institute for Mesoamerican Studies, State University of New York at Albany.

Historia de los Mexicanos por sus Pinturas

1941   In *Nueva Colección de Documentos para la Historia de México*, edited by Joaquin García Icazbalceta, 3:209–40. Mexico City: Salvador Chávez Hayhoe.

Histoyre du Mechique
1905   Edited by Edouard de Jonghe. *Journal de la Société des Américanistes de Paris* 2:1–41.

Hunt, Eva
1977   *The Transformation of the Hummingbird: Cultural Roots in a Zinacantan Mythical Poem.* Ithaca, N.Y.: Cornell University Press.

Joralemon, Peter David
1976   The Olmec Dragon: A Study in Pre-Columbian Iconography. In *Origins of Religious Art and Iconography in Preclassic Mesoamerica,* edited by H. B. Nicholson, 27–71. Los Angeles: UCLA Latin American Center Publications.

Karttunen, Frances
1983   *An Analytical Dictionary of Nahuatl.* Austin: University of Texas Press.

Klein, Cecilia F.
1987   The Ideology of Autosacrifice at the Templo Mayor. In *The Aztec Templo Mayor,* edited by Elizabeth Hill Boone, 293–370. Washington, D.C.: Dumbarton Oaks.

Kolata, Alan L.
1984   The Tree, the King and the Cosmos: Aspects of Tree Symbolism in Ancient Mesoamerica. *Field Museum of Natural History Bulletin* 55 (3): 10–19.

Lathrap, Donald W.
1977   Gifts of the Cayman: Some Thoughts on the Subsistence Basis of Chavín. In *Pre-Columbian Art History: Selected Readings,* edited by Alana Cordy-Collins and Jean Stern, 333–51. Palo Alto, Calif.: Peek Publications.
1985   Jaws: The Control of Power in the Early Nuclear American Ceremonial Center. In *Early Ceremonial Architecture in the Andes,* edited by Christopher B. Donnan, 241–67. Washington, D.C.: Dumbarton Oaks.

León-Portilla, Miguel
1963   *Aztec Thought and Culture: A Study of the Ancient Nahuatl Mind.* Translated by Jack Emory Davis. Norman: University of Oklahoma Press.
1974   *La Filosofía Náhuatl.* Mexico City: Universidad Nacional Autónoma de México.
1988   *Time and Reality in the Thought of the Maya.* 2d ed. Norman: University of Oklahoma Press.

López Austin, Alfredo

1987   The Masked God of Fire. In *The Aztec Templo Mayor,* edited by Elizabeth Hill Boone, 257–91. Washington, D.C.: Dumbarton Oaks.

Marcus, Joyce

1976   The Iconography of Militarism at Monte Albán and Neighboring Sites in the Valley of Oaxaca. In *Origins of Religious Art and Iconography in Preclassic Mesoamerica,* edited by H. B. Nicholson, 123–39. Los Angeles: UCLA Latin American Center Publications.

1978   Archaeology and Religion: A Comparison of the Zapotec and Maya. *World Archaeology* 10:172–91.

1983a   On the Nature of the Mesoamerican City. In *Prehistoric Settlement Patterns: Essays in Honor of Gordon R. Willey,* edited by Evon Z. Vogt and Richard M. Leventhal, 195–242. Albuquerque: University of New Mexico Press.

1983b   The Conquest Slabs of Building J, Monte Albán. In *The Cloud People: Divergent Evolution of the Zapotec and Mixtec Civilizations,* edited by Kent V. Flannery and Joyce Marcus, 106–8. New York: Academic Press.

Miller, Arthur G.

1986   *Maya Rulers of Time.* Philadelphia: The University Museum, University of Pennsylania.

1989   Comparing Maya Image and Text. In *Word and Image in Maya Culture: Explorations in Language, Writing, and Representation,* edited by William F. Hanks and Don S. Rice, 176–88. Salt Lake City: University of Utah Press.

Molina Montes, Augusto F.

1987   Templo Mayor Architecture: So What's New? In *The Aztec Templo Mayor,* edited by Elizabeth Hill Boone, 97–107. Washington, D.C.: Dumbarton Oaks.

Norman, V. Garth

1973   *Izapa Sculpture.* Part 1: *Album.* Papers of the New World Archaeological Foundation, no. 30. Provo, Utah: Brigham Young University.

Parsons, Lee Allen

1986   *The Origins of Maya Art: Monumental Stone Sculpture of Kaminaljuyu, Guatemala, and the Southern Pacific Coast.* Studies in Pre-Columbian Art and Archaeology, no. 28. Washington, D.C.: Dumbarton Oaks.

Pasztory, Esther
  1976   *The Murals of Tepantitla, Teotihuacan.* New York: Garland Publishing.
  1983   *Aztec Art.* New York: Harry N. Abrams.

Porter, James B.
  1989   Olmec Colossal Heads as Recarved Thrones: "Mutilation," Revolution
          and Recarving. *Res: Anthropology and Aesthetics* 17/18:23–29.

Quirarte, Jacinto
  1977   Terrestrial/Celestial Polymorphs as Narrative Frames in the Art of Izapa
          and Palenque. In *Pre-Columbian Art History: Selected Readings,*
          edited by Alana Cordy-Collins and Jean Stern, 53–62. Palo Alto, Calif.:
          Peek Publications.

Robertson, Merle Greene
  1983   *The Sculpture of Palenque.* Vol. 1: *The Temple of the Inscriptions.*
          Princeton, N.J.: Princeton University Press.
  1985   *The Sculpture of Palenque.* Vol. 3: *The Late Buildings of the Palace.*
          Princeton, N.J.: Princeton University Press.

Sahlins, Marshall
  1985   *Islands of History.* Chicago: University of Chicago Press.

Schávelzon, Daniel
  1980   Temples, Caves, or Monsters? Notes on Zoomorphic Façades in Pre-
          Hispanic Architecture. In *Third Palenque Round Table,* pt. 2, vol. 5,
          edited by Merle Greene Robertson, 151–62. Austin: University of Texas
          Press.

Schele, Linda
  1987a   *A Cached Jade from Temple 26 and the World Tree at Copán.* Copán
          Note 34. Tegucigalpa, Honduras: Instituto Hondureño de Antropología
          e Historia, and the Copán Acropolis Archaeological Project.
  1987b   *The Figures on the Central Marker of Ballcourt AIIb at Copán.* Copán
          Note 13. Tegucigalpa, Honduras: Instituto Hondureño de Antropología
          e Historia, and the Copán Acropolis Archaeological Project.
  n.d.   World Images and Statecraft at Teotihuacan and in the Maya Lowlands.
          Paper presented at the 51st Annual Meeting of the Society for American
          Archaeology, New Orleans, 1986.

Schele, Linda, and Mary Ellen Miller
  1986   *The Blood of Kings: Dynasty and Ritual in Maya Art.* Fort Worth,
          Tex.: Kimbell Art Museum.

Schele, Linda, and David Stuart

1986   *Te-Tun as the Glyph for "Stela."* Copán Note 1. Tegucigalpa, Honduras: Instituto Hondureño de Antropología e Historia, and the Copán Acropolis Archaeological Project.

Smith, Mary Elizabeth

1973   *Picture Writing from Ancient Southern Mexico: Mixtec Place Signs and Maps.* Norman: University of Oklahoma Press.

Soustelle, Jacques

1959   *Pensamiento Cosmológico de los Antiguos Mexicanos (Representación del Mundo y del Espacio).* Translated by María Elena Landa A. Puebla, Mex.: Federación Estudiantil Poblana 1959–1960.

Sugiyama, Saburo

1989   Burials Dedicated to the Old Temple of Quetzalcóatl at Teotihuacan, Mexico. *American Antiquity* 54:85–106.

Sullivan, Thelma D.

1986   A Scattering of Jades: The Words of the Aztec Elders. In *Symbol and Meaning Beyond the Closed Community: Essays in Mesoamerican Ideas,* edited by Gary H. Gossen, 9–17. Studies on Culture and Society, vol. 1. Albany, N.Y.: Institute for Mesoamerican Studies, State University of New York at Albany.

Taube, Karl A.

1986   The Teotihuacan Cave of Origin. *Res: Anthropology and Aesthetics* 12:51–82.

Tedlock, Barbara

1986   On a Mountain in the Dark: Encounters with the Quiché Maya Culture Hero. In *Symbol and Meaning Beyond the Closed Community: Essays in Mesoamerican Ideas,* edited by Gary H. Gossen, 125–38. Studies on Culture and Society, vol. 1. Albany, N.Y.: Institute for Mesoamerican Studies, State University of New York at Albany.

Thompson, J. Eric S.

1970   *Maya History and Religion.* Norman: University of Oklahoma Press.

Townsend, Richard Fraser

1979   State and Cosmos in the Art of Tenochtitlan. *Studies in Pre-Columbian Art and Archaeology,* no. 20. Washington, D.C.: Dumbarton Oaks.

Umberger, Emily

1984   El trono de Moctezuma. *Estudios de Cultura Náhuatl* 17:63–87.

Vogt, Evon Z.
1981   Some Aspects of the Sacred Geography of Highland Chiapas. In *Meso-american Sites and World Views*, edited by Elizabeth P. Benson, 119–38. Washington, D.C.: Dumbarton Oaks.

Willey, Gordon R.
1973   Mesoamerican Art and Iconography and the Integrity of the Mesoamerican Ideological System. In *The Iconography of Middle American Sculpture*, 153–61. New York: Metropolitan Museum of Art.

4

The Modern Gallery Exhibition as a Form
of Western-Indigenous Discourse

J. Edson Way

A characteristic of the growth witnessed in American museums in the last twenty-five years has been the increased significance accorded the educational function of these institutions, especially compared to the purely entertainment value of museums as an option for leisure time. Expanded staffing and budgets for the education department at most museums, the proliferation of educational outreach programs, and interactive exhibition techniques to engage and challenge the visitors' curiosity have been other developments, along with "blockbuster" exhibits, to heighten the public's expectation of museum performance. Furthermore, the leadership coming to the museum profession from those involved in "client-centered" children's museums has spurred the often-latent interest of museums in providing an appropriate experience for their visitors in contrast to a more passive approach to audience engagement.

These developments, which are part of a drive for a more democratic role for museums in contemporary society, are at least partly the result of a greater concern within the museum profession for a socially responsible role for our institutions, acknowledging the challenge of addressing the needs of a pluralistic community. This awareness is accompanied by a greater reliance on public monies whether from admissions fees or grants from government or private cultural agencies seeking the broadest public benefit from the funds they disburse. The effect has been to popularize the museum in the community and to increase public appreciation of the museum as a credible vehicle for the preservation of the best "museum quality" objects, the most authoritative presentation of knowledge regarding the objects, and the fairest interpretation of their significance. Furthermore, there is a general public assumption that museums embody an abstract ideal as the arbiter of standards of beauty, cultural value, and scientific importance. In this context, when viewing an exhibit of ethnic arts or ethnographic objects, one may assume that one's curiosity about the exotica created by another people is being addressed with the highest standards regarding these ideal values with a view to attaining an objective statement of reality regarding the items exhibited and their significance to the viewer as well as to the people who made them. This assumption may not be warranted. In the face of such authority, the public does not generally perceive that museums offer only current opinion.

With regard to the preservation and presentation of the works of other peoples, museums are societal institutions that carry a historical load that usually excludes the people of origin from involvement in the presentation of their works to the museum's visitors. With few exceptions, this has been the circumstance surrounding objects drawn from non-Western cultural origins. Non-Western peoples have had their works interpreted for them, not by them, for the museum's public. And despite a growing appreciation within the museum profession of the potential educational benefit and public appeal to be gained from such an approach to presenting non-Western materials, discourse between indigenous and Western peoples in the gallery of the museum remains more potential than reality.

Museum Discourse as an Artifact of the West

The essential fact to note about the modern gallery exhibition as a form of Western-indigenous discourse is that museums and their galleries are an artifact of the Western world (Burcaw 1975). They grew out of events in Western political and social history, and as part of that history, they came into contact with indigenous peoples around the globe. Initially, during the "age of discovery," this contact was only at a distance, through intermediaries who supplied museums with the objects, information, and sometimes the very people themselves, obtained from far-off places that had been contacted more directly by other emissaries of the West. In most cases this was accomplished by representatives of the military and/or the church, who were pursuing their own varied agendas throughout the non-Western world. Subsequently, other colonizing agencies became the primary source of contact for museums before they ultimately attempted to contact the indigenous peoples directly through exploratory and collecting expeditions.

We can assume that, throughout this early period, discourse in the sense of a dialogue with native people was limited. Little if any of it, beyond object identifications, found its way into the galleries, which, even in "enlightened" institutions, tended to provide ethnocentric explanations or to exemplify the evolutionary or typological theories of museum curators. The journey from the indigenous population to the museum gallery was usually greater than can be measured in miles, and any attempt at dialogue between native creators and museum curators usually resulted at best in muffled echoes of the native voices as projected through material objects and interpreted by non-native museum staff members.

Many of the functions we attribute to museums today were not unique to the West. Some non-Western cultures have practiced collecting in response to an interest in antiquarianism or the pursuit of exotica. Others have created institutional displays of individual or group wealth and have expressed the collectors' aesthetic. Further, the preservation and presentation of other cultures' political or social histories have been the purpose of various institutionalized means outside the West. But only in the West, or in locales heavily influenced by the West, has the institution of the museum as an entity separate from other social institutions been developed, and that relatively recently for the mass of men and women (Alexander 1979). Thus the goals or missions of museums reflect the Western cultural values of their place of origin. When the institution has been exported to the non-Western world, the set of intrinsic museum values has been exported as well. With the growth of independence movements around the world and the founding of ethnic, regional, or national museums outside the West, the dominant Western museum culture itself has tended to determine the form, content, and expression of displays in the galleries of these institutions exported from the West. Dialogue has not been a priority.

If we accept the premise that history is written by the victors, it should be no surprise that museums throughout history have functioned to present the objects collected by the victors and to promote the interpretive perspective derived from the victors' viewpoint. Beginning in Europe as private royal or noble collections, early museums reflected the aesthetic, social, and political tastes and interests of their founders. Edward P. Alexander's book *Museum Masters* (1983) offers several examples. With the rise of nations and the movement toward democratization in European history, the great private collections increasingly came to be considered worthy of national ownership as part of the national patrimony, whether created locally or obtained by conquest. Museums came to be viewed as part of the national treasure even when the majority of the people were denied access to them. The museums documented the achievements of the celebrated few in the nation who won great wealth or who earned distinction through artistic creation, scientific achievement, the exploration of uncharted regions, or military conquest.

The value of the objects in the collections, unless they were made of precious materials, was in the testimony they gave to the importance of the owner. This was certainly true of the vast majority of ethnographic collections amassed in conquered territories. The artifacts in these collections were exhibited as curiosities or as objets d'art from the hands of conquered peoples. Seldom was their intrinsic cultural value acknowledged unless doing so served to document the "strangeness" of native customs, that is, their divergence from the accepted (Western) norm. Rarely did intrinsic non-Western aesthetic values survive the transport, and in those rare cases in which they did, such values were subject to the vagaries of European fashion and taste among the cognoscenti—the popularity of "chinoiserie" and "objets à la japonais" in the eighteenth and late nineteenth centuries come to mind.[1]

While most museum professionals today would probably accept the brief historical outline above regarding the treatment of other people's objects in the past, many would be very uncomfortable in acknowledging just how recently it was that museums accorded similar treatment to other *peoples.* Further, a genuine alarm has been created in some areas of the museum world today by native peoples' demand that museums modify their practices regarding the treatment of both ethnographic objects and the indigenous people themselves. We are being challenged to enter into a dialogue with native people in order to introduce intrinsic native values into exhibits, to acknowledge indigenous sensibilities regarding material culture and the nonmaterial systems they represent, and to accord indigenous peoples the opportunity to comment on their own cultural practices and the appropriate degree of cultural explanation allowable before that explanation perpetuates, even with benign intent, their exploitation.

Writing in 1910 in the *Anthropological Papers of the American Museum of Natural History*, Aleš Hrdlička described the experience of a group of Inuit/Eskimo from Smith Sound, Greenland:

> In 1896 Lieutenant Peary brought six of the Smith Sound natives to New York, and they were housed in the Museum. However, scarcely had they arrived when the majority of them began to cough and became ill with the bacillus of tuberculosis. Within less than nine months four of them died from acute phthisis, one had to be sent back, the same fate threatening, and one, a boy of about eight at that time, after having been adopted and brought up in New York and after having passed through the initial stages of lung, as well as light grades of gland and skin tuberculosis, was, at his demand, also sent back to his native country.
>
> These six individuals the writer was able to examine during life and, in one instance, immediately after death; he further secured and described the brain of one of the men and made a preliminary report on the others, which were subsequently reported upon in detail by Spitzka. Finally, he was able to examine the skeletal remains of the four who died, as well as several additional skulls and skeletons collected in later years in the Smith Sound region by Mr. Peary. The results of these various observations are here recorded.
>
> *The Living.* The party consisted of, 1., an elderly man (Nooktah or Nuktun); 2., a middle-aged-man (Kishu, Kussuk or Kessuh); 3., a young man (Yaragapsuk or Ujaragapsuck); 4., an elderly woman (Atana or Atangana); 5., a girl of about twelve (Aviag), daughter of 1. and 4.; and 6., a boy of about eight years of age (Minnie or Minik), son of 2. For convenience, these individuals will be referred to simply under the numerals. Number 2 was examined post-mortem.

> *Description of the Living.* When the Peary party of Smith Sound Eskimo arrived in New York, they were remarkable in the main for two features: one, the decidedly red color of their faces and the other, their pleasant facial expression. The facial red was somewhat dusky and altogether characteristic for these people. It was most pronounced over the upper parts of the cheeks, as weather-roughness is in most whites, and during their stay in New York it gradually weakened until it was nearly all gone, leaving the face a dusky yellow.
>
> The color of the bodies of these people was that of a yellowish-brown stained wood, decidedly lighter than the average Plains or Southwestern Indian. As their health failed, the color became gradually more sallow. The eyes were brown. (Hrdlička 1910:222)

While Hrdlička's terse account may speak to us of a human tragedy played out in museum halls over some years' duration, it is actually only an extreme case in its mode of telling and represents a fairly common practice in "progressive" museums of that time. I say progressive because it was in fact an attempt at discourse but one in which the control over the dialogue was not shared equally by both parties, the Western institution and the native people. Furthermore, this example and others from that time contain the germ of contemporary attempts at discourse through the employment of native demonstrators, "informants," or "adjunct educators" in museums, whose job it was to communicate with the museum public in ways impossible for inanimate objects selected by curators.

Perhaps the most famous case of museum-as-domicile and native-as-educator is that of Ishi, "the last wild Indian in North America." Ishi, the sole survivor of a band of the Yahi in California, quit his attempts to hide from the non-Indian residents of California in the summer of 1911 and appeared one morning in the horse corral of a remote ranch adjoining his homeland. His appearance caused a sensation and his existence came to the attention of Professor A. L. Kroeber, who arranged to take him to the Anthropology Museum at Berkeley. In Theodora Kroeber's account of his life there, she states in part:

> On the ground floor there was even a small room, occupied frequently by Indians who came for a few days or a few weeks to get acquainted, to be linguistic informants, perhaps merely as guests, as Professor Kroeber and others in the field had been guests of their house or village. It was a

comfortable arrangement for them; they added color and variety to the serene round of life of a preparator or assistant, under whose chaperonage they became acquainted with the city. So it was that when Ishi arrived, Indian guests were a normal part of museum living, and his own sense of strangeness was made less acute through his new acquaintances' feeling of ease and accustomedness. They were merely more interested in his coming than in that of a "civilized" red man, and somewhat more particular to try to make him feel at home, but he fitted a slot already made, with the difference that instead of being a transient visitor he became a permanent member of the group. (Kroeber 1964:123)

However, the subtle difference between being a museum guest and celebrity and a museum specimen is made clear in Theodora Kroeber's description of the formal dedication of the museum, which occurred a few months after Ishi's arrival:

> What should Ishi's role in the reception be? Emaciated and weak as he was from the near starvation of his last months in the hills, he could scarcely be expected to stand in the receiving line, to face the stares of hundreds of strange and curious however friendly faces. His clothes would pass muster, to be sure, and he was possessed of a sense of correctness and neatness of personal appearance, but his small perfect feet were bare. And his English vocabulary was limited to a very few words.
>
> It was suggested that Ishi might be in one of the smaller exhibition rooms for as much of the long party as he wanted to take part in, in this limited and quiet way, and to this Ishi agreed. He was excited about the party which as he understood it was to be on the sensible lines of an Indian house warming to which you invited your friends for a feast, an exchange of news and some singing and dancing. There was, to be sure, no singing and dancing at the reception, but there were refreshments, and there were the exhibition cases of interesting objects to be pointed out and exclaimed over. Ishi stayed for the whole long party, hovering observantly in the background. From time to time Kroeber left the receiving line to bring a Regent, an artist, some person who had asked specially to meet Ishi. (Kroeber 1964:134)

Ultimately, Ishi, too, succumbed to disease and died after some years of demonstrating his native technology, participating in the manufacture of native tools for the museum's collections, and making sound recordings for the museum's linguistic research. Roy Wagner has summarized this historic episode of human-being-as-museum-specimen as well as cultural ambassador:

> In this light it is scarcely astonishing that Ishi, the last surviving Yahi Indian in California, spent the years after his surrender living in a museum (T. Kroeber 1964). Museums had by then assumed fully the role of a reservation for Indian culture, and we are told that in good weather Kroeber and others would take Ishi back into the hills so that he could demonstrate Yahi techniques and bushcraft. In spite of Kroeber's deep sympathy for Ishi, one cannot help feeling that he was the ideal museum specimen, one that did the anthropologist's job for him by producing and reconstituting its own culture. This suggestion makes it easy to forget that Ishi's job was primarily that of living, and that he had merely exchanged his existence for a formaldehyde sinecure. But this, again, is precisely the point; by accepting employment as a museum specimen, Ishi accomplished the metaphorization of life into culture that defines much of anthropological understanding. (Wagner 1975:27).

By demonstrating his erstwhile livelihood, Ishi came to symbolize through his words, his knowledge, and his products an abstract construction — "Yahi culture" — the actuality of which had ceased to exist in nature and which the museum sought to record and preserve in its vaults. But Ishi had no control over his destiny, and though he was able to converse with others in the museum, he was not able to enter into a dialogue as an equal with the museum over the scope of its presentation of his ethos except by withholding information obtainable from no other source. In that fashion he would be able to exercise some control.

Western-Indigenous Dialogue

The process of dialogue involves a formal exchange of views leading ultimately to greater understanding, if not consensus. Among the many and diverse responsibilities assumed by museums today, education is perhaps the one with the greatest currency, if one can judge by the (relative) explosion in numbers of museums adding "educators" or "education departments" to their rosters. Because this interest in promoting education in museums comes at the same time as a greater awareness of minority-rights issues in Western, particularly American, society, it should be no surprise that museum curators and directors are attempting to improve the quality of their educational offerings while demonstrating their sensitivity to minority cultures by entering into a dialogue with the indigenous peoples whose lives and works are the subject of our exhibitions. Yet in doing so, museums need to be willing to deal as equal partners and give up some of the traditional powers accorded them by history. Further, they must occasionally confront the fact that the "show-all, tell-all" approach to exhibitions and the pursuit and presentation of knowledge for its own sake may be strongly at odds with the basic values of indigenous cultures under consideration. In such circumstances, museum personnel must learn to listen to the native perspective and tailor their exhibitions to present the native explanation or view as one with its own historical integrity even if it is at variance with the explanatory or aesthetic system devised in the Western empirical tradition.

I am reminded of an explanation of the history of Navajo weaving I was presenting in the context of a historical Navajo textile exhibit and in the company of a traditional Navajo weaver in the gallery of a Southwestern museum. Having presented the traditional anthropological dogma that the Navajo loom and weaving technology had been borrowed from Anasazi-Pueblo weavers resident in the Southwest at the time of the Navajo entry from the north some 600 years ago, I was stopped in my self-confident tracks by the weaver's opening line of her weaving demonstration: "In spite of what Dr. Way has just told you, we Navajo know that it was Spider Woman who taught us to weave during Creation Times" (Pearl Sunrise, personal communication, 1986). She then went on to explain how the weaving technology of her family was passed on to her, including not only warping of the loom and preparing the various colors of yarn for the weft but also the importance of having good thoughts and a calm mind while weaving in order to have the textile come off the loom even and balanced and correctly harmonious.

Hearing in her own words of the manual, mental, and even spiritual training necessary to the making of a skilled weaver was more than simply a "charming" evening at the museum. Rather, it served to change the standards and add to the list of criteria we each employed on that occasion in our own critical analyses of the historical textiles hanging on the gallery walls. With her assistance, our eyes were opened to a new set of possibilities for appreciating the results of these long-dead women's efforts. She also inspired new speculation on the breadth of the impact of the introduction of the new commercially spun and dyed yarns made available in the 1890s. Economic conditions made the new yarns desirable from the perspective of the conservation of labor, but how were these new materials incorporated into the round of textile making beyond the warp and weft? We may not know the answer, but now we know enough to ask the question.

This simple example demonstrates, I think, what we may gain if museum personnel engage indigenous peoples in dialogue in which their own explanations add to the breadth of our appreciation and the depth of our understanding. This requires, however, that they seek the native perspective, not merely the native name or procedure.

Part of the issue involved is recognizing the importance of the context in which pieces of indigenous "art," as we have traditionally defined it, are made. While we may admire a Sioux riding crop as a purely sculptural form, we would miss much of the richness of the piece that comes from an understanding of the role of such an object beyond its use to hit a running horse. If that were its only function, an unadorned willow switch would work as well. In this concern for providing context, then, as well as an occasion for discourse, one model to be considered is that of the "living museum," such as Plimouth Plantation in Massachusetts or the living archaeological museums of Britain or Scandinavia. Upon consideration, however, I think that the load of history argues against such attempts in the presentation of non-Western cultural traditions.

My concern is the fear that we might confuse the living museum with a human zoo. In this respect, Haberland (1987) cites the Volkerschauen of nineteenth-century Germany, which were presentations of "companies" of native people booked by theatrical entrepreneurs to tour Europe as educational exhibits if not cultural ambassadors. Too often have I seen the assumption of racial as well as cultural superiority on the part of a museum visitor preclude the possibility of understanding the indigenous system being demonstrated. This response can expose the demonstrator to demeaning interactions with a segment of the museum public that is incapable of accepting a fellow human of different hue or belief system as an equal with something of value to say beyond the merely quaint. Besides, the most widely known historical precedents for such an attempt are the traveling Wild West shows of the nineteenth century or the more sinister human freak shows of circuses and carnivals.

It is the responsibility of the museum to enter into a discourse with indigenous peoples and to present the results of that discourse rather than to provide living-museum opportunities for public interaction with indigenous peoples. Without the museum as an active intermediary and editor, I fear that the cost in indigenous self-esteem exacted by the few in the museum's public may outweigh the possible benefits to the many. For the time being, it is the museum profession which must take the lead by according indigenous people the status of colleagues in the preparation of exhibitions on their cultures, a status higher than that implied by the term *informant*.

A further consideration lies in the inclusion in standard ethnographic exhibitions of a section dedicated to how the indigenous population views and copes with the representatives of the West with whom they have come in contact. It is at least enlightening, if not always comforting, to see oneself as others do. Consider African colonial woodcarvings of Europeans and Americans in the collections of the Field Museum or the Musée de l'Homme. African carvers present Europeans in poses drawn from their own artistic traditions but distinguishable by the material artifacts that make them seem so odd to the native observer. Top hats, monocles, bustles, binoculars, parasols, and bicycles appear in these works. Japanese woodblock prints portray Admiral Perry and his men with their distinctive Caucasian noses and bushy whiskers. Contemporary *koshare* and *koyemshe* clowns at Pueblo ceremonies mimic the behavior of the National Football League as portrayed on television—down to the victory dance moves after a touchdown—and the more ludicrous antics of the tourists, literally in their own backyards. Navajo painter Quincy Tahoma likewise illustrates the plague of the tourist with humor in his painting *Tourist Season*. A clichéd Navajo woman in front of a loom and with a child in a cradleboard poses for the camera, which is wielded by a squatting man accompanied by his wife in a bandanna and short-shorts.

Most shops on the Plaza in Santa Fe today either carry or can direct buyers to sources of now-traditional "Storyteller" figures reinterpreted as

Santa Claus or a teddy bear, or anthropomorphic turtles made by Pueblo potters. A decade ago, a recently arrived Cambodian peasant refugee was asked by a student of mine through a translator, another American student, if the refugee thought Americans were pretty or attractive people. After some nervous thought he replied, "They act very nice to me, but their eyes don't match their hair." Visions such as these of the outsider from the native perspective constitute a subject area with real potential for dialogue, and one that has not been explored by museum professionals in sufficient depth.

We are told in the Western tradition that in the beginning was the Word. Eventually in the gallery we must come back to words. One need not be a trained psycholinguist to recognize the effect of the combined weight of words like *primitive, simple, archaic,* and *residual,* which are still found in the text of labels in museums, as is the consistent use of the past tense. More subtle are the qualifying statements that begin with words like *while, however,* and *but,* which occur in the context of praising statements regarding indigenous cultures but which temper that praise. While we might say that we admire a given cultural system, we *do* damn with faint (and qualified) praise. (The last two sentences illustrate my point.) There is also the implied relative merit or status carried in terms like *craft, art, artifact, folk art,* or even the word *custom* as it refers to some deviation from the Western norm in effect in a given cultural area.

Terms of reference to a people may also carry a historical or political load that may not be understood by the museum-based author of label copy. *Indian, native, tribe, aboriginal* — these terms, like *colored* in another period of American history, may all carry negative connotations in various populations and contexts today. Deliberate sensitivity, which is increasingly common in the era of the lawsuit, may serve to alleviate some of the obvious excesses of the past, but it is no guarantee against unintentional slights or clumsy and transparent attempts at current notions of cultural and ethnic solidarity. The surest way to avoid awkwardness is to employ the actual voice of the people themselves. Label copy or catalog text based on quotations from the people may serve both to avoid mainstream biases and to offer the museum visitor a sense of immediacy that is only possible in actuality by participation with the indigenous colleague. This effect was well demonstrated in the traveling exhibit "Women of Sweetgrass, Cedar and Sage," produced by Atl-Atl, an arts support cooperative based in Phoenix, Arizona. The exhibit toured the United States from 1985 to 1987, and in it contemporary Native American women spoke in the catalog text about their work. No one else could have said it better. Given the opportunity to speak, they gave us their words and more.

While my ruminations on gallery verbiage may illustrate the benefit to be gained from the involvement of indigenous people as partners in determining how information about their cultures is presented, it does not address the more profound and, for most museums, the more threatening issue of what is appropriate for presentation to the public in the first place. This issue confronts the foundations of freedom of inquiry and the public's right to know, which are often at odds with an indigenous society's values. The museum may want to tell the world through its exhibitions things that, in the eyes of the members of such a society, are none of the world's business. Presenting a culture's belief system, showing ritual objects, or describing ceremonies in words may violate that culture's right to privacy, may expose tribal secrets to people unprepared to respect them, and may even be understood to put the uninitiated viewer and the world in general at risk, to the great concern of the people of origin. The perennial ethical dilemma of the anthropologist — developing the trust of his or her host population in order to learn about them and then possibly betraying that trust by sharing their secrets — becomes acute in the material world of the museum gallery.

Unfortunately, examples of the betrayal of indigenous trust abound: the display of medicine bundles and their contents; the display of grave-goods and skeletal remains at many archaeological museums; and perhaps the "finest" example, the incredibly life-like, full-size dioramas of Hopi ritual presented at the Field Museum in Chicago. The average visitor may feel the mystery behind this exhibit, but to most Hopi the exhibition is a betrayal and a dangerous sacrilege. How much of the non-Western art in the world's museums is based in ceremony and ritual, and to what extent does it desecrate the original belief system by the form of its presentation to the world in a truncated fashion and out of context? Think of Bambara antelope "sculptures" cut from their raffia drapery. What would the people of origin think if they knew? And what could the people of origin do if they did know? Until fairly recently, the answer to the last question was, not much. Museums were founded by the powerful.

Native American Discourses

Native American perspectives on museums and the museum profession are extremely varied and not universally negative. While museums are indeed generally viewed as takers rather than givers in the Native American experience, it is generally conceded that museums have preserved much of the richness of the material culture of many groups, material that would have been destroyed or jettisoned in the face of pressures to adopt Euro-American customs and give up "old-fashioned" ways. Now that the immediate, overt pressure to give up native lifestyles and material culture is lessened, however, many modern native people would like to retrieve the objects surrendered or abandoned by their forebears, and this desire places them in conflict with the policies of most museums. The museums did preserve these objects, but for whom, the native people ask, and how did the museum obtain the objects in the first place? Is an old bill of sale valid if the transaction was the result of cultural coercion? And if the courts are to decide, are they not rooted in the same historical tradition as the museums? These are questions laden with emotion, and they are delivered with great vehemence. But they are directed at much larger historical issues for which the museum is merely a tangible symbol.

It should not be assumed that there is a consensus within a united, monolithic Native American perspective on such matters as museums and their past and future role. Many Native American groups recognize the potential for enhanced cultural esteem to be gained from the establishment of native owned and operated local museums to house indigenous arts. They also recognize the potential for economic development through museum activity. Yet in spite of such widespread interest, the North American Indian Museums Association, established in 1979, is today practically defunct (Hanson 1980).

The Hopi Tribal Museum Project, which is designed to create a museum under local control to present the Hopi worldview, encounters difficulty in arriving at a local consensus about the nature of that worldview, if it exists, and how much of it should be displayed. The fact that the Hopi and other groups find it difficult to apply the model of the museum to their own circumstances in spite of their desire to do so stems not from an intrinsic argumentativeness or inability to cooperate in such a complex venture. Nor can it be attributed solely to conflict between "progressives" and "conservatives" within the community. Rather, the problem is that the model does not work toward the Hopi's social goals. With all the cultural diversity that is possible within the broad stream of their tradition, to select a single representative of that tradition to the exclusion of equally valid alternatives, or to select a place-specific representative to the exclusion of neighboring Native American and Western traditions, is to misrepresent the complexity of the whole (Rosanda Suetopka-Thayer, personal communication, 1988). A concern for the value, validity, and complexity of the details — though not very important, perhaps, to the typical museum professional "from outside" — leads to the lack of agreement. And if Native Americans are also concerned that their cultures may disappear due to pressure from outside, the preservation of the details, a basic museum purpose, becomes of paramount importance, though it also increases the chance of group deadlock.

Returning to the example of Ishi, once in the museum he came to represent a cultural abstraction — Yahi culture — with no alternative source of information that might produce a different interpretation. This is not the case for autonomous, diverse Native American groups of individuals in the complex present of culture change and cultural preservation. The reduction of a culture to a single representative for museum consumption ultimately comes to resemble the historical model of a single individual's achievements or power resulting in the establishment of a museum to perpetuate his or her individual interpretation of what is beautiful or valuable or in some other way worthy of preservation and presentation.

The museum profession is showing some signs of increased willingness to consider new ways of interacting with indigenous people. In Canada a conference held at the Glenbow Museum in Calgary in September 1986 addressed the topic "Museums and Native Collections." The purpose was to explore the possibility of forming a single policy for Canadian museums confronted with requests for the return of cultural materials to native peoples (Ames et al. 1988). The participants considered not only the possible legal actions initiated by such claims but also raised the "extra-legal" claims based on sentimental or moral grounds which might generate public interest and challenge the museums' popular standing. A discussion paper that resulted from the meetings enumerates the issues and the ways that museums might work in partnership with native peoples.

Times are changing, and the balance of power is shifting. Led (and in some cases threatened) by laws safeguarding the ownership of objects considered to be part of both a national and a tribal or ethnic patrimony, museums are rethinking their ethical positions regarding certain classes of "sensitive" objects. In 1988 the American Association of Museums published a "Policy Regarding the Repatriation of Native American Ceremonial Objects and Human Remains." Museums are coming to see that tangible benefits may accrue from their entering into discourse with indigenous people, tangible in ways other than improving the quality of the information presented in their galleries. Spurred by legal precedents such as the Zuni Tribe's successful claim in federal court to ownership of all war gods in any collection obtained by whatever means, and by international agreements such as UNESCO's statements on national cultural treasures and the International Council of Museums' policy regarding the international trade in art objects, museums are learning caution and in some instances consideration regarding indigenous peoples' rights to their cultural properties and the belief systems that such objects represent. That museums, often considered cultural paragons, have too often been followers rather than leaders in changing Western society's standards concerning relations with indigenous peoples is a reflection of their collective institutional history in the development of the West.

Elsewhere in this volume it is argued that the West has appropriated non-Western art and has imbued it with the West's own system of values. *Plus ça change, plus c'est la même chose.* The more it changes, the more it is the same. Around the world, indigenous people facing cultural change in the context of emerging political and economic circumstances are attempting to appropriate the institution of the museum and to apply it to their own purposes. In this country the Seneca Iroquois National Museum in Akwesasne, New York, the Oneida Museum in Oneida County, Wisconsin, the St. Francis Mission Museum in South Dakota, and the Navajo Museum in Window Rock, Arizona, are but a few examples of the more than 120 museums established to conserve individual Native American groups' views of their heritage and which are staffed in full or in part by tribal members or by employees of the particular tribes (Hanson 1980).

The Plains Indian Museum in Cody, Wyoming, is a regional museum of national importance that takes its inspiration from a dedicated staff and administration, including its curator, George Horse Capture, a Gros Ventre. The National Museum of Anthropology in Mexico celebrates a perhaps fictive but nonetheless remarkable national heritage comprised of the combined cultural resources of Mexico's indigenous peoples. Regional, often indigenous museums are also being developed in China, Zaire, and other parts of the world. To the extent that indigenous identity is not subsumed to national citizenship, these museums will reflect a discourse between nationalist representatives in museum administrations and representatives of the varieties of indigenous peoples within the national borders. In any event, such efforts depend on the tolerance of cultural pluralism and internal ethnic political stability.

In the meantime, in this country the national museum of the United States, the Smithsonian Institution, is seeking ways to engage North America's indigenous peoples in a discourse concerning their material cultural properties held by the museum. The Smithsonian's Native American Museum Program of the Office of Museum Programs, headed by Dr. JoAllyn Archambault of the Standing Rock Sioux, is seeking increasingly effective ways to inform all Native American groups of the existence at the Museum of collections related to their cultural past. The program seeks ways to involve representatives of these groups in supplementing the information available on the collections and disseminating the information concerning these historic materials among the peoples of origin. The task is exciting, challenging, and just beginning.

It is most significant that the editors of this volume included the issue of Western-indigenous discourse in the consideration of imagery and creativity because it demonstrates an inclination toward collaboration that is not yet universal. It also demonstrates the expectation that such discourse would be cost-effective for museums in spite of probable increases in exhibition budgets. This is an expectation we share. The benefits range from the immediate and tangible to the esoteric and ephemeral. They include issues as basic as clear title and ownership of cultural properties, a concern for the quality of information put before the museums' public, the possibility of less ethnocentric and therefore presumably more accurate or "true" portrayals of the diversity present in the human species and the human condition on this small planet we share.

NOTE

1. This brief review of ethnographic collections cannot consider the special case of collecting, displaying, and marketing pre-Columbian art and other artifacts. For a thorough recent examination of this question, see Messenger 1989. For a more general discussion of the development of museum anthropology, see Karp and Lavine 1991; Stocking 1985.

REFERENCES CITED

Alexander, Edward P.
　1979　*Museums in Motion: An Introduction to the History and Functions of Museums.* Nashville: American Association for State and Local History.
　1983　*Museum Masters: Their Museums and Their Influence.* Nashville: American Association for State and Local History.

Ames, M. M., J. D. Harrison, and T. Nicks
　1988　Proposed Museum Policies for Ethnological Collections and the Peoples They Represent. *Muse* [Ottawa] 54 (4): 22–28.

Burcaw, G. Ellis
　1975　*Introduction to Museum Work.* Nashville: American Association for State and Local History.

Butler, Barbara H.
　1981　China Journal. *Museum News* 59 (6): 33–38.

Deetz, James
　1983　The Artifact and Its Context. *Museum News* 62 (1): 25–27.

Haberland, Wolfgang
　1987　Nine Bella Coolas in Germany. In *Indians and Europe,* edited by Christian Feest, 49–63. Aachen: Forum II, Edition Herodot, Rader-Vorlag.

Hanson, James A.
　1980　The Reappearing Vanishing American. *Museum News* 59 (2): 44–51.

Hrdlička, Aleš

1910   Contribution to the Anthropology of the Central and Smith Sound Eskimo. Anthropological Papers of the American Museum of Natural History, vol. 5, pt. 2. New York.

Karp, Ivan, and Steven D. Lavine, eds.

1991   *Exhibiting Cultures: The Poetics and Politics of Museum Display.* Washington, D.C.: Smithsonian Institution Press.

Kroeber, Theodora

1964   *Ishi in Two Worlds.* Edited by Phyllis Mauch Messenger. Berkeley: University of California Press.

Messenger, Phyllis Mauch, ed.

1989   *The Ethics of Collecting Cultural Property: Whose Culture? Whose Property?* Albuquerque: University of New Mexico Press.

Stocking, George W., Jr., ed.

1985   *Objects and Others: Essays on Museums and Material Culture.* Madison: University of Wisconsin Press.

Wagner, Roy

1975   *The Invention of Culture.* Englewood Cliffs, N.J.: Prentice-Hall.

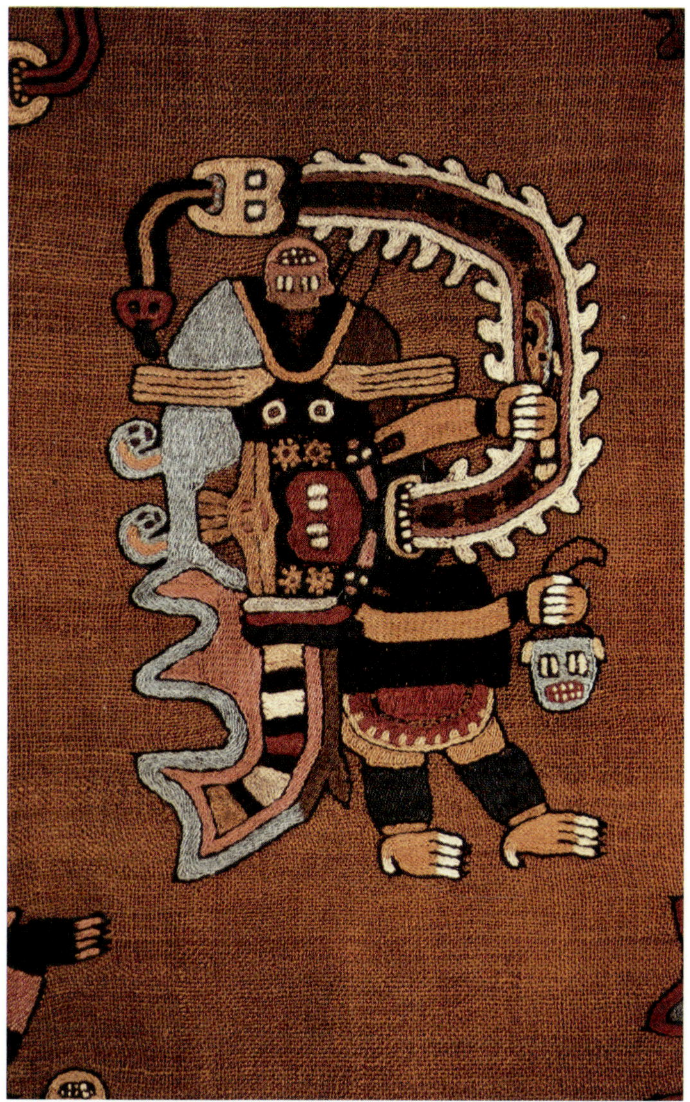

Plate 1. Detail from the embroidered mantle shown in Figure 5.5, presumably from the Paracas site. The anthropomorphic mythical being carries a trophy head in the right hand. Another trophy head is held between the jaws of the killer whale headdress. (Museum of Fine Arts, Boston, acc. no. 16.31)

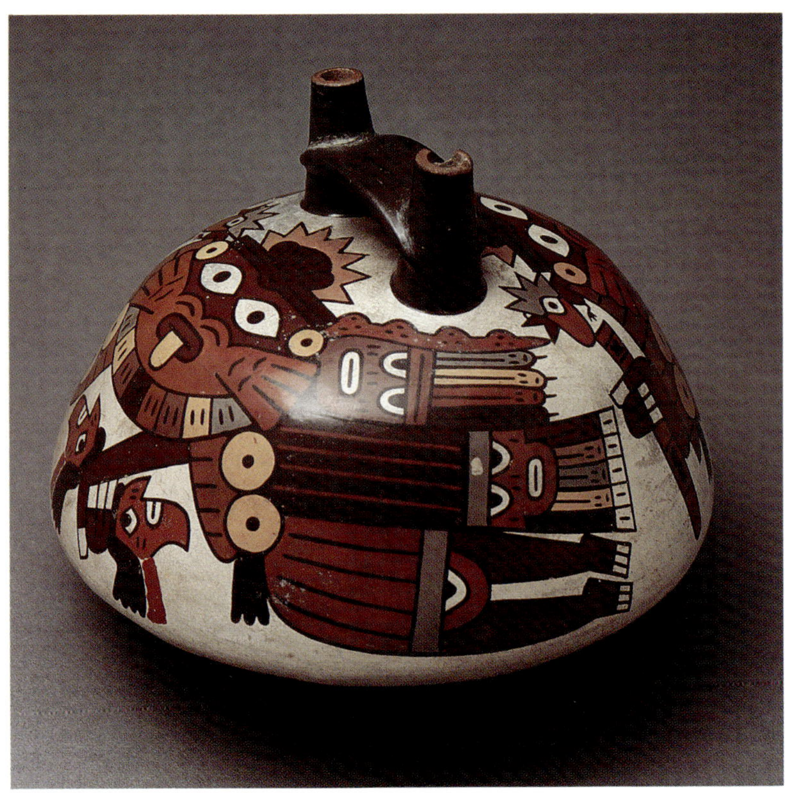

Plate 2. A Nasca double-spout-and-bridge bottle portraying two anthropomorphic mythical beings or masked ritual performers. Note the trophy heads held in the hand. (Art Institute of Chicago, Buckingham Fund, acc. no. 1955.2128; photograph by Kathleen Culbert-Aguilar)

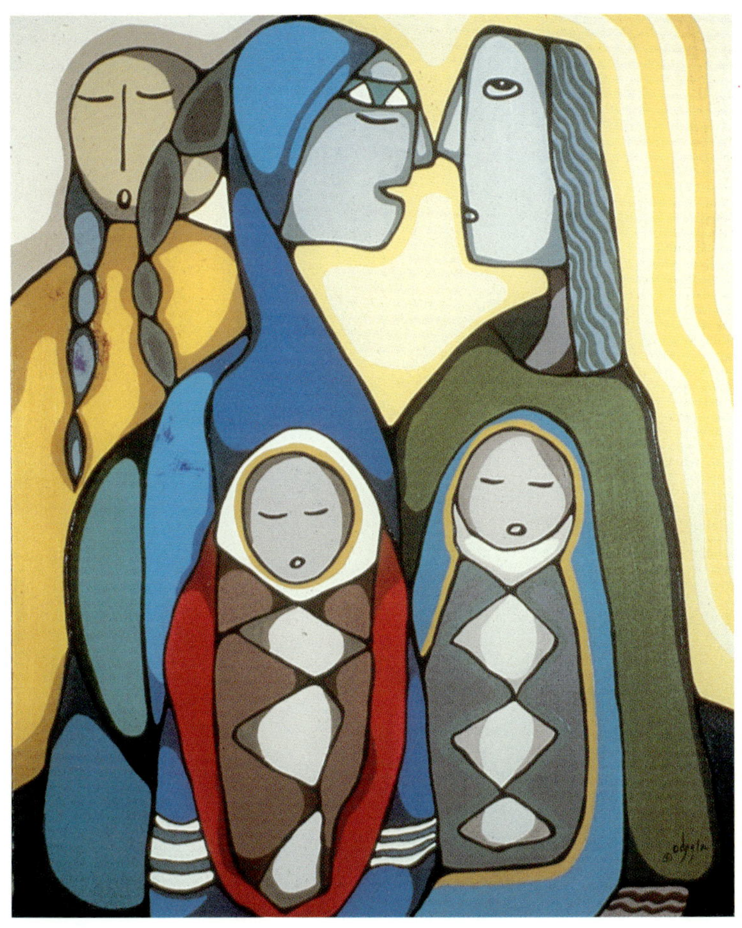

Plate 3. Daphne Odjig (Ojibway), *A Comparing Experience*, 1983 (IANA no. 84-0119)

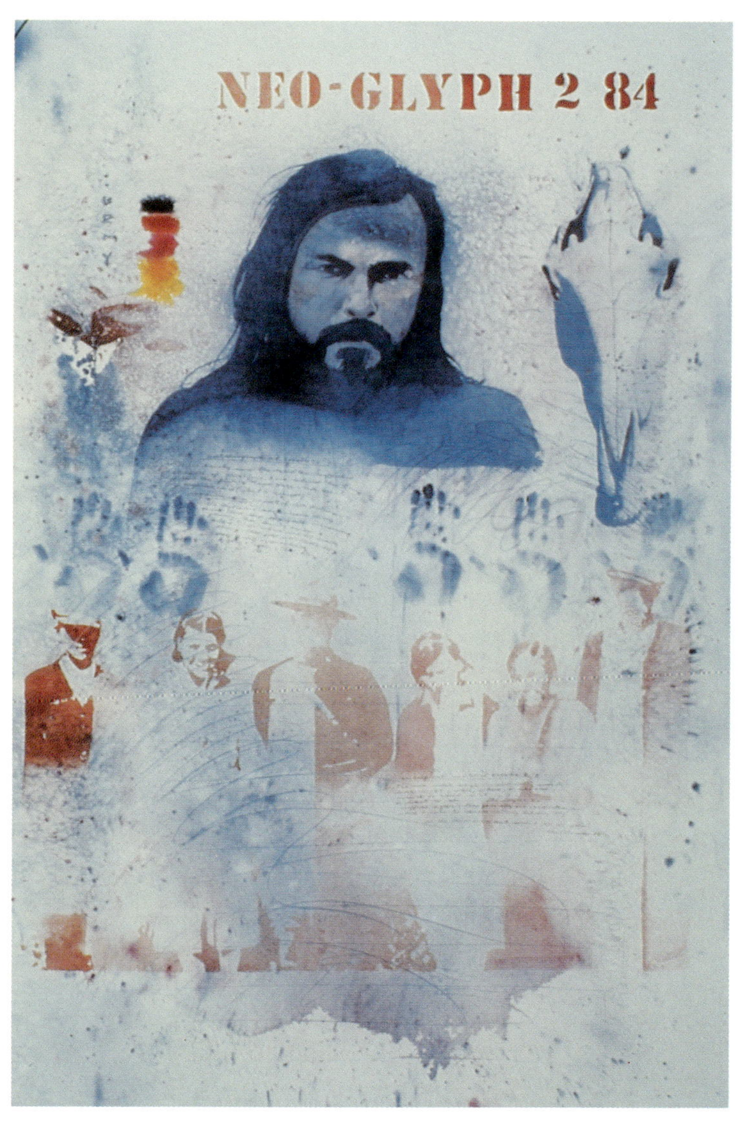

Plate 4. Carl Beam (Ojibway), *Neo-glyph 2*, serigraph, 180. (IANA no. 84-0405)

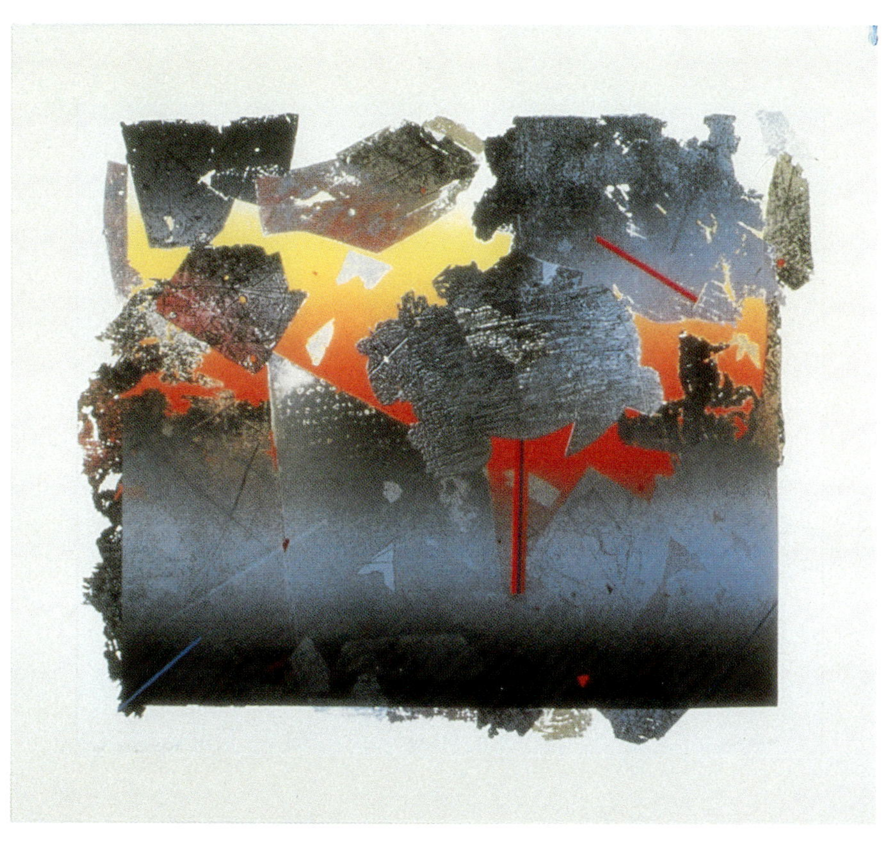

Plate 5. Jane Ashe Poitras (Cree), *Cree Ribbon Shirt,* print (IANA no. 84-0652)

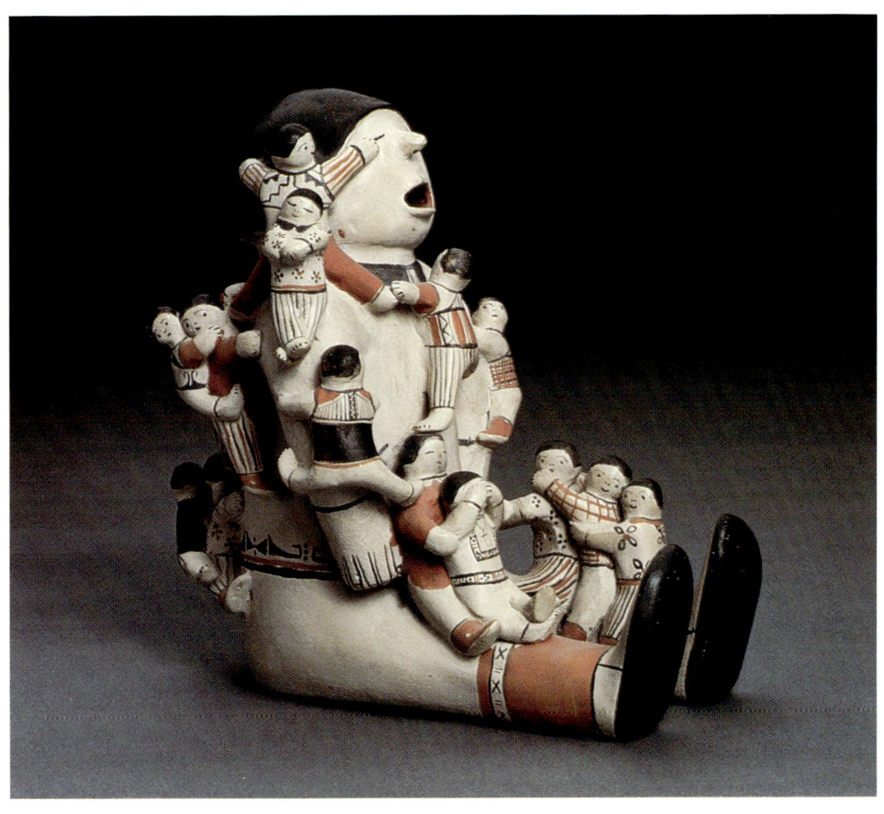

Plate 6. A Storyteller by Helen Cordero with sixteen children, shaped in 1971. (Courtesy of Al Anthony, Adobe Gallery; photograph by Glenn Short)

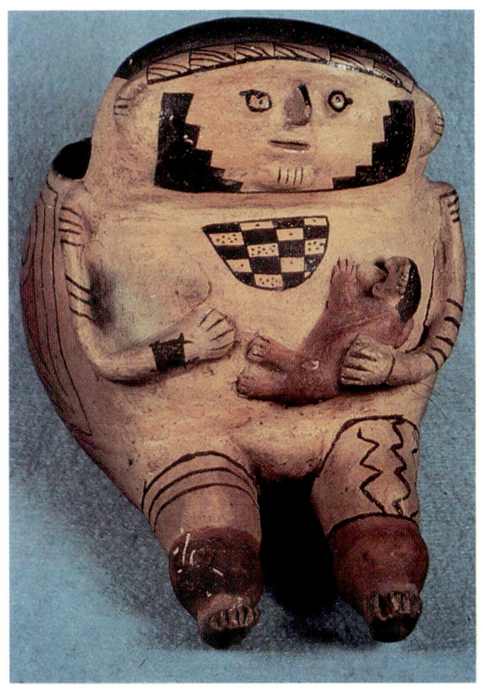

Plate 7. A Casas Grandes mother-and-child effigy jar from A.D. 1060–1340. (Courtesy of the Arizona State Museum, neg. no. 64018., acc. no. 03724)

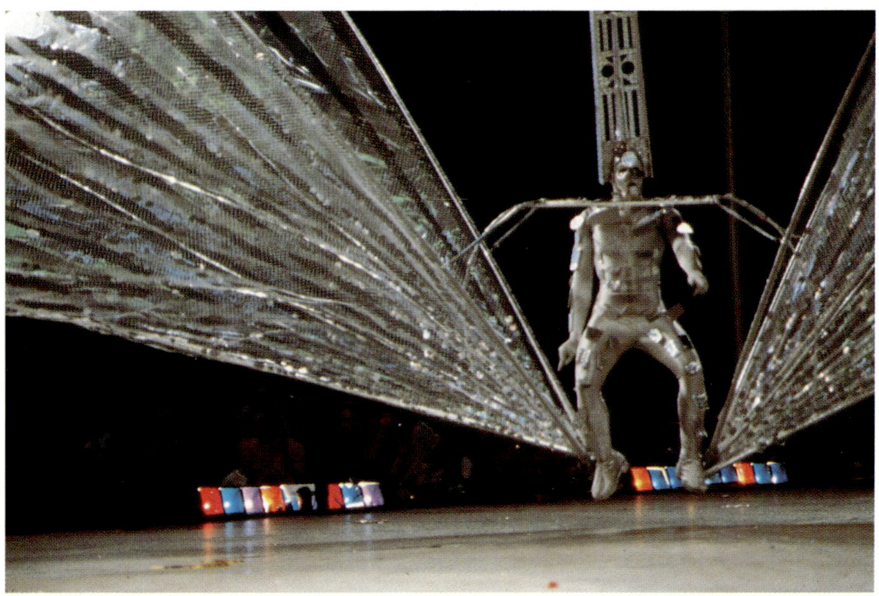

Plate 8. The King Callaloo costume Peter Minshall created for Carnival in 1984. The character's "wings" represent water splashing as he walks on the water.

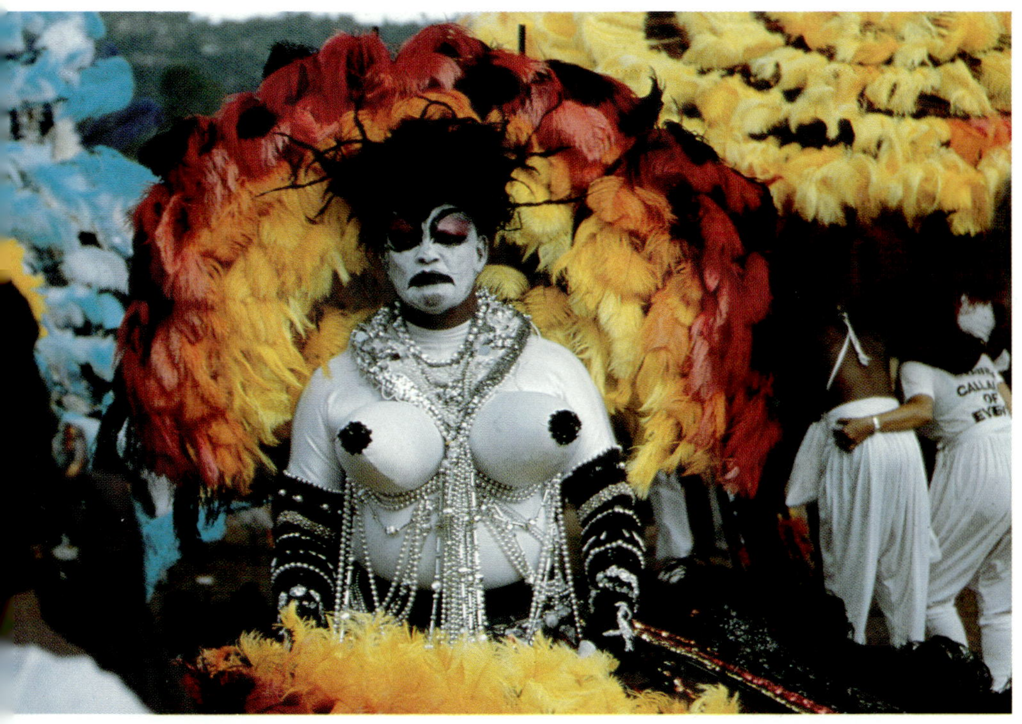

Plate 9. The Madame Hiroshima character portrayed by Hugh "Bote" Bernard for the Callaloo band of 1984. The large breasts represent bombs, and the plumed back section the mushroom-shaped cloud left by the explosion of an atomic bomb.

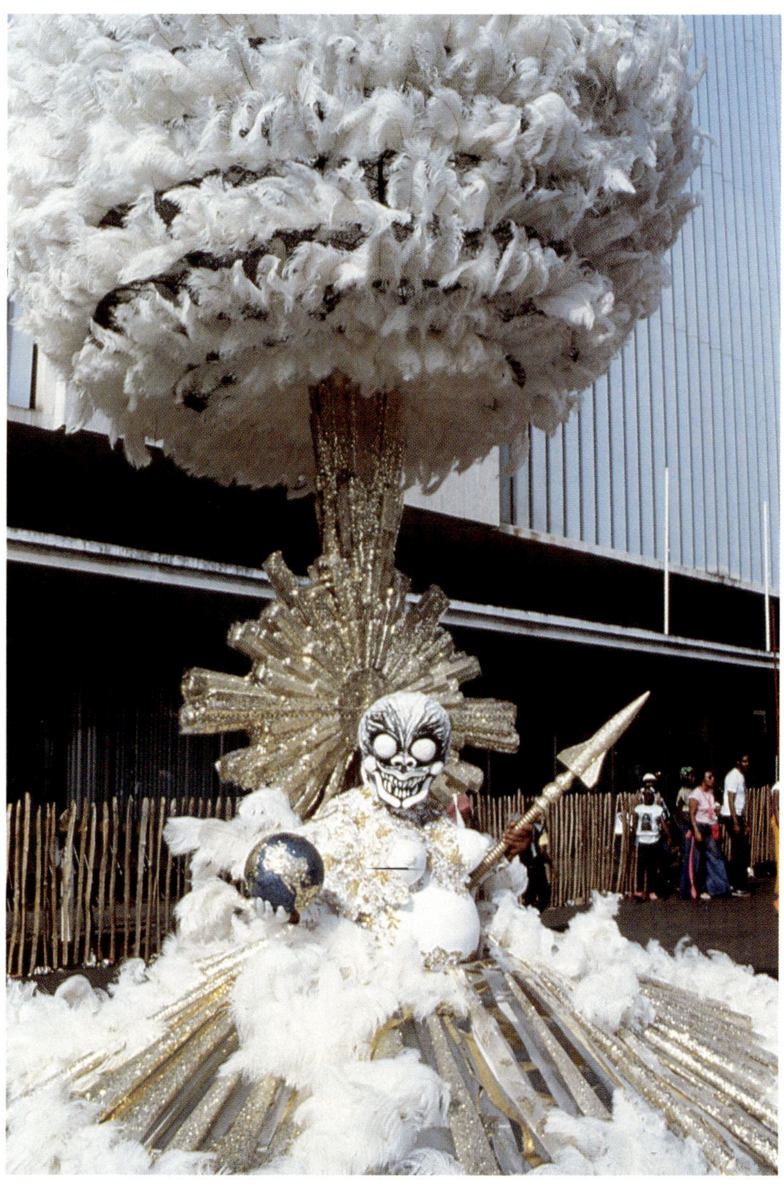

Plate 10. The Adoration of Hiroshima, created for Minshall's 1985 Golden Calabash band. With a missile scepter in one hand and a globe of the world in the other, this character rules the earth with the threat of destruction. (Photograph courtesy of Roy Boyke)

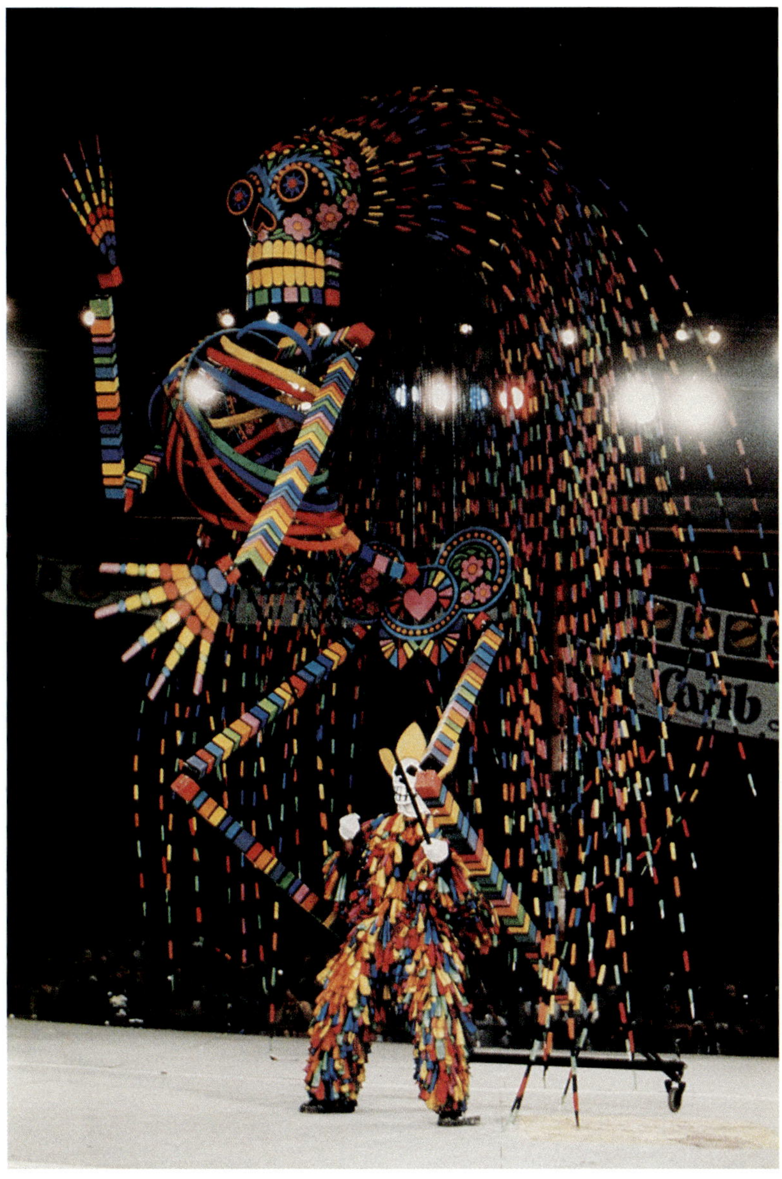

Plate 11. The Merry Monarch, designed by Minshall and performed by Peter Samuels on the Queen's Park Savannah stage during the 1987 Carnival.

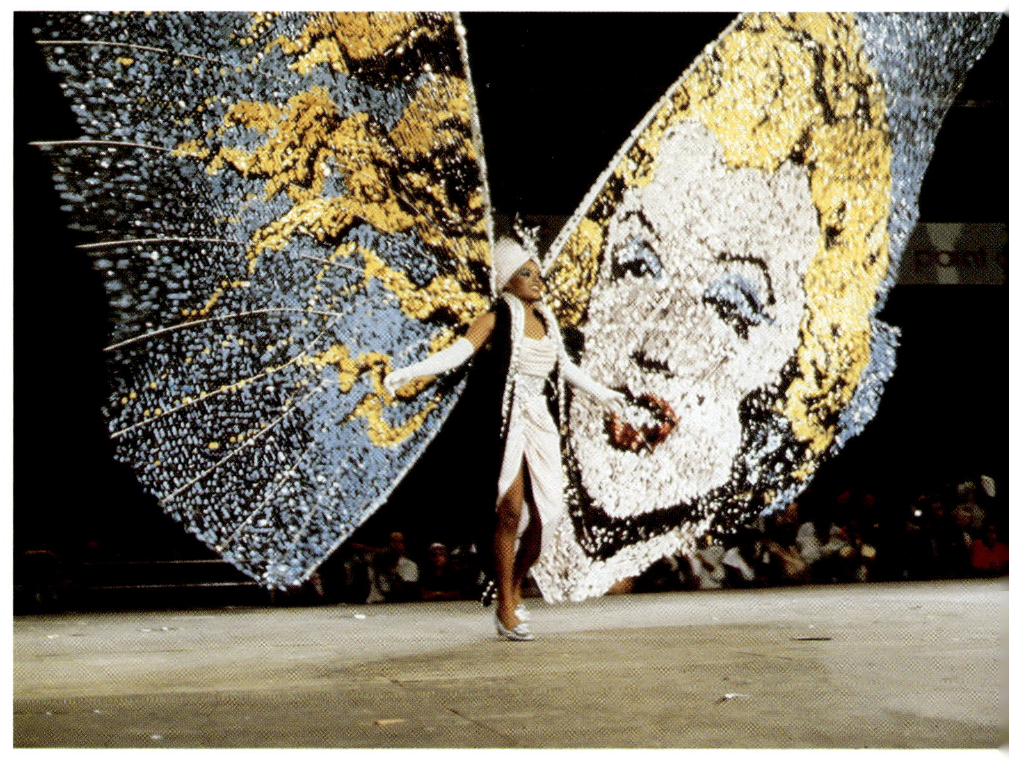

Plate 12. The Marilyn Monroe image on a butterfly costume from the 1982 band Papillon. (Photograph courtesy of Noel Norton)

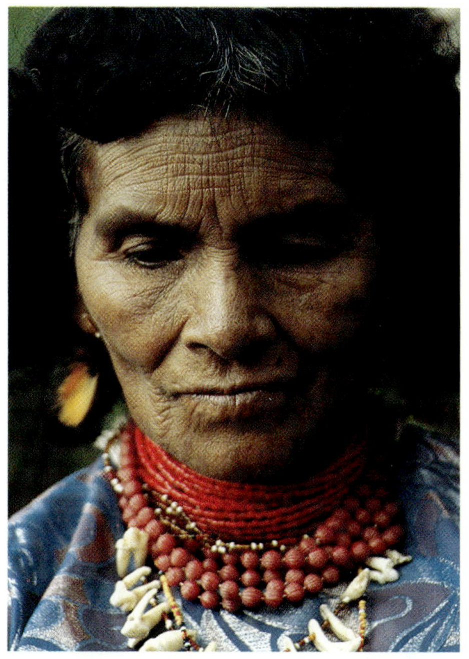

Plate 13. Clara Santi Simbaña, master potter.

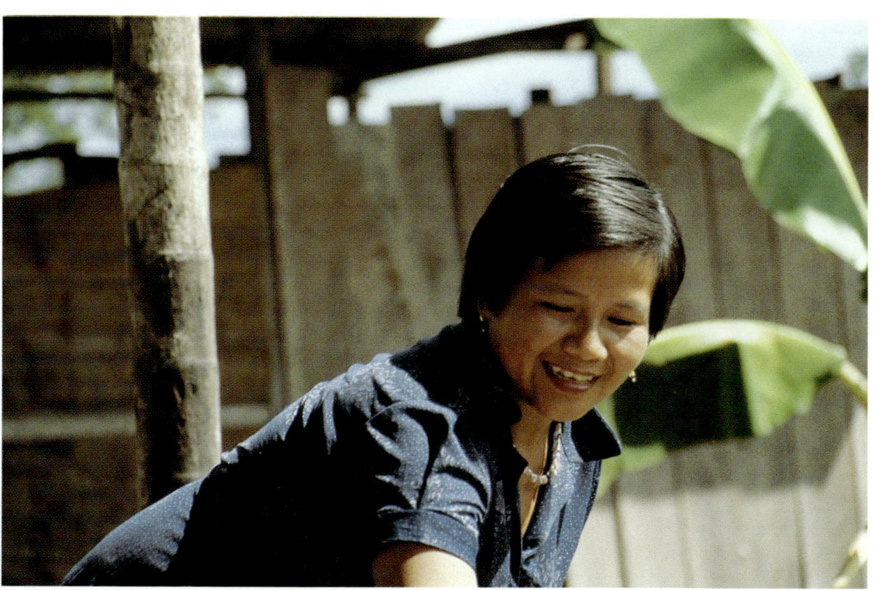

Plate 14. Esthela Dagua Malaber, master potter.

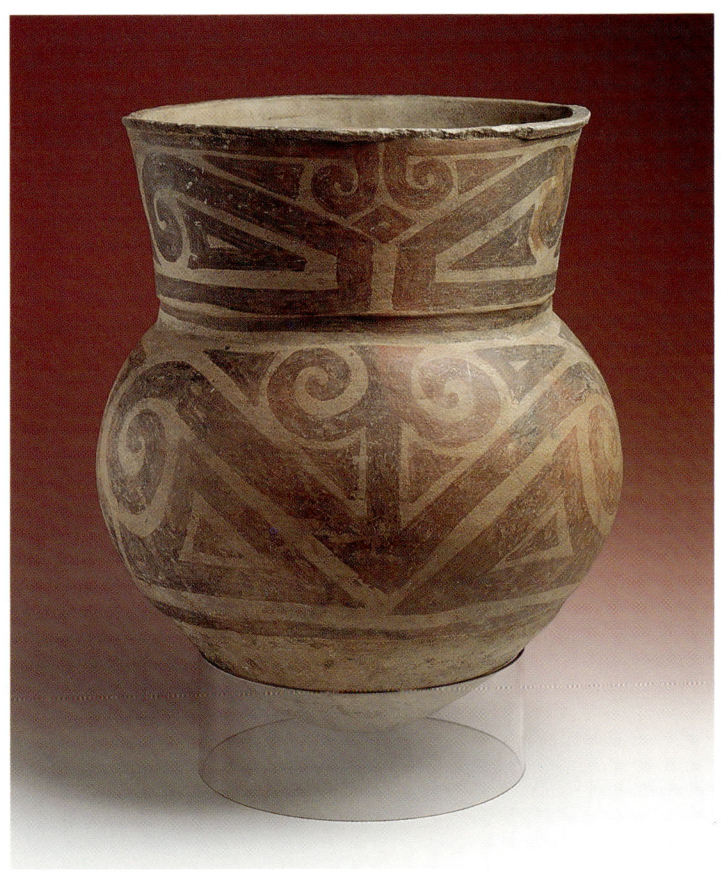

Plate 15. A Charapa Cocha urn found by Alejandro Taish and presented to César Abad of Puyo.

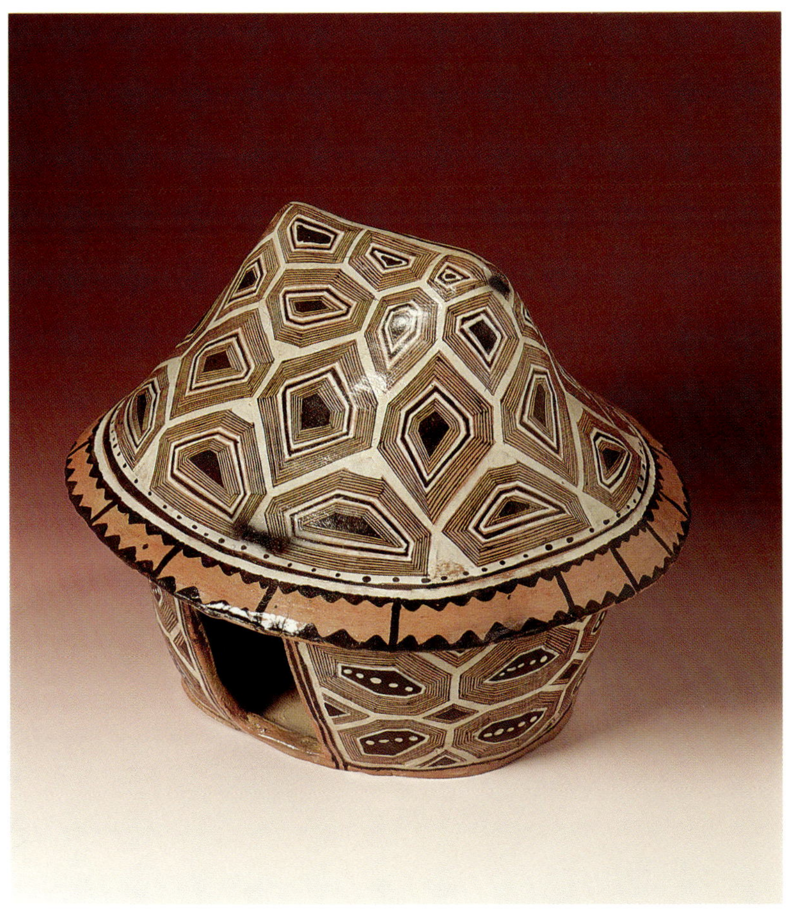

Plate 16. A ceramic house made by Esthela Dagua in 1989. It was inspired by a Charapa Cocha urn and a contemporary Charapa Cocha Achuar house.

5

Style and State in Ancient Peru

Helaine Silverman

Throughout Latin America, modern nation-states have appropriated the arts of indigenous pasts to their ideological heritages while relegating the arts of contemporary peoples to the domain of tourism and handicrafts. These countries exalt the "high level" of the arts of their pre-Columbian inhabitants while decrying the "poverty" of contemporary artistic products, seldom analyzing the causes of earlier developments and their subsequent decadence (Lumbreras 1974a:170). Nowhere is the contradiction between past and present arts more obvious than in Peru, whose American Popular Revolutionary Alliance party (APRA) proudly uses a major icon of pre-Hispanic Chavín culture, the "mother culture of Peruvian civilization" (Tello 1960), as its official symbol (Figs. 5.1 and 5.2).

Several major ideological decisions intervened in APRA's very conscious choice of an emblem. We can argue that, in choosing a Chavín motif, the APRA leaders reached back in time to the beginnings of a great art style much as the party purportedly sought to create a new Peruvian society, free from the trappings of imperialism. In choosing a Chavín motif for the party's standard, APRA consciously emphasized its own independent and populist ideology.

Chavín culture had been identified and defined by a mestizo Peruvian archaeologist, Julio C. Tello, as the font from which all of the later great Peruvian cultures emerged. Tello himself was the product of the era of popular movements in Peru, from about 1919 to 1939, that gave rise to Víctor Raúl Haya de la Torre (the founder of APRA), Luis Alberto Sánchez (APRA vice-president of Peru from 1984 to 1990), and other leading social science intellectuals such as Jorge Basadre, Luis E. Valcárcel, and José Carlos Mariátegui. Defying the scorn of the European landowning class, the non-European Tello argued that Chavín culture arose autochthonously in the highlands, the heartland of Peru's contemporary indigenous Indian population, not on the European-dominated coast and certainly not as a result of contact with a "more advanced" culture area. Tello's theory must be understood in the context of the class struggle then occurring in Peru as well as on the empirical grounds that showed it to be correct.

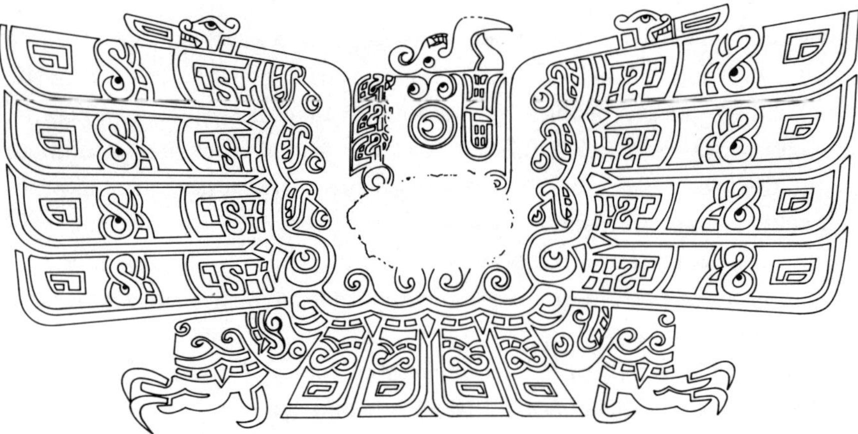

Figure 5.1. Roll-out of a Chavín bird (eagle, condor) from a cornice slab at Chavín de Huantar (Tello 1923:Fig. 74; redrawn by Steven Holland). John H. Rowe (personal communication 1991) notes that the stone on which this great bird was carved was used as a grinding stone sometime after the arrival of the Spanish and that the design in the bird's body was worn off. Tello's drawing shows the hole this later use created in the image. Tello's original drawing is not a very good representation of the original, and his drawing is reversed left to right. This error has not been corrected here.

The 1940s saw an explosion of archaeological research in Peru. As North American investigators working in the Central Andes accumulated massive amounts of data, they were forced to create a comprehensive scheme to understand and determine the chronology of the many pre-Columbian societies. Using diagnostic art styles as time markers, they devised a scheme of evolutionary stages of cultural development (Fig. 5.3; J. Rowe 1962). These were proposed and imposed on the Peruvian past by North Americans working in a foreign country (see Bennett 1948; Steward 1948; Strong 1948; Willey 1948). This developmental chronology was subsequently replaced by a basically objective scheme of abstract early, middle, and late time periods devised by John Rowe (1962).

Upon assuming the position of Director of the National Museum of

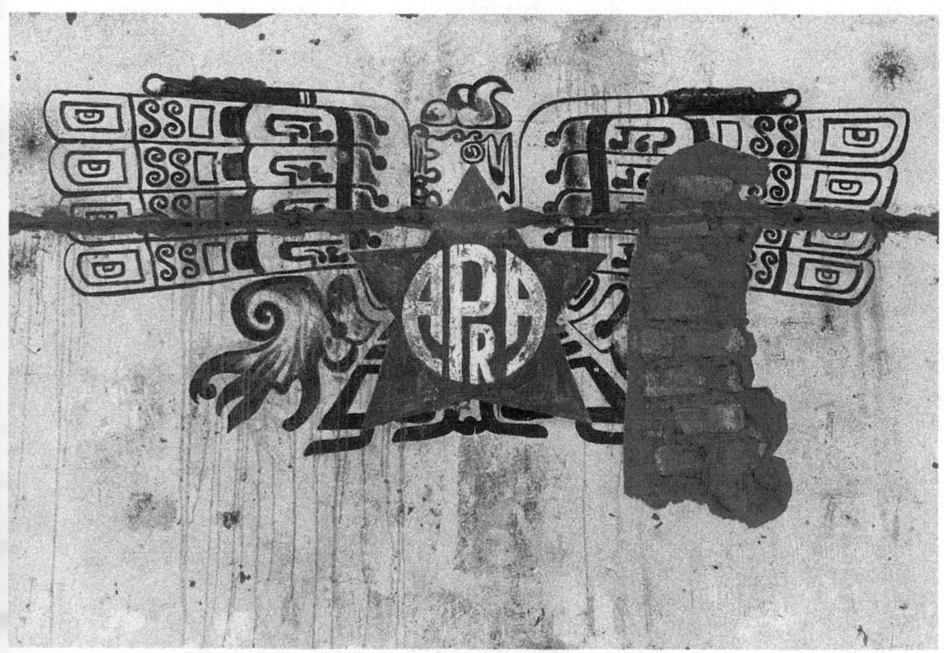

Figure 5.2. APRA's emblem painted on a wall in the town of Palpa on the south coast of Peru. When the APRA adopted this Chavín image, it covered up the hole in Tello's original drawing by placing the APRA logo over the damaged section. Note that the APRA bird faces the wrong way too. (Photograph by Helaine Silverman)

Anthropology and Archaeology in 1973, Luis Lumbreras promptly abandoned the foreign cultural-chronological terminology used for years by Peruvian and North American archaeologists working in the Central Andes. He placed a new chronological chart on display in the museum entryway as part of his conscious policy of restructuring the National Museum to create a "public museum" out of an "elite museum" (Fig. 5.4; Lumbreras 1974a: 167). Lumbreras' scheme sought to universalize, de-imperialize, and at the same time Peruvianize the Central Andean past. It was an attempt to reclaim Peru's culture history and national heritage and to participate in a political agenda for the present and future. Appointed at the height of General Juan Velasco Alvarado's leftist military revolutionary regime, Lumbreras' didactic reorganization of Peru's prehistoric cultural development clearly reflected his and the government's worldview. It also harked back to Tello in its concern with the dynamic relationships between man and the environment that were seen as having primary importance. The temporal factor was considered of secondary importance.

Lumbreras (1974a:162) unambiguously heralded this new interpretive processual chronology as the correct method of analyzing Peru's past. In it he followed a Marxist approach to culture process, organizing Peru's vast prehistory into an organic history of the nation that could be read, appreciated, and visited by all people. He envisioned the museum as a center for the action-oriented education of the masses in the social and cultural history of their country. Lumbreras' chronological chart sought to explain the causes of the manifest social inequalities visible in the archaeological record (and in contemporary Peru) and to show that exploitation was not inherent in human nature but was instead the result of a particular process. He wanted museum visitors to be impressed not just by the objects on display but also by the social processes that had produced them. These were described in the entryway chart under the rubric of changing relations of production through time. The chart compared Peru with other ancient civilizations and showed each historical trajectory to be the result of a process through which different groups came to play distinct roles in production. In that process the urban elite eventually stopped producing food and instead came to control the productive forces of society, expropriated the means of production, changed the social relations of production, and appropriated the product of production.

STYLE AND STATE IN ANCIENT PERU

Subsequent museum directors and archaeologists of different political persuasions have continued to argue over the "correct" chronology of Peru's indigenous past. The debates are not idle because chronologies organize national heritage as well as culture history. Decisions must be made about how to display collected antiquities and how to present ethnographies of living peoples as well. The stakes are therefore ideological as well as academic. Even the Incas appreciated the political aspects of the past, and they boldly related to the Spanish their self-serving version of the cultural history of the societies that had preceded and/or been conquered by them. In these stories the Incas depicted themselves as the civilized givers of light and bringers of order to the Andes. The Incas also established a museum in Cuzco for the private use of their own elites and historians. Ironically, the Incas subsequently became the subject of foreign elite collectors when Viceroy Toledo sent "Peruvian curiosities" to the Spanish king's museum at Madrid (see Chávez 1981:162).

The ancient Andean elites consciously appropriated art and exploited artists and artisans. Contributors to a state-of-the-art assessment of Peruvian culture history, *A Reappraisal of Peruvian Archaeology*, published in 1948, recognized the seemingly persistent association of exquisite, iconographically complex art styles — such as Paracas (Fig. 5.5 and Plate 1), Nasca

Bennett	Strong	Willey	Steward
Imperialists	Imperial	Inca	Empire and Conquest
City Builders		Expansionistic	
Expansionists	Fusion	Tiahuanaco	
Master Craftsmen	Florescent	Regional Classic —1000—	Regional Florescent
Experimenters	Formative	Negative —500— White - on - Red	Regional Development
Cultists		Formative Chavin —1 A.D.—	Inter - Areal Developmental
Early Farmers	Developmental	Pre - Ceramic	Basic Agricultural Beginnings
	Pre - Agricultural		Pre - Agricultural

Figure 5.3. The 1948 chronological schemes in *A Reappraisal of Peruvian Archaeology*. (Recompiled by Helaine Silverman)

ORIENT   LEVANT   EUROPE   AMERICA

Year	China	Japan	India / Pakistan	Egypt	Iraq	Europe	Mexico	Peru
1970	CHINA	JAPAN	INDIA / PAKISTAN	EGYPT	IRAQ	EUROPE — 2nd WORLD WAR	MEXICO	PERU
1900					OSMAN TURK	1st WORLD WAR		
1800		EDO	BRITISH COLONIAL			CAPITALIST EPOCH		COLONIAL HISPANIC
1700	CHI'NG		MUGHAL EMPIRE		SAFAVI	BURGEOIS	COLONIAL HISPANIC	
1600	MING	MUROMACHI				REFORM		
1500					CARA-QOYUNLU			TAWANTINSUYO EMPIRE
1400		KAMAKURA				RENAISSANCE (MARCO POLO)		
1300	YUAN				IL-KHAN		AZTECAS	
1200						FEUDAL EPOCH		
1100	SUNG					THE (CRUSADES)		REGIONAL STATES
1000	THE FIVE DYNASTIES	HEIAN			ABBAS	CAROLINGIAN EMPIRE	TOLTECAS	WARIEMPIRE
900			PALA		UMAYYA			
800	TANG	NARA		MOHAMMED				
700	SUI			SASSANIDES				
600	THE SOUTH AND		GUPTA			THE END OF		
500	THE NORTH DYNASTIES	TUMULS PERIOD				THE WEST ROMAN EMPIRE		
400	TSIN				SASANIDES	OFICIATING OF THE CHRISTIANITY		
300	THE THREE KINGDOMS				PARTHOS			REGIONAL DEVELOPMENT
200								
100	LATE HAN	YAYOI PERIODS	ANDHRA	NATIVITY OF CHRIST DEPENDENCY OF ROME		ROMAN EMPIRE	MAYAS	
100	OLD HAN		SHUNGA					
200	CHIN		MAURYA	PTOLOMAIC EMPIRE	SELEUCIDA EMPIRE	ROMAN REPUBLIC	TEOTIHUACAN	
300	ERA OF THE COMBATANT'S KINGDOMS		DEAT OF BUDDHA	GRECO ROMAN EPOCH				SUPERIOR
400						(ALEXANDER)		FORMATIVE
500				CONQUEST OF ALEXANDER				
600	(CONFUCIUS)		SHAISHNAGA	PERSIAN CONQUEST	PERSIAN CONQUEST	ETRUSCANS		
700	ERA OF SRING				NEO-BABYLON	PLATO	SUPERIOR	
800	AND AUTUMM			ETHIOPIAN SAINT PERIODS	LATE	FOUNDATION OF ROME	PRE CLASIC	
900					ASSYRIA			
1000	CHOU FROM THE WEST		HASHTINAPURA					MIDDLE FORMATIVE
1200	SHANG				GREECE	MIDLE PRE CLASIC		
1400				NEW EMPIRE	MYCENIC		OLMECAS	CHAVIN
1600	HSIA				ASSYRIAN AND BABYLON			
1800			CHANHUDARO	(HICSOS)	ISIN LARSA	INFERIOR PRECLASIC	INFERIOR FORMATIVE	
2000		JOMON PERIOD			THE THIRD DYNASTY (UR)			SUPERIOR ARCHAIC
2500	LUNG SHAN		MOHENJODARO	MIDDLE KINGDON	AKADIO FIRST DYNASTIES	HELADIC MINOIC		
3000	YANG-SHAO					(DIMINI) (SESKLO)	PURRON	
3500				DINASTIES I II III	SEMDET			
4000			RANA GHUNDAI	NAGADA	NASRURUK		ABEJAS	FORMATIVE ARCHAIC
4500					UBAID			
6000	SHA-YUAN	PRE JOMON PERIOD		BADARIENSE	HALAF	STARCEVO NEO LITHIC	COXCATLAN	
7000				FAYUN	HASSUNAN			
8000					JARMO		EL RIEGO	
9000					KARIM SHAHIR	MESOLITHC		SUPERIOR HUNTERS
10000					NATUFIENSE			
15000					KEBACENSE	MAGDELENIEN. SE	TEPEXPAN AJUEREADO	
20000				SEBILIENSE	AURIGNACOIDE	SOLUTRENSE		NO DIFERENCE COLLECTORS
30000							TLAPACOYA	
40000	CHOU KOUT TIEN							
50000	(OR DOS)			KHARGAN		AURIGNACIEN. SE		
75000			ANYATHIENSE		BARADOSTIENSE			
100000			MADRAS SOAN	MUSTERIENSE				
250000	SINANTHROPUS			LEVALLOISIENSE				
500000			PRE SOAN	ACHEULENSE				
1000000				ABBEVILLENSE / INDUSTRIES OF PEBBLES		HAO.		

Right-hand column (Universal development of the culture):

CONTEMPORANEUS PERIOD.
OCCIDENT SUBMITTED TO OTHER COUNTRIES OF THE WORLD NOW THEY HAVE BEGUN THE ERA OF THEIR LIBERATION THAT IS THE BEGINNING OF A NEW AGE OF HISTORY

CIVILIZATION AGE

SOME VILLAGES BECOME CITIES AND MEN DIVIDE IN COUNTRY AND CITY CLASES APPEAR THE STATES AND EXPLOTATION FROM SOME MEN TO OTHERS THE STONE REPLACED BY THE METALS AND THE INDUSTRIES DEVELOP AND WITH THEM COMERCE SOME MEN FIGHT OTHERS TO GET THE ECONOMIC AND POLITIC POWER IN THIS WAY THEY WRITE THE HISTORY OF TH COUNTRIES AND STATES.

THE VILLAGER COUNTRYMEN AGE

AFTER ONE REVOLUTION DEVELOPED BY NEW PEOPLE CALLED COUNTRYPEOPLE TH TOWNS LIVE FROM AGRICULTURE AND CATTLE RAISING IN VILLAGES AND STATES MAKING A SEMINOMAD OR SEDENTARY LIFE

THEY INVENTED POTTERY AND WEAVING

THE FOOD COLLECTOR'S AGE IN THAT TIME MEN'S ACTIVITIES ARE ASOCIATED TO HUNTING AND RECOLLECTION. THEIR LIFE IS NOMAD AND LIVE IN THE CAVES AND OTHER NATURAL PROTECTION THEY ONLY PRODUCE INSTRUMENTS OF STONE AND BONE.

UNIVERSAL DEVELOPMENT OF THE CULTURE

+ + + + + END OF THE COLLECTOR (COUNTRYPEOPLE REVOLUTION)

- - - - - - - BEGINNING OF THE URBANSOCIETY OR CIVILIZATION (URBAN REVOLUTION)

NATIONAL MUSEUM OF ANTHROPOLOGY OF PERU

Figure 5.4. The cultural-chronological comparative chart from the entryway of the National Museum of Anthropology and Archaeology in Lima.

(Plate 2), and Moche (Fig. 5.6) — with so-called theocratic social organization, and aesthetically routinized art styles — such as Chimú (Fig. 5.7) and Inca (Fig. 5.8) — with more "secular" or "militaristic" political systems (see Steward 1948; Willey 1948:14). The correlation between the nature of society and the kind of art produced was manifested in the various 1948 chronological schemes with terms such as Cultist, Master Craftsmen, and Empire and Conquest (Fig. 5.3).

One of the most interesting questions that remains is why certain ancient Peruvian societies portrayed their cosmology in rich iconographic detail while others did not. In this paper I examine the still-pervasive equation of theocratic states with masterpiece arts and militaristic states with routinized arts from theoretical and empirical perspectives. I first indicate inconsistencies and explanatory shortcomings of the earlier formulations with regard to the function and organization of art and craft. A sample of reasonably well documented ancient Andean cultures follows. Finally, I conclude by discussing recent changes in the approaches to the study of pre-Columbian art from iconographic literalism and chronological construction to art as ideology and the result of differential craft production-consumption strategies. The nature of the appropriation and exploitation *of* the past *in* the past must be understood if we are to comprehend cognate processes in the present. This chapter is an attempt to understand the relationship between style and state as played out in ancient Peru.

Art and Society in the Andes

Masterpieces were produced in the pre-Columbian Central Andes when cosmology was represented in art. Willey (1948:14) and Steward (1948: 103–4) attributed the creation and florescence of the great pre-Inca art styles to the political manipulation of religion, a legitimating trick no longer required or utilized once the Inca state became omnipotent. On the basis of the iconographic complexity and the evidence of state support of art for the state's own purposes, Willey and Steward argued that religion (or state-controlled religion) gave rise to great art styles. They conceived of such states as "theocratic" and considered them to be weaker in terms of power and control over human energy than secular states. Theocratic states justified the privileged position of their elite rulers through religious ideology.

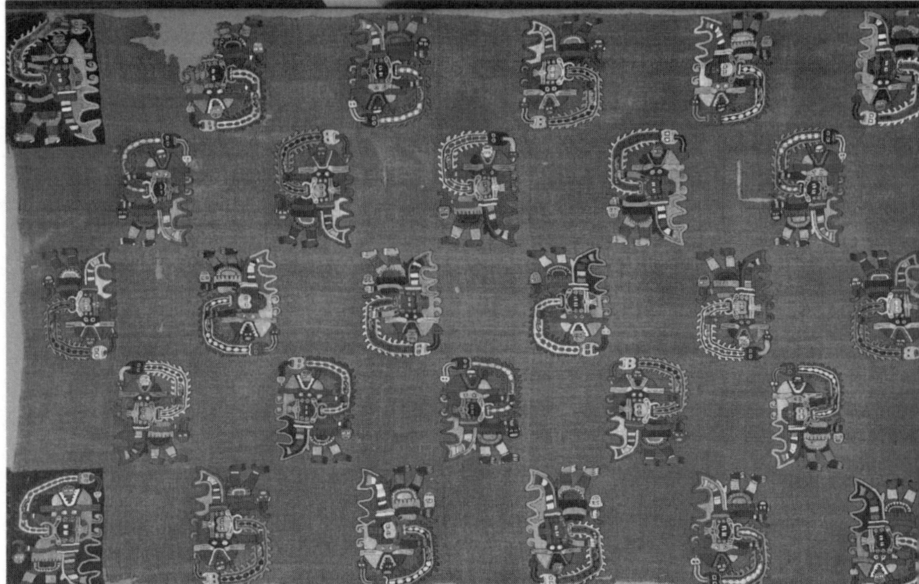

Figure 5.5. An embroidered mantle in the block color style, presumably from the Paracas site (size: 2.61 m × 0.90 m). The textile shows a series of anthropomorphic mythical beings in the killer whale aspect. A detail of the mantle is shown in Plate 1. (Museum of Fine Arts, Boston, acc. no. 16.31)

That worldview was represented in art, which was visible to all. Secular states, in contrast to theocratic states, were considered to be so strong that the ruling elite did not need to rely on religious sanction for their power. In such states, according to this argument, art declined in aesthetic (but not technological) quality or became routinized because it was no longer the medium of complex cosmological expression.

In 1948 the scholars determined whether a society was theocratic or secular by circular reasoning. They assumed that societies without a manifestly supernatural iconography were more secular than those whose artists portrayed mythical beings and whose populace built great pyramids. No pre-Columbian, pre-industrial society, however, can be regarded as secular as the term is used in the West today. Even the Inca empire, which the scholars in 1948 regarded as the most militaristic, most secular state, was

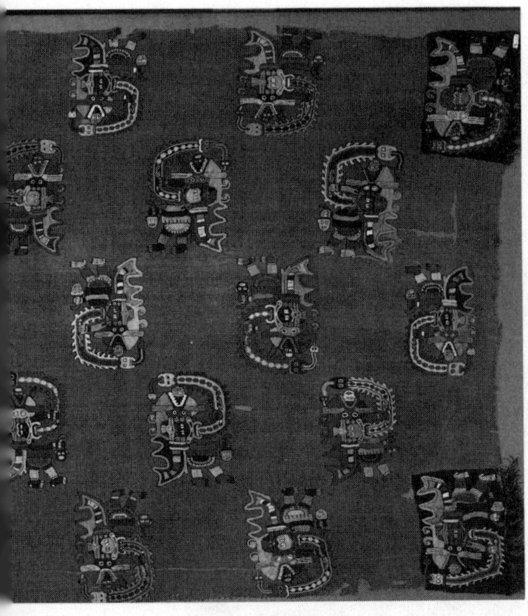

permeated with religious ideology. The emperor was the "son of the Sun," and a high priest ruled alongside him. Daily court activities revolved as much around sacred rites as affairs of state. The Incas garbed their politics in sacred ritual (Morris 1988) but also developed political machinery more powerful than in any previous state.

Today we realize that the ancient Peruvian art styles identified as florescent or Master Craftsmen all portray the dominant or elite ideology rather than various interpretations of social reality. Isbell (1984–85:93), for instance, indicates that Middle Horizon 1 Wari religious iconography conceptualized the cosmos in terms of a centralized and hierarchical structure that "organized all other domains, including the domain of humans." T. Topic (1977:344, 383) emphasizes that figural Moche art portrays elite individuals and that these representations become common at the time of

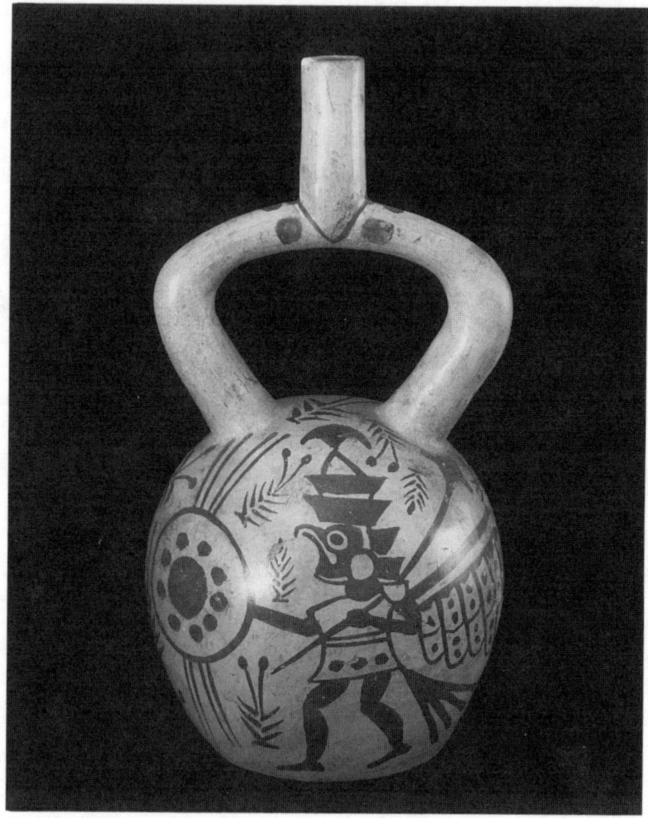

Figure 5.6. A Moche stirrup-spout bottle portraying an anthropomorphic warrior. (Krannert Art Museum, University of Illinois at Urbana-Champaign, acc. no. 67.29.74; courtesy of Maarten van de Guchte)

emergence of a conquest Moche state. Zuidema (1972) has labeled a major theme on Nasca pottery the "Nasca cosmic concept," which, by analogy with the Incas, is interpreted as indicative of social hierarchy and political dominance. Recently I called attention to the apparent deritualization and demythification of human figures in late Nasca times, when pottery shows vivid scenes of warfare, trophy-head taking, and chiefly individuals (Silverman, in press: chapter 15; Silverman 1988). On Wari ritual-offering pottery Cook (1985a) has recognized a similar shift from mythical beings to human figures, which she interprets as indicating the increasing role of centralized authority in the expansive Wari state.

Art has a distinct sociopolitical context as well as an aesthetic essence (see papers by N. Graburn, J. Nunley, S. Price, and J. E. Way in this volume). The relationship between style and society, and between producers and consumers, was as complex in prehistoric times as it is today (see Whitten and Whitten 1988 and papers by N. Graburn and S. Price in this volume). Not all ancient Central Andean societies portrayed social relations through art. Those that did, however, illustrated undisguised elite prominence rather than egalitarian social interaction. Such elite art reflects the structure of social and economic organization in these societies. Imagery, creativity, and relations of power were thus tightly intermeshed (see the essay by S. Gillespie in this volume).

In addition to its general or aesthetic meaning, it is incumbent on archaeologists to examine the specific meanings of art and the functions of

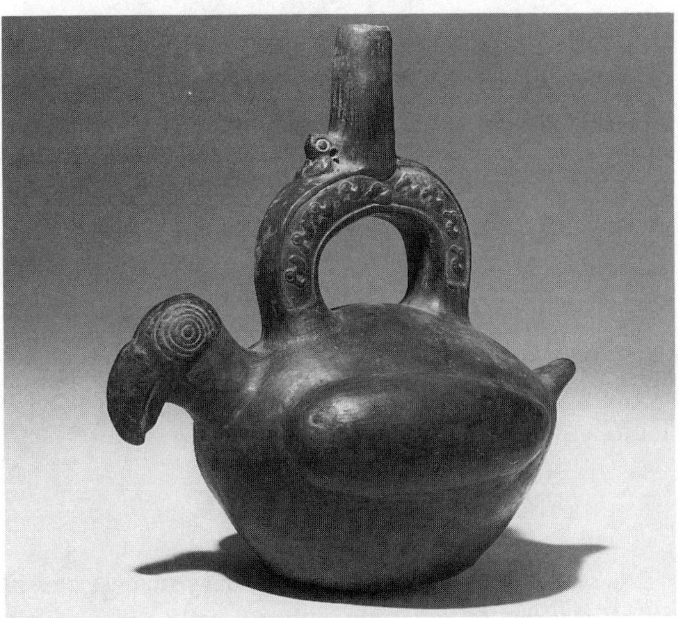

Figure 5.7. Chimú stirrup-spout bottle. (Baltimore Museum of Art, Bequest of Alan Wurtzburger, acc. no. 1960.30.99)

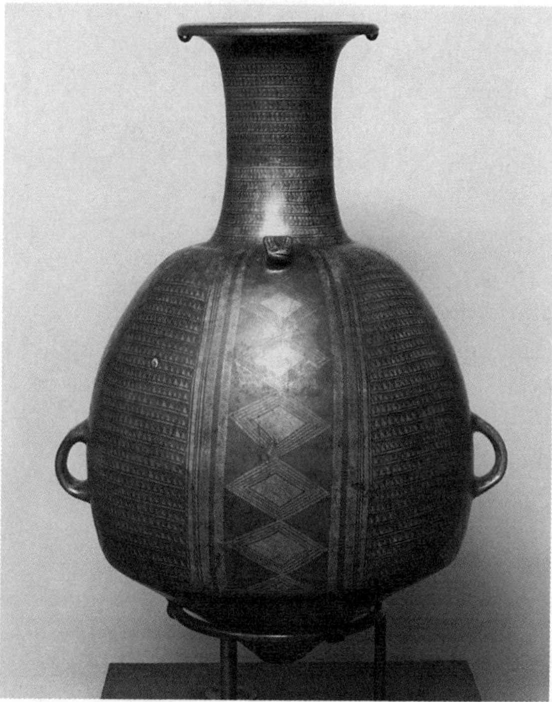

Figure 5.8. Inca aryballus vessel. (University Museum, Philadelphia, neg. no. 55516; courtesy of Clark Erickson)

a particular art in a given cultural context (see Willey 1973:153). As Lumbreras recognized in his approach to the chronological ordering of the cultural processes of ancient Peru, art is neither epiphenomenal nor exclusively superstructural. It is the product of distinct forms of organization of the means and relations of production. Art has an aesthetic quality, but it has a profoundly economic and sociopolitical one as well.

Art and Craft

Archaeologists study art because it is a system of symbolic expression materially encoded in form. At any moment, art is conjunctive within its own historical context and can be analyzed iconographically. Changes in art styles are usually gradual but can be abrupt. In the latter case, artworks are a significant body of evidence with which to document and explain social and cultural change. As in language, disjunction between form and meaning can occur (Kubler 1973; Kubler 1985:404; Panofsky 1960; Reese 1985: xxvii, xxix, xxxiii–xxxiv).

In archaeology, as in art history, the art studied typically comprises "works of art," the most elaborate, formally varying objects from which chronologies have been derived and iconographic systems defined and interpreted (see discussions in this volume by S. Price, N. Graburn, and J. E. Way on "primitive/anonymous" art vs. "authored/great" art). Borrowing from Kubler (1985:111–17), this kind of art can be called fine or sacred, and as such it contrasts with popular, plain, profane, folk, or utilitarian art. Sacred art comprises a religious art style that is highly symbolic and referentially nonsecular although it may carry an implicit, politically legitimating message. Unlike sacred art, popular art portrays quotidian things or events in accessible images rather than recondite symbols; it is an art liked by nearly everybody; and it is produced by and for the masses rather than the elite (Kubler 1985:112). As Kubler (1985:111) observed, there is an apparent functional difference between the two arts that is rooted in historical context and social structure. Following Gillespie (this volume), we could better express the difference not as a firm opposition but as a general contrast between elite and nonelite artworks, the difference being based "on the group in society which directed their production or for whose use they were intended."

In addition to the distinction between sacred/elite and popular/nonelite art, we must consider craft. Craft is art, but it also carries with it the implication of workshop and/or mass production, with the concomitant sacrifice of personal aesthetics referred to by Kubler. Art and craft are also frequently contrasted, with craft comprising those objects produced for utilitarian household consumption rather than elite aesthetic entertainment and class self-service. However, certain pre-Hispanic societies established urban craft workshops to satisfy the aesthetic, sumptuary, and daily needs of its elite city dwellers.

The distinction between art and craft seems to concern the differential locus of production and consumption, which is shown in a simplified form in Table 5.1. As ancient societies became more complex, economic specialization occurred. Among other things, no longer did the household produce exclusively for itself, and certain households were removed from subsistence activities to work full-time to fulfill certain industrial needs for the economically productive and nonproductive sectors of society. In the process by which pyramidal social class structures emerged and crystallized there occurred a concomitant revolutionary socioeconomic transformation of the household unit of production and consumption into a multihousehold sphere of production not coterminous with the means and consumption of that production. The professionalization of crafts was the direct outcome of the hierarchization and increasing complexity of society that can be traced in the material record of human history. Ancient Peru provides an excellent test case against which to assess whether the socioeconomic transformations that occurred with the rise of states and empires were associated with a "declining quality of workmanship" (Kubler 1984: 42) — the change from "qualitative" art to "quantitative" art noted by the 1948 Peruvianist scholars — and to study the relationship between sociopolitical complexity and the organization of artistic and craft production (for a chronological chart and map locating sites and cultures discussed in this article, see Figs. 5.9 and 5.10).

Table 5.1 Comparison of Access to and Distribution of Goods in Different Levels of Production and Consumption

Unit of Production	Unit of Consumption	Nature of Product Access and Distribution		
		Internal	Reciprocal	Asymmetrical
1. Individual	individual	x		
2. Individual	household	x		
3. Household	household	x		
4. Village	village		x	
5. Individual	elite			x
6. Household	elite			x
7. "Guilds"	elite			x

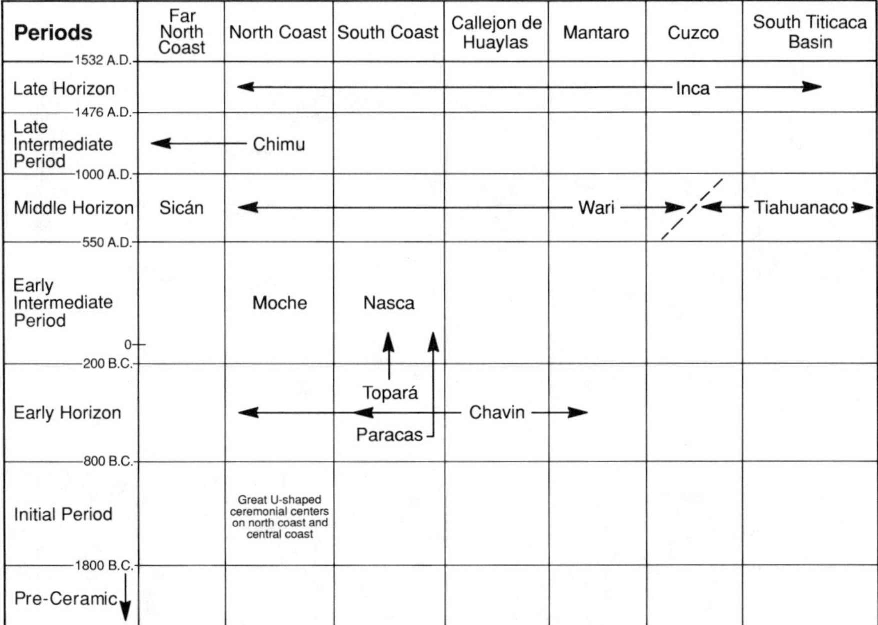

Periods	Far North Coast	North Coast	South Coast	Callejon de Huaylas	Mantaro	Cuzco	South Titicaca Basin
—1532 A.D.—							
Late Horizon		◀—				— Inca —	—▶
—1476 A.D.—							
Late Intermediate Period	◀—	— Chimu					
—1000 A.D.—							
Middle Horizon	Sicán	◀—			— Wari —	▶ ◀	— Tiahuanaco ▶
—550 A.D.—							
Early Intermediate Period		Moche	Nasca				
0—							
—200 B.C.—							
Early Horizon		◀—	◀— Topará / Paracas ⌐	— Chavin —▶			
—800 B.C.—							
Initial Period		Great U-shaped ceremonial centers on north coast and central coast					
—1800 B.C.—							
Pre-Ceramic ▼							

Figure 5.9. The chronology of the cultures discussed in this chapter.

"Cultists"

On the northern and central coasts of Peru during the "sacred millennium" between about 1800 and 800 B.C., a series of great ceremonial centers arose out of an already precocious late preceramic tradition of monumental architecture and incipient social differentiation (see, e.g., Donnan 1985; Fung Pineda 1988; Moseley 1975). Much of this Initial Period architecture was built in the form of great, individual U-shaped mounds that contained within themselves a readily understood message about the organization of society and the cosmos (Isbell 1977; Lathrap 1985), learned by the public through sanctioned visits to the ceremonial centers. The ceremonial centers functioned "not simply as a locale for particular ceremonies, but as a force in its own right that shape[d] supernatural power" (Lathrap 1985:242–43). Their layout focused supernatural power to a point that established an *axis mundi*. As such, the ceremonial centers were "mechanisms for the mainte-

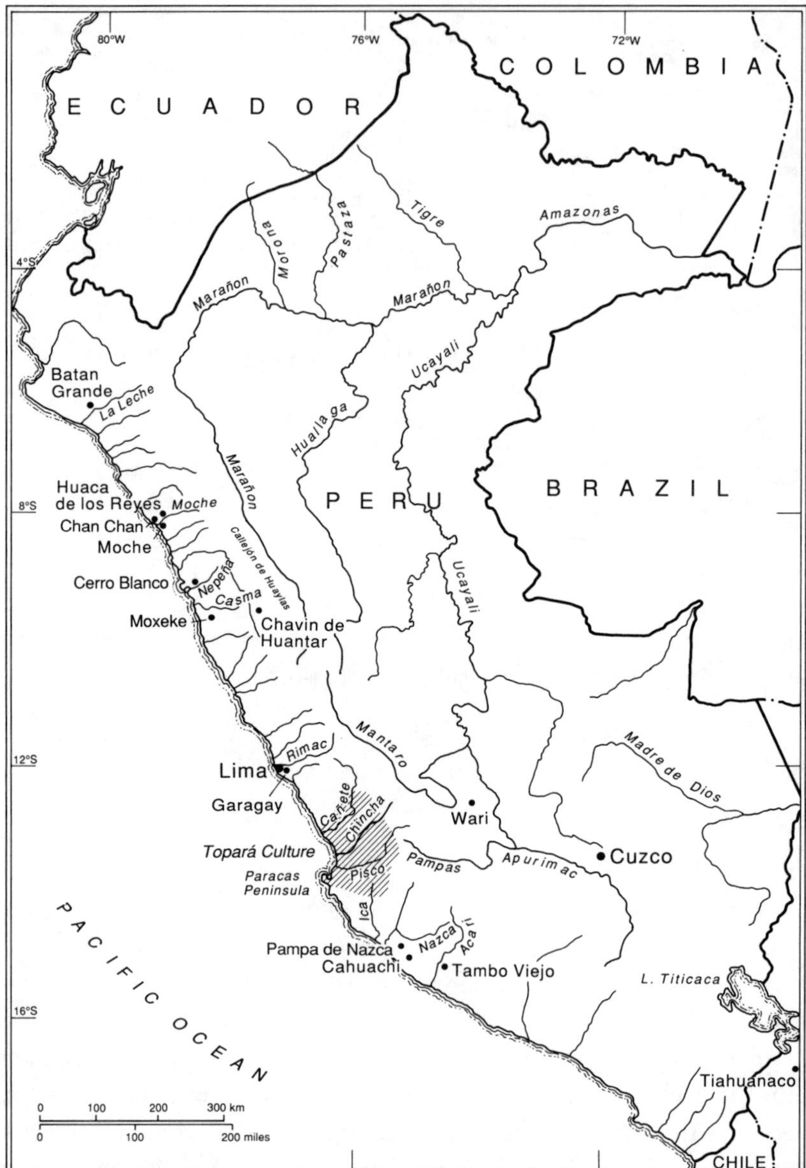

Figure 5.10. The cultures and sites discussed in this chapter. (Derived from Keatinge 1988:Figs. 3.1, 4.1, 5.1; redrawn by Steven Holland)

nance of stability and health of the polity" (Lathrap 1985:246) and were also a metaphor for Initial Period social organization (Lathrap 1985).

Individual dogma-bearing art objects from the Initial Period are rare in the archaeological record and craft production was overwhelmingly of a domestic and local nature (cases 1–4 in Table 5.1). In terms of socioeconomic differentiation, there is no evidence of full-time craft specialization in the Initial Period (cases 5–7). Priests or religious specialists were, however, buttressing their existence as a social group, separate from the rest of society, through their manipulation of ritual knowledge and the coordination of public works. Both the great U-shaped mounds and the monumental art inscribed on some of them (e.g., at Garagay and Huaca de los Reyes) were symbols of, and actual loci of, ritual power that could be converted to effective social power. Over time, aggregates or groupings of ritual specialists and those whose labor they directed evolved into true social classes and the relationship between art and power became more inextricably linked.

The Initial Period was followed by the Chavín or Early Horizon,[1] which lasted until 200 B.C. (Burger 1981). Chavín culture has been reconstructed largely on the basis of the art style found at the type site of Chavín de Huantar in the Callejón de Huaylas in the north highlands of Peru (Burger 1988; Rowe 1967). Chavín de Huantar consists of a U-shaped temple precinct with an associated residential area (Burger 1988). The temple was the repository of the maximal expression of Chavín religious ideology and cosmology, portrayed there in scores of elaborately carved stones emplaced in the temple or directly associated with it. Chavín-style art objects are found in a range of media over a wide area of ancient Peru.

The nature of Chavín's social, economic, and political organization has been debated extensively (see summary in Burger 1988), but running throughout the various interpretations is a "long-standing consensus that the Chavín horizon style is the symbolic expression of a religious ideology and that the Chavín horizon is the result of the diffusion of what may be referred to as the 'Chavín cult'" (Burger 1988:111). Willey (1974) posited a civilizing role for the great early religious traditions of Mesoamerica and the Central Andes, Olmec and Chavín respectively. Part of this "civilizing process" involved economic and occupational specialization sponsored by the corporate temple organization. Kubler (1984:44), considering the relationship of art to social structure, described the effects of priestly rule on artistic activity as radical: with the formation of a true temple cult, village styles and crafts became separated from canonized religious expressions. Burger (1988) has amply demonstrated the validity of this statement in his reconstruction of Chavín stylistic unification and associated local diversity during the Early Horizon.

The Chavín cult was intimately related to dramatic technological innovations applied to the production of Chavín-style art in textiles and metallurgy (Burger 1988:129–31). These innovations were time-consuming but provided "the means of manufacturing objects which were distinguishable immediately from other items and therefore especially suitable and effective as symbols or emblems of religious authority" (Burger 1988:130). Burger notes that this art is "presumed to be the work of full-time specialists who could dedicate themselves to developing an artistic style capable of communicating the power of Chavín religious ideology" (1988:130).

To Burger's conclusions I would add that these art objects were not only emblematic of the power of the religious ideology, they were also a real source of effective personal power, both ritual and social. This was so both because these objects were "awe-inspiring" (Burger 1988:131) and because their owner or manipulator was empowered by them in much the same way as the Olmec rulers (and later Mesoamerican elites) who physically and symbolically placed themselves at the mouths of caves to mediate between the other world and this one (see S. Gillespie, this volume). The art style communicated the power of Chavín religious ideology and concomitantly manifested and generated an increasingly hierarchical social reality.

"Master Craftsmen"

The Early Intermediate or "Master Craftsmen" Period, between about 200 B.C. and A.D. 600, was characterized by the emergence of distinct contemporary regional art styles. This contrasts with the relative artistic homogeneity of the preceding pan-Peruvian Chavín horizon (but see Burger 1988). The artistic regionalism of this period had important political correlates, which were clearly enunciated by the 1948 scholars. Willey (1948:12), for instance, described these styles as "national in scope," the "crystallized symbols of the national consciousness." He went on to explain that with "regional political and social control in the hands of ruling castes, it is not at all surprising that foreign art symbolism, as it might represent a threat to the status quo, was unpopular. Rather, it would have been to the advantage of the leaders to maintain a strong nationalism with its attendant isolationism." Today we regard these diverse regional art styles as the physical manifestation of territoriality and ethnic identity.

Among the various regional cultures encompassed by the "Master Craftsmen" label, three stand out for the unsurpassed beauty of their art: Paracas and Nasca on the south coast and Moche on the north coast. These may be used by way of examples for analysis. The Paracas culture was discovered and defined by Julio C. Tello (1959; Tello and Mejía Xesspe 1979) as a result of his spectacular burial finds on the Paracas Peninsula. About 18 percent of the hundreds of burials found by Tello contained massive amounts of fine cloth garments covered with iconographically complex images of the natural, social, and supernatural world (Paul 1980:25–26; Fig. 5.5 and Plate 1). This iconography probably explains man's relationship to and position in those realms. While all members of Paracas society would have shared in this dominant ideology, only a small group within the total population had access to the textiles decorated with the powerful symbols. Only they could wear them, and upon death these special garments were taken out of circulation to be buried with the elite, creating a continuous demand for their production on the part of new leaders (Paul 1980:96–103).

In addition to serving as primordial grave goods, the Paracas textiles were, in life, portable wealth, the result of one group's ability to mobilize and control the labor of others. The amount of time reflected in weaving, spinning, dyeing, and embroidering just one mummy bundle is enormous — anywhere from 10,000 to 30,000 hours (Paul 1990:30–33) — and would have involved the efforts of scores of individuals. Although there is no evidence of *aclla*-organized textile production as in the Inca empire (discussed below), we nevertheless see in Paracas society an early emphasis on textiles as an elite good of inextricably intermeshed political and ritual significance (see Paul 1990). The society that produced the fabulous Paracas textiles was clearly nonegalitarian in nature (see Silverman 1991).

Nasca art and society emerged out of the antecedent Paracas culture.[2] Nasca had its heartland in the Río Grande de Nazca drainage, where the largest and most numerous Nasca sites are located, not the least of which is the 150-hectare principal early Nasca cult center of Cahuachi in the Nazca

Valley (see, e.g., Silverman, in press; Silverman 1990a).[3] Nasca culture also flourished in the Ica and Acarí valleys.

Nasca pottery from thousands of looted tombs fills the world's museums and private collections. It consists of a highly varied repertoire of iconographically complex images portraying mythical themes (Plate 2), beautiful naturalistic representations of the plant and animal world, and lovely geometric designs. The vessels on which this iconography was painted encompass musical instruments (panpipes, drums, trumpets), useful bowls, dishes, vases, and cups, and prestigious double-spout-and-bridge bottles.

In contrast to the preceding emphasis on the textile medium in Paracas, Nasca society dedicated itself to the massive (but not mass-produced) production and consumption of fine pottery. Nasca pottery was portable art that conveyed important cosmological and, presumably, social information that was necessary for the proper functioning of society. It was buried in graves and was used and ritually broken at Cahuachi (Silverman 1990a: 230–31) and other locations. It circulated widely around the south coast. I suggest that, with the rise of Cahuachi and a series of lesser early Nasca ceremonial centers, there came increased demand for the iconographically elaborate ceramic vessels that were used in Nasca ritual (as musical instruments, as vessels used for ritualized food and drink consumption, etc.). This created an amplifying effect in terms of demand for the product (see Arnold 1985:161) and a concomitant increase in production. Pottery came into its own, then, in this south coastal region of Peru with the rise of the early Nasca cult, the shift to the ceramic medium being aided by the rapid technological improvements in slip-painting from Nasca 1 when it was rare, to Nasca 2 when the paint crackled, to Nasca 3 when a much greater degree of technical control and iconographic representation was achieved. It is also possible that Nasca society's emphasis of ceramic art resulted from the perception of textiles as too time-consuming and labor-intensive.

Within a couple of centuries of the demise of Cahuachi, which may have occurred around A.D. 300, Nasca ceramic art underwent a major stylistic change known as the bizarre innovation (Blagg 1975; Roark 1965). Formerly easily read motifs became disjuncted, visually complex, and abstract. In addition, this late Nasca pottery frequently depicts richly dressed humans ("chiefs"), often shown in positions of power, a prominent example being that of a man holding a trophy head in his hands or with trophy heads strung around the bottom of his tunic. The cultural correlates and causes of this artistic transformation seem to coincide with the growth of Wari, a powerful and expansive state in the adjacent Ayacucho highlands, and the increasing hierarchization of Nasca society (Silverman 1988, 1990b, 1990c). Technologically, Nasca pottery became even finer, with truer whites and more consistent colors, more even firing, and better surface finishes. Nasca ceramic art did not suffer from Cahuachi's decline; even the areal distribution of Nasca pottery remained the same.

Nasca society has been reconstructed as a conglomerate of culturally related, politically independent societies ("chiefdoms"), possibly grouped into two moieties, that worshipped and paid obeisance at Cahuachi until that site's demise (Silverman, in press: chap. 23; Silverman 1990a, 1990b). Nasca society appears to have changed in character from "religious," or priest- and cult-centered, in early Nasca times to more "political," or chief-led, in late Nasca times.

Thus far we know little about the organization of Nasca craft production, although its cultural context (see above) and technology (Blasco Bosqued and Ramos Gómez 1980; Carmichael 1986) are fairly well understood. Giuseppe Orefici (personal communication, 1988) and I have found little evidence for ceramic manufacture at Cahuachi, but there is good evidence of textile manufacture at the site (Silverman, in press: chaps. 18–19). We may tentatively hypothesize that fancy polychrome pottery was made both at the great ceremonial center and in individual settlements throughout the Nasca region. As noted above, Nasca ceramic production was apparently not disrupted by the decline of the principal cult center, although pottery would no longer have been made there (if it ever was).

Whereas ceramic specialists—part-time and perhaps some full-time— must have been responsible for obtaining and preparing the slip pigments and for painting the finest and most complex supernatural and representational images, some Nasca painted pottery is rustic enough in appearance to suggest local, "in-house" production and consumption (cases 2, 3, and perhaps 4 in Table 5.1). Ceramic specialists must have made the technologically complex panpipes that are ubiquitous at Cahuachi and that are also found in funerary caches and on the surface of Nasca sites throughout the Nazca drainage. In addition to the well-known ceramic and textile art, Nasca artists produced a corpus of mini-masterpieces in other media, such as carved gourds, gold facial ornaments, and stone vases. Nasca society also decorated its landscape with huge figures of animals (bird, whale, monkey, lizard, dog, spider, and others), mythical creatures (killer whale, anthropomorphic beings), and geometric designs (spirals, straight lines, and trapezoids). These are the great "Nazca Lines," or geoglyphs (see Aveni 1986; Reinhard 1985; Silverman 1990a, 1990b).

Contemporary with Nasca was the Moche culture on the north coast of Peru. Whereas Nasca society excelled at the production of vibrant polychrome pottery, Moche artists specialized in iconographically complex, bichromal (red or brown on white), fine-line drawings on mold-made pots and realistic and mythological portraiture on modeled vessels (Fig. 5.6). The technological factor of molds reflects the high demand for pottery by the Moche elite throughout Moche territory. Moche mass production is also indicated by the discovery of craft neighborhoods at the Moche site where there were corporate groups of artisans in the service of the elite. Thus, it is likely that Moche pottery was produced by full-time specialists residing at the capital site of Moche (see T. Topic 1982) and, presumably, elsewhere in the Moche realm. Even though much Moche pottery was formed in molds, in its painted decoration there was room for idiosyncratic variation. Donnan (1978:50) believes that Moche potters could have been artists affiliated with specific workshops, and he presents convincing evidence for the identification of the work of particular individuals.

Donnan (1976, 1978) has suggested that all Moche art was supernatural, religious, symbolic, and nonsecular in nature. Theresa Topic (1977: 344, 383) has challenged this view, suggesting instead that Moche art served elite and state purposes. The truth probably encompasses both positions and, as K. C. Chang (1983) argues for ancient China, art was a path to authority. It was the elite who sponsored and consumed the larger part of the output of Moche artisans: fine inlaid gold, shell, and stone jewelry; inlaid wooden staves; rich woven tapestries; and, of course, pottery. An extraordinary case in point is the recently discovered royal Moche tombs at Sipán in the Lambayeque Valley, which contain the richest grave goods ever reported in the New World (see Alva 1988, 1990).

Thus, the controversy over whether Moche art is religious or profane in nature obscures a more interesting issue. The Moche worldview or dominant ideology is expressed inseparably and in an intermeshed form in their iconography and media. Iconographically, we see the unmistakable portrayal of a class society with fixed social roles. That iconographic depiction of social reality was bolstered in material terms by two facts: (1) only the elite had access to the exotic luxury goods with which some of that art was rendered; and (2) some of those exotic materials, such as Spondylus shell, had a yet deeper symbolic meaning that inherently expressed the right of the elite to rule and their ritual role and ecological regulatory duties as rulers (e.g., Davidson 1982; Murra 1975a). Donnan's (1988) analysis of the grave goods from Sipán indicates that art and society were one: the Moche lords dressed identically to their representations on artworks and used many of these items of ritual paraphernalia in ceremonies identical to those represented.

The above comments would pertain best to objects used on public occasions when their implicit and, indeed, explicit message would be seen by all (Wobst 1977). The manipulation and functioning of jewelry, copper goblets and rattles, and rich textiles in such situations is obvious. Easily manipulated Moche pots, however, present a problem of visibility, because their small, intricate iconographic detail and powerful designs could not be seen by a distant audience. Scenes painted on Moche pots, however, give valuable insight into how such pottery was used. Apparently, the ceremonious Moche court consumed fine pottery in episodes of ritualized food presentation (Donnan 1976:Fig. 48), at state weaving installations (Donnan 1976:Fig. 47), and during occasions of ritualized sexual intercourse, hallucinogenic drug ingestion, and cannibalism (e.g., Donnan 1976:Fig. 1). Moche shamans and/or curers also had access to and in some way used elaborate ceramic vessels (Donnan 1976:Fig. 80a, Pl. 11).

Much Moche pottery ended up in tombs, sometimes in enormous quantities, as with a Sipán lord whose tomb contained more than a thousand pots (Alva 1988). But Moche pottery was not specifically made for interment. Donnan (1973:128) found sherds of elaborately decorated ceramics in habitation refuse during his explorations in the Santa Valley.

It might also be suggested that the Moche used pottery as metonymic ritual-stylized activity involving the substitution of one cause for another (Sapir 1977). Following Malinowski (1979:41, 42), I suggest that the act of making a ceramic representation of a potato propitiated the particular forces of nature and gods who brought forth potatoes; that the painting of a war scene (with real and/or mythical combatants) ensured success in battle; that the portrayal of the principal deity, Ai Apec, induced his powers to enter the human owner. While some Moche themes were perhaps the artistic property of society as a whole (e.g., potatoes or other food products), the right and ability to represent other ideas may have been the exclusive domain of the elite.

"Expansionists"

Specialized groups of craftsmen also characterize the Middle Horizon Wari state, whose heartland was the highland Ayacucho Valley east of Nazca. At the great capital city of Wari itself and at nearby Conchopata, archaeologists have found evidence of residential craft specialization. In the city of Wari there appear to be barrios whose inhabitants were devoted to the manufacture of particular classes of objects. At the foot of Robles Moqo, for instance, Gary Vescelius excavated a large ceramic workshop in a residential district (see Lumbreras 1975:126). Lumbreras (1975:126) suggests that other similar ceramic production areas exist at Wari. Further, at Conchopata, Lumbreras (1975:117, 123–24) uncovered a ceramic workshop replete with wasters (pottery damaged or deformed during the firing process), finishing instruments, and ceramic disk "hand-wheels." Near Ushpa Qoto, Lumbreras identified a surface area abounding in worked turquoise. This led him to suggest the presence of a barrio dedicated to this manufacture (Lumbreras 1975:128–29). Nearby there is an area of many fine projectile points made of flint (Lumbreras 1975:129), again suggesting the existence of a specialized craft district. Not all crafts, however, were organized at a suprahousehold level. Isbell, for instance, notes a lack of lithic workshops at Wari and suggests that "at least a fair amount of stone-working was going on at the domestic level" (1988:171).

Here it could be suggested that sumptuary goods lent themselves to the direct elite control of production, whereas subsistence crafts were pursued on the household level (so long as the raw materials were readily available). Lumbreras (1975:181–82) distinguishes these urban production centers of elite and export goods from the rural production centers that supplied domestic wares. At Conchopata, in addition to the specialized elite ceramic workshop and famous pottery offering deposit (see Cook 1985a), Lumbreras (1975) identified an area dedicated to the production of a local or internally consumed ceramic ware known as Huamanga. The Huamanga ceramists, in Lumbreras' words, "had rural ceramic workshops at the service of each population center and probably centers of artisanal production at the service of a given valley or agricultural region. For certain, none of these was in competition with the great ceramic center of Wari which produced elite pottery. This pottery was for limited use in Ayacucho itself, apart from Wari" (1975:182).

Wari iconography was embedded in the context of a state religion. Human figures are portrayed with notable differences in manner of dress and elite paraphernalia and also in association with supernaturals, combining with them in a hierarchy of elites, warriors, and captives (Cook 1985a: 83). This iconography has its correlate in the actual sociopolitical conditions of the Wari expansionist state (Isbell 1988; Isbell and Schreiber 1978).

Cook (1985b) shows a direct relationship between the ritual act of offering iconography-laden objects and the political domain of the Wari state. She argues that "ritual communication involves formalized and repeated acts and . . . this type of performance is a form of power that is characteristic of traditional authority situations." If this is so, then what is ritually offered should provide a clear indication of the surrounding sociopolitical milieu. Cook (1985b:22) demonstrates that there is an increased proportion of human figures relative to supernaturals on Wari pottery offerings in the period that coincides with the expansion of the Wari state (see Menzel 1964). She interprets this iconographic shift as evidence of the centralized authority's concern with human leadership. "The state," concludes Cook, "impinged directly upon religious and ritual domains in its legitimation process" (Cook 1985b:24).

Earlier than and contemporary with Wari is the great Tiwanaku civilization of the Lake Titicaca Basin in the South Andean altiplano. New field data for Tiwanaku (Kolata 1987a, 1987b) make it clear that the Tiwanaku city, state, and state cult supported a sector of specialized artisans who produced stone sculpture, fine textiles, pottery, jewelry, and metal objects (most notably bronze). Lumbreras (1975:119) considers the metallurgists the premier craftsmen of Tiwanaku society. The skill of the Tiwanaku metallurgists led to large-scale metalworking, and—unlike the situation in the rest of the Central Andes, where metallurgy was overwhelmingly devoted to the production of elite, nonutilitarian objects such as jewelry—in Tiwanaku society, tools and weapons were manufactured as well.

At Tiwanaku, as at Chavín de Huantar, an elaborate iconography was carved in stone that was integrally associated with temple architecture. The principal icon of Tiwanaku is a frontal standing human figure in elaborate dress with outspread arms who grasps a stafflike object in each hand (see Lumbreras 1974b:Fig. 153). This deity is associated with a class of secondary figures known as angels or profile attendants (Cook 1985a; Menzel 1964). Tiwanaku art also depicts felines and mythical animals (Isbell 1988:178).

Isbell (1988:179) and others have suggested that Tiwanaku's complicated iconography—although today most completely represented on monumental stone art—was actually developed on textiles, which have not been preserved in the wet altiplano environment of the Lake Titicaca Basin. Textiles, rather than stone or pottery, would have been Tiwanaku's primary medium for iconographic expression. Isbell's (1988) keen observation that the stone carvings themselves have the intricacy and two-dimensional aspect of textiles is also supported by the documented ritual and political importance of cloth in the Andes (e.g., Murra 1975b) and the ready availability of the raw material in the form of extensive herds of domesticated camelids with fine wool. Furthermore, exquisite textiles with Tiwanaku iconography have been found outside the Tiwanaku heartland, in dry coastal sites in far southern Peru and northern Chile and, rarely, in dry caves in the highlands (see, e.g., Conklin 1983; Oakland 1986).

Following Posnansky (1945), it can be argued that the main Tiwanaku icon mediates between the human and supernatural worlds. When humans clothed themselves in this iconography—as we saw at Sipán and with the Paracas Peninsula textiles—they assumed that mediating role and gained ritual and effective social power from the exercise of that office. But in Tiwanaku society, human contact with the other world was not achieved merely by impersonating the gods through dress. The frequent occurrence of carved wooden trays with Tiwanaku iconography in dry coastal sites has long been argued to be associated with the taking of a hallucinogenic snuff, probably Anadenanthera (see Torres 1987). Bone snuffing tubes are also known, and decorated wooden keros may also have been used in snuffing practice (Isbell 1988:179). Just as Cordy-Collins (1977) argued, in her essay on the role of hallucinogenic drug use in Chavín religion, that "the medium [drugs] was the message," it appears that ritualized drug consumption played an important role in the Tiwanaku cult.

"Cultists" Again

Newly defined Sicán culture (Shimada 1981, 1985) of the far north coast of Peru offers a very interesting case of interrelationships among art, technology, and internal and long-distance politics in terms of elite-sponsored and elite-administered arsenical copper production. From its political and religious capital at Batan Grande in the La Leche Valley, the Middle Sicán polity (A.D. 900–1100) coordinated intensive metallurgical activities whose purpose was to produce utilitarian objects (hoes, digging stick blades, spear points) and elite objects (*naipes*, or double-T shaped "primitive money"). From one Middle Sicán tomb at Batan Grande, some 500 kg of copper objects were recovered (Shimada 1985:375). Shimada (1985:375) notes that many of the ostensibly utilitarian copper objects associated with Middle Sicán come from tombs and show no evidence of use. This suggests that they were made as funerary offerings.

The enormous amount of copper associated with Sicán culture leads Shimada to conclude that "we are dealing with a procurement level beyond the production capacities of a cottage industry. . . . The control of the entire regional copper alloy production . . . was in the hands of the central authority of the Middle Sicán Culture" (Shimada 1985:376). This production encompassed not just the mining of the copper ore itself but also the provision of the huge amounts of fuel necessary for smelting (Shimada 1985: 376–77) and arsenic ore, whose source lay beyond Middle Sicán territory in the adjacent north highlands of Cajamarca. The fine tuning of all these factors necessary for Middle Sicán's intensive metallurgical industry led Shimada to argue for state intervention at all levels.

In addition to the evidence that copper, particularly the *naipes*, functioned as a medium of exchange or standard of value and status symbol in Middle Sicán society (Shimada 1985:390), other luxury exotics are also present in the archaeological record, such as Spondylus, lapis lazuli, emeralds and various semiprecious stones, and coral (Shimada 1985:391). The Middle Sicán elite was heavily involved in long-distance exchange and conspicuous consumption of sumptuary items. The value of these items lay, in large part, in the rarity of the raw materials rather than in the beauty of their final form. Indeed, although Shimada (1981) convincingly argues that Batan Grande was the long-term capital of a Sicán polity, a site whose primary functions revolved around a religious-pilgrimage-burial complex, and despite the ideological unification implied by the widespread and homogeneous "Sicán Lord" deity representation, this cultural focus did not manifest itself in a great art style. Instead, the Sicán state sponsored and controlled artistic production from procurement of raw materials to the final distribution of finished goods. The art style, albeit limited in vocabulary, conveyed a uniform and unambiguous message by virtue of the total cosmology encapsulated in the principal deity image and the raw materials out of which much of Sicán arts and crafts were made.

"City Builders"

There are excellent data on the organization (J. Topic 1982; Topic and Moseley 1983) and technology (e.g., A. Rowe 1984) of craft production in the Chimú kingdom of the north coast. John Topic's excavations in areas of small, irregularly agglutinated rooms (abbreviated as SIAR) in the Chimú capital city of Chan Chan on the north bank of the Moche River have revealed that most of these were organized in self-contained barrios. Within these barrios were residential complexes with abundant evidence of craft production — what Topic refers to as shops or workshops (J. Topic 1982: 153–55). Indeed, Topic (1982:161) has argued convincingly that the urban proletariat of Chan Chan consisted primarily of artisans rather than farmers or fishermen. Furthermore, these craftsmen had a certain degree of status in their capacity as retainers to the Chan Chan elite, as evidenced by their right to wear wooden ear tubes (J. Topic 1982:164).

Evidence of metalworking was especially common, as were workshops specializing in weaving and woodworking. John Topic also uncovered evidence pointing to a close relationship between an administrative complex and a nearby metalworking shop (1982:156). Clearly, craftsmen worked under the close supervision of Chan Chan's bureaucrats, yet there was significant autonomy within the barrios (J. Topic 1982:169–70).

The craft products of the barrios were destined to be consumed by the Chimú bureaucrats and nobility. Textiles recovered in SIAR contexts compare favorably in technical complexity with those found in a royal burial platform just east of a palace complex known as Ciudadela Laberinto (J. Topic 1982:163). The sacred and sumptuary nature of Chimú craft production in the city is indicated by a dedicatory cache of Spondylus shells encountered by J. Topic (1982:158) in an area of SIAR paralleling the eastern wall of one of Chan Chan's adobe palaces, Ciudadela Velarde.

Lumbreras has correctly observed that "the most outstanding form of Chimú craftsmanship was metalworking, especially gold" (1974b:188). The Chimú made greater and better use of gold (and silver) than any other ancient Peruvian culture. Chimú metallurgy was so esteemed that when the Incas conquered Chan Chan they took Chimú goldsmiths to Cuzco. Gold- and silversmithing had a clearly elite purpose: ceremonial vases were decorated with mythical and allegorical scenes; gold gloves bearing mythical and natural designs were fashioned; and the *tumi* sacrificial knife was made. In addition, all manner of jewelry and eating utensils were produced. Chimú textiles display the same sumptuary character. Particularly noteworthy is the use of exotic feathers in Chimú textiles and the frequent attachment of gold and silver plaques (A. Rowe 1984).

Chimú pottery (Fig. 5.7) affects scholars in one of two radically opposed ways. Lumbreras writes that Chimú pottery "attained a notable artistic development" (1974b:188). Lapiner, in contrast, emphasizes that this pottery was predominantly mass produced and that the mostly moldmade blackware is "drab and not very interesting artistically" (1976:260). The important points are that Chimú society produced and consumed enormous amounts of pottery and that pottery was not the medium designated to carry the bulk of this society's ideological message. In Chimú society the medium, again, was the message. The message being conveyed was only secondarily the one encoded in mythical iconography. It was primarily the physical manifestation — through the quotidian as well as ritual use of luxury exotics — of the Chimú origin myth which posited separate creations for the upper and lower classes (J. Rowe 1948).

"Imperialists"

The Inca empire was the culmination of the civilization process in the Central Andes. Occupational specialization, social class differentiation, and economic alienation reached a climax with the Inca institution of *aclla*, a group of women forcibly alienated from their home communities and normal reproductive role by the Inca state (Silverblatt 1987:85, 94). They performed lifelong imperial service as weavers, ritual specialists, and political pawns (Silverblatt 1987:85–108).

Inca textiles were technologically superb and were *the* prestige item in the Inca world (see, e.g., Murra 1975b; J. Rowe 1979). Even more than with the case of Chimú gold, the medium was the message. For the Incas, that medium was cloth, and paramount among its multilayered messages was that of state power. Murra (1975b:147) has gone beyond the usual aesthetic and technological interest in the great Andean textile tradition by asking how the enormous textile production of the Inca state was organized and how cloth was integrated into so many political and religious contexts. These are the same kinds of issues this essay has been addressing in its review of the relationship between style and state. As Murra (1975b) indicated, the Inca state's passion for cloth required it to extend the decision-making process to the most basic elements of textile production. Ethnohistoric documentation indicates that the Inca state provided the raw materials with which its textile demands were met. This means that the state expropriated the strategic resources of land, water, and flocks. In addition, the state demanded cloth production as labor tribute just as it demanded agricultural labor tribute.

The creation of the *aclla* went far beyond the sociopolitical implications of the craftsman barrios at Chan Chan, because those artisans, although in the service of the state, appear to have lived "normal" family lives. They were presumably in control of their own reproduction and we may speculate that their occupation was hereditary. The *aclla* were esteemed, honored, revered, and pampered (Silverblatt 1987:103–5), but they were a "guild-like group without precedence in Andean social structure" (Murra 1975b:170). Although the status of the *aclla* was significantly higher than that of the ear-tube-wearing Chimú craftsmen, they were totally controlled by the state, essentially retainers of the emperor. No evidence suggests similar treatment of other craft specialists in the Inca state. This is because of the multiple functions played by the *aclla* and the importance of cloth in the functioning of the Inca state (Murra 1975b).

Inca art — on textiles, pottery, and other media — is geometric, standardized, and abstract (Fig. 5.8; J. Rowe 1979:Figs. 1–11, 13–15). Inca art's message was conveyed by media and circumstance. Although Inca iconography does not depict cosmology in the rich, figurative detail of Chavín, Paracas, Nasca, Moche, Wari, or Tiwanaku, it is nonetheless a symbolic system of communication. The standardized designs found on Inca tunics (J. Rowe 1979) represent the status of the wearer in the Inca administrative hierarchy, and some of these designs may symbolize aspects of the empire itself.

Even though Inca art is visually nonmythical, it can be laden with religious significance, as with the ceramic, gold, and stone depictions of the corn used to make chicha, a beer consumed in great quantity in Inca politico-religious ceremony (see, e.g., Lapiner 1976:Figs. 689–92, 712). Also, contextually, some Inca art was used in ritual — for instance, knives and golden goblets used for sacrifices.

One other aspect of Inca society must be mentioned as we assess the nature and role of art in the Inca empire. The Inca elite indulged in collecting in a manner reminiscent of the West. Not only was there a zoo in Cuzco, capital of the empire, but also an elite museum, the *puquin cancha*, which was closed to all except the Inca and the imperial historians (Chávez 1981:162). Furthermore, both worlds — the Inca and the West — filled their museums with the looted artistic wealth of conquered or colonized peoples. It is not only Western art lovers and collectors who have admired and coveted "the physical possession of art objects from other peoples' worlds" (S. Price, this volume). But unlike the West, which has defined an art world of "Primitive Art" (J. E. Way, this volume), the Inca viewed the confiscated objects as fully equal to those of their own Inca manufacture. This interest in the art of competing cultures contrasts with the regionalism of the Master Craftsmen or Early Intermediate Period. It reflects the Incas' well-known policy of ethnic and religious tolerance. By possessing these foreign artworks, the Inca elite — like their later Western counterparts — sought "conceptual possession of their artistic intent" (S. Price, this volume). At the same time, the Incas also brought foreign craftsmen to their royal court, as in the case of the Chan Chan goldsmiths forcibly transferred to Cuzco following the Inca conquest of the Chimú empire (J. Rowe 1948). There, in the highland Inca capital, the Chimú craftsmen were made to apply their technological skills to the production of objects in the Inca mode, much of which was then appropriated by Pizarro as part of the immense ransom duplicitously demanded by the Spanish for the liberation of Atahualpa, the captured Inca emperor.

Conclusion

Pre-Hispanic art can constitute a rich body of cultural, economic, social, and political information if we consider the social power and economic relationships inherent in the nature, role, and organization of art in pre-Columbian societies together with aesthetics, iconography, and chronology.

The 1948 scholars did not sufficiently consider the nature and potentially heterogeneous and even contradictory roles of art and artistic production in the pre-Columbian societies they discussed. These topics have received new attention from archaeologists of a "post-processual" persuasion (e.g., Miller and Tilley 1984; Shanks and Tilley 1982; Shennan 1982). The topic is now entering the discourse of Central Andean archaeology. Kubler (1984:44) incisively wrote of art as a "social tool" by means of which public power can be concentrated through widely shared symbols. Similar interpretations can be found in works by Burger (1988), Cook (1984–85), and Murra (1975b), each of whom demonstrates the inherent political and symbolic manipulability of portable art. The development of widespread portable high art and crafts in the Central Andes occurred precisely at the emergence of regional polities (chiefdoms and states). Recognition of the causal relationship and interdependency between art and sociopolitical organization focuses our attention not only on the beauty of early elite art but also on the fact that it was physically, and socially, and politically manipulable. The eventual appearance of routinized, mass-produced art is not the outcome of societal militarism, as earlier conceived; rather, it represents the culmination of elite control over the means and relations of production and an emphasis on conspicuous consumption of items that were prestige-laden by virtue of their provenance and the labor and/or technology involved in producing them.

It is, of course, essential for archaeologists, historians, and ethnographers to study the inner meaning of a particular aesthetic genre as well as its general meaning. Luis Lumbreras recognized this need in his reorganization of the cultural chronology of ancient Peru. He also recognized that art is the product of the politico-economic distribution of wealth and power, including especially the means and relations of production. As archaeologists, it is incumbent on us to communicate a sense of the aesthetic worth of the ancient arts while recognizing and explaining the nature of the appropriation of that worth. The achievement of both goals balances interpretations of beauty and power. Such a paradigm also consciously recognizes the complementary and dynamic phenomena of inner worth and public value.

Ancient art, artists, and artisans were integral parts of a societal context that was neither static nor monolithic over time but was instead dynamic and heterogeneous. The manner by which archaeologists choose to study art — and the consequent approaches, theories, and chronologies they apply — represent decisions that may be political as well as scientific or academic. Art was manipulated in the past by the dominant class, and it continues to be manipulated in cognate ways today. And just as ancient rulers appropriated art and manipulated history, so too do modern nation-states like Peru take up emblems of the past to help them achieve present political, economic, and social goals and define a particular ideology against a competitive field of other players.

NOTES

1. The term *horizon* refers to an art style found over a very large area during a relatively brief period of time that interrupts or influences local regional sequences (e.g., Willey and Phillips 1958:29–34). The actual period of Chavín's maximal occurrence is perhaps 200 years (Burger 1981), corresponding quite nicely to this concept.

2. The nomenclatural distinction is based on the technological shift in painting fancy pottery with resin-based pigments applied after firing (Paracas) to slip paints applied prior to firing (Menzel et al. 1964:251).

3. The term *Nasca* refers to the archaeological culture, while *Nazca* refers to the geographical region, the drainage, the valley, and the modern town.

SILVERMAN

REFERENCES CITED

Alva, Walter

    1988   Discovering the New World's Richest Unlooted Tomb. *National Geographic* 174 (4): 510–48.

    1990   New Tomb of Royal Splendor. *National Geographic* 177 (6): 2–15.

Arnold, Dean

    1985   *Ceramic Theory and Cultural Practice.* New York: Cambridge University Press.

Aveni, Anthony

    1986   The Nazca Lines: Patterns in the Desert. *Archaeology* 39 (4): 32–39.

Bennett, Wendell C.

    1948   The Peruvian Co-Tradition. In *A Reappraisal of Peruvian Archaeology*, edited by Wendell C. Bennett, 1–7. Society for American Archaeology, Memoir 4. Menasha, Wis.

Blagg, Mary Margaret

    1975   *The Bizarre Innovation in Nasca.* M.A. thesis, Department of Art History, University of Texas, Austin.

Blasco Bosqued, Concepción, and Luis Javier Ramos Gómez

    1980   *Cerámica Nazca.* Valladolid: Seminario Americanista de la Universidad de Valladolid.

Burger, Richard L.

    1981   The Radiocarbon Evidence for the Temporal Priority of Chavín de Huantar. *American Antiquity* 46:592–602.

    1988   Unity and Heterogeneity in the Chavín Horizon. In *Peruvian Prehistory*, edited by Richard W. Keatinge, 99–144. New York: Cambridge University Press.

Carmichael, Patrick H.

    1986   Nasca Pottery Construction. *Ñawpa Pacha* [Institute of Andean Studies, Berkeley] 24:31–48.

Chang, K. C.

    1983   *Art, Myth, and Ritual: The Path to Political Authority in Ancient China.* Cambridge, Mass.: Harvard University Press.

Chávez, Sergio J.

    1981   History of Andean Archaeology. In *Museums of the Andes*, edited by Elizabeth Benson and William J. Conklin, 162–66. New York: Newsweek.

Conklin, William J.

1983   Pucara and Tiahuanaco Tapestry: Time and Style in a Sierra Weaving Tradition. *Ñawpa Pacha* [Institute of Andean Studies, Berkeley] 21:1–44.

Cook, Anita Gwynn

1984–   The Middle Horizon Ceramic Offerings from Conchopata. *Ñawpa*
85   *Pacha* [Institute of Andean Studies, Berkeley] 22–23:49–90.

1985a   Style and Time in the Evolution of Andean State Expansionism. Ph.D. diss., Department of Anthropology, State University of New York, Binghamton.

1985b   Ritual Tribute as an Expression of Huari Political Organization. Paper presented at the Roundtable on Huari Political Organization, Dumbarton Oaks Research Library and Collection, May 16–19, 1985.

Cordy-Collins, Alana

1977   Chavín Art: Its Shamanic/Hallucinogenic Origins. In *Pre-Columbian Art: Selected Readings*, edited by Alana Cordy-Collins and Jean Stern, 353–62. Palo Alto, Calif.: Peek Publications.

Davidson, Judith

1982   Ecology, Art, and Myth: A Natural Approach to Symbolism. In *Pre-Columbian Art: Selected Readings*, edited by Alana Cordy-Collins, 331–42. Palo Alto, Calif.: Peek Publications.

Donnan, Christopher B.

1973   *Moche Occupation of the Santa Valley, Peru.* University of California Publications in Anthropology, no. 8. Berkeley: University of California Press.

1976   *Moche Art and Iconography.* Los Angeles: UCLA Latin American Center.

1978   *Moche Art of Peru.* Los Angeles: Museum of Culture History.

1988   Iconography of the Moche: Unraveling the Mystery of the Warrior-Priest. *National Geographic* 174 (4): 551–55.

Donnan, Christopher B., ed.

1985   *Early Ceremonial Architecture in the Andes.* Washington, D.C.: Dumbarton Oaks Research Library and Collection.

Fung Pineda, Rosa

1988   The Late Preceramic and Initial Period. In *Peruvian Prehistory*, edited by Richard W. Keatinge, 67–96. New York: Cambridge University Press.

Isbell, William H.

1977   Cosmological Order Expressed in Prehistoric Ceremonial Centers. *Proceedings of the 42nd International Congress of Americanists,* 4:269–97. Paris.

1984–   Conchopata: Ideological Innovator in Middle Horizon 1A. *Ñawpa*
85   *Pacha* [Institute of Andean Studies, Berkeley] 22–23:91–126.

1988   City and State in Middle Horizon Huari. In *Peruvian Prehistory,* edited by Richard W. Keatinge, 164–89. New York: Cambridge University Press.

Isbell, William H., and Katharina Schreiber

1978   Was Huari a State? *American Antiquity* 43:372–89.

Keatinge, Richard W., ed.

1988   *Peruvian Prehistory: An Overview of Pre-Inca and Inca Society.* New York: Cambridge University Press.

Kolata, Alan L.

1987a   The Agricultural Foundations of the Tiwanaku State: A View from the Heartland. *American Antiquity* 51:748–62.

1987b   Tiwanaku and Its Hinterland. *Archaeology* 40 (1): 36–41.

Kubler, George

1973   Science and Humanism Among Americanists. In *The Iconography of Middle American Sculpture,* 163–67. New York: Metropolitan Museum of Art.

1984   *The Art and Architecture of Ancient America.* 3d ed. New York: Penguin Books.

1985   *Studies in Ancient American and European Art: The Collected Essays of George Kubler,* edited by Thomas F. Reese. New Haven: Yale University Press.

Lapiner, Alan

1976   *Pre-Columbian Art of South America.* New York: Harry N. Abrams.

Lathrap, Donald

1985   Jaws: The Control of Power in Early Nuclear American Ceremonial Centers. In *Early Ceremonial Architecture in the Andes,* edited by Christopher B. Donnan, 241–67. Washington, D.C.: Dumbarton Oaks Research Library and Collections.

Lumbreras, Luis G.

1974a   *La arqueología como ciencia social.* Lima, Peru: Ediciones Histar.

1974b   *The Peoples and Cultures of Ancient Peru.* Washington, D.C.: Smithsonian Institution Press.

1975   *Las fundaciones de Huamanga*. Lima, Peru: El Club Huamanga.

Malinowski, Bronislaw
1979   The Role of Magic and Religion. In *Reader in Comparative Religion*, edited by William A. Lessa and Evon Z. Vogt, 37–56. New York: Harper & Row.

Menzel, Dorothy
1964   Style and Time in the Middle Horizon. *Ñawpa Pacha* [Institute of Andean Studies, Berkeley] 2:1–105.

Menzel, Dorothy, John H. Rowe, and Lawrence E. Dawson
1964   *The Paracas Pottery of Ica: A Study in Style and Time*. University of California Publications in American Archaeology and Ethnology, 50. Berkeley: University of California Press.

Miller, Daniel, and Christopher Tilley, eds.
1984   *Ideology, Power and Prehistory*. New York: Cambridge University Press.

Morris, Craig
1988   A City Fit for an Inka. *Archaeology* 41 (5): 43–49.

Moseley, Michael
1975   *The Maritime Foundations of Andean Civilization*. Menlo Park, Calif.: Cummings Publishing Co.

Murra, John V.
1975a   El tráfico de mullu en la costa del Pacífico. In *Formaciones económicas y políticas del mundo andino*, by John V. Murra, 275–313. Lima, Peru: Instituto de Estudios Peruanos.
1975b   La función del tejido en varios contextos sociales y políticos. In *Formaciones económicas y políticas del mundo andino*, by John V. Murra, 145–70. Lima, Peru: Instituto de Estudios Peruanos.

Oakland, Amy
1986   Tiahuanaco Tapestry Tunics and Mantles from San Pedro de Atacama, Chile. In *The Junius B. Bird Conference on Andean Textiles*, edited by Ann P. Rowe, 101–22. Washington, D.C.: The Textile Museum.

Panofsky, Erwin
1960   *Renaissance and Renascences in Western Art*. Stockholm: Almqvist and Wiksell.

Paul, Anne
1980   Paracas Ritual Attire: Symbols of Authority in Ancient Peru. Ph.D. diss., Department of Art History, University of Texas, Austin.

1990   *Paracas Ritual Attire: Symbols of Authority in Ancient Peru*. Iowa City: University of Iowa Press.

Posnansky, Arthur
    1945   *Tihuanacu: La cuna del hombre americano*. Vols. 1 and 2. New York: J. J. Augustin Publisher.

Reese, Thomas F.
    1985   Editor's Introduction. In *Studies in Ancient American and European Art: The Collected Essays of George Kubler*, edited by Thomas F. Reese, xvii–xxxvi. New Haven, Conn.: Yale University Press.

Reinhard, Johan
    1985   *The Nasca Lines: A New Perspective on Their Origin and Meaning*. Lima, Peru: Editorial Los Pinos.

Roark, Richard P.
    1965   From Monumental to Proliferous in Nasca Pottery. *Ñawpa Pacha* [Institute of Andean Studies, Berkeley] 3:1–92.

Rowe, Ann P.
    1984   *Costumes and Featherwork of the Lords of Chimor*. Washington, D.C.: The Textile Museum.

Rowe, John H.
    1948   The Kingdom of Chimor. *Acta Americana* 6:26–59.
    1962   Stages and Periods in Archaeological Interpretation. *Southwestern Journal of Anthropology* 18:40–54.
    1967   Form and Meaning in Chavín Art. In *Peruvian Archaeology: Selected Readings*, edited by John H. Rowe and Dorothy Menzel, 72–103. Palo Alto, Calif.: Peek Publications.
    1979   Standardization in Inca Tapestry Tunics. In *The Junius B. Bird Pre-Columbian Textile Conference*, edited by Ann P. Rowe, Elizabeth P. Benson, and Anne-Louise Shaffer, 239–64. Washington, D.C.: The Textile Museum and the Dumbarton Oaks Research Library and Collection.

Sapir, J. David
    1977   The Anatomy of Metaphor. In *The Social Use of Metaphor*, edited by J. David Sapir and J. Christopher Crocker, 3–32. Philadelphia: University of Pennsylvania Press.

Shanks, Michael, and Christopher Tilley
    1982   Ideology, Symbolic Power and Ritual Communication: A Reinterpretation of Neolithic Mortuary Practices. In *Symbolic and Structural Ar-*

chaeology, edited by Ian Hodder, 129–54. New York: Cambridge University Press.

Shennan, Stephen
1982   Ideology, Change, and the European Early Bronze Age. In *Symbolic and Structural Archaeology,* edited by Ian Hodder, 155–61. New York: Cambridge University Press.

Shimada, Izumi
1981   The Batan Grande–La Leche Archaeological Project: The First Two Seasons. *Journal of Field Archaeology* 8:405–46.

1985   Perception, Procurement, and Management of Resources: Archaeological Perspective. In *Andean Ecology and Civilization,* edited by Shozo Masuda, Izumi Shimada, and Craig Morris, 357–400. Tokyo: University of Tokyo Press.

Silverblatt, Irene
1987   *Moon, Sun and Witches: Gender Ideologies and Class in Inca and Colonial Peru.* Princeton, N.J.: Princeton University Press.

Silverman, Helaine
1988   Nasca 8: A Reassessment of its Chronological Placement and Cultural Significance. In *Andean Anthropology,* edited by Virginia J. Vitzthum, 23–32. Michigan Discussions in Anthropology, no. 8. Ann Arbor: University of Michigan.

1990a   The Early Nasca Pilgrimage Center of Cahuachi and the Nazca Lines: Anthropological and Archaeological Perspectives. In *The Lines of Nazca,* edited by Anthony F. Aveni, 209–44. Philadelphia: American Philosophical Society.

1990b   Beyond the Pampa: The Geoglyphs in the Valleys of Nazca. *National Geographic Research* 6 (4): 435–56.

1990c   Nasca Settlement Pattern and Sociopolitical Organization: A First Run Through the 1988–89 Survey Data. Paper presented at the 18th Annual Midwest Conference on Andean and Amazonian Archaeology and Anthropology, Chicago.

1991   The Paracas Problem: Archaeological Perspectives. In *Paracas Art and Architecture: Object and Context in South Coastal Peru,* edited by Anne Paul, 349–415. Iowa City: University of Iowa Press.

in press *Cahuachi in the Ancient Nasca World.* Iowa City: University of Iowa Press.

Steward, Julian H.
1948   A Functional-Developmental Classification of American High Cultures.

In *A Reappraisal of Peruvian Archaeology*, edited by Wendell C. Bennett, 103–4. Society for American Archaeology, Memoir 4. Menasha, Wis.

Strong, William Duncan

1948   Cultural Epochs and Refuse Stratigraphy in Peruvian Archaeology. In *A Reappraisal of Peruvian Archaeology*, edited by Wendell C. Bennett, 93–102. Society for American Archaeology, Memoir 4. Menasha, Wis.

Tello, Julio C.

1959   *Paracas: Primera parte*. Lima, Peru: Empresa Gráfica T. Scheuch S.A.

1960   *Chavín: Cultura matriz de la civilización andina*. Lima, Peru: Universidad Nacional Mayor de San Marcos.

Tello, Julio C., and Toribio Mejía Xesspe

1979   *Paracas: Segunda Parte; Cavernas y Necropolis*. Lima, Peru: Universidad Nacional Mayor de San Marcos and the Institute of Andean Research of New York.

Topic, John

1982   Lower Class Social and Economic Organization at Chan Chan. In *Chan Chan: Andean Desert City*, edited by Michael Moseley and Kent C. Day, 145–76. Albuquerque: University of New Mexico Press.

Topic, John, and Michael Moseley

1983   Chan Chan: A Case Study of Urban Change in Peru. *Ñawpa Pacha* [Institute of Andean Studies, Berkeley] 21:153–82.

Topic, Theresa

1977   Excavations at Moche. Ph.D. diss., Department of Anthropology, Harvard University.

1982   The Early Intermediate Period and Its Legacy. In *Chan Chan: Andean Desert City*, edited by Michael Moseley and Kent C. Day, 255–84. Albuquerque: University of New Mexico Press.

Torres, Constantino Manuel

1987   The Iconography of the Prehispanic Snuff Trays from San Pedro de Atacama, Northern Chile. *Andean Past* 1:191–245.

Whitten, Dorothea S., and Norman E. Whitten, Jr.

1988   *From Myth to Creation: Art from Amazonian Ecuador*. Urbana: University of Illinois Press.

Willey, Gordon R.

1948   Functional Analysis of "Horizon Styles" in Peruvian Archaeology. In *A Reappraisal of Peruvian Archaeology*, edited by Wendell C. Bennett,

8–15. Society for American Archaeology, Memoir 4. Menasha, Wis.

1973   Mesoamerican Art and Iconography and the Integrity of the Mesoamerican Ideological System. In *The Iconography of Middle American Sculpture*, 153–61. New York: Metropolitan Museum of Art.

1974   The Early Great Art Styles and the Rise of the Pre-Columbian Civilizations. In *The Rise and Fall of Civilizations*, edited by C. C. Lamberg-Karlovsky and Jeremy Sabloff, 157–69. Menlo Park, Calif.: Cummings Publishing Co.

Willey, Gordon R., and Philip Phillips

1958   *Method and Theory in American Archaeology.* Chicago: University of Chicago Press.

Wobst, Martin

1977   Stylistic Behavior and Information Exchange. In *Papers for the Director: Research Essays in Honor of James B. Griffin*, edited by C. E. Cleland, 317–42. Anthropological Papers of the Museum of Anthropology 61. Ann Arbor: University Museum, University of Michigan.

Zuidema, R. Tom

1972   Meaning in Nazca Art. *Artstryck 1971*, 35–54. Göteborg, Sweden: Etnografiska Museum.

6

Ethnic Arts of the Fourth World

The View from Canada

Nelson H. H. Graburn

In late August of 1983, 110 Native Canadian artists plus a smattering of white people converged on the small town of Hazelton, British Columbia, a few hundred miles north of Vancouver. There, at the 'Ksan Indian Cultural Centre[1] on the banks of the Skeena River, was held the First National Native Indian Artists' Symposium. This gathering was conceived by the Indian Arts and Crafts Society of British Columbia and was supported by many local and national organizations. Its goal was to bring together artist representatives from all the major Indian communities in Canada. This pioneer effort, subsidized by public and private institutions, both local and national, embraced much of what typifies Fourth World art in Canada. A vast nation that includes many indigenous minority peoples, Canada serves here as a microcosm through which to examine both the theory and practice of the arts of the Fourth World.[2]

When one considers the panorama of Indian artists represented at 'Ksan—along with others not present at the conference, including the Canadian Inuit[3]—one may discern the general range of Fourth World arts and artistic ideologies. Consequently, in this essay I focus on the range of expression of modern native art in Canada, both because it has rarely been studied systematically (exceptions are Dickason 1972 and Hickman 1975) and because I hope that Canada may serve as a model for studying the arts of other modern nations having Fourth World populations. I have worked out a set of categories that seem to express this range, and my essay focuses on an analysis and discussion of them. Of course, one must note that throughout this chapter there are artists who do not fit any ethnic or stylistic mold perfectly. Some are "bridges" between ethnic/stylistic groups, and others are so idiosyncratic that, like many modern artists, they are difficult to place (see, e.g., Brody's classification of "Idiosyncratic" Indian artists, 1971:213).

Throughout the four days of the 'Ksan symposium, the participants met in the local high school to talk about the problems of being a Native Canadian artist, to hold "show and tell" sessions with the portfolios, slide sets, and maquettes they had brought, and to attend the opening of an Indian art exhibition at the Northwestern National Exhibition Centre in 'Ksan. Surrounding the "work" of the symposium were barbecues and potlatchlike feasts at 'Ksan and at local villages (including Kitwancool and Hagwilget), informal discussions, and a chance for some of the artists to sell their pieces.

Although eighty-six of the Indian artists came from British Columbia, there were also representatives from the Great Plains and the Eastern Woodlands, including the Iroquois. They ranged from avant-garde, modernist, and postmodernist painters at home in Taos or Paris to native monolingual traditional craftsmen flown out of their small bush settlements in the Northeast. The majority fell between these two extremes, typically being Indian artists concerned both with the continuity of embedded tradition and the commercial necessities of making a living. Discussion between people of such different backgrounds was often difficult,[4] and mediation was occasionally offered by white specialists in Indian arts, such as anthropologists, art historians, and a few dealers and collectors.[5]

Art as Artifact

At the least acculturated end of the range are the relatively unself-conscious artists and artisans who continue to produce artifacts characteristic of their native culture, unburdened by much knowledge of the art market or of the layers of meaning attached to the concept of "art."

For at least a century, the arts and crafts of most of the Fourth World peoples of North America have been subject to collection and the market (Cole 1985). Most of the earlier collecting was carried out for scientific and souvenir purposes. It has only been since the 1940s that these objects have attained status as art and have been circulated in the art market (Carpenter 1975).

The Indians and Inuit soon became knowledgeable about this demand, and the early evolution of their arts under its impact is analyzed in my book *Ethnic and Tourist Arts* (1976) and other works. To summarize, native craftsmen and women (dare we say artists at a historical point where their products were not considered art?) parted with, traded, or sold their creations to visiting Europeans with more thought for what they were getting in trade than for the ultimate destination of their productions. These were *Functional* arts in the broadest sense: they functioned as part of subsistence, religion, politics, and personal adornment in the native society.

As the native people became aware of the repeated demands for their manufactures, they started to make more of them, for trade as well as for their own needs. For instance, early in the nineteenth century the Inuit of the Hudson Strait awaited the arrival of the ships (sailing through into Hudson Bay) "as a sort of annual fair; their little manufactures of dresses, spears &c are reserved for the expected jubilee" (Chappell 1817:57–58). In response, they soon started making *Replicas*—artifacts that may or may not be distinguishable from those made for local use (or internative trade). In some cases replicas differed from functional specimens in that (1) they were not meant to be used (e.g., they were less strongly made, used different materials, showed changes in scale), and (2) because of market demand, they were made to look more exotic and were decorated if nonfunctional (Myers 1980). Sometimes these commercial ventures failed, as did, for example, the manufacture of Cree Craft by the Cree of Great Whale River and Wemindji (Graburn 1978).

Soon, because outsiders did not want full-sized copies of the originals, replica models emerged. Models are an important kind of souvenir among nearly all Fourth World natives of Canada. It was probably to such models that Chappell was alluding in the above quotation. Thus a vast range of miniaturized souvenirs developed — dolls, model boats and kayaks, weapons, house forms, baskets, and pouches. Until recently, none of these were designated as native "art."

Another form of souvenir also emerged in some contact situations. These were *Novelties* — items invented specifically for trade, either by producers who had become familiar with Euro-Canadians, their material culture, and their demands, or by Euro-Canadian buyers, who suggested items they thought would serve as suitable mementos of the native cultures. Perhaps most prominent among these novelties in Canada in the nineteenth century were what came to be called the argillite carvings of the Haida Indians — miniature friezes, sculptures, and plates illustrating both European and traditional Haida motifs in their distinctive formal art style. This innovation coincided with the demise of traditional Haida culture (Gunther 1966; Kaufmann 1976; Sheehan 1981; Wright 1982). In twentieth-century Canada, a similar "novelty" phenomenon was the explosion of soapstone and whale bone carvings (now called sculptures), which became a regular trade item in the 1950s and 1960s under the stimulation of the Canadian artist James Houston and resident Hudson's Bay Company traders in the Arctic (Graburn 1987; Houston 1952; see Fig. 6.1).[6]

Even earlier, other Canadian Indians had been producing novelty souvenirs, though most are less well remembered today. The Eastern Woodland Algonkians and Iroquois made quilled boxes, letter holders and openers, wastepaper baskets, beaded jewelry, velvet birds, and picture frames. The Great Lakes Algonkians produced a similar range of souvenirs, with more emphasis on birchbark items. Northern Plains novelties included more beadwork and hidework, medallions, "ledger book drawings" (Coe 1986: 138–41), and much that bore evidence of the fast-disappearing buffalo.

The production of many of these object types has persisted until the present day, while at the same time most truly functional objects ceased to be made as anything more than replicas. However, the consciousness of the producers themselves has changed; they know that they are creating for the market and that their livelihood may depend on such production. Frequently today, the native peoples in the rural and remoter parts of Canada do not understand why white people want such objects or what they do with them when they get them. The physical and social distance between

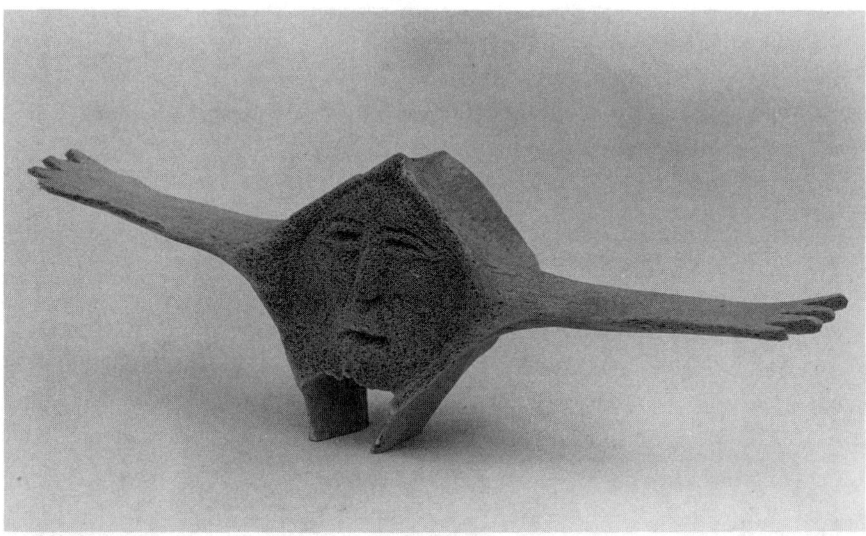

Figure 6.1. Joannassie Kaki (Inuit), whale bone carving, Pangnirtung, N.W.T., 1986.

the artists and craftspeople and the ultimate consumers is still great, though it is diminishing rapidly. For instance, many Inuit carvers and Naskapi/Cree artists, such as Sammy Paschene, Johnny and Emma Shecapio (Fig. 6.2), and Jean-Claude Paule (Huron), produce novelty and replica artifacts for sale, but until recently they had never seen them for sale in stores "down South," nor had they seen them in their ultimate destinations in white people's homes. Many times I have been asked by Inuit carvers, "What does the white man want with these things?" or, "Thank you for helping us by buying these lumps of stone; what do you do with them in your land?"

Even for such people, whose creations are in no way influenced by the Western art world, the social distance is breaking down. Increasingly, they are being "celebrated" by invitations to exhibitions, one-man shows, and conferences in the "South" or outside of Canada (with interpreters when they are monolingual in their native language). They have the chance to see the whole market chain through visits to cooperative and middlemen's warehouses, galleries, and retail stores and the final placement of their works in homes and museums. These artists are increasingly aware not

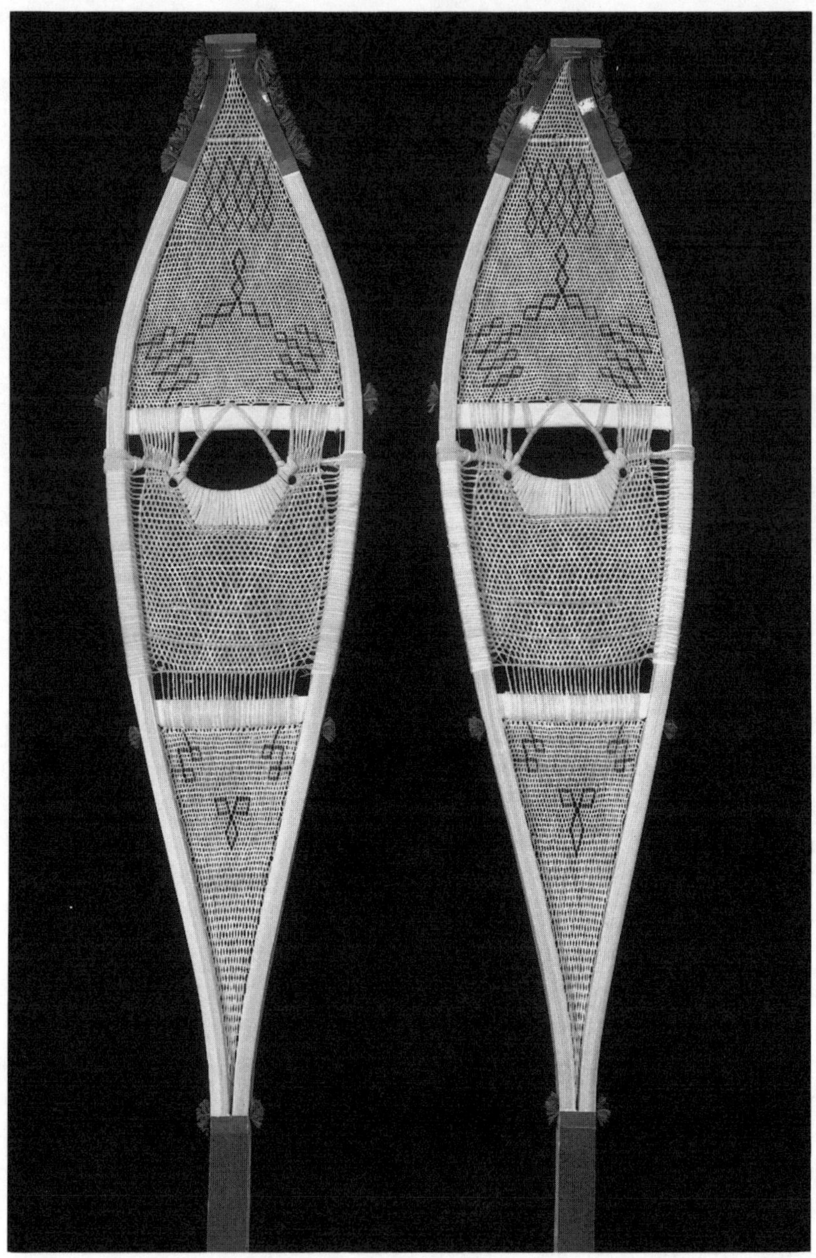

Figure 6.2. Johnny and Emma Shecapio (Cree), traditional snowshoes, Mistassini, Quebec. (IANA no. 85-0422B, ID no. 152766)

only of the market value of their work but also of the awe in which it (and they) are held. They are developing an understanding of the categories and values in the culture of the Euro-Canadians who control the system. Similar acculturative forces are at work in the hinterlands, which are increasingly visited by art experts and traveling exhibitions. There, magazines, television, and larger numbers of white residents transmit some of the same messages.

Early Assimilation

So far we have been considering the social and cognitive distance between the artists and artisans and the market chain by which their commercial works end up in our "art world" (Becker 1982). There are two more cognitive/cultural divisions that are equally important to our consideration of Canadian Fourth World artists. These are (1) knowledge of the general visual forms of Western art, which requires exposure to Western art (something generally unavailable to the native peoples discussed in the section above), and (2) knowledge of the background and execution of these art forms, which usually requires attendance at an art school.

In this section I consider the works of those who have the former knowledge though not the latter. These artists could be called "naive," following Howard Becker, who states: "They have not had the training people who ordinarily produce such works have had, and they know very little about the medium they are working in—about its history, conventions or the kind of work ordinarily produced in it" (Becker 1982:258–59). I choose the word *Assimilated*, as in my own earlier work (Graburn 1976: 8), to refer to those native artists who choose to work in the media of the Western mainstream art world rather than in genres associated with their traditional cultures.

Obviously, such artists had been exposed to some genres of Western art through personal contacts, school, print or electronic media or, less frequently, attendance at galleries and museums. More important, they must have had access to materials, whether they be brushes and paints, clay and wheels, or sculptural media and tools.

Nevertheless, for at least fifty years a small but increasing number of Inuit and probably a larger number of Indians have had the opportunity to "copy" Western art forms, usually filling them with their own subject matter. Among the Inuit, such unself-conscious artists include Peter Pitsiulak of Cape Dorset (Pitsiulak and Eber 1975; Graburn 1979), Peter Naujak of Rankin Inlet, Eddie Witaltak of Kujjuarapik, Simon Qitsualuk of Povungnituk and Akulivik, and Davie Atchealak of Pangnirtung. Peter Pitsiulak started painting in watercolors when he became an assistant to John Buchan (later Lord Tweedsmuir), who spent a year as a Hudson's Bay trader on Baffin Island before World War II. Much like the relationship between Albert Namatjira and the Australian watercolorist Rex Battarbee (Batty 1963), Pitsiulak learned by imitation the art practiced by the visiting "master" (Buchan 1951). After Buchan's departure, Pitsiulak went on to become a very successful sculptor and graphic artist, as well as one of the earliest Inuit photographers of note. Henry Ivaluakjuk, by contrast, was already a famous sculptor by the time he learned easel painting while in jail. He went on to add acrylic painting to his commercial repertoire and has frequent commissions for genre scenes. Simon Qitsualuk, a talented sculptor, is perhaps more typical of those Inuit who occasionally paint when they get materials from friends such as white schoolteachers. Like an increasing number of Inuit, he has been hired by local Inuit institutions to paint murals that would foster local pride and identity.

The most visible Assimilated art form among the Canadian Inuit is printmaking (see Fig. 6.3; Houston 1967; Goetz 1977; Blodgett 1991). This commercially successful genre was introduced to the Inuit of Cape Dorset in 1957 and 1958 by the same Mr. Houston who had promoted Inuit sculpture a decade earlier. Since then, five more villages have set up workshops with white artist-advisors to produce annual editions of prints for sale in southern Canada and elsewhere. Stonecut block printing was the first technique introduced, but the Inuit artists have also used stencil, copperplate engraving, lithography, and etching. Many of the artists mentioned in the above paragraph have also engaged in this pursuit. Trained in Western (and Japanese) printmaking techniques, using imported paper and ink and the institutions of the metropolitan art world (numbered annual editions, exhibitions, galleries, and museums), they remain "naive" in the sense that they are not school trained and know little of metropolitan art history.

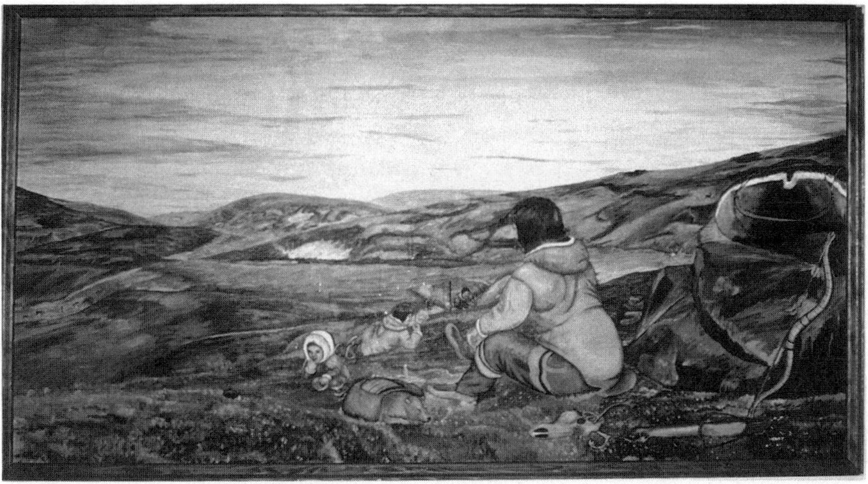

Figure 6.3. Joe Talirunilik (Inuit), *Hunting Animals in the Winter*, stonecut block print, Povungnituk, Quebec, 1968. (Photograph by Eugene Prince, Lowie Museum of Anthropology, Berkeley, California)

In early-historical eastern Canada, a few artists had access to the materials and techniques of Western "easel painting," usually through contact with Catholic missionaries (Harrison 1988:#109; Labelle and Thivierge 1981). This was rare and sporadic, however, until the outpouring of Indian "artists" in the mid twentieth century. Among contemporary Canadian Indians, Allen Sapp (Cree) is perhaps typical of the better known of this group (Peters 1970:10). He can neither read nor write and speaks very little English. Although he had minimal schooling and only occasional artistic advice from friends, his paintings fetched more than two thousand dollars each at auction in the 1970s. Like many of this kind, his art is a somewhat nostalgic evocation of "life as it was on the reservation," painted without sketches, entirely from memory (see Fig. 6.4). Similarly, Don Ningewance, an Ojibway also from northern Ontario, paints in an assimilated realistic style, portraying nature and reservation life in a manner that cannot be distinguished as Indian in authorship (Kenny 1978). His work sells moderately well, and for some it provides "relief" from the more powerful symbolistic works of his co-tribal Legend Painters (see below). Probably the two different artists appeal to different markets.

Although most Indian children are taught art in grade school, many of those who have become professional artists (rarely in the styles taught in school) have gone to art school since World War II. Though Allen Sapp mastered watercolor, pastels, oils, acrylics, and the palette knife almost "by accident" (as did Ningewance with drawing and acrylics), most of his Indian colleagues received practical training in all the main "assimilated" techniques in art school.

Resurgent Ethnicity: Eastern Woodland Legend Painting

In the mid-twentieth-century world of art-school-trained Indian artists, one of the giant exceptions is Norval Morrisseau (Fig. 6.5), an Ojibway from Lake Nipigon, Ontario. According to Warner,

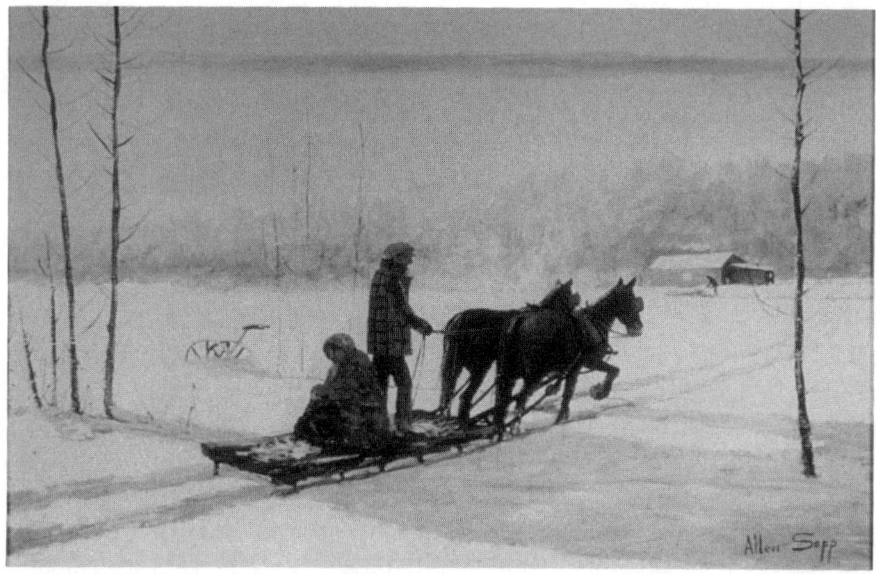

Figure 6.4. Allen Sapp (Cree), *Almost Home*, acrylic on canvas, 1981. (IANA no. 152920)

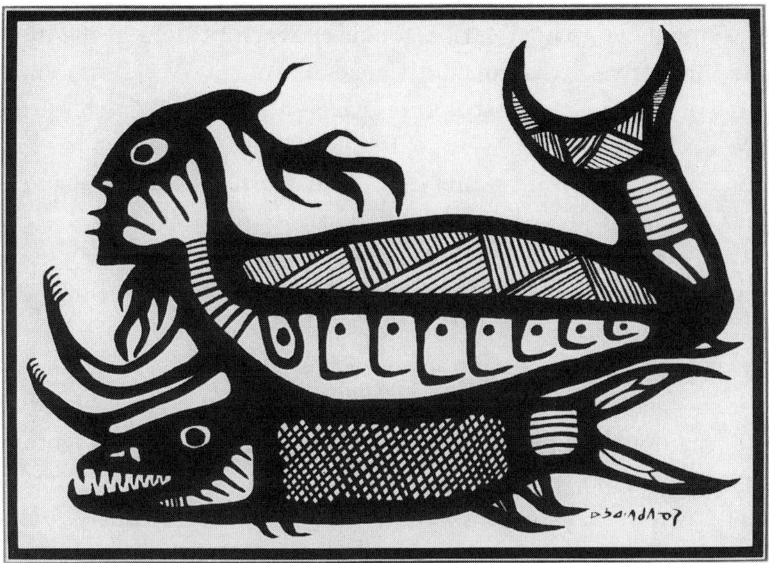

Figure 6.5. Norval Morrisseau (Ojibway), *101 — The Mermaid and the Fish Spirit,* oil on paper. (IANA no. 53.5474)

He began painting in 1959 after he received a "vision" telling him to do so. He is the first Indian to break Algonkian tribal taboos about setting down legends in picture form. . . . Tribal elders . . . were aghast that sacred Ojibway legends should be profaned, . . . being portrayed on paper and available to non-Indians.

Morrisseau first painted in the early 1960s on birchbark because it was the only material he had available. He felt very deeply he had been chosen to set down the great heritage of the Ojibway . . . before it disappeared for ever. In 1960 he was "discovered" by an art dealer, Jack Pollock, who brought thirty six of his paintings back to Toronto and sold them all within a twenty-four-hour period. (Warner 1978:60–61; see also *Tawow* 1 (1) [1970]: 14–15; and Pollock 1974:5–6)

Unfortunately, this account does not tell us whether Morrisseau had any exposure to Indian or Western arts before 1959 nor whence he obtained his painting materials. He went on to become one of, if not the, most famous and influential native artists in Canada (McLuhan 1984). More relevant for this essay is the inspiration that his work has provided to the well-known

Eastern Woodland "school" of (Algonkian) Legend Painting, the most important innovative "tradition" in Canadian Fourth World arts since the inception of Inuit soapstone sculpture (1949–50) and Inuit graphic prints (in the late 1950s). Though a "young" tradition, Legend Painting has had tremendous impact on white awareness of Indian arts (Townsend-Gault 1983) and on Canadian Indian artists of adjacent geographical areas (see below).

This new tradition has a number of distinctive artistic and sociocultural characteristics. First, in form it is without precedent in the traditional Ojibway culture, though it has some connections with the sacred scrolls of the Midewewin (Dewdney 1975). Second, without exception its content consists of beliefs about nature and the spiritual world of the contact-traditional Ojibway. Third, the style is fancifully representative of animal and human creatures, as a rule with black or darker outlines, often internally paralleled by other colors. Still other colors — usually somewhat brighter than earth tones — generally fill the form with curvilinear, slightly geometric blocks; this is normally achieved with "X-ray" or other internal depictions. Mouths (and often digits and horns too) are usually represented by curved and pointed lines, with similar somewhat "threatening" teeth, nails, lips, and other extremities. Finally, most distinctive is the presence of wavy or pointed black lines (like sperms' tails) emanating from the outside of the black/dark outline forms — less marked in Morrisseau's work than others. These wavy lines and a combination of one or more of the other characteristics seem to "signal" that these are Legend Paintings, differentiating them from all other Canadian native arts.

After the early success of Morrisseau's work, emulation of his style led to an outpouring of Legend Paintings from other Ojibway artists. Soon younger artists took up the style, whether or not they had been to art school. Almost all its practitioners are of Ojibway (or closely related Algonkian) descent, and the school has influenced the ethnic pride of these downtrodden people in a positive way.

Most instrumental has been the artist Daphne Odjig, an Odawa Ojibway artist older than Morrisseau. Odjig was already a self-taught practicing artist of eclectic abilities. Some of her earlier works, especially pen-and-ink drawings, recall the "naive" romantic realism of Allen Sapp, while others go far beyond the Woodland School in resembling mainstream expressionist arts (*Tawow* 1971Aa). According to John Warner, "she has absorbed the styles of several European art traditions in her own work, not the least of which influences is that of Pablo Picasso. . . . While she still does some works of this genre [Legend Painting] she is very self-conscious about being stereotyped as a legend painter" (Warner 1978:63).

Odjig encouraged a group of seven like-minded Indian artists (perhaps modeled after the famous Canadian "Group of Seven") to promote the production and exhibition of their Indian art. After their initial success, other artists were drawn to the style, and soon workshops were set up all over Indian Ontario and Saskatchewan. At first, sponsorship was by private collectors; later, government support ensured success; and today, important collections of this work may be found in national museums such as the McMichael Canadian Art Collection (also the host to the best collection of the Group of Seven). Odjig, an artist with a social conscience, has also been very concerned, in her work and in her professional and educational activities, to thwart injustices and dispel stereotypes about Canadian native peoples, especially her own Algonkian people (see Plate 3).

Another influential artist associated with Legend Painting is the late Benjamin Chee Chee (Ojibway). Although some of his work, perhaps the more widely known and distributed, is reminiscent of the rather "Disney-esque" aspects of Eastern Woodland art (see *Untitled #17*), he, like Odjig, refuses to be restrained by the label. Like some postmodernist Indian artists (see below), Chee Chee "rejects the label 'Indian artist' just as he rejected the traditional form and materials of 'Indian' art" (*Tawow* 1974:3). While his *Untitled #25* (Fig. 6.6) could perhaps be identified as exhibiting formal elements of Indian art, his *Untitled #15* resembles even more the work of the "process artists" than it does the highly sophisticated works of the Plains artists.

The Eastern Woodland School has had a very positive effect on the ethnic pride of Indian artists and nonartists, but its members suffer the predicament of artists the world over: they need a regular income. Consequently, popular and derivative versions of Legend Painting are mass-produced in the form of calendars and greeting cards. The fear of erosive commercial forces and the demand for stereotyped work are problems faced by Algonkian artists and other Indian artists alike.

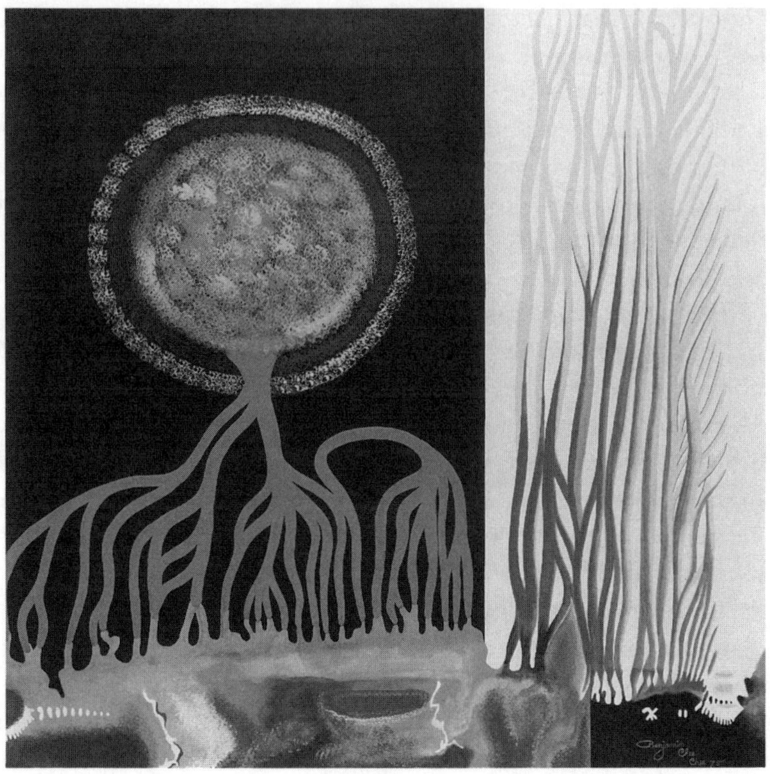

Figure 6.6. Benjamin Chee Chee (Ojibway), *Untitled #25*, acrylic, 1975. (IANA no. 85-0032)

Tradition Preserved: The Northwest Coast

Northwest Coast Indian art is perhaps the best known of all Canadian Fourth World art traditions. Impressive in its functional settings in the nineteenth century, mourned in its demise — like cathedrals in ruins — in the early twentieth century, it has long attracted the admiration of artists and anthropologists alike (Cole 1985). In the past twenty years, Northwest Coast art has experienced a powerful revival both as a functional ethnic-art form and as a commercial success. It is also significant that support from official national institutions has long placed Northwest Coast art at international expositions and venues, recently at Expo 70 in Osaka, Expo 86 in Vancouver, and in the new Canadian Embassy in Washington, D.C.

We cannot be concerned here with a history of this art, save to say that in the late nineteenth and early twentieth centuries it fell on very hard times due to the pressures on Indian culture (disease, corruption, missionization, population dispersal) and specific attacks on the art forms and their supporting institutions (banning the potlatch, stealing and collecting the artifacts, and destroying the apprenticeship system). This demise was more complete in the northern part than in the areas around Vancouver Island, most specifically among the Kwakiutl and the Westcoast (Nootka) Indians. In describing his landmark researches, Bill Holm wrote: "Unfortunately, I was unable to locate a qualified informant from the area covered, i.e., the coastal region from Bella Coola to Yakutat Bay. . . . [C]ontemporary work seen from the area reveals a lack of understanding by Indian craftsmen of the principles" of their traditional art style (Holm 1965:vii).

In spite of these setbacks, Northwest Coast Indian art is thriving today. Three factors account for most of the enhanced continuity and revival. In southern British Columbia, Kwakiutl and other arts were stimulated and encouraged by employment and commission, largely through non-Indian agencies, such as anthropological and public museums and public parks (Ames 1981). Among the more northern traditions, where Bill Holm found a complete break in continuity, it was he who provided the stimulus through his formal analysis of the essentially two-dimensional low-relief carving and painting style in his book *Northwest Coast Indian Art: An Analysis of Form* (1965). Holm (1965:vii–viii) adds that Bill Reid, an artist of Haida descent, contributed through his own discoveries and artistic works. Working with other Northwest Coast artists from both the south and the north, Holm and Reid impelled the revival of the classical quality that subsequently attracted native, scholarly, and commercial attention.

This revival was eventually solidified in 1973 with the founding of 'Ksan and the establishment of an art school and an Indian cultural centre there. Of this Blackman and Hall write:

A number of individuals, native and non-native, were influential in the early development of 'Ksan art, including Kwakiutl artists Tony and Henry Hunt and Doug Cranmer, Haida artist Robert Davidson, [white

artist and art historian] Bill Holm and most importantly, white artist
Duane Pasco, who spent more than a year instructing at 'Ksan. Much of
the recent 'Ksan art shows the stamp of Gitksan instructor Vernon
Stephens. (Blackman and Hall 1981:56n1)

A third factor contributing to the success and renewal of Northwest
Coast art, and which applies to all the Fourth World arts and is of a much
more general nature, has been the First World's general revival of interest
in the "primitive," the native, the folk, the non-Western arts, and eventually other cultural features, starting with the avant-garde early in this century, reaching institutional levels after World War II, and expanding
throughout the world in the 1960s. In the case of Northwest Coast art, the
public, hungry for recognizable non-Western (preferably Native Canadian)
art has latched onto available forms that are both aesthetically pleasing and
easily placed within this stylistic tradition.

Because Northwest Coast art is very distinctive and is perhaps better
known and publicized than other Canadian Fourth World arts, I will focus
on only two major and interconnected points here: (1) there is a strong
predilection to stay within the formal restraints of the traditional style,
regardless of medium and subject matter (Holm, personal communication,
1988), and (2) there is an equally strong feeling that the art, including the
commercial productions, must serve or be connected to the continuity-
giving spiritual, ceremonial, and genealogical heritage of the culture. Anything else is considered "selling out."

I believe that the former derives at least in part from the latter. The
Northwest Coast artists feel they are struggling for the survival and revival
of their culture. After a complete break in the north and the proliferation
of stylistically and technically sloppy souvenir productions in the south,
only the Kwakiutl and the Nootka of the west coast of Vancouver Island
provided spiritual continuity (through dance, language, and ritual) along
with the artistic continuity co-sponsored by white agencies. The Kwakiutl,
as the more ethnically successful group, provided a model of embeddedness
for the revivals in other areas, and Bill Holm and Bill Reid provided the key
to the stylistic revival in the north, in which, as mentioned above, a number
of Kwakiutl artists participated. Having been "given back" the art they had
lost, the artists strongly believe that they should never again depart from

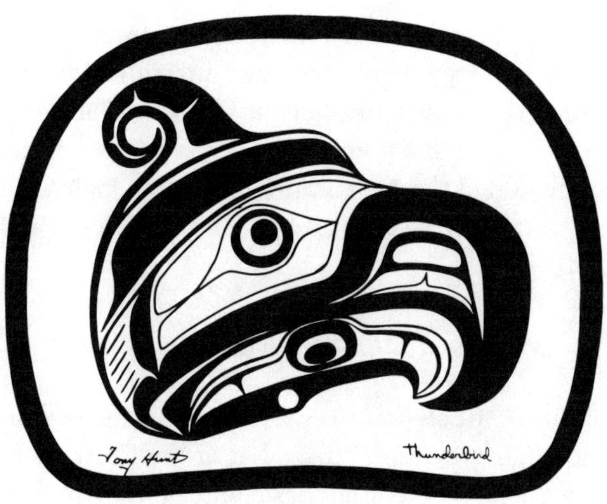

Figure 6.7. Tony Hunt (Kwakiutl), *Thunderbird*, print. (IANA no. 84-0127)

the ancestral style (which coincides with white demand) and that spiritual continuity is the way to keep on this path. As Frieda Deesing, a Haida graduate of 'Ksan, said, "On the West Coast we know our way, others may not. I learned a great deal from the white man. Bill Holm, Duane Pasco. We had lost the connection. People are now realizing what we've got to lose, by seeing what's in the museums from 100 plus years ago. Its up to us to continue our history."

Perhaps one key to the successful "embedded revival" is the revival of the apprentice system and the inception of a number of Indian-run schools or workshops for the transmission of the arts; thus many younger Indians can become successful professional artists without going through mainstream Canadian art schools (Holm, personal communication, 1988). Furthermore, much of the art is "community based" and, for the artists, other Indians are "the toughest and most important critics," according to Doreen Jensen, Git'ksan artist (personal communication to Julia Harrison).

This is not to say that Northwest Coast artists have not been innovative. With regard to the explosion of serigraphy by artists such as Tony Hunt (see Fig. 6.7), a medium which is more purely graphic than the traditional low-relief, wraparound wood-surface carving, Blackman and Hall (1981) discuss variations within the style and departures from the traditional subject matter, color, and choices of form, and Indian and white reactions to these innovations. Only recently have a few Canadian artists from this region attempted to stray far from the rules and forms of Northwest Coast art, following the lead of the American Tlingit artist James Schoppert, who has even taken to creating pieces based on Alaskan Eskimo and other traditions (Hoffman 1986:272).

Modernist Ethnicity: The Great Plains

The recent output of artists from the Canadian Plains is more difficult to label as a "school" or "tradition" than that of the Northwest Coast or the Legend Painters. As John A. Warner has pointed out, "The emerging forms of painting . . . have not yet coalesced into a single paradigm, if, indeed, they ever will. Modernist Indian painters experiment with mainstream contemporary styles such as cubism, surrealism, abstract expressionism and pop art, but usually manage to retain a sense of their Indian origins by the use of Indian symbols, motifs, themes and/or subject matter" (Warner 1985:46).

More than other Fourth World Canadian peoples, the Canadian Plains artists are influenced by their co-ethnics in the United States. For instance, Arthur Ammiotte, M.F.A., is an American Sioux who has taught in Canada since 1964 and who creates works with a very sophisticated blend of the type Warner described above (Loeb 1985). Sarain Stump (American Shoshone–Flathead-Cree) taught in Saskatchewan in the early 1970s, and his own art is a technically and formally striking blend of realism, expressionism, and social criticism. It has had a great influence on younger Plains artists such as Gerald McMaster, Del Ashkewe, and Edward Poitras (see below).

In some ways, these artists stand halfway between those who stress adherence to their particular ethnic traditional style and referents, such as the Northwest Coast artists, and those who have moved fully into the modern mainstream without tribal[7] referents, such as the postmodernist artists (see below). For these Plains artists, ethnic or tribal referents may be signaled in two ways. First, through the direct portrayal of Plains Indians, such as in the paintings of Cyril Assiniboine (Saltaux) (see *Pow Wow*

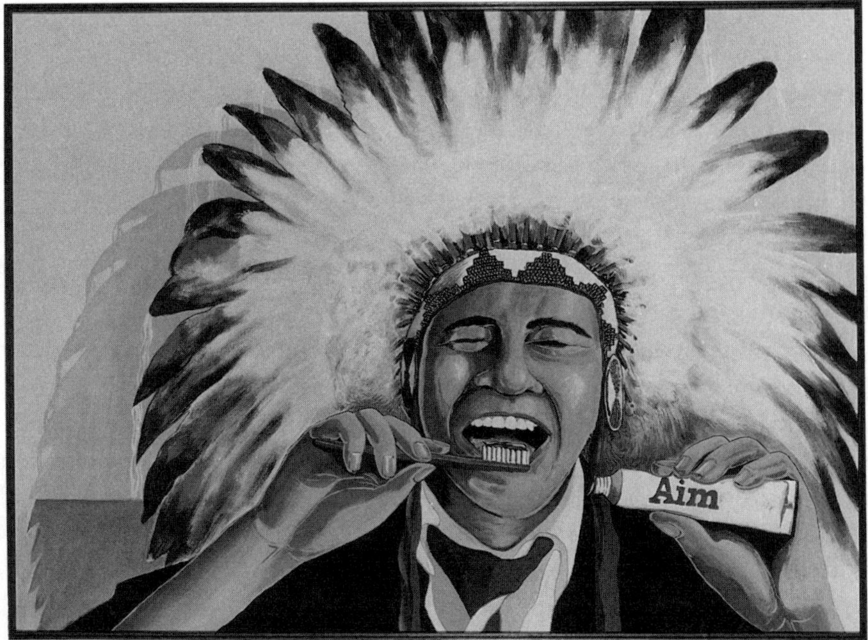

Figure 6.8. Alfred Young Man (Cree-Ojibway), *Indian in Pink and Blue*, acrylic. (IANA no. 87-1248)

Dancer 1982), or Alfred Young Man (see *Indian in Pink and Blue*, Fig. 6.8). This latter work also exhibits the contemporary social criticism — by showing a feathered (Plains) Indian brushing his teeth with a toothpaste labeled AIM — that is typical of many of the postmodernist painters. Young Man himself exhibits the less tightly identifiable, mobile, and well-educated characteristics of these artists. He was born in Montana and educated at the American Indian Institute of the Arts in Santa Fe and the Slade School of Art in London, and he holds a Master of Fine Arts degree from the University of Montana. Like other well-trained Plains artists, he teaches art at the college level (Warner 1985:50–53).

Alex Janvier (Plains Chipewyan) and Del Ashkewe exemplify the other direction in ethnic reference, the inclusion of formal motifs and color choices identified with Plains art: a hard edge and brightly colored geometrical forms within a variety of semiabstract styles, as in Janvier's *Other*

Worlds. Ashkewe was trained in commercial art in Toronto and, though he is an Ojibway, found his artistic identity while living on the Plains for seven years (Stephen Rothwell, personal communication, 1988). He is also capable of a hard realism (as seen in his *Great Blue Heron*) that is reminiscent of the Inuit artist Kananginak. Sturtevant (1986:42–43) points out that in addition to subject matter and symbolic devices in the content of the artwork already mentioned as clear signals of Indian ethnicity, the artist's identity may also be made obvious through the choice of title, a recognizably Indian name or, lacking that, a tribal attribution next to the name. Many of the modernist and postmodernist artists use one or more of the latter three devices.

In his article on the Canadian Plains, Warner (1985) also includes some artists who, though they are influenced by Plains art or live in urban areas of the Canadian Plains, I would include under the rubric Legend Painters. Among them is the talented and versatile Daphne Odjig, who, with her husband, lived in Winnipeg and operated an art gallery there. While her work encouraged some Plains Indians to adopt the newly invented Eastern Woodland Legend (Morrisseau) style, I do not think the influence was the other way around. Similarly, the eclectic Benjamin Chee Chee influenced both Plains and Algonkian Woodland artists, though I would place him with the latter group.

Postmodern Artists

One of the striking features of the 'Ksan symposium was the clearcut division between the majority of the artists, who hold to specific tribal or ethnic traditions, either stylistically or in depicted content, and those few artists who, though identified by tribe on their name tags, had broken away from feeling the need for a specific tribal affiliation in their art. In the intense conversations at the symposium, these latter rejected many of the majority suggestions as being unnecessarily restraining. The two "groups" often seemed to be talking at cross purposes and from different philosophical assumptions. In fact, some of the postmodern individualists just walked out and left the symposium a day or two before the end.

In a recent presentation, Joan Vastokas (1988) characterized postmodern Indian artists and their art as converging with other postmodern arts of the past twenty years. She defined their philosophy and their art by the following features: it is autobiographical, being concerned with self-identity rather than tribal identity; it has reverence for and reference to things traditional and spiritual, relating the past to the present; and it has a concern for craftsmanship, a bricolage of images, mixing media, and art as an exorcism of the ills of the present age. These artists, she avers, address global concerns of personal, cultural, and human survival, and they think that in their lives and art they should take a stand against oppression, violence, war, pollution, and the degradation of nature. She emphasizes that within the Society for Canadian Artists of Native Ancestry (SCANA) — an outgrowth of the original 'Ksan symposium — these are "artists who work independently."

An examination of their words, their behavior, and their works leads one to believe that these artists, among all Canadian Fourth World artists, have broken away from the self- and market-stereotyping that requires artistic evidence of tribal identity. It is as though they have decided, consciously or unconsciously, that their identity lies first as "artists" (in the white, mainstream mold) and secondarily as specifically "tribal" Indians (e.g., Benjamin Chee Chee, discussed above). Their works strongly recall those of the mainstream "process" artists of the 1960s and 1970s. Their semiabstract, mixed-media arts make reference to Indian motifs (eagles, old Indians, and teepees, for example) but with no necessary reference to their *own* tribal milieu. Their works are often concerned with social criticism in their references to wars and world crises as well as to dying and disappearing peoples and traditions. Sturtevant (1986) has suggested that this aesthetic may reflect a growing pan-Indian political consciousness.

Culturally, most of these artists obtained art-school training and degrees, and they have shouldered the burden of world art history, within which they place themselves. In their artistic development they may have avoided the already in-place "tribal" traditions in favor of going directly into "mainstream" art forms. Like the only two Canadian Inuit "nontraditional" artists, Abraham Anghik and David Ruben Piqtouken, many do not live in or near their native reservations or homelands; instead, they are more cosmopolitan and more oriented toward urban life and may have spent long periods outside Canada. A number are married to white spouses, who seem to act as their agents or managers, perhaps giving them a different relationship to the white art world.[8] Yet, because of the similarity of their work to mainstream art and the consequent lack of "Indianness," they find themselves in competition with all the world's artists and are less commercially successful than those who emphasize ethnicity and tradition (Vastokas, personal communication, 1988).

Many postmodern Indian artists are highly educated, with baccalaureate and advanced degrees. Some, like Tom Hill (Iroquois), have written extensively and have edited magazines. Others, such as Joane Cardinal-Schubert (Plains), were long separated from their heritage (like Bill Reid) and consciously sought it out when well into adulthood. Others were never "tribal": Edward Poitras (Regina Metis), for example, although he grew up on an Indian reserve, never felt he "belonged" (Vastokas 1988). After training with Sarain Stump at the Indian Cultural College in Saskatoon, he joined the Baha'i faith and sought a personal liminal identity through his art. Not all of them choose a formal postmodern style to express their pan-tribal or pan-human social criticism. For instance, Tom Hill, who is quite capable of painting in abstract expressionist and postmodern styles, often chooses ironic realism in his nontribal references to oppression, as in his *Allegory to MGM — A and B*.

Carl Beam, B.F.A. (Ojibway), like Tom Hill, attended the 1983 symposium. According to Vastokas, Beam perhaps typifies the ultimate convergence of native and postmodern Western arts, as in his self-referential *Neo-glyph 2* (Plate 4) and *Spirit of the Eagle*. It is interesting to note that one of his works was the first Native Canadian piece to be purchased (in 1986) by the National Gallery of Canada (Vastokas, personal communication, 1988), an institution notoriously resistant to accepting Fourth World creations, old or new, as genuine "art." Living outside Canada from time to time — in New Mexico and Paris — Beam has been heavily influenced by white and other artists such as Fritz Scholder, who himself has a very attenuated Indian heritage (Brody 1971:20–45). (For an excellent discussion of the institutional placement of Indian arts, see Phillips 1988.)

Joane Cardinal-Schubert, B.F.A., of equally attenuated Indian heritage, makes vague reference to her Plains background (as in *Spirit of the*

Last) but often through connections with the distant past, such as petro-glyphs, or contemporary world problems, such as Chernobyl. Jane Ash Poitras, M.F.A. (Cree), orphaned at the age of six, was for years a micro-biologist before finding her calling as an Indian artist. Though she refers to her tribal connections in *Cree Ribbon Shirt* (Plate 5), some of her work is visually more difficult to identify as Indian at all (such as *Alberta Ratroot*).

Other well-known artists in this postmodern group include Bob Boyer, Leonard Paul, and Pierre Sioui (see, for instance, Duffek 1989; T. Hill 1989). With the path already blazed for them, the members of this new generation of younger native artists has less compunction about breaking away from "tribal" or other ethnically identifiable traditions even if they do not have a full formal art-school training. Perhaps Sioui best exemplifies the freedom or even the obligation to engage the panhuman concerns of nuclear war, epidemics, genocide, and contemporary fears of death — topics which, though certainly germane to Indians, pertain to all of us. We should not forget that, like many other successful Canadians, a number of Indian artists have permanently forsaken Canada to work and reside in the United States, joining their artistic counterparts there but often breaking their connections to the Canadian ethnic heritage. For instance, Richard Glazer Danay, born in New York of Caughnawaga (Canadian) Mohawk parents, lives and teaches in California, and his works are as likely to be erotic spoofs on "Dear Abby" or to refer to his former occupation in New York high-steel construction work as they are to express anything "traditional" (Hoffman 1986:279).

At the 1983 symposium, artists of this type scorned those who were clinging to ethnic styles and content, with the veiled — and often heard — ac-cusation that the latter were "selling ethnicity," providing the public at large with easily identifiable symbols of nonthreatening Indianness. They, like the "New Indian" movement in the United States typified by the work of Fritz Scholder (Brody 1971), put art and social criticism first and were not afraid to present the ugly or the unexpected.

Warner (1986:197) distinguishes among "modern Individualists" those who continue and elaborate traditional reservation art, "those who employ new forms of expression but retain Indian symbolism," and those whose work is assimilated into mainstream Euro-American art. Many postmodern artists straddle the line or change their self-presentation during their careers.

Conclusions

This survey reveals a range of acculturation in both form and content among Canadian Indian arts of the post-contact period. At first glance, my classification may appear to have "evolutionary" overtones, but it must be stressed that all these forms are being produced today. We can say that some forms have existed for hundreds of years (the "traditional" arts), others for a century or so (replicas, models, and novelties), and still others have specific dates of "invention" (the Legend Paintings, for example). With regard to the "assimilated forms," Indian artists have long emulated various genres of mainstream art. Obviously the realistic, romantic "naive" forms have been produced for many decades, whereas the post–abstract expressionist "process" art has arisen only in the past two decades.

It is at this last point that Indian art has most fully merged with the mainstream, but at the same time some creations by white artists have merged with native arts in what is called "artifaking" (Holm 1978). Duane Pasco and Steve Brown, for example, make Northwest Coast masks, Cheryl Samuels makes Chilkat blankets, Bill Holm does the whole range of Northwest Coast material culture and arts, and Eugene Arima makes Inuit carvings as well as Kwakiutl masks (Duffek 1983; Holm 1978).[9]

Unlike the multigenre African artists described by Jules-Rosette (1985), the cultural and mental attitudes of these Native Canadian artists separate sharply according to the kinds of art they are producing. This accounts for the tense exchanges and frequent misunderstandings that occurred at the 'Ksan conference. There were two main positions, reflecting the geographical "culture area" styles; the uninitiated hardly entered into the discussions at all, not understanding the strongly held and expressed attitudes of others concerning art, spirituality, and tradition. The main divisions of opinion were between the Northwest Coast artists and the postmodern artists. The former, though realizing the need for commercial success, constantly referred to the gifts of their elders and ancestors, the necessity for the infusion of spirituality, and the "near-prostitution" of those who strayed far from tradition and emulated white artists. They made such statements as,

> You learn everything by heart from the elders, so now I speak my heart. You owe to where you come from. . . . Great artists are into ceremony, dance, singing, etc.

> Young artists change relatives the same as the white man. . . . They do not want to give or join, just to get.

> The responsibility of an artist is to give an honest response, not just to be a commercial success.

> Spirituality is the power to turn the raw into art. Urban artists have to fake it.

The Legend Painters tended to agree on the matter of ancestors and spirituality but could not claim that their art was traditional, only ethnic. Many of the Plains artists and the most assimilated protested the restraints of tradition and the groupthink of stereotypically Indian arts. They sought to claim their freedom as creative individual artists. As Carl Beam said,

> Now is the time for new things, it's part of the cultural revival. . . . All areas need revitalizing: It springs from the same old creative instinct, the need to define what's happening, in complex North America today. . . . We must be responsible and responsive to today. Times are changing; what remains is the spirit behind the forms. If not, we are living off our forefathers, unless *we* define the present. Indian people *will* dictate where art is going, no fucking archaeologist or anthropologist. You make an object for *you*. . . . Let nothing or nobody interfere with the creative process.

The long-assumed linkage between Indian ethnicity and artistic style is strongly negated by the following statements of Indian artists who adopt positions characteristic of mainstrain modern artists:

> Quality is inside the artist himself, we know when we are doing a sham or damn good. Authenticity — who cares, you are an Indian and a person — you do what you have to do.

> I am a Plains Indian, taught by a coastal Indian. I had trouble selling, so went away and learned another style. If a white man does art better than

an Indian, does that make the latter "authentic"? . . . The outsider decides what is authentic.

Given these attitudes expressed by Canadian artists of Indian heritage, can we say that all the different genres described above will continue to narrow so that in some distant future "Indian" art will disappear or assimilate into mainstream art? There is conflicting evidence on this point, but it should be noted that by the time of the next Canadian Indian Artists Symposium (described in Young Man 1988) the divisions were less apparent and the concerns expressed were mainly those of modernist and postmodernist, professional, market-oriented artists.

In the United States, Jamake Highwater has recently pointed out, "Most of the Indian artists who have had some degree of public recognition as producers of Indian art are now trying, like Scholder himself, to get out of the field as quickly and quietly as possible. And most of the artists of Indian heritage who have been accepted in the international world of art (Leon Polk Smith, James Havard, George Morrison, and others) pursue their careers with little or no public emphasis upon their ethnicity" (Highwater 1986:240). This public denial of ethnicity does not appear to have occurred in Canada.[10] As Vastokas remarked, artists like Carl Beam have great difficulty in succeeding as mainstream artists without emphasizing their Indian heritage in various ways. Perhaps the situation in Canada is different from that in the United States. For instance, there is evidence that the kinds of conflicts expressed above between "traditionalist" and "individualist" Indian artists is passé in the United States, at least as suggested in the remarks of the late T. C. Cannon (Caddo-Kiowa) quoted by both Highwater (1986:226) and Hoffman (1986:281). Perhaps Canada, with its national policy of multiculturalism (as opposed to the U.S. emphasis on the melting pot), is more supportive of the ethnically based cultural expressions of its "native" Fourth World peoples.

Further suggesting a new stage in the acceptance of Indian arts as "art" in Canada was the Art Amerindian '81 show in Ottawa in the autumn of 1981. Kay Woods described the show as "the first [national] collection of contemporary Indian art to be chosen by jury" and concluded that "it may well become a milestone in Canadian art, perhaps comparable to the beginning of public awareness and acceptance of Inuit art brought about over thirty years ago" (Woods 1981:33, 36). This "separate but equal" support of multicultural institutions is also signaled by the mandates of such national institutions as the Thunder Bay and the 'Ksan galleries and the Prince of Wales Heritage Centre to foster and mount exhibitions of native arts. Another manifestation is the enormous financial and logistical support of Canadian Inuit art over the past forty years compared to the minor and sporadic support for comparable institutions for Alaskan natives.

James Clifford suggests that "Non-Western cultural and artistic works are implicated by an inter-connected world cultural system without necessarily being swamped by it" (Clifford 1987:126). He specifically argues that ethnic arts — "endangered traditions" — will continue to be identifiable even though new definitions of authenticity, which no longer depend on a salvaged past, are making themselves felt. While I agree with Clifford that Native Canadian ("ethnic") arts will continue in new forms, his analysis is not sufficiently fine-grained. He writes as though all these "ethnic" arts exist because a need for expression exists among their "ethnic" creators, forgetting that the system is also market driven. By this I mean that in the above range of arts, all but the functionally traditional and the postmodern forms exist mainly because of outside support: it is non-Indian society that needs these nostalgically referential forms (see, e.g., Graburn 1986). Canada and the United States differ in their support for these contemporary traditions. Apparently Canada needs its modernist Indian artists to signal its multi-ethnic identity, whereas the United States and the international market exclude ethnic art from serious consideration. This effect of two different national cultural ideologies may be permanent, or, as in so many matters, Canada may follow along in ten years or so.

ACKNOWLEDGMENTS

I would like to acknowledge the help of Molly Lee of the Lowie Museum of the University of California at Berkeley, without whose knowledge of the intersections of anthropology and art history this paper would have lacked both breadth and clarity. I would also like to thank the members of the "Dissertation Write Up" seminar (U.C. Berkeley, Anthropology 250H), all nonspecialists in these fields, without whose feedback it might have lacked comprehensibility. It was also very fortunate that in 1988, before I completed this chapter, Professor Joan Vastokas of Trent University and Bill Holm of the Burke Museum were both invited to give public lectures in the Bay Area and to visit Berkeley. Both were generous in sharing their expertise in fields very relevant to the essay. They were brought to the Bay Area by Ann Brodsky and Tony Williams of the Society for Arts Publications of the Americas, in San Francisco, for their 1987–88 Canadian Lecture Series, which was generously supported by the Canadian Consul General and the Department of External Affairs of the Government of Canada. An earlier draft of this essay was read by Julia Harrison, Curator of the Glenbow Museum in Calgary, and by Jonathan King, Keeper of the Museum of Mankind in London, for which the author is very grateful. Many of their comments and suggestions have been included in this version of the work.

NOTES

1. 'Ksan is an Indian art center at the boundary of the Git'ksan and Carrier tribal lands. It emerged from attempts by Indians and non-Indians to found a museum for preserving the threatened traditional artifacts in the Seekan treasure house. In the 1970s, the Kitanmax (later shortened to 'Ksan) School of Indian Art was founded (*Tawow* 1971b). Since 1973 traditional Northwest Coast artists have taught there, and since 1978 it has also become a center for Indian activism.

2. For a more extended discussion of these concepts, see Graburn 1976, 1981.

3. No Canadian Inuit were invited because the organizers thought it was complicated enough to bring representative Indian peoples together without compounding their problems with the very different linguistic and artistic situation of the Canadian Inuit. However, the organizers expressed great interest in Inuit artists and hoped to invite them to any subsequent symposium. This has not occurred, however, at the later meetings held under the auspices of the Society for Canadian Artists of Native Ancestry (Young Man 1988).

4. There is an official, though unpublished, report on the symposium (Farber and Ryan, n.d.), but all quotes and observations in this paper are from the author's own notes.

5. Non-native participants included Carole Farber, University of Western Ontario; Marjorie Halpin, University of British Columbia; Alan Hoover, British Columbia Provincial Museum; Carmen Lambert, McGill University; George Mac-

Donald, National Museum of Man, Ottawa; Joan Ryan, University of Alberta; Polly Sargent, Indian Art Patron, Hazelton, B.C.

6. Unless otherwise stated, all photographs in this essay are courtesy of the Indian Art Centre, Department of Indian and Northern Affairs, Ottawa, and all works are from the Centre's collection. The Eskimo (Inuit) works are of various or unknown ownership.

7. In this essay, I use the term "tribal" in the nonanthropological sense, as used by the Indians themselves in this and other forums (see Farber and Ryan n.d.; Young Man 1988).

8. This is reminiscent of Ed Bruner's seminal article on change in Mandan-Hidatsa kinship terminology (1955), in which he showed that those who were able to use the social patterning of white American kinship terminology (regardless of the language they spoke) were those who had or had had a white person in the nuclear family.

9. Other white artists incorporate stylistic features and images of native arts into their mainstream creations (e.g., Jack Butler, Mark Tobey, and Jack Shadbolt; see M. Ames's remark in Young Man 1988:11). One could pose the question, When Indians do mainstream art, why is that not also called artifaking?

10. Some of these artists see their art as therapeutic in resisting the temptations of the white world in providing a personal bridge of continuity to their roots. A few, such as Clyde Prosper and Curtis Mason, have found their way to a livelihood as artists and to their Indian roots while in prison (*Tawow* 1980). The Inuk artist Henry Evaluakjuk, of Iqaluit, also learned to paint while he was in jail.

REFERENCES CITED

Amadio, Nadine
   1986   *Albert Namatjira: The Life and Work of an Australian Painter.* Melbourne: Macmillan.
Ames, Michael M.
   1981   Museum Anthropologists and the Arts of Acculturation on the Northwest Coast. *B.C. Studies* 49:3–14.
Batty, Joyce D.
   1963   *Namatjira: Wanderer Between Two Worlds.* Melbourne: Hodder and Stoughton.
Becker, Howard
   1982   *Art Worlds.* Berkeley: University of California Press.

Blackman, Margaret B., and Edwin S. Hall

1981   Contemporary Northwest Coast Art: Tradition and Innovation in Serigraphy. *American Indian Art* 6 (3): 54–61.

Blodgett, Jean (ed.)

1991   *In Cape Dorset We Do It This Way: Three Decades of Inuit Printmaking*. Kleinburg, Ontario: McMichael Canadian Art Collection.

Brody, J. J.

1971   *Indian Painters and White Patrons*. Albuquerque: University of New Mexico Press.

Bruner, Edward M.

1955   Two Processes of Change in Mandan-Hidatsa Kinship Terminology. *American Anthropology* 57:840–49.

Buchan, John [Lord Tweedsmuir]

1951   *Hudson's Bay Trader*. New York: W. W. Norton.

Carpenter, Edmund

1975   Collecting Northwest Coast Art. Introduction to *Form and Freedom: A Dialogue on Northwest Coast Indian Art*, by Bill Holm and Bill Reid. Houston: Rice University Press.

Chappell, Eward

1817   *Narrative of a Voyage into Hudson's Bay in His Majesty's Ship Rosamund*. London: Mawman.

Clifford, James

1987   Of Other Peoples: Beyond the "Salvage" Paradigm. In *Discussions in Contemporary Culture*, edited by Hal Foster, 121–50. Seattle: Bay Press.

1988   *The Predicament of Culture: Twentieth-Century Ethnography, Literature and Art*. Cambridge, Mass.: Harvard University Press.

Coe, Ralph T.

1986   *Lost and Found Traditions: Native American Art, 1965–85*. Seattle: University of Washington Press.

Cole, Douglas

1985   *Captured Heritage: The Scramble for Northwest Coast Artifacts*. Seattle: University of Washington Press.

Dewdney, Selwin

1975   *The Sacred Scrolls of the Southern Ojibwa*. Toronto: University of Toronto Press.

Dickason, Olive P.

1972   *Indian Arts in Canada.* Ottawa: Indian and Northern Affairs.

Duffek, Karen

1983   "Authenticity" and the Contemporary Northwest Coast Indian Art Market. *B.C. Studies* 57:99–111.

Farber, Carole, and Joan Ryan

n.d.   Report [on] National Native Indian Artists' Symposium, August 25–30, 1983, Hazelton, British Columbia. Coordinated by Doreen Jensen and Reva Robinson. Unpublished.

Goetz, Helga (ed.)

1977   *The Inuit Print / L'Estampe Inuit.* Ottawa, Ontario: National Museum of Man.

Graburn, Nelson H. H.

1976   Introduction to *Ethnic and Tourist Arts: Cultural Expressions from the Fourth World,* edited by Nelson H. H. Graburn, 1–32. Berkeley: University of California Press.

1978   "I like things to look more different than that stuff did": An Experiment in Cross-Cultural Art Appreciation. In *Art in Society,* edited by M. Greenhalgh and J. V.S. Megaw, 51–70. London: Duckworth.

1979   Peter Pitsiulak at the McCord Museum. *RACAR* [Royal Academy of Canadian Art Review] 7 (1–2): 105.

1981   1, 2, 3, 4 . . . Anthropology and the Fourth World. *Culture* 1:66–70.

1983   Art, Ethnoaesthetics and the Contemporary Scene. In *Art and Artists of Oceania,* edited by Sid M. Mead and B. Kernot, 70–79. Palmerston, N.Z.: Dunmore Press; and Mill Valley, Calif.: Ethnographic Arts Publications.

1986   Inuit Art and Canadian Nationalism: Why Eskimos? Why Canada? *Inuit Art Quarterly* 1 (3): 5–7.

1987   Inuit Art and the Expression of Eskimo Identity. *American Review of Canadian Studies* 17:47–66.

Gunther, Erna

1966   *Art in the Life of the Northwest Coast Indians.* Portland, Oreg.: Portland Art Museum.

Harrison, Julia (ed.)

1988   *The Spirit Sings: Artistic Traditions of Canada's First Peoples.* Calgary: Glenbow Museum.

Hickman, James
  1975   The Quiet Birth of the New Indian Art. *Imperial Oil Review* 59 (2):
          14–23.

Highwater, Jamake
  1986   Controversy in Native American Art. In *The Arts of the North Ameri-
          can Indian: Native Traditions in Evolution*, edited by Edwin Wade, 223–
          42. New York: Hudson Hills Press.

Hill, Tom
  1989   *Indian Art '89*. Brantford, Ontario: Woodland Cultural Centre.

Hoffman, Gerhard
  1986   Frames of Reference: Native American Art in the Context of Modern
          and Postmodern Art. In *The Arts of the North American Indian: Native
          Traditions in Evolution*, edited by Edward L. Wade, 257–82. New York:
          Hudson Hills Press.

Holm, Bill
  1965   *Northwest Coast Indian Art: An Analysis of Form*. Seattle: University
          of Washington Press.
  1978   Artifaking: Perception Enhancement by Doing. Paper presented at the
          77th Annual Meeting of the American Anthropological Association,
          Los Angeles.

Houston, James A.
  1952   In Search of Eskimo Art. *Canadian Art* 9:5.
  1967   *Eskimo Prints*. Barre, Mass.: Barre Publishing.

Jules-Rosette, Bennetta
  1985   *The Messages of Tourist Art: An African Semiotic System in Compara-
          tive Perspective*. New York: Plenum.

Kaufmann, Carole
  1976   Functional Aspects of Haida Argillite Carvings. In *Ethnic and Tourist
          Arts*, edited by Nelson H. H. Graburn, 56–69. Berkeley: University of
          California Press.

Kenny, George
  1978   To Capture Life's Beauty: Don Ningewance, Feature Painter. *Tawow* 6
          (2): 22–23.

Labelle, Marie-Dominique, and Sylvie Thiverge
  1981   Un peintre huron du XIXe siècle: Zacharie Vincent. *Recherches Amér-
          indiennes au Québec* 11 (4): 325–37.

Loeb, Barbara
  1985   Arthur Amiotte's Banners. *American Indian Art* 10 (2): 54–62.

McLuhan, Elizabeth
  1984   *Norval Morrisseau and the Emergence of the Image Makers.* Toronto: Art Gallery of Toronto.

Myers, Marybelle
  1980   *Things Made by Inuit.* Montreal: La Fédération des Coopératives du Nouveau Quebec.

Peters, Mary Jane
  1970   Allen Sapp. *Tawow* 1 (3): 10–11.

Phillips, Ruth B.
  1988   Indian Art: Where Do You Put It? / C'est de l'art indien: Où va-t-en le placer? *Muse* 6:64–71.

Pitsiulak, Peter, and Dorothy Eber
  1975   *People From Our Side.* Bloomington: Indiana University Press.

Pollock, Jack
  1974   Norval Morrisseau: A View from His Agent. *Tawow* 4 (4): 5–6.

Schwarz, Herbert T.
  1969   *Windigo and Other Tales of the Ojibways.* Illustrated by Norval Morrisseau. Toronto: McClelland & Stewart.

Sheehan, Carole
  1981   *Pipes That Won't Smoke: Coal That Won't Burn.* Calgary: Glenbow Museum.

Sturtevant, William C.
  1986   The Meanings of Native American Art. In *The Arts of the North American Indian: Native Traditions in Evolution,* edited by Edwin Wade, 23–44. New York: Hudson Hills Press.

Tawow
  1970   Norval Morrisseau. *Tawow* 1 (1): 14–15.
  1971a   Daphne "Odjig" Beavon. *Tawow* 2 (1): 21–23.
  1971b   'Ksan. *Tawow* 2 (1): 30–31.
  1974   [Benjamin Chee Chee] Indian Artist. *Tawow* 4 (1): 1–4.
  1980   [Indian] Art [in Prison]. *Tawow* 8 (1): 21–25.

Townsend-Gault, Charlotte
  1983   Defining the Role. In *Visions: Contemporary Art in Canada,* edited by Robert Bringhurst et al., 123–56. Toronto: Douglas & McIntyre.

Vastokas, Joan
  1988   Into the Mainstream: Native Art and Post-Modern Values. Canadian
          Lecture Series, no. 5, May 19, 1988. San Francisco: Society for Arts
          Publications of the Americas.

Warner, John A.
  1976   Allen Sapp, Cree Painter. *American Indian Art* 2 (1): 40–45.
  1978   Contemporary Algonkian Legend Painting. *American Indian Art* 2 (1):
          58–69.
  1985   New Visions in Canadian Plains Painting. *American Indian Art* 10 (2):
          46–53.
  1986   The Individual in Native American Art: A Sociological View. In *The
          Arts of the North American Indian: Native Traditions in Evolution*,
          edited by Edwin Wade, 171–202. New York: Hudson Hills Press.

Woods, Kay
  1981   Art Amerindian Contemporary Tradition. *Arts West* 6 (10): 33–36.

Wright, Robin K.
  1982   Haida Argillite — Made for Sale. *American Indian Art* 8 (1): 48–55.

Young Man, Alfred
  1988   *Networking: Proceedings from National Native Indian Artists' Sym-
          posium IV.* Lethbridge, Alberta: Society for Canadian Artists of Native
          Ancestry.

7

Shaping Selves, Reshaping Lives

The Art and Experience of Helen Cordero

Barbara A. Babcock

In the beginning Itc'tinaku considered how the people should live. She said to herself, "My old father and my old mother must go down to the people and be Clay (*mitsi*) Old Woman and Clay Old Man." In Shipap she made the old man and woman into Clay Old Woman and Clay Old Man. The old woman began to mix the clay with sand and soften it with water. When she had finished she made it into a ball and wrapped it in a white manta. She began to coil a pot with her clay, and Clay Old Man danced beside her singing while she worked. All the people gathered in the village and watched her all day long. When she had made her pots so high (about eighteen inches) and the old man was singing and dancing beside her, he kicked it with his foot and it broke in many pieces. The old woman picked up his stick and chased him all around the plaza. She overtook him in the middle of the kiva. They made friends again and she took the broken pot and rolled it into a ball again. The old man took the pot and gave a piece of it to everybody in the village. They each took it and made pottery as Clay Old Woman had made it. This was the time they learned to make pottery. Clay Old Man told them never to forget to make pottery. In those days they only indented it with the marks of their fingers. Ever since when we do not make pottery these two masked dancers come with the dance to remind us of the clay they gave to the people. They tell us not to forget our grinding stones and always to grind our own corn flour.

"The Institution of Pottery," from Ruth Benedict
Tales of the Cochiti Indians

Beginnings

When Helen Cordero shaped the first Storyteller doll in 1964, she made one of the oldest forms of Native American self-representation her own, reinvented a longstanding Cochiti tradition of figurative pottery, engendered a revolution in Pueblo ceramics, and reshaped her own life as well as that of her family, her pueblo, and countless other Pueblo potters. Helen's "little people," as she calls them, have become prize-winning and world-famous collectors' items. Storytellers and related figurines are now being made by no less than two hundred other potters throughout the Rio Grande Pueblos, and she has had to come to terms with what it means to be "a big Indian artist."[1] Every figure she shapes represents and recreates images of personal history and family life, cultural experience, and Keresan mythology.

Her most famous creation, the Storyteller, is both a portrait of her grandfather and a reenactment of storytelling—both an objectification of personal experience and an interpretive commentary on that other verbal art whereby the stories of her people are passed on from generation to generation (Fig. 7.1). In both her figures and the stories she tells about them and about herself, Helen Cordero continues these two traditions—pottery making and storytelling—through which Pueblo culture is transmitted and identity maintained. Less obviously, Helen is also continuing a family tradition of sharing oneself and one's home with an Anglo outsider—of constructing and reconstructing an Indian self in response to an Anglo other, of acting as a cultural broker and interpreter.

In this essay I want to talk about these stories, potteries, and relationships; describe how Helen Cordero has shaped her experience and told her own life history with her hands; and examine how these "little people" have in turn reshaped her life and that of countless other Pueblo women, producing changes of political and economic as well as aesthetic consequence in present-day Pueblo life. I also want to discuss some of the issues

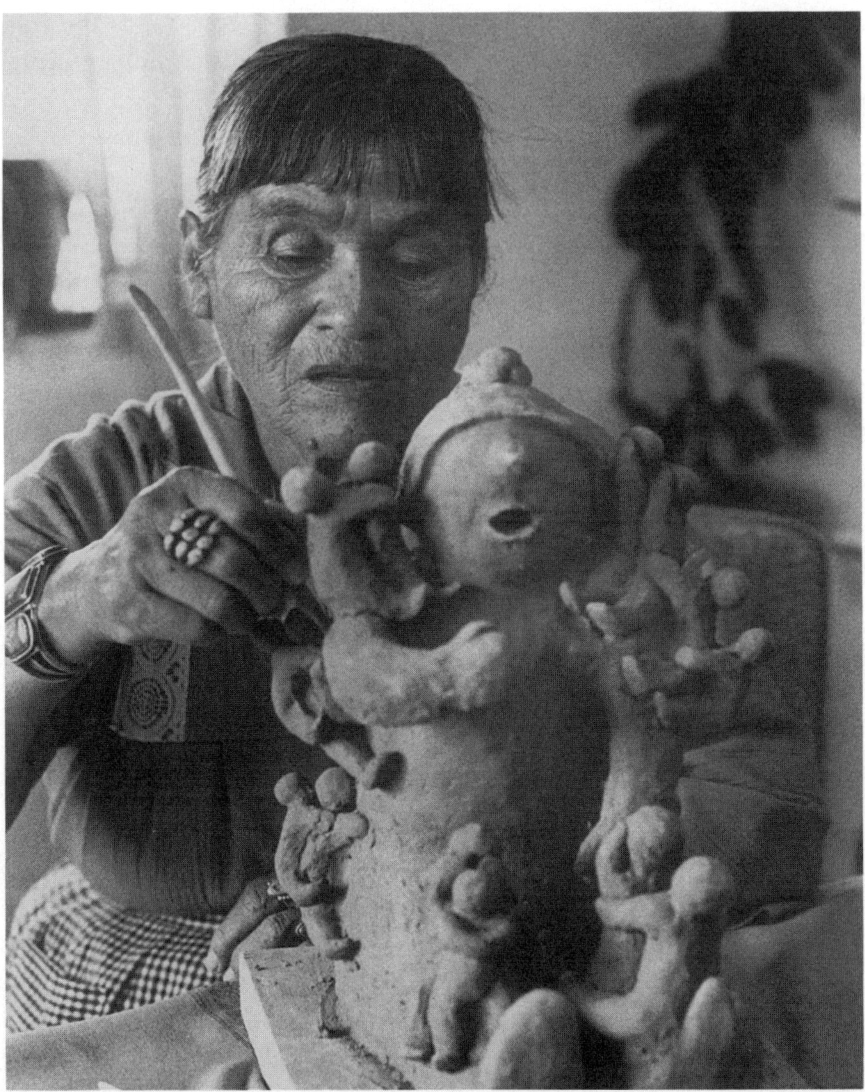

Figure 7.1. Helen Cordero at home in 1979 shaping a Storyteller with twenty-five children. (Courtesy of the Denver Museum of Natural History, neg. no. 4-79082-9A; photograph by Dudley Smith)

that Helen's art and experience and my efforts since 1978 to, as she says, "make it into a big book" raise for the cross-cultural construction, presentation, and interpretation of life histories.

Stories and Storytellers

Pueblo stories are models of and for "generativity," a power to survive that is both instinctual and psychosocial.[2] Like their ancestors, the contemporary Keresan storytellers Simon Ortiz and Leslie Silko will tell you that "the only way to continue is to tell a story and there is no other way" (Ortiz 1977:9); that stories are "life for the people"; and that "you don't have anything if you don't have the stories" (Silko 1977:2). When asked why he wrote, Ortiz replied, "your children will not survive unless you tell them something about them — how they were born, how they came to this certain place, how they continued." To the question, Whom do you write for? he replied, "for my children, for my wife, for my mother and father and my grandparents and the reverse order that way so that I may have a good journey on my way back home." Pueblo stories were and are one of the primary modes in which the family, the clan, and the community regenerate themselves in that they both describe and create "chains" linking generation to generation and back again and involve what Silko describes as the vital dynamic of "bringing and keeping the people together" (Silko 1981:59).[3] Moreover, in the embedded style in which they are structured and told, the stories themselves are models of reproduction: "Often the speakers or tellers go into the stories of the words they are using to tell one story so that you get stories within stories. . . . [W]hat is essential is this sense of story, and story within story, and the idea that one story is only the beginning of many stories, and the sense that stories never truly end" (Silko 1981:56) — that every one is "a seed of seeds."

Whether one is considering stories or things or ceremonies, "the structure of Pueblo expression resembles something like a spider's web — with many little threads radiating from a center, criss-crossing each other. As with the web, the structure will emerge as it is made and you must simply listen and trust, as Pueblo people do, that meaning will be made" (Silko 1981:54) and that all of the meanings are ultimately related. This is a telling metaphor of cultural expression, for Spider Woman is the "mother of all," the maker of Pueblo identity who is in turn made and remade in the stories. That storytelling involves these threads back to the ancestors and that one's identity is so constituted is expressed as well by the common practice of opening the door when stories are told so that the ancestors may come in. Leslie Silko recalls her Aunt Suzie saying, "Let them come in. They're here with us within the stories" (Silko 1981:71). Or, as Helen says of her grandfather and her portrait of him, "he had lots of stories and lots of grandchildrens and we're all in there, in the clay."

From the Pueblo point of view, stories, like "potteries" and like kinship systems, connect the reproductive aspect of generation with the cultural basis of thought: transmission. Nowhere is this more evident than in the image of the storyteller with which Silko prefaces *Ceremony*, her novel about the power and importance of stories: "He rubbed his belly. / I keep them here / [he said] / Here, put your hands on it / See, it is moving. / There is life here / for the people" (Silko 1977:2). When asked about the origin of her very similar ceramic image of a storyteller (Fig. 7.2), Helen recalls that folk-art collector Alexander Girard asked her to make a larger "singing mother" or "madonna" with children of the sort that she herself had made and that had been made at Cochiti for more than a century, and "when I went home and thought about it, instead of womens, I kept seeing my grandfather. That one, he was a really good storyteller and there were always lots of us grandchildrens around him."

In addition to telling stories to his many grandchildren and being known in the pueblo as a gifted storyteller, a leading member of one of the two clown societies, and a *mucho sabio*, Santiago Quintana (Fig. 7.3) was a valued friend and informant of several generations of anthropologists and observers of Pueblo life. He wanted his traditions preserved and maintained, and he went to great lengths to assure that *they* got it right." In the 1880s he befriended Adolph Bandelier, who quoted from him at length in his journals and who made him one of the protagonists in his ethnographic novel *The Delight Makers* (1971 [1890]), situated in Frijoles Canyon, to which he was first taken on burro by Santiago. In 1897, Frederick Starr recorded most of his Cochiti census from Santiago, traveled with him to Frijoles Canyon, and greatly enjoyed his company. "Santiago," Starr noted in his diary, "is a great talker."[4]

Several years later, when naturalist and writer Charles Saunders visited the pueblo, he was greatly impressed by this man who was both an adventurer and one "who stands vigorously for the old order." In *Indians of the Terraced Houses* (1973 [1912]), he recounted a conversation with Santiago about his trip to California. Edward Curtis photographed him and quoted him extensively in volume 16 of *The North American Indian* (1976 [1926]). On one of her first ethnographic trips to New Mexico in 1912 or 1913, Elsie Clews Parsons visited several pueblos on horseback with her Santa Clara Indian guide, Pedro Baca. They spent a day and night with Santiago Quintana and his family, and she recalled that Santiago "was

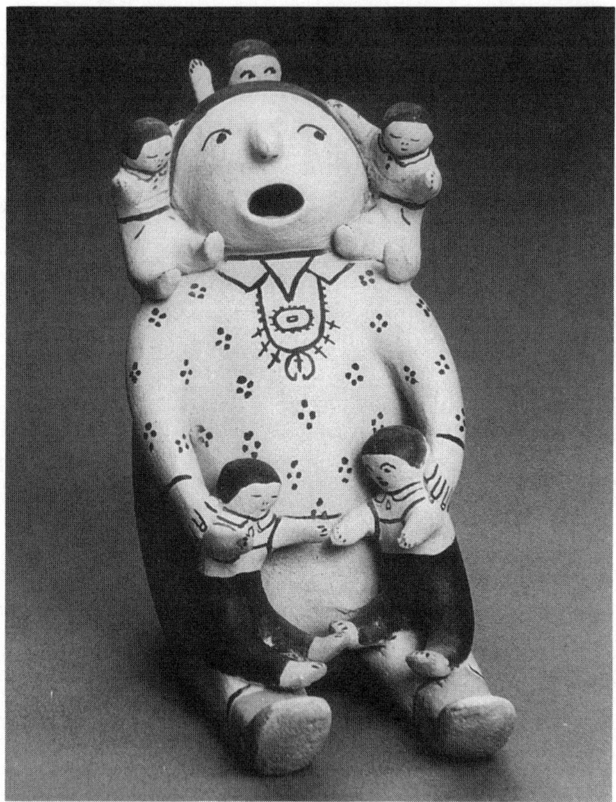

Figure 7.2. The first Storyteller doll made for folk art collector Alexander Girard in 1964. (Courtesy of the Museum of International Folk Art, acc. no. A. 79.53-41; photograph by Glenn Short)

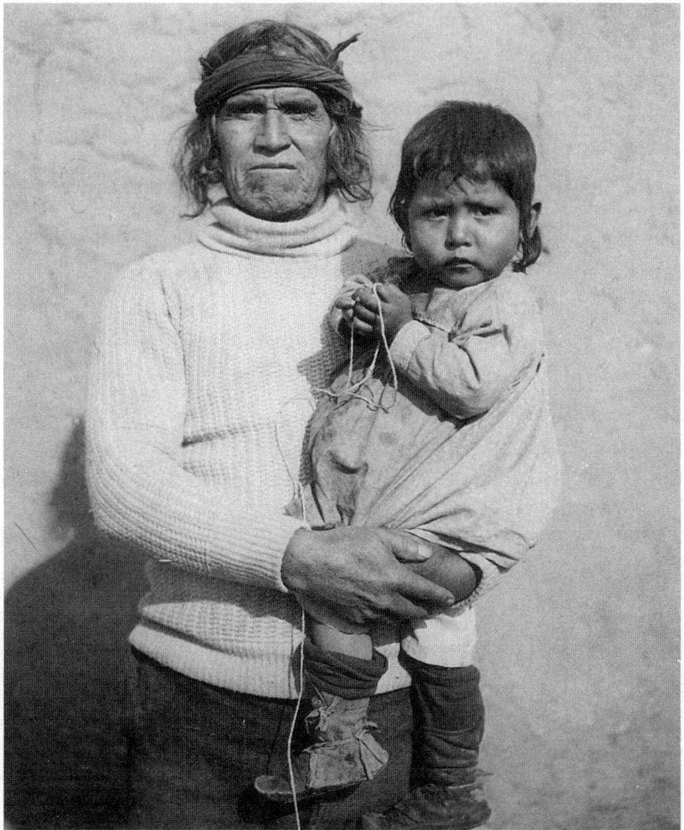

Figure 7.3. Helen's grandfather, Santiago Quintana, photographed in 1906 with one of his many grandchildren. (Courtesy of the Smithsonian Institution, neg. no. 80-5499; photograph by Fr. Simeon Schwemberger)

holding the baby, they were all joking or laughing and one of the girls devoted herself to keeping the bowls full."[5]

In the 1920s, Parsons and Boas's student, Ruth Benedict, collected many Cochiti tales from Santiago and wrote warmly of him in letters from the field to Margaret Mead:

My old man is ninety and a great old character. . . . He speaks excellent Spanish and I can follow a good deal when he talks it — I am angry that I have to bother with interpreters at all, but I do. He hobbles along on his cane, bent nearly double, and is still easily the most vivid personage in the landscape — he has the habit of enthusiasm and good fellowship. (Benedict 1973:300)

In the introduction to her collection of Cochiti narratives, Benedict again described this favorite storyteller and the distinctive stories he told:

> Informant 4 was a very different individual from the others, as can be seen in the material recorded from him. He spoke Spanish fairly and had been an adventurer all his life. He is very old now, but a leading member of the *principales*, in great demand in those acculturated Mexican ceremonies in which repartee must be carried on in what is considered to be Spanish. He liked best to give true stories . . . and his tales of the mythological heroes always emphasized their success in turning the mockery that had directed against them against those who had mocked them. (Benedict 1981 [1931]:xiii)

When outsiders ask her what her figures are, or what they mean, or to what she attributes her success, or what it feels like to be famous, Helen invariably replies: "I don't like to be called famous. My name is Helen Cordero. It's my grandfather, he's giving me these. He was a wise man with good words, and he had lots of grandchildrens and lots of stories, and we're all in there, in the clay."

When Helen shaped that first portrait of her grandfather in 1964 (Fig. 7.2), she modified the "singing mother" tradition in two significant respects: (1) she made the primary figure male rather than female, and (2) she placed more than a realistic number of children on him — the first Storyteller had five children; subsequent ones have had as many as thirty (for one with sixteen children, see Plate 6). By 1970 Helen had developed the distinctive face that has become her trademark: "His eyes are closed because he's thinking; his mouth is open because he's singing" (Plate 6). The proportions of this figure "bringing and keeping the people together" are social proportions, and its very structure replicates the reproductive pattern and embedded structure of Pueblo stories. Its subject is explicitly relationship — between past and present, old and young, male and female, words and things. From his body sprout countless children and grandchildren, and from his open mouth, as from the *sipapu*, emerges "life for the people" in the shape of stories. If you abstract the heads of these figures and concen-

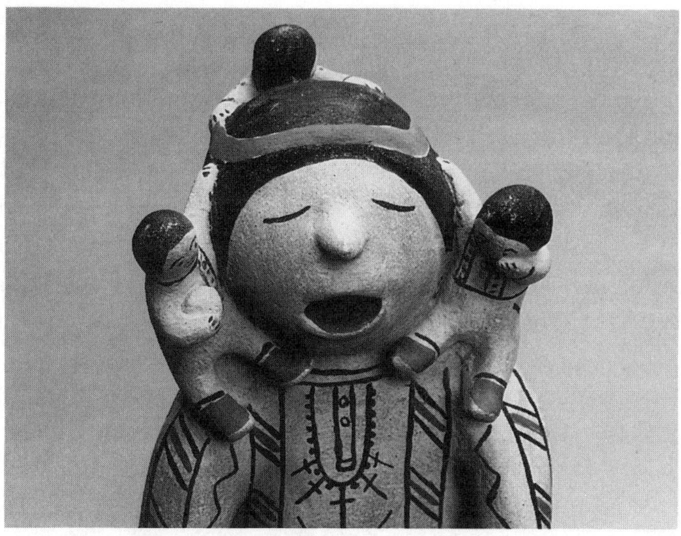

Figure 7.4. Head of a 1968 Storyteller. (Courtesy of Sallie Wagner; photograph by Glenn Short)

trate on shape alone (Fig. 7.4), you will see replicated again and again the primordial Pueblo pottery raincloud design (Fig. 7.5). Not only is this visible idea everywhere to be seen in Pueblo art and life, but the rainclouds themselves are believed to be inhabited by the ancestors, and when they are summoned in songs and dances for rain, the clouds are addressed as "our grandfathers," who answer by bringing the rain, and thus the entire cycle begins again.[6]

The history of the Storyteller is itself an expression of this reproductive dynamic, for the first Storyteller was the beginning of countless "little people." Helen herself has made more Storytellers than she can or will count — "It's like breads, we don't count" — and her clay portraits of family and pueblo life are by no means limited to Storytellers. If, as she says, "for a long time pottery was silent in the pueblo," it is by no means so today. Several members of Helen's family and over fifty other Cochiti potters are producing Storytellers and related figurines (see Fig. 7.6). Moreover, the voice of the Storyteller has spread throughout the Rio Grande Pueblos, where potters are shaping Storytellers in the clays, paints, and designs distinctive to their pueblos. When you talk to any of these potters, they will tell you stories about the mother or aunt who taught them to make "potteries" and about the grandfather or grandmother who told them stories, and then they will tell yet again the stories they told.

That first Storyteller was the beginning of many, Helen's and others', in part because she made it "in the old way, the right way," and in part because it bespeaks powerful personal involvement: "I don't know why people go for my work the way they do. Maybe it's because to me they aren't just pretty things that I make for money. All my potteries come out

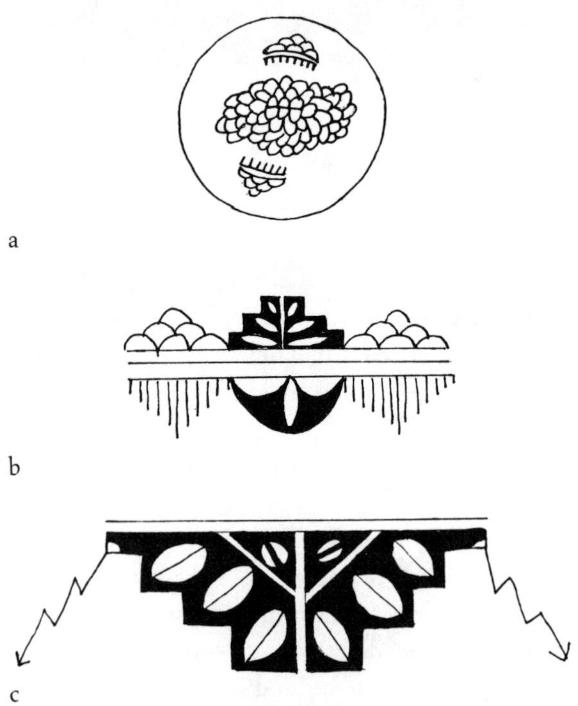

Figure 7.5. Traditional Cochiti and Santo Domingo raincloud pottery designs: (a) interior decoration of a ceremonial bowl, ca. 1875–1900 (after Chapman 1977: 32); (b) shoulder banding design on a Cochiti jar, ca. 1910 (School of American Research); (c) pendant rim design on a Cochiti dough bowl by Juanita Arquero, ca. 1965 (private collection). (Drawings by Barbara Babcock)

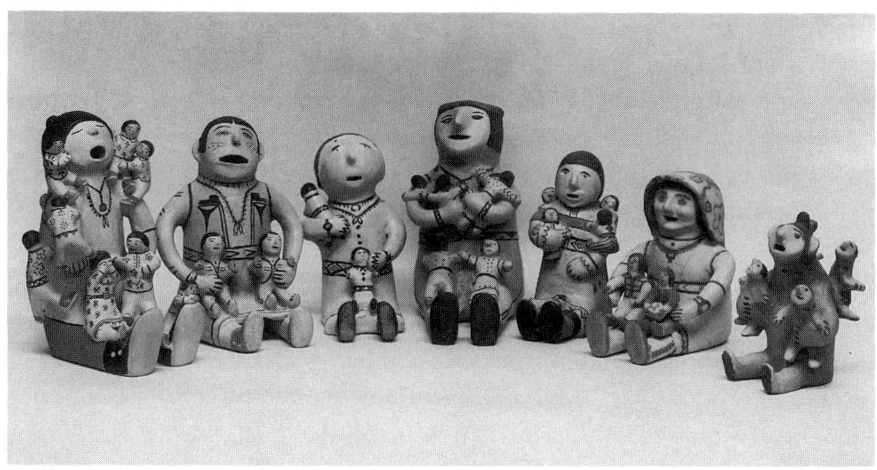

Figure 7.6. Cochiti Storytellers in the "What is Folk Art?" exhibit at the Museum of International Folk Art, Santa Fe, 1973. Left to right: Helen Cordero, Felipa Trujillo, Aurelia Suina, Juanita Arquero, Frances Suina, Seferina Ortiz, and Damacia Cordero. (Courtesy of the Museum of New Mexico, neg. no. 70433)

of my heart. They're my little people. I talk to them and they're singing." But in largest part it is because it speaks in terms of cultural constants — stories, generations, and the persistent problems of community organization and survival. Like their subjects, Storyteller figurines have themselves become a means of bringing and keeping Pueblo people together, attesting to the power of the hand as well as the word and demonstrating that cultures and the individuals within them constitute, reflect upon, and reconstitute themselves not only through what they say and do but also through articulations of the material world.

Potteries and Persons

Both the Storyteller and his historic and prehistoric ceramic ancestors (Plate 7) are symbolic forms through which and in which Pueblo conceptions of the person, the social order, and cosmology are articulated and displayed. As my preceding discussion implies, these conceptions center around the idea of fertilization, of generation — the key symbol or root metaphor of

Pueblo culture. While it is impossible to ignore the pervasiveness of pottery in Pueblo life, it is easy to forget that pottery making involves a transformation of the natural world into commodities of cultural value and personal significance as well as economic necessity, that this primary mode of production is also a cultural mode of reproduction, and that, as Weiner (1982: 33) argues regarding Samoan fine mats, these objects, though physically detached from the social self, nonetheless embody the very basis of the creation and regeneration of the social self. In traditional Pueblo belief, clay itself is regarded as a living substance, and according to Cushing (1886:510–15), a pot acquires a kind of conscious and personal existence as it is being made. "In other words," Margaret Hardin notes, "a pottery vessel was not thought of simply as an inert manufactured object. Rather, it was active, endowed with a life of its own. As a receptacle for water and food, it held, and was in turn, a source of life" (Hardin 1983:33). Moreover, the painted designs with which these containers of food and water were decorated — clouds, lightning and rain, leaves, flowers, and seedpods in an endless profusion of combinations — simultaneously had one dominant theme: a prayer for rain for the crops.

As archaeologists have demonstrated, as Cushing so finely described in *Zuni Breadstuff* (1920), and as the Cochiti story about the origin of pottery reproduced as an epigraph at the beginning of this essay reflects, settled Pueblo existence as it developed in the southwestern United States and as it was lived until the latter part of the nineteenth century was inconceivable without rain, without the cultivation of corn, and without pottery to store water and grain. The last lines of the Cochiti story about Clay Old Man and Clay Old Woman telling the people not to forget their corn and grinding stones, is therefore not the non sequitur it initially seems, for both modes of production are necessary to "how the people should live," as well as being technologically similar and cosmologically related.

In addition to descriptions of how the people came to make pottery, such as Benedict collected, every recorded Pueblo origin myth also describes the creation of life itself as occurring in part through the process of pottery making. This is notably so in Keresan emergence stories, in which Iyatiku (Bringing to Life) and her sister, Nautsiti (More of Everything in the Basket) are sent up into the light, to this earth, by Itc'tinaku (Thought Woman, Spider Woman) with baskets crammed full of seeds and clay images from which they create all forms of life. Several of these seeds and "little images" actually enable the two sisters to reach their goal: the pine tree that they climb up, the badger who makes the hole in the earth big enough for them to climb through, and the locust who smooths the hole by plastering.[7] What these myths reflect and what archaeology confirms is not only that clay has life-giving power but also that for almost as long as they have shaped utilitarian vessels necessary for life from the clay of the Southwest, Puebloan peoples have formed ceramic images of themselves, their gods, and the animal and vegetable world around them. Figurative pottery in the form of effigy vessels, figurines, and appliquéd or painted designs on both figurative and nonfigurative shapes is found in all prehistoric Pueblo cultures and dates from at least A.D. 300.

Further indication that clay figures are connected not only to the creation but also to the maintenance and reproduction of Pueblo identity is the practice of collectively representing Keresan townspeople in male and female clay images kept by the *cacique* (the religious leader of the pueblo). As Parsons observed at Santo Domingo, the *cacique* "takes care of his people by looking after 'his children' just as the Mother (Iyatiku) whom he represents looked after the images in her basket" (Parsons 1939:vol. 1, pt. 2, p. 336).[8] And as Parsons also recorded, throughout the pueblos, small figurines, which are frequently unbaked and unpainted and which are made of cornmeal or clay, are central to rites and prayers of increase, particularly those associated with the winter solstice and/or Christmas. Images of domestic animals are placed on kiva or church altars and are thereafter buried in the corral "so that there will be more of them" (Parsons 1919: 279). Similarly, a woman wanting children will make a clay "baby," take it to the altar, and then place it on a small cradleboard in a special place in her home; or she may be given a clay or wooden baby in a miniature cradle by one of the kachinas, which she then cares for and regards as "the heart of the child" (Dumarest 1918:141). Such clay figures are taken to be "the seed from which the real objects will grow" (Parsons 1939:574).

Making and exchanging "potteries" is a vehicle for personal and tribal identity in a much more pragmatic and everyday way as well. Long before Anglos introduced the idea of "signatures," individual potters were distinguished and identified by their styles, as were families and pueblos. Old family potteries were and are passed on from generation to generation, carefully tended, used or displayed on ceremonial occasions, and valued not only as a source of traditional designs but as a way of telling and maintaining family history.[9] With the encroachment of the Anglo world in the last hundred years and the expansion of an Anglo market for Indian objects, Pueblo "potteries" have become increasingly important as a distinctive cultural voice, as containers of Pueblo values. Although the majority of Pueblo pottery is now made for Anglo shelves rather than local use, it is still important to Helen and other potters that it be made, in her words, "in the old way, the right way." Despite — or perhaps because of — the importance of Anglo patronage to the survival and revival of Pueblo ceramics, "in a very real way the survival of the craft symbolizes the survival of the people — an involvement with tradition and a material link with the ancestral past far more basic than patrons' interest in archaic patterns" (Brody 1976:76).

Not all life stories are told in words, and in countless ways Helen Cordero has told me that her "potteries" are her autobiography and that her art has given her "the privilege to imagine, to recollect, to think and to feel in *forms*" (Focillon 1948:47). In a very literal as well as a symbolic sense, Helen's "little people" are life-giving and life-sustaining. In 1968 and 1971, her oldest son and daughter were killed in automobile accidents. At the time, recognition of her work was spreading and the ever-increasing demand for her "potteries" and her presence at shows and demonstrations helped her to deal with her loss. "When God took away my babies, he gave me my little people to keep me going. If I hadn't had my work, I think I would have just gone down myself." This embodiment of personal meaning in "autographic objects" and the reciprocal relationship of Helen's art and life points up a need to consider life histories and the construction of self not only in narrative and performative but also in material terms.[10]

Despite repeated assertions that people use things as well as words and deeds to create culturally constituted modes of existence for themselves, that objects are essential in the production and reproduction of cultural persons and social relations, too many social scientists have neglected the relationships between people and the objects they make and use, privileging language instead in the expression of self. Given the importance of photographs, memorabilia, and heirlooms as repositories of personal meaning and vehicles of continuity, and given the ease with which stories may be elicited through objects, collectors of life histories would do well to consider the meaning of things and the importance of what Georg Simmel called "objective culture," and what Annette Weiner describes as a "model of reproduction" and "elementary cycling."[11] This is so, I contend, even when the narrator does not literally talk with her hands.

Since Helen does tell her life story in clay, let me now describe some of the forms other than the Storyteller into which she has shaped her experience and interpreted her life. Another interesting re-enactment of storytelling is the Children's Hour, in which the children are grouped around rather than placed on the Storyteller. Helen describes this figure as follows: "These are older kids listening to him. He used to say, 'Come children, it's time,' and I remember us all around him out at the ranch, and that's how I thought of the Children's Hour." In addition to it being physically impossible for older children to be sitting on their grandfather, this ensemble and Helen's remarks about it connote integration with differentiation and individuation and a greater emphasis on the grandfather's pedagogical rather than nurturant role, which is characteristic of an adolescent state of affairs.

The structural hierarchy of the Storyteller and the Children's Hour is inverted in the other multiple-piece scene that she regularly makes, the Nativity, in which the entire community — people, animals, foodstuffs, and goods — is organized around the infant. While this is the very essence of the Christian nativity scene, she emphasizes that, unlike the first *nacimiento* that she made for Alexander Girard, these are "Indian nativities." All the figures are dressed in Indian costume, "what we wear when we dress up nice," and they carry "what we take to the Infant Jesus on Christmas morning." "The man with the sack over his shoulder is carrying what the boys use for their dancing. Costumes. The Indians knew that Jesus was a boy and would need what the boys use. The cows and horses are close to the baby to keep him warm. They all have the Cochiti brand." The artistry of this scene is not realized entirely in clay. The cottonwood bows and arrows, the cradleboard ("For the newborn baby, we always use the cradleboard to lay him on"), and the stable are made by her husband Fred and her son George. Again, as was the case with the Singing Mother or Madonna figure, Helen has taken a traditional Christian image and transformed it into very personal and very Pueblo terms.

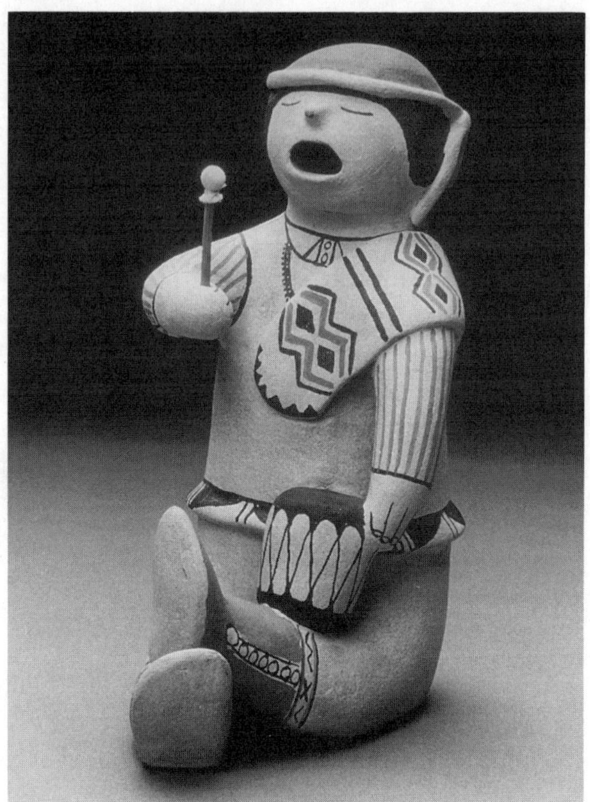

Figure 7.7. Drummer, 1970. (Courtesy of Dr. & Mrs. Zigmund W. Kosicki; photograph by Glenn Short)

Many of Helen's "potteries" as well as their accessories bear Fred Cordero's imprint. In the beginning, Helen was afraid to paint her people, and Fred both taught her and helped her paint for several years. Her Drummer (Fig. 7.7) is her portrait of Fred, who in addition to being a fine drum maker is the leading singer and drummer for the Pumpkin kiva and has held many ceremonial and political offices in the pueblo, including governor. Drums are the heart of Pueblo life and ritual, and have kept its rhythm for centuries. Throughout the pueblos, Cochiti has long been famous for its drums, which are made for and sold both to other pueblos for ceremonial

THE ART OF HELEN CORDERO

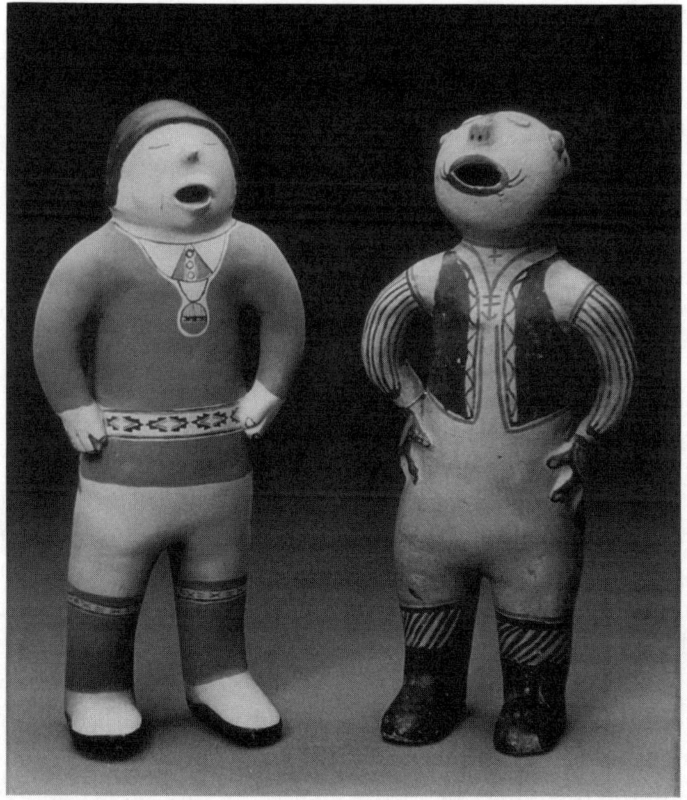

Figure 7.8. Nightcrier, 1976 (left), and Cochiti *mono*, ca. 1895. (Courtesy of Forrest Fenn; photograph by Glenn Short)

use and to Anglos for decorative purposes. In recent years the drum has become an important symbol of community identity — the landscape is dominated by two water towers painted to look like drums, and the end of every pew in Cochiti's St. Bonaventura Church is decorated with an incised drum.

Like the Drummer, the standing Nightcrier figure that Helen makes is also a familiar Cochiti ceremonial personage, and sometimes he too is personalized by being given a governor's cane of office "so that he looks like Grandpa" (Fred). Helen made the first Nightcrier in 1976 after she saw an old (ca. 1895) Cochiti figure at the Fenn Galleries in Santa Fe. She looked at it standing in its nicho on the stairway and said, "He's sad. Nobody should sing alone." She measured it and went home and made the first of these large standing figures, who now sings with his century-old friend (Fig. 7.8).

Potteries, however, are not only described as being or being like family members or significant pueblo personages. The reverse also occurs, and I have been struck on several occasions by the extent to which Helen's works of art, as Focillon observed, "create formal environments which impose themselves on human environments" (Focillon 1948:63). I once took Helen a Parkhurst photograph taken of her mother in the 1920s that I had found in the Museum of New Mexico (Fig. 7.9). She exclaimed, "Look at her. She's so pretty. She looks just like my Water Carrier" — a seated or standing female figure with an *olla* on her head. The same sort of reciprocal interchange occurs with old Cochiti potteries, which are sometimes, as in the case of the Nightcrier, an inspiration to Helen for a new shape or a new design. In other cases, the older forms are evaluated and interpreted both technically and aesthetically in terms of Helen's own work. While she acknowledges her debt to and frequently admires old Cochiti figurines, she is quick to point out that she conceives and names her own figures differently: "Those old ones, they called them *monos* [a Spanish term meaning monkey, mimic, silly fool, or mere doll]. Some people here and some of the dealers still call them like that. I tell them, 'No, these aren't *monos*. These are dolls. They're my little people.' I don't like to call my potteries by that word because they used that for the figures that you knock over and break with a ball at the carnival."

One of Helen's more recent and very appealing creations is a turtle carrying children on his back (Fig. 7.10). When she talks about this figure, it is clear that he is regarded both as a model of an important event in Keresan mythology and a model for a desirable present occurrence: "He's not only a turtle. He's somebody who helps out, and he's very big in spirit. A long time ago when there were wars and the people were fighting among themselves, the turtle came and volunteered to take the kids away. Now, he's taking these ones on a long journey — very slow and very sure — to learn the old ways." Sometimes the shell that carries the children is decorated realistically with a saddle blanket of Pueblo textile design; in others it is treated

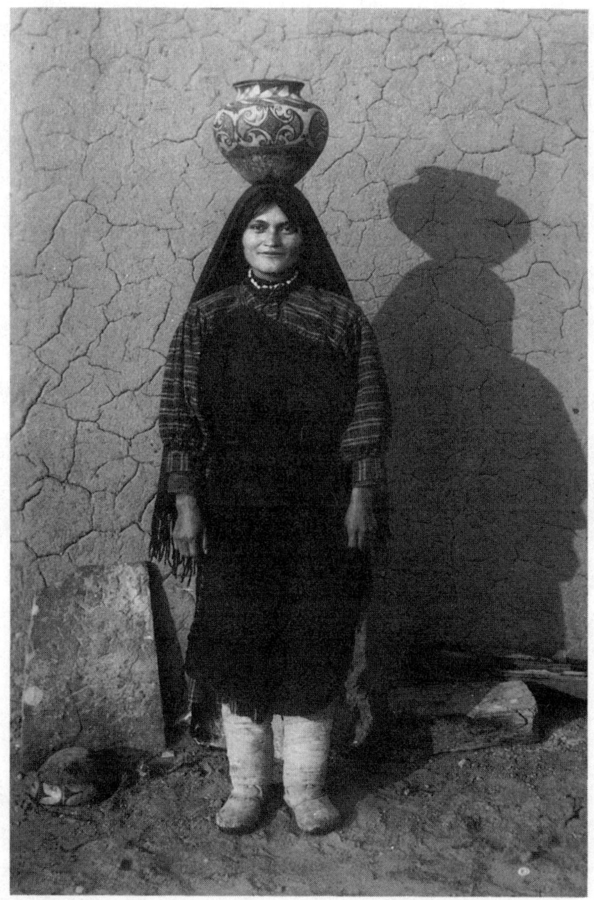

Figure 7.9. Caroline Trujillo Quintana Pecos, ca. 1920. (Courtesy of the Museum of New Mexico, neg. no. 2326; photograph by T. Harmon Parkhurst)

like an inverted bowl, and the edge is painted with traditional pottery rim designs representing plants or rain clouds — designs, I again emphasize, that are omnipresent in Pueblo iconography as prayers for rain and icons of fertility, and are by no means limited to ceramic design. Whether we are dealing with the relationship of her art to her personal and cultural experience or, as in this case, the relationship of her clay shapes to other forms of

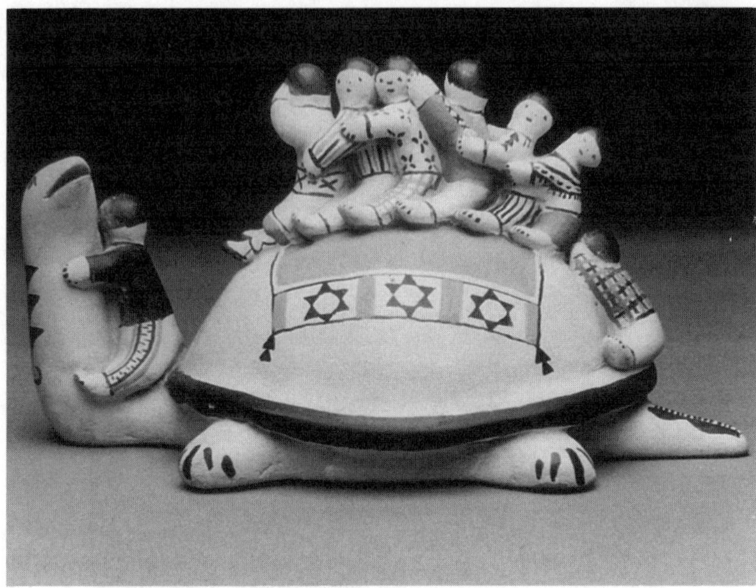

Figure 7.10. Turtle, 1980. (Courtesy of R. K. McCord; photograph by Glenn Short)

Pueblo art or systems of signification, it is no simple matter of representation and reflection but is instead a complicated relationship of continuity and reciprocity, and of economic and political consequence as well.

Rewriting Scripts, Reshaping Selves

Like most students of Pueblo pottery, I had naively assumed that potteries and politics had nothing to do with each other. Then, in the summer of 1982, a Cochiti tribal official tried to stop the women from demonstrating and exhibiting their pottery, and I was forced to see that the Storyteller revolution engendered by Helen Cordero had caused a profound dislocation in the economy of cultural representations and gender roles. Cultural expressions such as potteries are not only a way of seeing the world but also a way of changing it, and that is perforce political. Through her pottery, Helen has redefined the terms of her existence and rewritten the traditional

Pueblo woman's script. In contrast to her life prior to the mid-1970s, she can now go where she wants, buy what she wants, and more or less do what she wants. I once teased her about her new harvest gold, ice-dispensing refrigerator. She turned to me and said, quite seriously: "I'm getting me what I always wanted." Another time she related how Fred had objected to so many Anglos coming to their house, and she said, "I just told him, 'Daddy, it's my work and you'll just have to stand it.'"

For centuries, pottery making was a primary and privileged mode of expression for Pueblo women, and the exchange of pottery, which was controlled by men, played a significant economic role in Rio Grande Pueblo culture. More recently it has become an important vehicle both of identity maintenance and identity change in the transition from a subsistence to a cash economy.[12] With the latter, in addition to the automobile and an Anglo market that names and wants to know its artists, Pueblo women have assumed activities that were once their husbands' prerogatives. But more than simply reshaping traditional roles, pottery making has enabled Pueblo women who were "muted" and discouraged from putting themselves forward to be articulate and to call attention to themselves.[13] With her pottery, Maria Martinez of San Ildefonso became an internationally celebrated artist and provided other Pueblo women potters such as Helen with an alternative career pattern. When I first met Helen, she had been a prizewinning potter for more than a decade. After we had talked for over an hour, she asked why I was asking her all these questions. When I replied that I was thinking about writing an article on Storytellers, she remarked without hesitation, "There are three books about Maria and none about me." And, indeed, like Maria, she has, through traditional Pueblo women's work, both revised the standard female script and realized a very nontraditional career and sense of self.

Beyond the Essential Primitive, Writing Otherwise

As the preceding dialogue implies, whatever the text that is ultimately produced and labeled a life history, it is not a thing but a relationship. It is a thing only in the sense that it is an artifact of the ethnographic encounter. This particular relationship, moreover, does not consist simply of Helen living and telling, and me writing — of a textualized other and an interpreting self. Whatever our encounter produces is a complicated interpersonal construction in which several different agendas are being negotiated. In the case of Helen's book, there are at least four: (1) Helen's idea of what her book should look like, including what is and is not important in her life and what, as a traditional Pueblo woman, she can and cannot tell the outside world. She wants a book, but she doesn't want "to spill the beans." (2) The generic constraints of an artist's biography, in particular the primitive or folk artist's life story, in which the art has been far more important than the artist and his or her culture. (3) The model of the life history, especially the life histories of American Indian women, beginning with Ruth Underhill's *Papago Woman*. Like life histories in general, these are dialogues presented as monologues in the voice of the indigenous woman and framed by that of an Anglo authority. (4) My own ideas of what a postmodern dialogue constructed between two women might look like — a dialogue within which earlier textualizations and other voices such as Helen's grandfather's and Ruth Benedict's are reinscribed, and visual as well as verbal images of Cochiti, Helen's family, and her art are incorporated.

I now realize, as Crapanzano (1977, 1980) has pointed out, that these conventions and constraints are operative not simply on the life historical text that is produced but also on the very dialogue that produces those texts. In 1978 I spent a lot of time, for example, trying to determine how many Storytellers Helen had made, because that mattered to Anglo consumers and anthropologists, both of whom have a tendency to reduce art to economics. It took me a long time to hear what she was really saying when in exasperation she remarked, "It's like breads, we don't count," and to recognize the commodity fetishism of material culture studies that had shaped my questions. After that, I too stopped counting and began to try to understand what it means to liken breads to potteries, to not count, and how this primordial art is differently conceived from a Pueblo woman's point of view. I also started attending more carefully to how Pueblo women and pottery are imaged in various Anglo art worlds.

What agendas 2 and 3 share, and what is implied in the very terms *life history* and *biography*, is a bounded, essential notion of self, of identity that is unfolded in a coherent and chronological narrative. Just as all ethnography consists of the textual integration of cultural fragments, all life stories entail recuperating a self and a past through writing and the fiction of a beginning, a middle, and an end.[14] I am not sure why we in the West have invested so much in these fictions, but on the basis of what I've experienced and described to you in part, I am sure that Helen Cordero has never conceptualized her life in the form of biography or life history. Helen is always "in a hurry" and rarely sits still long enough even to talk about her life. When she does, at my prompting, the stories come in bits and pieces in the interstices of a busy life. And why should she bother, since she has already objectified, integrated, and transformed herself and her experience in her dolls? Time spent talking is time away from making potteries.

I wonder how common this situation is, and how many, if any, life histories have been written as they were told. Or even if edited, how many are intentionally informed by a collaborative relationship between the written other and the writing self? Are substantially if not stylistically dialogic? As both James Clifford (1983) and Vincent Crapanzano (1980) have argued, writing the lives of others cannot and should not be conceived as an act of singular authority. Who am I to say where the person named Helen Cordero begins or ends, and how am I to gather the countless fragments, images, and voices of Helen's life into a whole that is neither a seamless, linear distortion nor a "riot of confusion"? Who am I to presume to reweave a spider web of culturally patterned relationships?

The problems that Helen and I have had in, as she puts it, "gathering all these words and pictures together" have also convinced me that it is not a simple project to try to speak for the other woman. Yet it is at the same time an essential project, for women writing the biographies or recording the life histories of other women are enacting something fundamental about feminism as a commitment to friendship and about feminist method as "the collective critical reconstitution of the meaning of women's social experience as women live through it" (MacKinnon 1983:255; see also Geiger 1986). As I attempt to assemble and reassemble the words and images and memories of Helen's experience that I have collected, I realize that a life history with a beginning, a middle, and an end is as much an androcentric fiction and distortion as is an objective, impersonal, and authoritative style of presentation. Helen Cordero neither conceives nor represents her life in anything resembling the life histories that we have read and studied criteria for, and for me to do so would be to reinscribe a very inappropriate patrilineal syntax. Moreover, it is essential that the relation of author to subject (and vice versa) inform the narrative, becoming part of a "new relation, that of woman to woman across time and cultures, helping us to create the public space so long denied us" (Minnich 1985:288). Together, Helen Cordero and I help each other to speak.

As an alternative to the conventional life history or typical artist's biography, I would like to suggest a polyphonic patchwork model — a collaborative piecing discourse that Miriam Schapiro has termed *femmage* (Meyer and Schapiro 1978:66–69). Based on an aesthetic of connection and relationship, of quilting — that woman's art par excellence — femmage involves collecting and creatively assembling old and seemingly disparate elements into a functional, integrated whole. That seems to me to be an accurate description of what life-history making is all about, but I think it is time that we let the pieces and the relationships and the stitching begin to show, that we begin to engage in what James Clifford (1983:137) has called polyphonic exposition. I used plural nouns in the title of this essay because I wanted to call attention to the plurality, relationality, and indeterminacy of identity that has not sufficiently informed life history writing and that, in this case, is inescapably the nature of the Pueblo conception of the person. Relationships, Henry James once remarked, never really end; the best we can hope to do is to inscribe a circle in which they might happily appear to do so.

NOTES

1. Unless otherwise indicated, these and other statements in quotation marks were made by Helen Cordero in conversations with me between 1978 and 1985.

2. For discussions of the concept of generativity, see Erikson 1963, 1964, 1974; and Kotre 1984.

3. For a very suggestive Jungian analysis of the importance of "chains" of generations in creation myths as a way of being linked "with historical continuity, i.e., from the inside, with one's ancestral soul, to be connected with the archetypal foundations of the psyche, as counter-magic against dissociation," see von Franz (1978), esp. chap. 11; quotation is from p. 204.

4. Frederick Starr's unpublished diary of his 1897 trip to Cochiti is in the University of Chicago Library Archives. The pages are not numbered.

5. Elsie Clews Parsons' unpublished manuscript, "In the Southwest," is in the American Philosophical Society Library. I am presently editing this material for publication with the University of New Mexico Press. The essays are not numbered consecutively.

6. For further discussion of these aspects of Pueblo ritual and religion, see Kurath 1960, Lange 1968, and Parsons 1939.

7. In addition to the summary statements of Pueblo origin myths made by Parsons (1939), see Cushing 1896, 1920; Stirling 1942; White 1932a, 1932b, 1935, 1942, 1962; Boas 1928; and Benedict 1981 [1931]. The motif of creation through the molding of meal, dust, or clay is not limited to origin myths but rather is widely found throughout Pueblo narratives.

8. For further discussion of the *cacique*'s "children" and associated beliefs and practices among the Keresan pueblos, see White 1932b, 1935, 1962; Lange 1968:241–48; and Bandelier's *Journals*, edited by Charles H. Lange, Carroll Riley, and Elisabeth M. Lange (1966, 1975).

9. For discussions of fertility as the dominant idea or master trope of Pueblo culture, see especially Haeberlin 1916, Cushing 1920, and Benedict 1934.

10. For discussions of "autographic objects" in which considerations of density and repleteness are coupled with a stress on origins and a history of production, see Mitchell 1986:153.

11. See Arendt 1958 and Csikszentmihalyi and Rochberg-Halton 1981 for discussions of the material creation of personal and cultural existence. See Simmel 1984 for a further discussion of "objective culture" — the world of cultural forms and their material artifacts, which define and shape human life and which, however simple and mundane, are essential elements in the production and reproduction of cultural persons and social relations. For an elaboration of the concept of "elementary cycling" and "the model of reproduction," see Weiner 1980 and 1982. The latter is based on the premise that "any society must reproduce and regenerate certain elements of value in order for the society to continue. . . . These elements of value include human beings, social relations, cosmological phenomena such as ancestors, and resources such as land, material objects, names and body decorations" (Weiner 1980:71).

12. On the importance of Pueblo pottery in the transition from a subsistence to a cash economy and gender-specific roles in the making and marketing of pottery, see Reynolds 1986 and Snow 1973. For discussions of the social and political as well as economic consequences of this transition for Rio Grande Pueblo life, see Babcock 1988 and Wade 1986.

13. For lengthier and more detailed discussions of Cochiti pottery and the politics of discourse, of female power and male dominance, and of women as a

"muted" rather than an "articulate" group vis-à-vis the dominant communicative system of the society, see Ardener 1975 and Babcock 1988.

14. See Clifford 1983 and Crapanzano 1980 for critiques of the concepts of identity, authority, and linearity that have informed the Western inscribing of non-Western lives.

REFERENCES CITED

Ardener, Edwin

1975   Belief and the Problem of Women and the 'Problem' Revisited. In *Perceiving Women*, edited by Shirley Ardener, 1–27. London: Malaby Press.

Arendt, Hannah

1958   *The Human Condition.* Chicago: University of Chicago Press.

Babcock, Barbara A.

1986   Modeled Selves: Helen Cordero's "Little People." In *The Anthropology of Experience*, edited by E. Bruner and V. Turner, 316–43. Urbana: University of Illinois Press.

1988   "At Home, No Womens Are Storytellers": Potteries, Stories, and Politics in Cochiti Pueblo. *Journal of the Southwest* 30:356–89.

Bandelier, Adolph F. A.

1966   *The Southwestern Journals of Adolph F. Bandelier, 1880–1882.* Edited by Charles H. Lange and Carroll Riley. Albuquerque: University of New Mexico Press.

1970   *The Southwestern Journal of Adolph F. Bandelier, 1883–1884.* Edited by Charles H. Lange and Carroll Riley. Albuquerque: University of New Mexico Press.

1971   *The Delight Makers.* New York: Harcourt Brace Jovanovich.
[1890]

1975   *The Southwestern Journals of Adolph F. Bandelier, 1885–1888.* Edited by Charles H. Lange, Carroll Riley, and Elisabeth M. Lange. Albuquerque: University of New Mexico Press.

Benedict, Ruth

1934   *Patterns of Culture.* Boston: Houghton Mifflin Co.

1973   *An Anthropologist at Work: Writings of Ruth Benedict.* Edited by Margaret Mead, New York: Equinox Books.

1981   *Tales of the Cochiti Indians.* Albuquerque: University of New Mexico
[1931]   Press.

Boas, Franz

1928   *Keresan Texts*. Publications of the American Ethnological Society, vol. 8.

Brody, J. J.

1976   The Creative Consumer: Survival, Revival, and Invention in Southwest Indian Arts. In *Ethnic and Tourist Arts*, edited by Nelson Graburn, 70–84. Berkeley: University of California Press.

Bunzel, Ruth

1972   *The Pueblo Potter: A Study of Creative Imagination in Primitive Art*. New York: Dover Publications.

Chapman, Kenneth M.

1950   *Pueblo Indian Pottery of the Post-Spanish Period*. Santa Fe: School of American Research.

1977   *The Pottery of Santo Domingo: A Detailed Study of Its Decoration*. Albuquerque: University of New Mexico Press.

Clifford, James

1983   On Ethnographic Authority. *Representations* 1:118–46.

Crapanzano, Vincent

1977   The Life History in Anthropological Field Work. *Anthropology and Humanism Quarterly* 2 (2): 3–7.

1980   *Tuhami: Portrait of a Moroccan*. Chicago: University of Chicago Press.

Csikszentmihalyi, Mihal, and Eugene Rochberg-Halton

1981   *The Meaning of Things: Domestic Symbols and the Self*. Cambridge: Cambridge University Press.

Curtis, Edward S.

1976   *The North American Indian*. Vol. 16. New York: Johnson Reprint
[1926]   Corporation.

Cushing, Frank Hamilton

1886   *A Study of Pueblo Pottery as Illustrative of Zuni Culture Growth*. 4th Annual Report of the Bureau of American Ethnology, 437–521.

1896   *Outlines of Zuni Creation Myths*. 13th Annual Report of the Bureau of American Ethnology, 321–447.

1920   *Zuni Breadstuff*. Indian Notes and Monographs, vol. 8. New York: Museum of the American Indian.

Dumarest, Fr. Noel

1918   *Notes on Cochiti, New Mexico*. Memoirs of the American Anthropological Association, no. 23, 135–236.

Erikson, Eric
  1963   *Childhood and Society.* New York: Norton.
  1964   *Insight and Responsibility.* New York: Norton.
  1974   *Dimensions of a New Identity.* New York: Norton.
Focillon, Henri
  1948   *The Life of Forms in Art.* New York: Wittenborn, Schultz.
Geiger, Susan N. G.
  1986   Women's Life Histories: Method and Content. *Signs* 11:334–51.
Haeberlin, H. K.
  1916   *The Idea of Fertilization in the Culture of the Pueblo Indians.* Memoirs
          of the American Anthropological Association, no. 3, 1–55.
Hardin, Margaret Ann
  1983   *Gifts of Mother Earth: Ceramics in the Zuni Tradition.* Phoenix: Heard
          Museum.
Kotre, John
  1984   *Outliving the Self: Generativity and the Interpretation of Lives.* Balti-
          more: Johns Hopkins University Press.
Kurath, Gertrude
  1960   Calling the Rain Gods. *Journal of American Folklore* 72:290, 312–15.
Lange, Charles H.
  1968   *Cochiti: A New Mexico Pueblo, Past and Present.* Carbondale: South-
          ern Illinois University Press.
MacKinnon, Catherine A.
  1983   Feminism, Marxism, Method, and the State: An Agenda for Theory. In
          The Signs Reader: Women, Gender, and Scholarship, edited by
          Elizabeth Abel and Emily K. Abel, 227–56. Chicago: University of
          Chicago Press.
Meyer, Melissa, and Miriam Schapiro
  1978   Waste Not, Want Not. *Heresies* 4:66–69.
Minnich, Elizabeth Kamarck
  1985   Friendship Between Women: The Act of Feminist Biography. *Feminist
          Studies* 11:287–305.
Mitchell, W.J.T.
  1986   *Iconology: Image, Text, Ideology.* Chicago: University of Chicago
          Press.
Ortiz, Simon J.
  1977   *A Good Journey.* Berkeley: Turtle Island.

Parsons, Elsie Clews

1919   Increase by Magic: A Zuni Pattern. *American Anthropologist* n.s. 21:279–86.

1939   *Pueblo Indian Religion.* 4 vols. Chicago: University of Chicago Press.

n.d.   "In the Southwest." Unpublished manuscript. American Philosophical Society Library.

Reynolds, Terry R.

1986   Women, Pottery, and Economics at Acoma Pueblo. In *New Mexico Women: Intercultural Perspectives,* edited by Joan Jensen and Darlis A. Miller, 279–300. Albuquerque: University of New Mexico Press.

Saunders, Charles Francis

1973   *The Indians of the Terraced Houses.* Glorieta, Tex.: Rio Grande Press.
[1912]

Silko, Leslie

1977   *Ceremony.* New York: Viking Press.

1981   Language and Literature from a Pueblo Indian Perspective. In *English Literature: Opening Up the Canon,* edited by Leslie A. Fiedler and Houston A. Baker, Jr., 54–72. Baltimore: Johns Hopkins University Press.

Simmel, Georg

1984   *On Women, Sexuality, and Love.* Translated by Guy Oakes. New Haven: Yale University Press.

Snow, David H.

1973   Some Economic Considerations of Historic Rio Grande Pueblo Pottery. In *The Changing Ways of Southwestern Indians: A Historic Perspective,* edited by A. Schroeder, 55–72. Glorieta, Tex.: Rio Grande Press.

Starr, Frederick

1897   New Mexico Trip, September, 1897. Manuscript diary. University of Chicago Library, Archives.

1899   A Study of the Census of the Pueblo of Cochiti. Davenport Academy of Sciences *Proceedings* 7:33–45.

Stirling, Matthew

1942   *Origin Myth of Acoma and Other Records.* Bureau of American Ethnology Bulletin, no. 135.

von Franz, Maria

1978   *Patterns of Creativity Mirrored in Creation Myths.* Zurich: Spring Publications.

Wade, Edwin L.
1986   Straddling the Cultural Fence: The Conflict for Ethnic Artists Within Pueblo Societies. In *The Arts of the North American Indian: Native Traditions in Evolution*, edited by Edwin L. Wade, 243–54. New York: Hudson Hills Press.

Weiner, Annette
1980   Reproduction: A Replacement for Reciprocity. *American Ethnologist* 7:71–85.
1982   Sticks and Stones, Threads and Bones: This is What Kinship is Made Of. Paper presented at the Conference on Feminism and Kinship Theory, Bellagio, Italy.

White, Leslie A.
1932a   *The Acoma Indians.* 47th Annual Report of the Bureau of American Ethnology, 17–192.
1932b   *The Pueblo of San Felipe.* Memoirs of the American Anthropological Association, no. 38.
1935   *The Pueblo of Santo Domingo.* Memoirs of the American Anthropological Association, no. 43.
1942   *The Pueblo of Santa Ana.* Memoirs of the American Anthropological Association, no. 60.
1962   *The Pueblo of Sia.* Bulletin of the Bureau of American Ethnology, no. 184.

8

Collective Fictions

Performance in Saramaka Folktales

Richard Price and Sally Price

During the past two decades the study of expressive culture has witnessed a reorientation, aptly glossed by Dell Hymes (1975) as a "breakthrough into performance."[1] Art objects (from Africa, Oceania, and Native America) that had been gathering dust in museum cases began to be recontextualized "in motion," with the help of contemporary ethnography, video, and multimedia presentations (see, for example, Thompson 1974). Folktales that had been silenced on the printed page were given new life, not just through structuralism, deconstruction, and other new textual modes of analysis but also by ethnographic recontextualization and attention to the performative dimension of their telling (Abrahams 1983; Basso 1987; Cosentino 1982; Crowley 1966; Falassi 1980; Hymes 1981; Seitel 1980; Sherzer and Woodbury 1987; Tanna 1984; Tedlock 1972). Visual or verbal arts, previously analyzed largely in static, normative modalities (almost as *langue* rather than *parole*) began to be examined in their quotidian settings as lively arts within the context of ongoing expressive cultures.

Folklore studies among the Suriname Maroons[2] have not yet caught up with these scholarly trends. The available published collections (for example, Herskovits and Herskovits 1936, Hurault 1961, and numerous pamphlets by members of the Summer Institute of Linguistics) continue to favor written over oral communication. Often, "informants" have been asked to tell a tale (in artificial and often "taboo" circumstances) — in an investigator's temporary quarters, phrase by slow phrase, to an interpreter who, phrase by slow phrase, rendered a version to the investigator, who then wrote "it" down. Or, in the case of the Summer Institute of Linguistics, potential Christian converts (usually children) learning to read and write have been given the exercise of writing out a tale in their own language. Although a faithful Lévi-Straussian might argue that none of this matters (since the "structure" of the tale would in theory be recoverable by the analyst even from corrupt texts like these), it is our experience as ethnographers that there is little relationship between such tales (which are, ultimately, little more than artifacts of their elicitation) and those that form such an integral part of the Maroon moral and aesthetic universe. The folktales of the Saramaka Maroons, which are told only at wakes (or, rarely, in horticultural camps away from the villages), reflect central cultural values and aesthetic principles. Viewed from the perspective of performance, they reveal much about what it means to be Saramaka.[3]

Saramaka folktales (*kóntu*) are closely associated with funeral celebrations. The immediate goal of every Saramaka funeral (which serves ultimately to usher a recently deceased member of the community into the world of the ancestors) is "to bury the deceased with celebration [*pizíi*]." Amidst the hectic weeks of drumming, dancing, singing, feasting, and complex rituals that contribute to these festivities, the telling of folktales — which takes place during the night after the actual burial (as well as, for some deaths, on subsequent nights) — constitutes a special moment for people of all ages. The setting is more intimate than other funeral-related gatherings, typically involving some thirty to forty kinsfolk and neighbors sitting on stools before the deceased's doorstep. Together, they in effect agree to transport themselves into a separate reality that they collectively create and maintain: *kóntu-kôndè* ("folktale-land," an earlier time and a distant place), where animals speak, where the social order is often inverted, where Saramaka customs have been only partially worked out, and where the weak and clever tend to triumph over the strong and arrogant. For Saramakas, folktales are sharply distinguished from history; *kóntu* are fictions with deep moral lessons for the present, not accounts of "what really happened."[4] Sitting by torchlight or the light of the moon, the participants at a tale-telling wake come face-to-face with age-old metaphysical problems and conundrums. By turns frightened by the antics of a villainous monster, doubled over with laughter at a lascivious song, or touched by a character's sentimental farewell, they experience an intellectually and emotionally rich evening of multimedia entertainment.

Such a session is privileged in terms of the social solidarity it expresses. Individuals (whether neighbors or kin) whose daily lives include frequent and strongly felt frictions of various sorts lay aside their differences for an evening to honor the dead. This shared sense of community contributes much to the effectiveness with which *kóntu* provide a stage for the discussion of morality. Everyone present can react in concert to the actions of the characters in folktale-land; with competing personal interests no longer a factor, people who normally quarrel over just such issues can agree on what is right or wrong, justified or outrageous, cunning or foolish. And as people of all ages are present when tales are told, *kóntu* represent an important crucible for socialization.

The stock characters in Saramaka folktales number in the scores and have diverse provenances. Some, like the "scrawny little kid" (usually the youngest sibling, who saves his sister from disaster), appear throughout Afro-America (Abrahams 1985:22);[5] others, like the ubiquitous "devils," have at least partial Christian European roots; still others, like Anasi the Spider (and his numerous progeny) or — more remarkably — Elephant (an animal whose memory is preserved by Saramakas at a remove of three centuries) are African to the core. The bulk of *kóntu-kôndè* characters are humans, more or less like Saramakas themselves, and familiar animals of their own South American rain forest — Jaguar, Deer, Cayman, Howler Monkey, Hummingbird, Anaconda, and a host of others. And there are, in addition, frequent cameo appearances by special figures such as Death and the Great God. One memorable character is the mysterious stranger whose impressive dancing inspires Anasi to run up to him and offer a congratulatory embrace; only after the damage has been done does he, and the other spectators who smell his soiled body, realize that the stranger was Shit himself. The characters that inhabit folktale-land are familiar to all Saramakas, and their individual gifts and foibles are frequently alluded to, by way of comparison, in everyday discourse about the here and now.

The plots of Saramaka tales—by turns dramatic, fabulous, riotous, and sentimental—combine the ordinary with the extraordinary. Many of their initial settings are familiar to Saramakas from everyday experience, and characters move the action forward on the basis of quite ordinary motives (such as greed, revenge, altruism, or fear). But while Saramaka parents, for example, must deal with the temporary loss of a daughter who marries out, it is only in tales that she goes off to the land of a husband who is an elephant, cayman, or eagle; while Saramaka men commonly call on magical charms to help them in hunting, it is only in tales that a feather plus a magic word allows them to kill without another weapon; and while Saramakas often argue about who has the right to raise a particular child, it is only in tales that they rip the child in two and each take half.

Some tales depend on a character's raw cunning, as in the story of the boy who tricked a tough-skinned white boss into feeling pain or the tale of the young girl who escaped from the devil by a sexual distraction. In others, the magical component is more central, as when characters are revived from the dead, usually by the squeezing of special juices into their eyes, or when a magical ordeal determines the fate of those who have transgressed a taboo. Frequently, an underdog hero benefits from the advice of a supernatural being or a character in possession of special ritual knowledge. Thus, the Old Woman of the Forest whispers the magical word *aditô* to Goat, whose relatives are being killed off by Jaguar, enabling him to kill the physically more powerful members of the latter's clan, much to their mutual astonishment. In another tale, whose plot unfolds somewhat along the lines of *The Wizard of Oz*, Great God himself lays out techniques by which a young boy can solve a whole string of characters' dilemmas. Sometimes the ritual aid assumes a tangible form, such as a needle that can kill the devil or a magical bundle that turns a fart into a deadly weapon.

Plots can also advance through the *rejection* of good advice. Stubborn children regularly get into trouble by disregarding the advice of their elders—for example, the two sisters whose mother had told them to take the more overgrown of two paths into the forest but who instead opt for the well-cleared one and meet up with a lecherous devil. Many tales center on a quest for the solution to a problem (for example, a boy's pilgrimage to the land of the devils explicitly in order to discover drums), but others bring about change inadvertently (as in the tale about how Anasi's interactions with Old Man Death ended in a fight in which Anasi sought refuge in his own village, bringing Death out of the forest and into human society, where he has been a part of life ever since). And the plots of many tales center on some kind of contest—a wrestling match to decide which of two men will get a woman, a life-and-death endurance contest between a dancing boy and a drumming devil, or a dance competition to determine whether Anasi will get to sleep with a beautiful young girl.

In terms of themes, some tales chronicle the origins of institutions and other aspects of life as known today: how, for example, particular stretches of forest, once inhabited by devils or monsters, came to be habitable by humans; how drums, fire, or sickness were introduced to the Saramaka world; how various animals came to look or act the way they do; or why it is that men and women live together, that men may have more than one wife, or that men must give presents to their wives. Other tales are concerned with central structural tensions in Saramaka life, for example those so common in a matrilineal society between consanguineal and affinal kin, those between men and women who are participating in a polygynous marriage system, or those between Saramakas and outsiders—the coastal bosses for whom Saramaka men must work for wages, the Christians who attempt to introduce their religion, or the schoolteachers who hold the powerful key to literacy. Still other tales have cosmological overtones: the separation of day from night, the land of the living from that of the dead, or the waters from dry earth. But the thematic core of most tales is moral, communicating such central ideological concerns as the need to be wary of non-Saramakas.

Before taking up performance in Saramaka folktales, it would be well to make a brief detour into Saramaka performance more generally.[6] From a broad comparative perspective it can be argued that Saramakas exhibit an unusual appreciation of nuances in voice, accent, gesture, and posture. Playfulness, creativity, and improvisation permeate conversation, making even everyday speech a lively art. Spontaneously invented elliptical phrases frequently substitute for standard words so that, for example, a watch may become a "back-of-the-wrist motor," food "under-the-nose material," a stool "the rump's rejoicing," and (in the folktale presented below) swimming "underwater work." Speech play assumes other forms as well: verbal dueling by young men (involving the improvisation and recital of run-on strings of wittily phrased insults); the casual insertion of foreign-language expressions (e.g., from French Guiana creole, coastal Suriname creole, Dutch, or English); and elaborate secret play languages (usually developed by groups of young men). Saramakas' interest in individual mannerisms inspires frequent verbal and gestural mimicry. The expressive, dramatic quality of Saramaka life comes through also in the spontaneous songs and dances that are sparked by mundane but happy events. We once saw an elderly woman who had been fishing without success for more than an hour catch a tiny fish. Dropping into a sitting position in the shallow water, she broke into a sinuous dance of celebration with her upper torso. Another time, a woman with a new enamel bucket on her head noticed one of us passing her door and sang out a spontaneous little song: "The red bucket suits my 'sister-in-law,' look how the red bucket suits my 'sister-in-law.'"

Saramaka performances, at all levels of formality, are characterized by total participation and the highly structured (though at the same time fluid) nature of interplay among participants, rendering inappropriate the analytical use of Western distinctions between "audience" and "performer." For example, certain stylized contrapuntal patterns recur in everyday speech and gossip, the formal rhetoric of ritual and judicial sessions, public song/dance/drum performances, and the telling of tales. Normal conversations are punctuated by one of the listeners, who offers supportive comments such as "That's right," "Yes indeed," or "Not at all." Even when men living on the coast send tape-recorded messages back to their villages, they leave pauses after each phrase so that the "conversation" may assume its proper two-party form when the tape is played.

In formalized settings, such as tale-telling, stylized responses become more frequent, and the responsibility for providing them is assumed by a particular individual; discussions involving the Tribal Chief, for example, are always conducted with the rhetorical aid of a third party, who explicitly represents the "public" presence. Prayers also assume an antiphonal structure as participants support the speaker's words at frequent intervals with slow hand clapping and a specially intoned declaration of "Great thanks." Solo work songs are repeatedly interrupted by the comments of others present, and popular song forms are built on the alternation of a soloist and a responsive chorus. Whatever the specific context, this fundamental contrapuntal pattern expresses the ongoing, active engagement of people other than the principal speaker or performer.

A closely related feature of Saramaka performance is role-switching between a temporary soloist and other participants. For example, song/dance/drum "plays" are characterized by the emergence of a succession of individual soloists, each of whom briefly enjoys center stage and then yields to another. In other words, in terms of the structure of participation, Saramaka performances resemble a jazz jam session rather than the playing of a piano concerto, and such structuring supports the balance between the complementary Saramaka values of individual virtuosity and full communal participation.

Many kinds of cultural events in Saramaka, including tale-telling, exhibit a common diachronic structure characterized by repeated interruptions. An initial exposition is interrupted by another, which in turn may be interrupted by a third, with subsequent portions of each unfolding — often with further interruptions — throughout the performance. (The link between adjoining segments is usually a thin, and often obscure, associative thread.) For example, either a divinatory seance with an oracle or a formal court session might proceed from A (the first case) to B, to a continuation of A, to the end of B, to a continuation of A, to the beginning of C, to the whole of D, to another continuation of A, to the end of C, and finally to the end of A. This practice of interrupting and overlaying segments strung out through time is closely related to central features of Saramaka musical performance, as with drummers' or singers' staggered points of entry and the pervasiveness of polyrhythms.

These very general features of Saramaka performance (which are paralleled by fundamental Saramaka concepts about the unfolding of events through time) are part of the historical synthesis that the original maroons and their immediate descendants forged during the late seventeenth and early eighteenth centuries. Ethnographic evidence makes clear that features such as antiphonal speech and song, verbal indirection, ellipsis, play, "interruption" as a syntagmatic principle, and interactive participation in performative events were already firmly established by the second half of the eighteenth century (see R. Price 1990). On the plantations of coastal Suriname, slave songs were described from a European viewpoint as "melodious but without Time; in Other respects [they are] not unlike that of some Clarks reading to the Congregation, One Person Pronouncing a Sentence Extemporary, which he next hums or Whistles, when all the others Repeat the Same in Chorus, another sentence is then Spoke and the Chorus is Renew'd a Second time & So ad perpetuum" (Stedman 1988 [1790]:516). German missionaries from that period complained that their sermons were frequently disrupted: "One [Saramaka listener] said, 'Teacher, today we understand your words.' Another said, 'What you say is the truth.' A third, 'I see that our Obia men have deceived us.' A fourth, 'I believe that the great God is the only one'" (R. Price 1990:254). Unfortunately, we have little specific information about eighteenth-century folktales, since neither the missionaries nor the Dutch civil servants who lived among the Saramakas seem to have been interested in such matters.[7]

An evening of *kóntu* usually begins with riddling, a long string of witty prompts and responses exchanged by two people at rapid-fire pace, ideally without pause. After a few minutes of riddles, someone calls out "*Mató!*" the opening formula for *kóntu*, and someone else responds, loudly, "*Tòngóni!*"[8] At this signal, everyone present steps over the invisible barrier into folktale-land.

Once begun, each tale should be "interrupted" or "cut into" by several minitales (or "tale-nuggets"); Saramakas use the word *kóti* (to cut [into, across, or off]) in talking about this interruptive pattern. Each tale-nugget briefly evokes a longer tale, often simply through a song that plays a pivotal role in the fuller version. The aesthetic success of an evening of tale-telling depends explicitly on the frequency of people "cutting in" with such nuggets; when a tale is allowed to proceed too long without one, people chide one another until someone cuts in and restores the evening's rhythmic momentum. As in other Saramaka speech settings, formal "responses" are regularly interjected into the narrative; a particular individual (called a *píkima*, a responder) accepts responsibility for the task for the duration of a tale, punctuating most of the teller's phrase endings with the conventional "*íya*," but occasionally varying for effect ("That's true," "Really!" or "Right") and shifting to the negative ("Certainly not!" "No way," or simply "No") as the narrative requires. For interruptive tale-nuggets, it is usually the teller of the main tale who serves as responder.

To participate in an evening of tale-telling is to join speakers and listeners in the collective creation and maintenance of a fictional but richly significant separate reality. Its specialness is underscored by various devices: before launching into a ribald song, a man might say "When you're doing tale-telling like this, there are certain things you say, so everybody please excuse me. If fathers-in-law are present . . . If mothers-in-law are present, we're not doing that kind of [polite] talking. Today is for Anasi stories, not for father-in-law or mother-in-law matters! We mustn't take offense." And a number of the most striking performative features of *kóntu* serve to enhance the persuasiveness of this other reality. Saramaka tale-tellers (and "interrupters") situate themselves right at the center of the action; they were "there" when it happened. Various rhetorical devices contribute to this eyewitness effect. One is the common practice of asserting almost formulaically that "When [for example] Cayman was carrying the boy across the river [or the two brothers were setting out to seek wives, or the devil was leering at the young girl], I was standing right there! And I saw Squirrel wrestling with Mouse [or Dog chasing Goat, or the Old Woman sweeping her doorstep with her breasts]." Others are more participatory: "Well, just when Jaguar was dragging that stream for fish, I was standing there on the shore, and he asked me to help out." Similarly, current place names and relationships are frequently inserted at the outset of a tale to create verisimilitude and familiarity, and listeners often insert themselves into the story by remarking on how *they* would have handled a particular dilemma or challenge. Speakers also use frequent shunts between tenses or perspectives to enhance the sense of a story's immediacy. One moves quickly, for example, from a description of what "people" used to do to get wage labor jobs on the coast to "You'd go and ask the white man," which, in turn, might be complemented by some version of the "I was there" rhetoric. Similarly, one finds passages that move rapidly from "They went along" or "They were doing such and so" to "The wind is coming up."

Direct discourse serves as another concretizing device, and it permits a variety of emotional effects. Speakers frequently mimic characters, sometimes with facial expressions and gestures as well as speech. Foreign words and accents crop up frequently, evoking, for example, the speech of urban bosses, French gendarmes, or Hindustani shopkeepers; and the devil characteristically speaks Sranan, the creole language of the coast. All active tale-tellers cultivate stylistic specialties. One male teller is especially appreciated for the sweet, innocent voice of an adolescent virgin about to be hoodwinked by a devil; another brings down the house with his nasalized, stuttering rendition of Anasi the spider, as he engages in one or another mischievous trick. One elderly woman is the undisputed master of onomatopoeic descriptions, such as the exquisitely innocent "*píí páá, píí páá*" of devils who are feigning sleep, the rambunctious "*a tiá gbéngbelen, a tiá gbéngbelen*" when they are *really* snoring, or the "*Hólo bigódo, hólo gwégede*" as plates of food are tossed into the devil's upturned asshole and clang downward to join the motley assortment of pots, human bones, and other detritus that rests in his belly.

Tale-telling sessions are supremely interactive, involving not only tellers, responders, and those who "cut into" the *kóntu* with tale-nuggets, but also others who put in their own two cents' worth. The comments and questions of all of these contribute visibly to reality maintenance. Extraordinary characters and situations are constantly made to seem reasonable; what would be nonsensical outside of folktale-land is repeatedly brought into the realm of logic. Like well-meaning tourists in a foreign country, participants at a tale-telling session struggle to learn the rules of appropriateness in this other milieu. For example, we will see below how a woman named Akóbo frequently engages ongoing exotic events through commentary: "Imagine a husband who carries you on his back! And with your basket on your head!" Some brief interjections place a listener right into the story, at least in an "as if" mode: "*I* would have been happy to dig up the gold when that happened." Other such side comments tell the characters what to do (or not to do), much in the way someone identifying with a character in a horror film might gasp "No! Don't open the door!" Still others simply express support for a seemingly unlikely part of the story: "Well yes, Jaguar and Goat would have become friends, because when you live next door to someone, you become friends."

Folklorists interested in performance have developed a variety of textual strategies and notational devices to deal with the problem of representing oral materials on the printed page. In deciding how to present Saramaka *kóntu* to a non-Saramaka audience, we have adapted a number of these and developed some of our own as well. Like Basso (1987), Burns (1983), Cosentino (1982), Dauenhauer and Dauenhauer (1987), Seitel (1980), Tedlock (1972, 1983), and others, we try to help the reader imagine an actual oral performance with translations that pay careful attention to stylistic features such as rhythm, structure, and phrasing. While indebted to these pioneers in folklore transcription, our mode of presentation is also molded by the specifics of Saramaka discourse. In the spirit of Abrahams (1986), we have chosen, more than most of our predecessors in the field, to stress the communal, interactive aspects of tale-telling. Rather than basing our phrasing on the relative or absolute duration of narrators' pauses (as in Seitel 1980 or Tedlock 1972, 1983) or on the literary analysis of versification (as in Hymes 1981), we segment our text at points when the speaker's narration was audibly "cut" by a conventional response, a listener's question, generalized laughter, or extraneous conversation that interrupted the story's continuity.

Prompted by the conviction that Saramaka *kóntu* make little sense outside their performance setting, our book and this essay present seriatim everything that fell within our tape recorder's range, from a mother reprimanding her child for knocking over a lantern and people arguing about the right way to chorus a particular song, to the tale-teller excusing himself for some slip of the tongue or a listener announcing that she's sleepy and is only going to stay for one more story. We include (as ex post facto "stage directions" in our texts) nonverbalized aspects of the recording, such as various kinds of laughter, clucks of moral disapproval, murmurs of sympathetic condolence, exclamations of indignation, and so forth, as well as indications of the gestures and dances that contributed to the appreciation of the performance. It is our conviction that an understanding of those devices, routines, and incidents that make *Saramakas* laugh, exclaim, feel sad, and so forth is one important avenue leading to our understanding of meaning.

We do not reconstruct those pieces of the performance that are missing from our tapes even when we have reason to believe that they were part of the original performance. For example, if our microphone did not pick up the standard opening exchange (*Mató! . . . Tòngôni!*), it does not appear in our translation. And when collective laughter drowns out the conventional "responses" that punctuate a narrative segment, no such response appears in the text. The actual experience of any individual present at such a session is imperfect in much the same way that a tape recording is, and it could be argued that to reconstruct those elements that we know "should" be present would create an artificial, hypercorrected text.

Distinctive personalities emerge through the interactions of speaker and listeners. The elderly Kandámma fulfills her well-established role as instructor in esoteric meanings; Antonísi, the main teller's rather shy younger brother, aborts his telling of a comical interruptive nugget when his giggling runs out of control; Akóbo is true to form in her persistent self-insertion into the heads of various characters; and Asabôsi, the deceased woman's daughter, dutifully takes on responsibility for the success of the wake by prodding people to volunteer more tale-nuggets.

We have chosen a tale told in 1968 about midway through the wake held after the burial of an elderly woman named Sindóbóbi. Volunteered by Kasólu, a classificatory grandson of Sindóbóbi from a downstream village, it is a relatively straightforward telling, with none of the wild hysteria that sometimes characterizes more sexually explicit tales or the performances by more histrionic tale-tellers. Twenty-one years after the recording was made, we met up again with Kasólu, this time at the French missile base in French Guiana where he and his brothers (who had been at that wake) were providing manual labor. They were able to clarify those allusions and double entendres that depended on the explication of the participants. That experience revived our sense of the strong entertainment value of *kóntu*, as the half dozen men who attended our afternoon sessions reacted to the unfolding plots on our tapes with the same emotional involvement as on the night of Sindóbóbi's burial.

The tale itself deals with some heavy themes — the impelling solidarity of siblings even when they do not know of each others' existence; the emotional costs of virilocal residence, which isolates a woman from her family; the ambivalence of both brothers-in-law and "formal friends," who juggle solidarity and hostility in a precarious balance; the separation of edible foods from those prohibited to humans; the division of the world into land, air, and water (here represented by Elephant, Eagle, and Cayman); the alternation of night and day; the relationship between body and soul (which allows the killing of a monster by an attack on his physically separated "heartbeat"); the issue of mortality and rebirth (as the temporary replacement of a severed head brings the reptilian monster briefly back to life); and the delineation of nature and culture (in this case, the establishment of a boundary around the territory in which an anthropophagous snake has been vanquished).

But at the same time, the ambience during this narration was consistently light and fun-filled, with comments focusing on the specifics of the story rather than on its cosmological and moral messages. There was real empathy for the mother who watched her last child leave home in search of his sisters, cautious disbelief at the announcement of Jaguar's alleged death, curiosity about where a woman would hold her basket if she had a husband who carried her on his back, joy at the recognition scenes between brother and sister, concern over the appropriate etiquette for those encounters, amusement at the inevitable appearance of Anasi as soon as there was glory to be claimed, nervousness at moments of oblivious relaxation when danger was clearly at hand, incredulity when the tale's hero declared his feelings of affection toward the twelve-headed monster, and some discussion of that monster's gullibility when the boy claimed he was going off to urinate and would be right back. Insofar as the tale carried deeper significance, this was communicated via the low-level concerns of *kóntu-kôndè* characters, reacting to rather extraordinary situations through the application of rather ordinary and everyday principles of social interaction.

Kasólu's tale, along with the various "interruptions" of it, illustrates many of the performative features of Saramaka tale-telling sessions. We present it here in support of our contention that it is the interactive, communal nature of such sessions that not only lends Saramaka folktales their value as entertainment but also empowers them as vehicles for the expression and negotiation of central cultural principles.

The conventions we use in the following translation (spelled out in greater detail in R. and S. Price 1991:23–37) include the following: "Responses" from a designated responder appear between slashes (e.g., /*íya*/), with the responder's name given only when a new person takes on that role. Significant pauses appear as three ellipsis points between slashes (/ . . . /). Especially loud speech is printed in uppercase. Multi-voice portions of songs (either choral responses to the soloist or supportive joining with the soloist's voice) are set in bold italics. Saramaka words are set in italics; clarifications of obscure phrases, translations or explanations of songs, and our own ex post facto "stage directions" are given in brackets.

Kasólu:	*Mató!*
Antonísi:	*Tòngôni!*
Kasólu:	So there they were. /Antonísi: *íya*/

There was a woman who had three daughters. (This isn't a singing tale, y' hear? So you can cut into it with a song very nicely, and a little dance too!) A woman had three daughters /*íya*/
and those girls were more beautiful than you can imagine. / . . . /

Asabôsi: [to a child who's crying] My goodness, don't hang onto me like that!

Kasólu: So many men asked them to marry them that there weren't any men left in the whole world who hadn't.

Abátelí: Except that I myself didn't ever get there. If I had been around, they certainly would have wanted me.

Kandámma: You're right. They would have.

Kasólu: Well, all the young men had already asked, but Elephant was still left. /*íya*/
Elephant set out *vúúún* — /*íya*/
He and Cayman [long pause], as well as Eagle. /*íya*/
The three men set out along a path /*íya*/
and they went to propose marriage. They kept asking people for directions. /*íya*/
And finally they got there. /*íya*/
They turned themselves into sharplooking young guys, really handsome. So they got there. That's all. / . . . / Once they got there, they went to propose marriage. Elephant asked for the oldest one. /*íya*/
Eagle asked for the middle one. /*íya*/
Cayman asked for the youngest one. /*íya*/
Well, once they all got there, nothing to it. Those women, well it was like something came over them. They all started pointing out which one they wanted.

Antonísi:	[breaking in] At that time, I was standing there.
Kasólu:	What was happening?
Antonísi:	Okay! Well, what's-his-name — [clears throat ostentatiously] Goat. /Kasólu: *ÍYA!*/
Antonísi:	Goat and what's-his-name — the Village Animal [i.e., Dog] — /right!/ They were going to run after a woman.
Kasólu:	[chuckling] How were they going to run after her?
Antonísi:	You want to know how they ran?
Kasólu:	Yeah, how did they run?

Antonísi:	[doing a little dance mimicking the funny way that Dog was running]
	    Mbèè, mbèè Selína. Na f'i éde mi e dêdè
	    Mbèè, mbèè Selína. *Selína, mbèè . . .*
	[*Mbèè mbèè* is the braying sound of Goat. Selína is the woman's name. *Na f'i éde mi e dêdè* means "I would die for you." A couple of voices join in the "*mbèè, mbèè Selína*," but the song never really gets to a clear alternation of solo and chorus before being cut short by giggles. In 1987, Antonísi explained to us that the song alludes to a story in which Dog made love to the woman that Goat had lined up for himself, and that's why people always say that wherever Dog is absent, that's where Goat will go hunting. That is, Goat tries to avoid Dog, because Dog interferes, takes things away from him, and generally causes him grief.]

Antonísi and others:	[hysterical laughter]
Antonísi:	[still laughing] Let's just forget it, guys. I can't go on talking. No, I really can't go on. It's too much for me.
A man:	Go on with the other story.

PRICE AND PRICE

Antonísi:	Go on with your story!
Kasólu:	Well, as for the women themselves, /Antonísi: Right./ The oldest one points out the one she wants. /íya/ She points at Elephant, saying, Okay, this is the husband she wants. /íya/ The other one said the same thing to Eagle. /íya/ The youngest one said it to Cayman. /íya/ Those guys! Even before they arrived, the women started wanting them. /íya/ They asked for wives, /íya/ beautiful wives. /íya/ The girls' mother didn't like it. /íya/ But the daughters said they wouldn't listen. /íya/ They went ahead and took husbands. /íya/ There they were with their husbands. The next day dawned. They went on like this for many days. Well, the way it is in folktale-land is just like, well, let's admit it, the things that happen in Saramaka don't happen there, 'cause in Saramaka, families loan out wives, /íya/ but in Western countries they give wives. /íya/ In folktale-land they give you a wife. /íya/ But Saramakas—Bush Negroes lend them. /íya/ So what they did there was they actually gave those men wives. /íya/ They really gave them, for them to take away, and even to bury them after they died.[9] /íya/ That's just how it was. /íya/
Kandámma:	Well, at that very moment—/Kasólu: íya/ Well, Jaguar's mother had died. /That's right./ They washed the body and laid it out. They did everything properly. Then Jaguar went to Howler Monkey to ask him to help perform papá.[10] /íya/
Others:	[laughter]

Kandámma: So Howler Monkey came. Howler Monkey came for the *papá*-play. /hm!/
He was there at the *papá*-play for a little while.
And then Howler Monkey sang a song. Jaguar's mother was dead. /*íya*/
She was there with a club and a machete. /*íya*/
The mother, that dead-as-a-doornail person— They took a club and put it on one side of her. They took a machete and put it on the other side. /*íya*/
And Howler Monkey was supposed to come help perform the *papá*. /That's right./
So Howler Monkey came and he sang:

Konoi: Was it at the funeral house that they went to play *papá*?

Kandámma: It was at the funeral house that they went to play *papá*.

Others: [laughter]

Kandámma: *Ahéééé, ee ahéééé! Ahóóó, ee ahééé!*
Ambê yéi ká Tatá Domó dêdè wan tuú tuú dêdè-oo,
ma a dê ku ahitigóó ku agwamtoóku-ooo.
        /*íya*/
Ahééé, ee ahóóó! Ahééé, ee ahééé!
Ambê si ká Domó dêdè wan tuú tuú dêdè-ooo,
ma a dê ku ahitigóó ku agwamtoóku-ooo.
[Line 1 is a series of exclamations. Lines 2–3 mean "Who'd ever believe that if Father Jaguar died for real, he'd have a club and a machete with him there?" Although these two lines are largely in Saramaccan, the terms for club (*ahitigóó*) and machete (*agwamtoóku*) are Komantí words that are used in *papá* singing.][11]
Go ahead with your story.

Kasólu: Okay! Well, once they had been given wives, they

	said, "Okay, women, no problem. We'll leave in the morning.
Asabôsi:	[exclamation]
Kasólu:	We'll go off together." (They agreed.) They got everything together until they were all ready, and then they set out on the path. / . . . / They left. They continued on for a while, and then they said, "Women, stay here." ("All right," they said.)
Asabôsi:	[complaining] This tale isn't being answered well.
Kasólu:	Well, one of them had borrowed one limb. Let's say you'd borrowed an arm from some person. /Antonísi: *íya*/ Now you go back, pull off the arm, and give it back. Then you return and put on your animal limb. /*íya*/ The next one went off and came back and put on his cayman's limb. /*íya*/ The last one went off and came back and took his wing. /*íya*/
A woman:	Uh oh, things are already getting really bad!
Kasólu:	So back and forth they went, taking off limbs and putting others on, and then one of them turns around to ask, "Wife, are you afraid?" /*íya*/
Akóbo:	[apprehensively] Uh oh!
Kasólu:	She says to her husband, "No, Husband, how could I be afraid? I loved you so much I married you." / . . . / Well, how could she answer otherwise?
Overlapping women's voices:	[discussion of the dilemma of how to act in such a situation]
Kasólu:	Because if you said anything else, that'd be the end of your relatives. /*íya*/

Kandámma:	That would really be the end!
Kasólu:	Then they kept on going. /*íya*/ Elephant turned completely back into an elephant. /*íya*/ Just the way an elephant is. /*íya*/ Eagle turned into an eagle. /*íya*/ Cayman turned into a cayman. /*íya*/
Kandámma:	With his bugging-out eyes!
Kasólu:	Cayman starts limping along, *katja, katja*. /*íya*/ Eagle can't even walk. /*íya*/ He cried out, *hòòò!* His wings were really bothering him. /*íya*/
Akóbo:	I bet he's going to fly.
Kasólu:	As for Elephant, he's very uncomfortable too. /*íya*/ Finally he said, "Wife —" /*íya*/ ("Yes," she said.) "This business's bothering me, this walking. /*íya*/ It really is hindering us a little. If you could just jump onto my back, with your basket, and secure everything so it's not in your way, and then take hold of me, /*íya*/ we could head on out. We'd get to our village as quick as can be. Wouldn't even take half an hour." /*íya*/ He said, "Wife, that's all you have to do." / . . . / She climbed right on. /*íya*/
Konoi:	She's as good as dead already.
Kasólu:	She got on and gave a kick, *gbem*, /*íya*/ *gbem gídi, pííí*, and off they went. / . . . / They went to their village. /*íya*/
Akóbo:	Imagine a husband who carries you on his back!
Others:	[laughter]
Akóbo:	And with your basket on your head!

Kasólu: Eagle said, "Oh, Wife, the way we're walking along here, something's bothering me. /*íya*/
The way we're doing things, the way we're going along here — If you could just get under my wing, /*íya*/
along with your basket, and hold onto me, /*íya*/
it seems to me we could make it." /*íya*/

Asabôsi: Where's she going to put the basket?

Kasólu: "Mm," she said, "all right." She said, "I'm not afraid." /*íya*/
He flew off, /*íya*/

Akóbo: [speaking on top of Kasólu] How's she supposed to be afraid?! She's taken him as a husband!

Kasólu: and they left without a trace. /*íya*/
They went to their village. Cayman is walking along there and he says, "Wife, something's bothering me. /*íya*/

A woman: [speaking on top of Kasólu] Well, his teeth — they must be one of the things that are bothering him.

Kasólu: The way we're doing things, the way we're walking on the shore here, /*íya*/
it's difficult for me. /*íya*/
If you could take your basket and get on the back of my head, right on the point of my head here, holding on to your basket, we could make it. Hold on to me right here. /*íya*/
Quickly, quickly." He jumped into the water.

A woman: [speaking on top of Kasólu] The water's getting *tjen! tjen!* [filled with ripples]

Kasólu: She said, "No problem." Swoosh! In a moment, they're right there in their village. /*íya*/
They came out of the water. /*íya*/

Akóbo: Well, the woman there — does she know underwater
              work?

Kasólu: Mmm. They came out of the water. /íya/
              Once they arrived there, they stayed there a
              VERY LONG TIME — for really quite a number
              of years! /íya/
              Their mother and father never heard from them
              again. They said, "Uh huh, we told them so. /íya/
              We told them that those men there were not the
              sort of men they should marry. Here we are, and
              we don't hear a single word from them. They're
              finished." /íya/
              They really didn't know what to do. All the [classi-
              ficatory] mothers and fathers were back there. But
              the girls were off with their husbands. /íya/
              So things went along like that, until one day a boy
              was born [back in their village]. /íya/
              So there the boy was for a long time. Well! He
              eventually became familiar with ritual things, and
              after a while an *óbia* talked to him and said, "The
              fact is that you have three sisters. /íya/
              Your sisters are such and such, and they took
              husbands at such and such a time." /íya/
              ("I see," he said.) Then after a while he came to ask
              his mother and father about it, and he said,
              "Mother — " (She replied.) "When you gave birth
              to me, was I the only child you had in the world?"
              /íya/
              They said, "Yes, son. You're the only child we have.
              We've never had any other children." /íya/
              ("I see," he said.) Things went along for a long
              time. Then he asked them — he said, "Mother, the
              thing I asked you both about. You haven't really
              answered me. Am I the only child you've ever
              had?" /íya/

"Yes," she said. And then she said, "Son — " (He
replied.) She said, "You're not the only child we've
had. /íya/
We had three sisters before you were born. /íya/
But they took husbands in such and such a way.
The fact is, they married trouble. /íya/
It's already been so many years since they left." He
said, "Really?" ("Yes," they said.) He said, "I'm
going to go find them." She said, "Well, all right."
/íya/
He got everything ready, and when the time came
he said he was going after them. His parents told
him not to. And then the mother started crying.
/íya/
She couldn't bear to hear such a thing. /íya/
He said, "I'm ready." He'd prepared [ritually] till he
was as ready as he could be. /íya/
The boy — he said he would go. / . . . / He prepared
[ritually] one of his hats. /íya/
He prepared a hunting sack. /íya/
And then he set out, *gwelei!* He said, "Let my
'hat' — "[12] He said for his hat to take care of him.
/íya/
"Let my 'hat' take care of me." He set right out and
got to the path along Elephant's creek, /íya/ *tjálá!*
He kept going on and on until he arrived. /íya/
Now, when he got there he saw the woman sweeping around her door, swish swish swish. He gave
her a "Greetings, Aunt." She replied, "Greetings,
Boy." /íya/

Akóbo: [surprised at the formal archaic greeting that has
just been exchanged] Oh!! "Greetings, Boy"!!

Kasólu: He said, "How are you?" "Quite fine," she said.
"Good," he said. "Say, woman, please, I'd appreciate
it if you'd give me a little water to drink." /íya/

She said, "Boy?" ("Yes," he said.) She said [here Kasólu begins speaking in an exaggeratedly girlish voice:] "It's been so many years since I first came here." /íya/
("Yes," he said.) "Well, I never meet a soul anymore. Whatever brought you here? Look where you crossed the stream over there and came all the way here to ask me for a little water to drink. /íya/
Don't you know that my husband could show up here and kill you?" /íya/
"Woman," he said. (She replied.) "Is that how mean you are? /íya/
IF YOUR BROTHER were the one who came here, would you be cruel to him like this?" They embraced each other over and over again. /íya/
They hugged and hugged. She said to him, "Boy, the way my husband is, /íya/
when he gets here, if he sees you, he'll certainly kill you." /íya/
He said, "No way! Your husband can't kill me, /íya/
'cause I'm [ritually] quicker than your husband. If he tries to fool with me, I'll kill him."

Others: [exclamations of surprise]

Kasólu: He asked, "When your husband's coming, will you know it?" She said, "I'll know." /íya/
So that's all.

Kandámma: Was it his sister he met?

Kasólu: It was his sister, his oldest sister.

Kandámma: [an exclamation of sympathy]

Akóbo: The oldest sister is the one who married the big guy.

Kasólu: Yes. They were there for quite a while. /íya/
In the evening they cooked and ate. /íya/
Then, after a while, sure enough, there he comes

[guttural rumbling sound]. The forest is breaking. /*íya*/

The ground is shaking. /*íya*/

She said, "Here he comes." The brother threw his hunting sack right down. He told her how to hide him. He hid himself in a certain place there, and you couldn't see him at all. /*íya*/

When the husband arrived, he saw that the wife looked all despondent. He called to her: "Woman, what's wrong?" "Nothing," she said. He tossed down — when he got there he tossed half of his hunting kill over there. He took the other half and tossed it down over here. /*íya*/

He said, "Woman, what's wrong?" "Nothing," she said. "It's nothing." "Mm?" he said. He came over and shook her shoulder gently. He said, "Woman, what's wrong? Ever since I came here, so many years ago, /*íya*/

I've never seen you like this. / . . . / The way you're acting today, there's got to be something wrong." "No," she said. /*íya*/

She said, "Husband, there is something that's bothering me." ("Yes," he said.) /*íya*/

"Since you and I arrived here — since you arrived here — well, I have a mother and a father, you know." /*íya*/

"Yes," he replied.

Asabôsi: [breaking in] At that time I was standing there.

Kasólu: *Íya*. And what did you —

Asabôsi: Well, there was a certain woman named Agangaai /Kasólu: uh-huh/

who never got tired of singing and dancing. /that's right/

Even if the wind came up, really blowing up, she just kept on performing. /that's true/

Agangaai, i sá kíi m. M hmm.
Agangaai, i sá kíi m. **M hmm.**
Di hánse fa a du m te. **M hmm.**
A du m te mooi ta yáa sónu. **M hmm.**
Agangaai, i sá kíi m. **M hmm.**
["Agangaai, you could kill me, mm–hm// Your beauty really does something to me, mm-hm/ It's enough to make the sun come up, mm–hm/ Agangaai, you could kill me, mm–hm." Because Asabôsi has a noticeable speech defect, both we and the Saramakas who listened to the tape had great difficulty arriving at a transcription. The "chorus" is only two voices — Asabôsi and Akóbo.][13]

A man: No one's chorusing the song! [reprimanding:] The chorus is what makes a song really sweet.

A woman: It's not that no one's chorusing. It's that I'm the only one who's doing it.

Asabôsi: Continue your story. /íya/

Antonísi: *Íya!*

Kasólu: All right. Then she said [in a plaintive voice], "When you come back, /Antonísi: *íya*/
you always toss half the meat over there and you bring the rest over here. /*íya*/
Well, I just feel as though it might be my own people. I don't know anything about the people you killed and set down there. /*íya*/
That's why I sat down [i.e., became dejected]." He said, "Mm. Wife, you can't play around with me like that!" /*íya*/
She said, "What if I feel as though, if a brother of mine, or some relative, came here, you would kill him?" He said [protesting indignantly in no-pause speech]: "If a relative of yours came here, you and I would sleep in separate hammocks,[14] if your brother came here, /*íya*/

the things I'm separating out over there, they're the
ones that could kill me, the ones I kill and set over
there are evil, /*íya*/
and the meat that I put over here— /*íya*/
If your brother came here," ("Yes," she said) "you
and I would sleep in separate hammocks." /*íya*/
Her brother jumped out: "Brother-in-law,
greetings!" They hugged and hugged. The husband
said, "Brother-in-law, jump on my back!" /*íya*/
Mm! He jumped on his back. He ran *bwelé, bwelé,
bwelé*. He carried him around like—well, it was
almost like something in the city [i.e., they were
riding all over]. /*íya*/
He took him all around to show him his various
hunting places, one by one, and then brought him
back home. /*íya*/
He said, "Brother-in-law, this is my home [i.e.,
you're always welcome]." ("Yes," he replied.) /*íya*/
The brother slept there with him three nights.
/*íya*/
"Brother-in-law—," he said. (The other replied.)
He said, "I'm going to leave. /*íya*/
I'm going to visit my other sister, going to her
village, going to see if I can find her and see how
she's doing." /*íya*/
The husband said, "No problem, Brother-in-law."
/ . . . / He walked out to the path with him. /*íya*/
He pulled out one of the claws of his left hand,

Others: [exclamations of surprise]

Kasólu: and gave it to him. "Brother-in-law—," he said.
                 (The other replied.)

Akóbo: He pulled out his own claw for him!!

Kasólu: Yes. He said, "When you go off, /*íya*/
                 if you run into difficulties that you can't handle and
                 your life is in real danger—" /*íya*/

"Yes," he said. "Go to the path /íya/
and gather some dry leaves. Strike your flint and
light a fire [to heat the claw]. I'll come to you as if
I were going to kill you. But you must be in serious
need. If you're not," ("Yes," he said) "then I will
kill you, Brother-in-law. You mustn't call me for
nothing. /íya/
I don't have anything else I can offer you.[11] /íya/
Then he went away *zéngee, téé djaláa. /íya/*

Kandámma:	Well, way back then, /Kasólu: *íya*/

I was right there. /That's right./
And the devil was in the tree at the Chief's
doorway. /That's right./
He was killing people so much that they were all
dying off. /That's how it was./
Well, the boy went to an *óbia* man, who told him,
"With the tree at the chief's doorway and people
being finished off in the village — it must be that
the devil is inside the tree." /Well, that's right./
So he told the others in the village, "Today I'm
going to do something here. Let everybody close
the door to their houses. /íya/
No one should be outside." /íya/
They said, "Well, what about you?" He said, "No,
I'm the one who's going to be doing all this. All the
rest of you, close the doors to your houses."

A man:	[laughing] He was that ritually strong?!
Kasólu:	*Íya.*
Kandámma:	Then he went to the base of the tree. And he sang:

    Asinailonpu-oo, Tatá Asinailonpu a tá
       tíngi-ee.
    Asinailonpu-oo, Tatá Asinailonpu a tá
       tíngi-ee.
    Un da mamá mi siná púu dadjá.
    Un da tatá mi siná púu dadjá.

Tatá Gángama fu Alakwáti, Alakwáti tjóló tjóló tjóló tjóló tjóló tjóló. /íya/
[In this song, the boy is taunting the devil, Father Asinailonpu, by saying that he stinks (lines 1–2) and by referring to his mother and father (lines 3–4), inciting him to come out and fight so that he'll be able to kill him. And thanks to him, a devil no longer hides up in a tree next to the door of the chief's house.]

Others:　　　　[gentle laughing]

Kandámma:　　And once he had spoken, /íya/
that devil just shook the tree *huyaa.* /íya/

Others:　　　　[exclamations of apprehension]

Kandámma:　　Here he comes!

A woman:　　　I'm trembling!

Kandámma:　　It's that he had been in there killing people. /íya/
But then the boy called him, "*Tatá Asinailonpu a tá tíngi Gángama fu Alakwáti.*" That's the same as "*Alakwáti tjóló tjóló.*" /íya/
Go right ahead.

Others:　　　　[murmurs of appreciation]

Kasólu:　　　　Then he arrived at the path by Eagle's creek.
/Antonísi: *íya*/
He walked along until he got to the young woman who was sweeping around her doorstep, swish swish. /íya/

Akóbo:　　　　He's got to Eagle's place.

Kasólu:　　　　He walked up and said, "Greetings, young woman." "Greetings, boy," she replied.

Others:　　　　[laughter at the girl's disparaging term of address]

A woman:　　　[sarcastically] All the sisters answer the same way.

Akóbo:　　　　Yeah, they're all equally gracious!

Kasólu: He said, "Sister, I came to ask you if you'd be willing to give me a little water to drink." "Mm," she said. [Gently scolding:] "Listen, boy, why did you come to me here? Look how you crossed the creek there and came all the way here just to ask me for water. What makes you think Eagle won't come here and kill you? /íya/

I've been here so long and I've never seen anyone else." He said, "Woman, are you so unkind? /íya/ If a little brother of yours, born after you left, were to come to see you, is this how badly you'd treat him?" /íya/

They hugged over and over again. /íya/

Overlapping
voices: [exclamations and comments]

Kasólu: They hugged and hugged. She said, "Boy —" (He replied.) She said, "I took a husband here, as you see." ("Yes," he said.) "Well, he's not a husband. /íya/

Evil! / . . . / But there's no way out. We're already married." /íya/

("I see," he said.) "If he were to come and see you here, he could kill you." "Mm," he said. "If he were coming, would you know it?" ("Yes," she said.) He said, "Your husband couldn't kill me by himself. /íya/

If he came to kill me —" ("Yes," she said.) "I would kill him." /íya/

She said, "All right." She cooked some food and they ate. So there they were until a certain point. /íya/

The wind came up like something else! No joke! She said, "Well, he's on his way. /íya/

At this very moment he's coming home." He came along till he was very close. The boy was already

hidden, just as he had been before. */íya/*
The husband arrived. He brought something to set
down over there. */íya/*

Akóbo:

[talking over the end of Kasólu's sentence] My god,
the woman who was their mother must be thinking
that another one of her children is gone!

Kasólu:

Another one's gone. The husband set something
down over there. */íya/*
He took half of it and set it down here. */íya/*
He came up to his wife, who was sitting there
dejected. */ . . . /*
He addressed her: "Wife, here I am." She greeted
him. He said, "Why is it you're sitting there like
that?" She said, "It's nothing." He said, "Well, the
way you're sitting there — since you and I came
here — " ("Yes," she said.) "I've never seen you
sitting like that. */íya/*
There must be something going on */íya/*
that makes you sit like that." */íya/*
"No, no," she said. She said, "Husband, there's
nothing wrong. It's just that it's been so many years
since you and I came here." ("Yes," he said.) "And
every time you come here, you always set things
over there, */íya/*
and half of what you're carrying you set down over
here. Well, I don't know. I have so many relatives. I
never know if they're my relatives or what, and
that's why I'm sitting here like this. */íya/*
Those are the things I'm thinking about." He said,
"No, Wife, don't play around like that. The things
that I kill and throw down there are evil things that
try to capture me to kill me. */íya/*
That's what I kill and set down there. */íya/*
And the [edible] meat is what I bring over here."
/íya/

("I see," she said.) "But if my brother — ," he said,
"if your brother came here — " ("Yes," she said.)
He said, "You and I would sleep in separate
hammocks." /íya/
The boy jumped right out and called, "Greetings,
Brother-in-law!" "Brother-in-law, greetings!" he
replied. They hugged over and over again. /íya/
They hugged. He said, "Brother-in-law, Brother-in-
law, Brother-in-law! Come over here under my
wing." /íya/
[laughing:] He went *zuuu*, and held him tight.
/íya/
They flew off and glided around. He showed him
lots of places where he liked to hunt. /íya/
Then he brought him back and set him down.
/ . . . / The boy said, "Brother-in-law, I've come to
visit you." ("Yes," he said.) They spent three whole
days talking to each other. They slept there three
nights. /íya/
Then the boy said, "Brother-in-law, I'm going to
leave. /íya/
I'm going off to Cayman's village." /íya/
"All right," he said.

Overlapping
voices: [indistinct comments]

Kasólu: He walked him to the path. When they got there,
he pulled a claw out of his right foot. /íya/
The other one had pulled out of the left. This one
pulled out of the right hand. /íya/
And he gave it to the boy. He said to him,
"Brother-in-law, when you go, if you run into a
problem that's too much for you, /íya/
if it's really about to kill you — " /íya/
("Yes," he said.) He said, "Just come out /íya/
and go to the path there, gather some dry leaves,

strike your flint to light a fire. But, Brother-in-law,
if you don't absolutely need help — " ("Yes," he
said.) /íya/
"You and I will have a real problem. /íya/
I'll kill you." "That's all right," he said. /íya/
Then he set out and walked all the way /íya/
to the path by Cayman's creek. /íya/
He continued along until he got there. /íya/
When he looked around, he saw the young woman
sweeping her doorstep. /íya/
He gave her a "Greetings, Aunt." She said,
"Greetings, Boy." /íya/

Akóbo:	It's that same "Boy" all over again. [she laughs]
Asabôsi:	Don't they have any other way to address him besides "Boy"?
Kasólu:	Yes, well, [chuckling:] it was the way things were done in the old days. He said, "Woman, I've come to ask if you'd be willing to give me a little water to drink." She said, "Look at how you've come down the path along the creek there." /íya/ ("Yes," he said.) "What makes you think Cayman won't come and catch you here? Over by the creek is where you could've drunk water, but you didn't want to. /íya/ Just wait till he comes here. Let him rip off your kneecap and then you'll see!"[15] /íya/ He said, "Woman, is that how unkind you are? If a younger brother that was born after you left came to see you, is that how badly you'd treat him?" /íya/ They hugged over and over again.
Overlapping voices:	[various exclamations]
Kasólu:	They hugged and hugged. /íya/

She said, "Boy—" (He replied.) She said, "The guy
I've married—he's a disaster. /*íya*/
The way you've come here—"

A woman: So why did she marry him then?

Kasólu: "Well, I'm not sure he wouldn't kill you." He said,
"Woman, your husband couldn't kill me by
himself. /*íya*/
When he's on his way, will you know it?" "Of
course," she said. "As soon as he's on his way, I
know it." "Okay," he said. / . . . / So they visited
with each other for a while. /*íya*/
They'd cook food and they'd eat, and they talked to
each other the way sisters and brothers do. /*íya*/
They talked about family things. Then the time
came. The water started to shake /*íya*/
and tremble. She said, "There! He's coming!" /*íya*/
("Yes," he said.) Then the water really started to
shake violently. The boy hid himself. /*íya*/
His hunting sack is where he hid. He had a hunting
sack with him. /*íya*/

Konoi: When he hid, and when the man got there, didn't
he notice the hunting sack?

Kasólu: No, he had hidden all his things. The way it was,
the boy had gotten to be more dangerous than the
other guy. The guy was on his way. The boy was
really [ritually] quick.

Kandámma: Quickest kid in the world!

Kasólu: Mm hm! So there he was. He was right there when
the guy arrived. He tossed half the fish way over
there. /*íya*/
Well, that guy—fish is what he hunted. /*íya*/
He brought the other half and tossed it down in
front of his wife. / . . . / There they were. The
woman came over, completely silent. The animal

PRICE AND PRICE

<table>
<tr><td></td><td>came over, katja, katja, katja, katja.
He said, "Wife, what's wrong?"</td></tr>
<tr><td>Akóbo:</td><td>My god, that husband's really baaad!</td></tr>
<tr><td>Kasólu:</td><td>"Why are you so sullen? Since you and I came to this place, years ago, I haven't ever seen you so sullen. What's wrong with you today? /íya/
Is something the matter?" She said, "It's nothing, Husband. But do you know what's bothering me?" (He replied.) "Ever since you and I came here — " ("Yes," he said.) "Whenever you kill something, you toss some away before you bring the other half of it and toss it down for me here." ("Yes," he said.) "I have a family out there. I have relatives out there. /íya/
I've got a father and a mother out there, and I don't know how they are. Because you can't bring them here to visit." /íya/
"Yes," he said. He said, "Wife, I can't kill those things that I hunt and toss down over there, 'cause they're evil and they want to kill me. /íya/
Those I kill and throw over there. But if your [matrilineal] family were to come here — " ("Yes," she said.) "Like your brother — " ("Yes," she said.) "You and I would sleep in separate hammocks." /íya/
[laughing:] She's tricking him. The brother said, "Brother-in-law, greetings!" /íya/
The other answered, "Brother-in-law!" They hugged over and over again.</td></tr>
<tr><td>Asabôsi:</td><td>How would he have hugged him?</td></tr>
<tr><td>Kasólu:</td><td>[chuckling] They hugged and hugged. There they were, running all around, calling out to each other. The guy said, "Let's go over to the water's edge." /íya/</td></tr>
</table>

They went in the water. The boy jumped right onto the back of the guy's head. / . . . / They swam around. He took him to show him around for a long time. They came back again. /*íya*/
They stayed together. They were there for quite a while. /*íya*/
It was several days that he slept at his brother-in-law's. /*íya*/
Now, there was another village just downstream. /*íya*/
A snake lived there. /*íya*/
He couldn't stand boys. /*íya*/
The boy said he would go visit the village nearby, just to visit. /*íya*/
That village was just downstream. /*íya*/
So he set out. So Cayman said that since he was going there to visit, he would be happy to walk him to the path. The boy said he was going to a village, the village just downstream there. /*íya*/
So he walked off with him. He pulled a claw out of his left hand /*íya*/
and gave it to him. /*íya*/
"Brother-in-law — ," he said. (He replied.) "When you go — " ("Yes," he said.) "If you run into a difficulty you can't handle, and you think you might die — " /*íya*/
("Yes," he said.) "Just go over to the path there /*íya*/
and gather some dry leaves, strike your flint, and light it up. /*íya*/
Then I'll come at you as if I were trying to catch you. /*íya*/
But if the problem isn't really big — if I get there and don't see the problem — " ("Yes," he said.) "I'll kill you." /*íya*/
"That's all right," he said. / . . . / Then he left.

Asabôsi: [breaking in] At that moment I was standing right there. /Kasólu: *íya*/
Now, the cure for all problems used to be *tonê* leaves.[16] /That's right./
Well, Spider was the only one in the world who knew how to summon the *tonê* god from the water.

Kasólu: That's true; you can't tell a tale that doesn't include him!

Asabôsi: You really can't. When the time came, he went to the river. /That's right./
Then he sang out, to summon the *tonê* god from the river: /That's right./
"Asúngúlú gwantan, asúngúlú gwantan, donkúlo."
> *Zuma weee, un bái zuma weee.*
> *Zuma weee, e-alêke **zuma weee.***
> ***Zuma weee, un bái zuma weee.***
> ***Zuma weee, e-alêke zuma weee.***

[This is in fact a song used to call the *tonê* god from the river. It says, "*zuma weee*, you call out *zuma weee*."]
Continue your story. /*íya*/

A woman: That was Anasi bringing *tonê* out of the water.

Kandámma: You mean that even though he's a good-for-nothing, he's still sort of an okay guy?

Kasólu: He took his hat and headed off, continuing on till he got to the village there. /Antonísi: *íya*/
He arrived right at the village /*íya*/
quick as could be. Well, the snake who lived there couldn't stand seeing boys. /*íya*/
He had twelve heads. /*íya*/

Overlapping voices: [exclamations of astonishment]

Kasólu: And he ate boys till there weren't any more left. /*íya*/

Then he went on to women.

Akóbo: In the village where the boy was going?

Kasólu: Yeah. Well, the women he ate there — the women would be catching lice for him. */íya/*
And while they were catching lice for him — when a few of them were catching lice for him — he'd look them over and decide which one to eat next. */íya/*

A woman: I would have left those lice right where they were!

Kasólu: Right. Now he's the one in charge in that village, so whatever he says, goes. */íya/*
He's got twelve heads.[17]

Akóbo: And he's someone who never dies.

A man: Twelve heads he's got?!

Kasólu: He's already eaten the men. */íya/*
But there are still women around, so it's women he gets. */íya/*
Well, he looked up and there was the boy coming toward him. */íya/*
And he saw him. And the girls are still catching lice for him, because he hadn't fully noticed the man yet. */íya/*
But now he's starting to push the women aside */íya/*
because he's seen the man, and he wants to eat him instead. */íya/*
He went over to him, walked right over till he reached him, and gave him a "Greetings, *Máti* [Friend]." And the snake replied, "Greetings, *Máti.*" */íya/*

Someone: The [twelve] heads are all over the place.

Akóbo: They're everywhere!

Kasólu: He said, "*Máti* —" (The boy replied.) He said, "I like you so much that I'd like to become your *máti.*" The boy said, "Me too. I'm fond of you too, *Máti.*"[18] /*íya*/

Kandámma: You mean the boy liked the anaconda?!

Others: [laughter]

Akóbo: He saw the snake's body with all those heads and decided he liked him?!

Kasólu: Mm. The snake loved the boy. When the boy greeted the snake as "*Máti,*" the snake replied the same way, said he loved the boy like a *máti,* and the boy replied by saying he had an affection EVEN GREATER than the affection you'd need to become *máti.* /*íya*/

The snake said that, well, it was decided. They would be *máti.* He said, "*Máti,* the reason I love you enough to become your *máti* — " /*íya*/

(The snake's the one who's saying this.) He said, "*Máti,* it's because, the way things are." He said, "Well, *Máti,* it's because you couldn't kill me by yourself."

A woman: Oh! The snake?

Kasólu: The snake. The boy said, "No, I couldn't kill you by myself." /*íya*/

The snake said, "*Máti,* the way things are here — " ("Yes," he replied.) "Well, my heartbeat isn't here on shore where I am. /*íya*/

My heart — " (The boy replied.) "My heart is located far under the water. /*íya*/

It's down with Awó Mmá, [laughing:] with the goddess of the river. That's where it is. /*íya*/

Well, could you get it? /*íya*/

Could you make it to there?" /*íya*/

The boy said, "No way. You couldn't get there. [Correcting a slip of the tongue:] I couldn't get there." /*íya*/

"That's right," the snake said. "And if you did get
there, / . . . / my heart — " ("Yes?" said the boy.)
/íya/
"It's inside an iron chest. /íya/
So if you could find the iron chest, would you be
able to break it open?" /íya/
"No," he said. "You wouldn't be able to break it.
And," the snake continued, "even if you managed
to break the iron chest — " ("Yes," said the boy.)
"My heart is a white bird. /íya/
And if the white bird flew out, there'd be no way
you could catch it." /íya/
"Yes," said the boy, "it's true, *Máti*, you can't be
killed." He said, "I really love you enough to
become your *máti*." /íya/
The snake replied —

Akóbo: [anticipating] "You and I will become *máti*."

Kasólu: The boy said, "Well, *Máti*, you and I will be *máti*."
/íya/
He said, "Yes, well, wait just a minute, *Máti*." (The
snake replied.) "Let me go urinate. I'll be right
back." /íya/
The boy left in a flash and zipped into the forest.
/íya/
He pulled out Cayman's claw in an instant and
quickly made the fire under it, and Cayman arrived
in a flash. He said, "Look, my friend, what's up?
What did you call me for? What's the big deal?

Others: [laughter]

Kasólu: You'll force me to kill you." He said, "Friend — "
(he replied) He said, "It's nothing much that I called
you for. Except that since I came here — " ("Yes,"
he said.) "There's this snake and there's this game
we've been playing with each other." ("Yes," he
said.) "And there's an iron chest down with the

goddess of the underwater." ("Yes," he said.) "And I called you so you could get it for me." He said [with surprise]: "Hm! I've just been hunting. /íya/ And when I was hunting this morning," he said, "it was right there on the crack of the iron chest that I sat down to rest! /íya/

Others: [laughter]

Kasólu: When I sat down on top of it, I really rested," he said. /íya/
"Let's stay here and talk a while." /íya/
The boy said, "Friend, don't play around with me like that. Let's not sit and talk. The snake will kill me. And if you let the snake kill me — if you let the snake kill me, I will kill you. /íya/
Go and get the chest for me!" /íya/
Splash! He plunged into the water. /íya/
After a while he came back with it *séngéé*, and he said, "*Máti*, I've done it already." /íya/
[Laughing:] The iron chest was there but he didn't know what to do next. /un-un/

Others: [laughter]

Kasólu: Now at that moment — /íya/

Akóbo: The snake is there, all ready to eat him.

Kasólu: The snake was right there. /íya/
And he was beginning to feel tired in his heart. /íya/

Others: [exclamations]

A man: He felt it coming already!

Kasólu: Well, the heart that had been underwater had been brought ashore. /íya/

Asabôsi: He's already getting tired.

Kasólu: His heart was beginning to be tired. /íya/

Kabuési: They should make a fire and put the chest on it [to kill the bird].

Kasólu: And things were already starting to seem bad. He couldn't eat women anymore. /íya/
Before, when there were men around, he used to eat men. /íya/
And when the men were finished, he went on to the women who were delousing him. /íya/
And when he saw the boy approaching, he pushed the women away. /íya/
Well, what those girls did, when the guy went to bring back the chest — well, the snake began to feel tired. /íya/
He said, "*Máti*, I'm done for." Then the cayman went back home. /íya/
The boy was there for a while. /íya/
And then he went out /íya/
and he took out the one that Elephant had given him. /íya/
Elephant came instantly. /íya/
Mmm! He came right up to him. /íya/
He said, "Friend—" /íya/

Akóbo: [breaking in] At the time when he arrived, I myself was there too.

Kasólu: *Iya.* What was it like?

Akóbo: At that time, Spider was asking for a wife. He was going off to look for a wife. [She giggles.] /Kasólu: íya/
And people had told him the woman's name, and now he was walking along repeating the name so he wouldn't forget it. /íya/
He was singing [she laughs as she sings]:
  Zegemôni-ee, tjèè tjèè tjèè.
  *Môni-ee, **tjèè tjèè tjèè**.*

Môni-nò, **tjèè tjèè tjèè.**
Zegemôni-ee, **tjèè tjèè tjèè.**
Môni-ee, **tjèè tjèè tjèè.**
Môni-nò, **tjèè tjèè tjèè.**
[The woman's name was Zegemôni, or Môni for
short. The chorus, *tjèè tjèè tjèè,* is for rhythmic
effect.]
Go on with your story.

Kasólu: Okay! So he appeared instantly. /Antonísi: *iya*/
He said, "Friend, why did you call me? What's the
big problem?" /*íya*/
The boy said, "Friend, I've got this chest here, /*íya*/
this iron chest, and I'd like you to break it for me."
/*íya*/
He said, "That iron chest there? /*íya*/
That's the one? /*íya*/
This thing here." He touched it like this, squeezed
it a bit. It was just like, you know, something very
soft. /*íya*/
It was as if he had picked up a papaya, /*íya*/
a very ripe papaya. /*íya*/
[In a very relaxed tone:] "Let's sit and talk together,
Friend. /*íya*/
That job's nothing." /*íya*/ The boy said, "I said to
break the thing for me! /*íya*/
There's a guy who's playing around with me!"
("Yes," he said.) "And you're going to let him kill
me! /*íya*/
That iron chest there, I want you to break it for me!
I'm having an argument with this guy. /*íya*/
So just break it for me." /*íya*/
The other took hold of it *buwáá,* /*íya*/
smashed it open *pònyôn.* The iron chest's — [Cor-
recting himself:] It flew off *vún vún vún* /*íya*/
vún.

A woman: From being broken?

Kasólu: No, it was the white bird [and not the chest] that
                was going like that. /íya/
                He had already finished with the chest. /íya/
                Elephant left. He said, "Friend, I've finished my
                part. /íya/
                There's nothing more I can do for you." /íya/
                And at that time /íya/
                the snake's heart was really getting tired.

Akóbo: [anticipating] He started squirming.

Kasólu: He just didn't know what to do any more. He'd turn
                and squirm, just didn't know what to do.

Akóbo: He didn't know what to do, but did he know where
                the boy was?

Kasólu: The boy didn't go back to him. Once they had
                talked that time and they became *máti*, he told him
                to wait a minute, that he was going off to urinate.
                Well, if I were visiting you and I said, "Wait for me
                here. I'm going off to urinate," you couldn't stop
                me. Because I certainly wouldn't urinate there
                inside your house!

Asabôsi: That's true, I wouldn't urinate in your house.

Kasólu: Exactly. And once the boy went off —

Akóbo: He's gone off to urinate, and he hasn't returned yet.

Kasólu: — the snake's heart started feeling tired. And then
                the white bird escaped. /íya/
                It flew out, and so the boy went on to Eagle's claw.
                /íya/
                He struck the flint, he went to the edge of the forest
                just like before. /íya/
                He lit it and put it there, and instantly Eagle
                arrived. He said, "Friend? Brother-in-law? What's
                up?" "Nothing," he said. /íya/

"Brother-in-law, did you see the bird flying off
there?" ("Yes," he said.) "I want you to catch it and
kill it for me. /íya/
I need to have its head cut off before it gets where
it's going." /íya/
Eagle said, "Brother-in-law, sit down and let's talk a
while." /íya/

Overlapping voices:	[laughter and comments]
Konoi:	You mean they're letting the boy's bird escape?!
Kasólu:	He said, "There's no place /íya/

where the bird can go that I can't get to it. /íya/
He's got to alight on a tree along the way, Brother-
in-law." /íya/
"Yes," he said. "It's got to rest on a tree. /íya/
It's sure to. /íya/
So let's just sit and talk, and when the time comes
I'll go kill it." /íya/
"Brother-in-law," said the boy. (Eagle replied.) He
said, "Don't let the bird go. You'll make the snake
kill me. /íya/
That white bird that's flying there — I want you to
catch it and kill it." /íya/
Eagle said, "Come on, let's tell stories." /íya/
"Brother-in-law of mine, don't be like that!" Eagle
flew off, *vúún*. He cut off the white bird's head
gélém /íya/
gwaa gwíi. Night fell on the village. The snake was
falling, and it was the dead of night. /íya/

Akóbo:	The snake is dying.
Kasólu:	He was ALREADY dead!
Kandámma:	The chief of them all.
Akóbo:	The chief of that place.

Kasólu: It was the dead of night. Everything was dark. For all the people who were there, all those people, it was completely dark.

Akóbo: The big man of that place that they used to catch lice for!

Kasólu: The boy left the place, just walked right out.

Akóbo: Was it because the snake's time to die had come that he told all about himself?

Kasólu: Well, if you're going to go ahead and do things like that — he just went too far. /íya/
That thing is that the snake had killed all the available men, and that's why he went on to the women. /íya/
Since they caught lice for him, they were really providing a service for him, but he still wanted to eat the ones who caught lice. /íya/
The boy rushed out, took his knife, and went up to the snake. /íya/
He pulled the snake's head on over, and he cut it *sóko sóko kélén* [sounds of sawing and then severing], /íya/
pulled it off and slipped it *zuu*, /íya/
into his sack. Then he went off to Cayman's place. It had already gotten light. After he cut off the head, it got light as could be again.

Kandámma: The head had made it dark.

Overlapping
voices: [laughter and comments]

Kasólu: And he went off. /íya/
So that's how it was for a while, and then people wanted to investigate what had happened. /íya/
They said [in a tone of bewildered astonishment:] "Well, how is it that the snake here died? /íya/

Because, well, not a thing in the world had been
able to kill that guy." /íya/
After a long time one of the girls told the whole
story. One of the girls who had caught lice for the
snake, one of those who caught lice for him, that he
had wanted to eat. /íya/
Well, there she was until at one point she said,
"You know what?" (Others replied.) "They sent a
boat after them — " (Whoops! I got it wrong. /íya/
I got that part wrong.) /íya/
After they said those things, /íya/
night came and then it got to be dawn. He cut off
the head and took it. /íya/
Then they asked who it was who had killed the
snake. And Anasi said it was him! /íya/

Konoi: But he hasn't got any of the snake's heads.

Kasólu: He went out and walked into the forest. /íya/
He killed snakes. / . . . / He killed snakes until he'd
gotten twelve heads. /íya/
He was going to bring them back to stick them on.
Anasi said he was the one. He kept on trying
without success. /íya/
He'd put them together, but they didn't fit. Well,
when you bring back a snake's head, /íya/
it must fit perfectly.

Akóbo: Right. All twelve of them.

Kasólu: Then you know who killed it. /íya/
He kept trying. He had cut twelve and brought
them back, but some were bigger than others. He
kept trying till he was exhausted.

Akóbo: He'd try them all out on each neck.

Kasólu: He couldn't get them to fit. /íya/
Then the girl, the one they had been asking about
this, one of those girls said — [with sudden

enlightenment:] oh, SHE knew! /íya/
A man had come there from Cayman's village. /íya/
And he and the guy had had some words. /íya/
And during the discussion they talked a lot, and at
the end they decided to become *máti*, and they
talked some more and the boy left. /íya/
Well, after he left, it wasn't even a half an hour
before the snake's heart started feeling weak, and
after a little longer, as it got dark, /íya/
the snake died. Well, since they didn't understand,
that's why they paddled their canoe over to there.
/íya/
They paddled their canoe over to where the boy
was. The boy was still right there in Cayman's
village. /íya/
They arrived and told him what had happened. He
said, "Mm. Really?" /íya/
("Yes," they said.) "Well," he said, he would come
have a look. /íya/
But it wasn't him, not him. /íya/
The boy set out and continued until he got there.
/íya/
He reached into his hunting sack. /íya/

Konoi: Well, if the snake were already put back together,
           wouldn't he come back to life?

Kasólu: The boy had already cut him apart. Even if he were
           put back together, he wouldn't be able to revive
           enough to do himself any good.

Akóbo: That guy was already dead!

Kasólu: So the boy reached right into his hunting sack,
           /íya/
           and pulled out the head he had there. /íya/
           He fitted it on, *biingá babala baa* [sound of the
           snake starting to move again, proving that the boy

was the one who had killed it]. Night fell
immediately! /*íya*/

They screamed in fear. He pulled the head right off.
/*íya*/

He put it on again, *biingá babababababa*. And took
it off. /*íya*/

He put it on again, *biingá ba*. And night fell. Then
he pulled it off again. /*íya*/

He left. / . . . / Then the Chief came along and
split off one side of the village. /*íya*/

That made a village, let's say about the size of
Paramaribo. /*íya*/

So the boy and his sisters and their relatives came
there to live. And that's the part of the world we're
living in here.

Akóbo: With the brothers-in-law?

Kasólu: Yes, with the brothers-in-law. It's the part of the
earth the boy had, with his mother, where he
brought his relatives. That's the part of the world
we're in here.

A woman: Whatever happened to the snakes' heads that Anasi
had?

Akóbo: [laughing] He just threw them away.

Kasólu: They just rotted.

Akóbo: It's that he wanted to be chief!

Kasólu: And that's the end of my story.

NOTES

1. This paper presents materials that are further developed in *The Evenings in Saramaka* © 1991 by The University of Chicago Press. All rights reserved. Fuller acknowledgments appear there. The 1966–68 fieldwork during which we recorded most of our corpus of tales was funded by a grant (to R. Price) from the

National Institute of Mental Health; the translations were supported by a more recent grant (to S. Price) from the Editions Program of the National Endowment for the Humanities. To both of these agencies we express our gratitude. We also wish to thank those Saramakas in the Netherlands and in French Guiana who worked with us on the tales in 1986 and 1987 after Suriname's civil war made it impossible to continue work in that country. We dedicate these pages to Kasólu, who died in early 1992.

2. The English word *maroon* derives from the Spanish *cimarrón*, a term with Arawakan (Native American) roots that by the early 1500s had come to be used in plantation colonies throughout the Americas to designate slaves who successfully escaped from captivity.

3. The Saramaka, today some 22,000 people, are one of six Maroon (or "Bush Negro") groups in Suriname that together constitute well over 10 percent of the national population. Their ancestors were among those Africans sold into slavery in the late seventeenth and early eighteenth centuries to work Suriname's sugar plantations. They soon escaped into the dense rain forest — individually, in small groups, sometimes in collective rebellions — where for nearly a hundred years they fought a war of liberation. In 1762, a full century before the general emancipation of slaves in Suriname, they won their freedom. Those present-day Saramakas (the very great majority) who continue to live in their traditional riverine villages, deep in the rain forest, are heirs to a way of life forged two centuries ago. Until the 1980s, when Suriname's civil war disrupted many aspects of that life, it had changed less radically through time than that of many peoples on the fringes of the Western world.

The Saramaccan language may well be the world's oldest extant Afro-American creole (for recent assessments, see Alleyne 1987 and Smith 1987). Possessing a syntax that emerged from West African progenitors (Alleyne 1980), approximately half of its lexicon derives from one or another of the scores of African languages that were spoken by the seventeenth- and early eighteenth-century maroons; another 20 percent derives from Portuguese (the language of most of the slavemasters from whom these maroons escaped) — including the word *kóntu* for "folktale"; another 20 percent from English (the language of the original seventeenth-century European settlers of Suriname); and 10 percent from Dutch and Amerindian languages (R. Price 1976).

For various reasons (among which racism and ethnocentrism predominate), Suriname Maroons have always had a bad press in regard to language, speech, and folklore. Apparently intelligent visitors (like V. S. Naipaul and John Walsh) conclude that they speak a kind of "baby talk" (Naipaul 1962; Walsh 1967); the 1971

Guinness Book of World Records awarded their language the palm for being the world's "least complex," allegedly possessing "only 340 words"; and Jean Hurault has made the fanciful assertion that their folktales (which are in fact filled with ribald incidents) "are never of a licentious character" (Hurault 1961:268).

4. For Saramakas, both *kóntu* and First-Time knowledge are central cultural resources, an important part of their collective identity, but they occupy separate spheres. Though the morals of folktales, as well as certain rhetorical devices, may overlap with those of particular First-Time (historical) stories, Saramakas maintain a clear distinction between the two, both in the contexts in which they are communicated and the kinds of characters and incidents they depict.

5. Africanists and Afro-Americanists will recognize in Saramaka tales not only a number of the characters and plots but also many performative features: the insistent use by tale-tellers of the "intrusive 'I'" (widespread in Afro-American folktales [Abrahams 1983:2]), onomatopoeic renditions of such acts as snoring (common in African tale-telling [Paulme 1986:3]), and others.

6. Portions of the next several paragraphs are abstracted from S. and R. Price 1980:167–70.

7. One tale was written out by the missionaries (in German), undoubtedly because it "explained" why whites and blacks had separate stations in life, but though it is somewhat difficult to plumb because of the corrupt form in which it was recorded, it appears to be more a part of Saramaka men's ironic "tomming" repertoire with whitefolks than the kind of folktale that would be told during an evening of *kóntu*. (For the text of this tale, see R. Price 1990:297, and for a discussion of diverse versions from Africa and Afro-America, see R. and S. Price 1991.)

8. When *kóntu* are told informally in horticultural camps, the only place they are ever told other than at wakes, the opening formulae shift to "*Híliti . . . Dáiti*," the formulas used at wakes for riddles. An example of a riddling string is presented in S. and R. Price 1980:184–85.

9. Saramaka women, even those who spend the bulk of their time in their husband's village, retain strong ties to their matrilineal village, where they will eventually be buried.

10. *Papá* is the Saramaka music of death, played by specialists on the night before burial and, many months later, on the night before the ghost is chased forever from the village.

11. Note that the song refers to *Father* Jaguar, but that Kandámma seems here to have altered the story to mesh more closely into the tale it is interrupting. In 1987 in Cayenne, another Saramaka told us a related tale, which has almost the same song: There was a king who promised his daughter in marriage to the man who could bring him the tails of a twelve-tailed *makáku* (a kind of monkey). Anasi

feigned being dead at the side of a creek, with a club in one hand and a machete in the other. The one-tailed *makáku* had seen from up in the tree how he had walked to the creek and fallen down on his back "dead," holding the machete and club. He came down to the ground and said he didn't have the expertise to bury someone who had died holding a club and machete. So he called the two-tailed *makáku* (by singing a nearly identical song) to help. The two-tailed *makáku* then called the three-tailed *makáku*, and so on until finally the twelve-tailed *makáku* arrived. Anasi jumped up and killed him, and won the king's daughter.

12. Here, Kasólu shifts from the Saramakan word for hat, *kaapúsa*, to the Sranan equivalent, *hati*.

13. Upon listening to the recording of this tale-nugget in 1987, the Saramaka men in Kourou told us a version of what they thought was the same tale: It used to be that when a man asked for a wife, she would engage him in a dance contest. If she outdanced him (i.e., if he got tired and gave up), she'd kill him. In the tale, Anasi seeks the hand of a very beautiful woman named Agangaai, who could out-dance any man. As they danced around and around each other, Anasi flattered her with this song of praise. In the end, Anasi won the contest. Thanks to him, since then men have not had to undergo this ordeal.

14. In Saramaka, tying hammocks side-by-side and spending the night in each other's company is a gesture of friendship and solidarity among men. By saying that he would not sleep with his wife, Elephant is telling her what a good host he would be for any of her male relatives who might visit.

15. Saramakas say that when a cayman attacks a person, it usually strikes the knee.

16. The *tonê óbia*, one of whose songs Anasi is singing here, controls the rains via the *tonê* gods that dwell in rivers.

17. When we played this tape to Saramakas in French Guiana in 1987, several responded spontaneously to this phrase by exclaiming, "*Bóóta!*" — referring to Desi Bouterse, the military strongman of Suriname.

18. *Máti* is a highly charged volitional relationship, usually between two men, that dates back to the Middle Passage. *Máti* were originally "shipmates," those who had sailed out from Africa and had survived the journey together. By the eighteenth century, *máti* was a life-long relationship entered into only with caution and in the case of very strong mutual affection and admiration (R. Price 1990). Today, an often-cited Saramaka proverb holds that, *Máti ganyá i, án o láfu* (When your *máti* betrays you, he won't smile — that is, he'll be deadly serious). And, for a man, perhaps the most strongly forbidden of all sexual partners is the wife of a *máti*, since between *mátis* there should be absolute trust.

REFERENCES CITED

Abrahams, Roger D.

  1983   *The Man-of-Words in the West Indies: Performance and the Emergence of Creole Culture.* Baltimore: Johns Hopkins University Press.

  1985   *Afro-American Folktales: Stories from Black Traditions in the New World.* New York: Pantheon.

  1986   Complicity and Imitation in Storytelling: A Pragmatic Folklorist's Perspective. *Cultural Anthropology* 1:223–37.

Alleyne, Mervyn C.

  1980   *Comparative Afro-American.* Ann Arbor, Mich.: Karoma.

  1987   *Studies in Saramaccan Language Structure.* Amsterdam: Centre for Caribbean Studies.

Basso, Ellen B.

  1987   *In Favor of Deceit: A Study of Tricksters in an Amazonian Society.* Tucson: University of Arizona Press.

Burns, Allan F.

  1983   *An Epoch of Miracles: Oral Literature of the Yucatec Maya.* Austin: University of Texas Press.

Cosentino, Donald

  1982   *Defiant Maids and Stubborn Farmers: Tradition and Invention in Mende Story Performance.* Cambridge: Cambridge University Press.

Crowley, Daniel J.

  1966   *I Could Talk Old-Story Good: Creativity in Bahamian Folklore.* Berkeley: University of California Press.

Dauenhauer, Nora Marks, and Richard Dauenhauer

  1987   *Haa Shuká, Our Ancestors: Tlingit Oral Narratives.* Seattle: University of Washington Press.

Falassi, Alessandro

  1980   *Folklore by the Fireside: Text and Context of the Tuscan Veglia.* Austin: University of Texas Press.

Herskovits, Melville J., and Frances S. Herskovits

  1936   *Suriname Folk-Lore.* New York: Columbia University Press.

Hurault, Jean

  1961   *Les Noirs Refugiés Boni de la Guyane Française.* Dakar: Institut Français d'Afrique Noire.

Hymes, Dell

1975   Breakthrough into Performance. In *Folklore: Performance and Communication*, edited by Dan Ben-Amos and Kenneth S. Goldstein, 11–74. The Hague: Mouton.

1981   *"In Vain I Tried to Tell You": Essays in Native American Ethnopoetics.* Philadelphia: University of Pennsylvania Press.

Naipaul, V. S.

1962   *The Middle Passage.* London: Andre Deutsch.

Paulme, Denise

1986   Un Conte bete et son narrateur. *Gradhiva* 1:1–8.

Price, Richard

1976   *The Guiana Maroons: A Historical and Bibliographical Introduction.* Baltimore: Johns Hopkins University Press.

1990   *Alabi's World.* Baltimore: Johns Hopkins University Press.

Price, Richard, and Sally Price

1991   *Two Evenings in Saramaka.* Chicago: University of Chicago Press.

Price, Sally, and Richard Price

1980   *Afro-American Arts of the Suriname Rain Forest.* Berkeley: University of California Press.

Seitel, Peter

1980   *See So That We May See: Performances and Interpretations of Traditional Tales from Tanzania.* Bloomington: Indiana University Press.

Sherzer, Joel, and Anthony C. Woodbury, eds.

1987   *Native American Discourse: Poetics and Rhetoric.* Cambridge: Cambridge University Press.

Smith, Norval S. H.

1987   The Genesis of the Creole Languages of Surinam. Ph.D. diss., Universiteit van Amsterdam.

Stedman, John Gabriel

1988   *Narrative of a Five Years Expedition Against the Revolted Negroes of*
[1790]   *Surinam.* Edited by Richard Price and Sally Price. Transcribed for the first time from the original 1790 manuscript. Baltimore: Johns Hopkins University Press.

Tanna, Laura

1984   *Jamaican Folk Tales and Oral Histories.* Kingston: Institute of Jamaica.

PRICE AND PRICE

Tedlock, Dennis
>1972   *Finding the Center: Narrative Poetry of the Zuni Indians.* New York: Dial.

>1983   *The Spoken Word and the Work of Interpretation.* Philadelphia: University of Pennsylvania Press.

Thompson, Robert Farris
>1974   *African Art in Motion: Icon and Act.* Berkeley: University of California Press.

Walsh, John, with Robert Gannon
>1967   *Time Is Short and the Water Rises.* New York: E. P. Dutton.

9

Peter Minshall

The Good, the Bad, and the Old in Trinidad Carnival

John Nunley

Great artistic traditions have a life of their own; they experience good times, bad times, exuberance, vitality, and near fatality. These traditions are often altered by the creations of performers and artists who, through great effort, adapt these traditions to their own aesthetic aims. Western classical music, for instance, was severely tested by Schönberg's Serial Music, which in its democratic approach rendered all notes equal, freeing them of the dominant, subdominant and other diatonic structures that arranged notes in a musical hierarchy. Likewise, opera has sometimes had outstanding individuals who have brought the tradition renewed vitality. This essay examines another artistic tradition of great merit and longevity, one that has experienced great moments through the efforts of its best artists. That tradition is Trinidad and Tobago's Carnival, which is held on the pre-Lenten calendar dates of the Christian holiday cycle. An artist who has occupied a pivotal position in this tradition is Peter Minshall. His masquerade bands from 1983 to 1985, examined here, had an impact on the content, symbols, style, and sources of Carnival, which has been the central cultural event in the country for more than one hundred fifty years.

Trinidad and Tobago were originally settled by Amerindians known as the Caribs and Arawaks, who came from the north coast of South America.

After Columbus discovered the West Indies for the Old World, the Spanish claimed the islands, using them to mount operations aimed at discovering gold in South America. Later, in 1777 and 1783, the French from the West Indian Islands were invited to establish plantations and to develop the land in other ways. The French brought their slaves to the colony, and the population of the colony increased from about 1,000 in 1760 to more than 12,000 by 1787 (Carr 1975:27). Because the Spanish government had failed to establish organized defenses, a British fleet captured Trinidad in 1797, and thus Trinidad and Tobago passed into the hands of the English (Carr 1975:28). By the early nineteenth century, Spanish, French, English, black slaves, and Amerindians co-existed, though the latter group of peoples was nearly exterminated. After emancipation in 1838, the English, who greatly expanded the plantation system, were compelled to look for a new supply of labor and a system to recruit it. That system was indentured servitude, and under it Chinese, Africans, and East Indians were recruited to work on the plantations for several years in return for free passage to the colony. They were then freed to establish their own enterprises. With these new settlers came East Indian cultural practices, including a Moslem tradition known as Hosay, and also many Hindu customs, including Devali, Pagwa, and the worship of Shiva, Vishnu, Ganesha, and numerous other deities of the Hindu pantheon. The great civilizations of Africa, Europe, and India converged on this very small landmass, creating a cultural mix frequently referred to as Callaloo.

It is important to understand the Callaloo metaphor, because it is central to the masquerade bands created by Peter Minshall in the early 1980s. Callaloo is a soup with a variety of ingredients, commonly including crab, curry spices, chicken, hot peppers, coconut meat and milk, and very importantly, a large heart-shaped leaf locally called dasheen and commonly known as taro. Other recipes include an even greater variety of ingredients, but however it is made, diversity is clearly the key to its character. Just as the soup improves in taste, becoming sweeter as the diverse ingredients blend, so has Trinidadian culture become better as it has increased in diversity. The ingredients it has adopted from three civilizations have blended into a sweet Callaloo mix. Trinidadians note that the heart-shaped dasheen leaf adds heart to the soup and by extension adds heart to the mixture of humanity that is Trinidadian society. Cultural diversity, though it sometimes causes severe social tensions in the community, remains positively valued. Carnival artists have a large selection of themes and motifs from which to draw, and Minshall has been the consummate appropriator.

Carnival, better known as mas, is celebrated by the masquerade bands on Monday and Tuesday of the pre-Lenten holiday and abruptly ends on midnight of Ash Wednesday. Preparations for mas begin in the previous early fall when the artists launch their bands. On these occasions, they invite their followers and the general public to see the drawings for the various costumed sections and the larger costumes known as the kings, queens, and individuals. Following the launchings, many volunteers and professionals produce the costumes for the members, who range in number from about 200 to 4,000. Minshall's bands usually number about 2,500. Competitions for the roles of kings, queens, and individuals occur a week prior to Carnival at the specially built stage before the grandstands on the Queen's Park Savannah. For three nights these costumed characters perform before the public seated in the stands and those watching them on television. The judges rank the characters each night until first place in all categories has been established on the Sunday evening before the Monday masquerade. Jouvay (from the French *jour overt*, to open the day) begins about 3:00 A.M. on Monday. In this opening of Carnival, participants dress in last year's costumes or old clothing and smear themselves from head to foot with ochre, mud, and oil (Fig. 9.1).[1] Starting from all points in the city of Port of Spain, the 60,000 or so masqueraders converge in their bands on Independence Square, where steel bands and other drum ensembles provide the musical muscle that drives mas. It is by this ritual that Carnival participants pass through the threshold into the ritual space of renewal. On Monday afternoon the masqueraders join their bands, parade the streets, and cross the Savannah stage. Tuesday marks the serious competition, in which everyone dresses in complete costumes and remains within his or her costume section so that the entire band looks good before the judges and the public. This is a time of liberation but also a time of stress among the artists who become involved in controversy. Minshall is an artist who thrives on such controversy.

The first masquerade band of the Minshall trilogy, called River, appeared in the 1983 Carnival. It featured the Mancrab as king and Washerwoman as queen. Mancrab — constructed of metal, paper, and wood — was

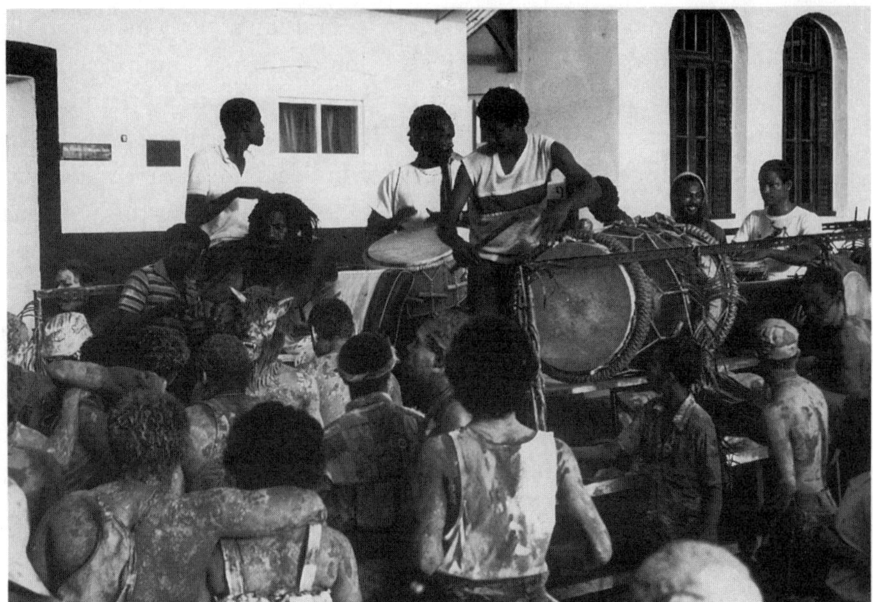

Fig. 9.1. Jouvay participants celebrating the opening of Carnival with music, dance, drinks, and food. Port of Spain, 1988.

inspired by the outer-space automatons that appear in Hollywood films like *Star Wars*. The creature displayed six pincerlike arms that moved to the motion of the dancer. At the center of the costume and over the face of the masquerader was placed a papier-mâché mask of simple construction which matched the contours of the human face (Fig. 9.2). Attached to the heavy black boots were two poles on each foot. Standing sixteen feet high, the four poles supported a canopy of white silk twenty-five feet square. This costume was worn by Peter Samuels, a longtime associate of Minshall and frequently a king character in his bands. Each night of the kings' competition, he danced to the music of the East Indian–derived tassa drums, which included large double-headed wooden drums, smaller ceramic drums, and brass cymbals. Tassa music is very militant in character, sounding the call of battle. The violent, distorted patterns in which the silk moved was made possible by the motion of the poles, which responded to the movements of the dancer and occasional gusts of the trade winds. As the dancing became more violent, the masker released paint from a compressor within the costume. Traveling up small, unnoticed tubing attached to the four poles, the red paint at first barely left a trace of itself in sprinklings in the silk, yet before the dance was over the silk had been turned into a blood-stained shroud, symbolizing the death, destruction, and pollution represented by the Mancrab creature.

Opposed to this frightening character was the queen of the band, Washerwoman, played by the artist's half sister, Sherri Ann Cuelho. Dressed in a white full-length skirt tied at one end to the waist, this beautiful queen sambaed onto the stage. Two poles on her shoulders were used to attach clotheslines, on which were hung pieces of cloth in various abstract shapes. As she moved to the music, the shapes waved in the thick night air, creating brilliant flashes of white on the Savannah's stage. Washerwoman also carried a basket and with it pantomimed the washing of clothes.

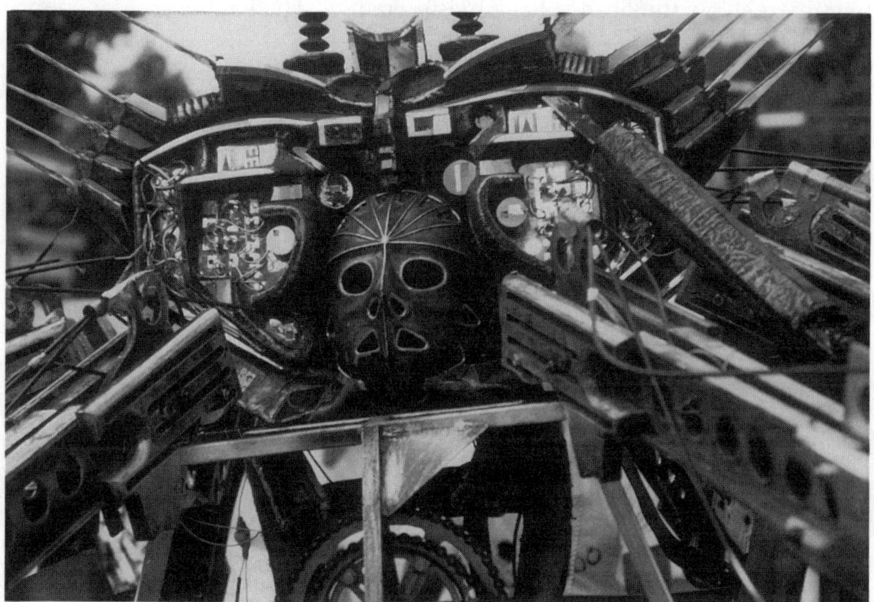

Fig. 9.2. The Mancrab character created by Peter Minshall for the River band at the Trinidad Carnival in 1983. The costume was carried in the streets of Port of Spain on Carnival Monday and Tuesday.

In the story "Callaloo and de Crab," which was adapted from a Trinidadian folktale, Mancrab was jealous of the powers of this beautiful queen, who protected her river people from the crab's pollution and greed. Through the course of the Carnival, the Mancrab was determined to capture the admiration of the river people by offering them technology. Jealous of the power of love symbolized by a magical calabash filled with pure water, which was controlled by the queen, Mancrab planned to destroy that protective love. With slick black oils and beautiful chemicals that composed a rainbow, this villain painted the river. The colors stood for the luxury and profits bought by technology. The river people were attracted to the promised wealth and fought with one another to fill their basins with the colored water. This turning away from purity by the people broke the heart of the queen, causing her death.

On Carnival Monday the Minshall band assembled near the Queens Park Savannah. More than 2,000 people, all dressed in white, paraded beneath a half-mile canopy of white nylon parachute fabric attached to poles held high above the heads of the masqueraders. The band was divided into sections, each representing a different tributary to the main river, represented by the nylon canopy. Each section wore a distinctive style of costume. One section, produced by the late Ken Morris and called River Gods, included ten dancers in white full-length skirts with bright copper masks crowned with white feathers attached to copper frames that loomed over the heads. They also wore breastplates similar to those of ancient Roman legionnaires. The band paraded through the streets of Port of Spain as a mighty and pure river with its tributary sections, the menacing Mancrab, and the beautiful Washerwoman.

In the transition to Mardi Gras (Fat Tuesday), the queen had died and the king had begun to work his magic on the river. The half-mile-long canopy had been dyed blue, yellow, green, and red, the colors of the rainbow. However, at this point the river people were not yet polluted. The queen's death was indicated by her blood-stained clothes suspended from the lines. River performed in the streets from noon until 5:30 before approaching the Savannah stage. The red shroud of the Mancrab, suspended from the four poles and carried by the king's attendants, could be seen dancing in the wind a quarter mile from the stage. Its presence was amplified by the sound of the tassa drums, which gradually increased in volume as the group moved closer to the stage.

The first Minshall group to appear on the stage was composed of sixteen sacrificial dancers who performed with magical calabashes before the stands. Suddenly the music stopped and the audience became silent. Everyone watched the movement of the priestesses. Slowly they turned to the south stands and raised the calabashes. They then turned to the north stands and completed the same movement and then turned back to the south stands. At this moment they raised the calabashes high above their heads and then slowly downward over their breasts, then they tilted the bowls toward their bodies, spilling the blood-red liquid all over their pure white costumes and skin. The river people had made their sacrifice to the god of technology, greed, and pollution. Moments later, the triumphal king entered the stage, his red umbilicus spewing his guts. At the end of this cord came the dead Washerwoman, covered in the monster's polluted fluids. The tassa drums played their staccato rhythms as the creature moved in triumph across the stage. Captured by the joys of technology, the river people climbed onto the stage and danced for several minutes, celebrating the victory of their new leader. Bottles of dye and compressors of paint showered everyone with color. Thus the stain of technology was shared by all.

The 1984 band, Callaloo, represented the second part of the trilogy. Its main characters included King Callaloo, the Mancrab costume from the year before, the Bird of Paradise as the queen, and an individual called Madame Hiroshima. The band sections were collectively called the Children of the Moon and were the river people transformed.

Competing on the Savannah stage, "Callaloo, Dancing Tic-Tac-Toe Down the River," was portrayed by Peter Samuels, and he represented Everyman—black, white, red, brown, yellow; every color, race, and culture. This costume incorporated African motifs, including a fifteen-foot-high carved balsa-wood plank that projected from the head of the masquerader. The geometric designs carved into this structure from its base to its top were derived from West African designs found on *sigi* masks of the Dogon people of Mali. Using the same principal of motion as in the last year's costumes, fiberglass poles were attached to the dancer's feet. The poles and ribs of lesser diameters supported sequined mylar material, which sometimes spread in fan shapes and at other times in a multitude of different shapes, depending on the motion of the dancer (Plate 8). The bodysuit of silver material was studded with amuletlike packets that reflected the stage lighting. Armed with the functional power of light, Callaloo was prepared to defeat his enemy, a creation of Mancrab's technology known as Madame Hiroshima.

Madame Hiroshima, played by Hugh "Bote" Bernard, was crowned with a large cluster of red, black, and yellow ostrich plumes in the shape of an atomic mushroom cloud (Plate 9). Her large, conical breasts echoed the shape of bombs, and her large hoop skirt was decorated with thousands of sequins and feathers matching the colors of the mushroom.

The third character, the queen of the band, played by Sherri Ann Cuelho, was called the "Bird of Paradise: She Has Spread Herself Before Me, and I Shall Never Be the Same Again." This birdlike creature was made of materials dyed the colors of fire and supported by fiberglass ribs. Rising as much as fourteen feet from the ground, the Bird of Paradise struck sensational forms in brilliant orange and red reflections.

On the night of each performance the story was developed further. Before Washerwoman had died, she had given birth to a son, Callaloo, whose father was the spirit of the forest known in Trinidad as Papa Bois. This son was armed with the magic of love and hope, which would protect his people and him from evil, but, saddened by the loss of his mother and the degradation of his people from the River band, Callaloo prepared to die. Papa Bois, however, disguised as a *morocoy* (a land turtle) told him he must regain his faith, and this he accomplished by climbing a mountain and bathing in the healing flames of a large fire. Callaloo then returned to his people to teach them to love and respect each other and their individual differences. Peace and harmony were symbolized by the Bird of Paradise, who represented the unconquered spirit of the deceased Washerwoman.

Upset by this turn of events, Mancrab set out to invent a seductress who would win over Callaloo by offering him the ultimate power of technology. Taking Science as his mate, he produced Madame Hiroshima. This atomic creature had no effect on the young king, and with the advice of the Seven Deadly Sins, Mancrab instructed his daughter to corrupt the River people, or in this case the Children of the Moon. This tactic worked, and

Callaloo's heart was once again broken. The offspring of science and technology had conquered Everyman.

"Callaloo and the Children of the Moon," act one of the band, was presented on Monday of Carnival by the three main characters and about 2,500 members in twenty-nine sections. The sections were named after musical instruments or mythical characters that symbolized the races and cultures of Trinidad. Thus the violin section, the sitar section, and the pan (steel band) section represented the Western, East Indian, and African cultures, respectively. The band, then, was Everyman, a reflection of Callaloo. These all-white sections in various styles wore hooped substructures covered with cloth reflecting the crescent shapes of the moon.

The finale, "Callaloo and the Seven Deadly Sins," was presented on the following day. This act begins with the Children of the Moon waiting for the duel of Callaloo and Madame Hiroshima. Troubled by the corruptness of his people, the young king staggered before the temptress, who was poised to descend in deadly lust upon him. Just then, however, the Bird of Paradise, accompanied by a little band of children dressed in white, entered and saved Callaloo from destruction. Though the king was spared, the Children of the Moon mounted the stage and danced around seven tall structures representing the deadly sins, and in this respect Madame Hiroshima prevailed. From the top of each structure, colorful dyes were sprayed on the band members, thus staining them with science and technology.

Completing the trilogy in 1985 was the band Golden Calabash, which included two clashing bands, the Lords of Light and the Princes of Darkness. Although the kings and queens of this two-part band were never completed, a number of outstanding individual costumed characters concluded the ominous trilogy. Hugh "Bote" Bernard, who performed in place of the queen on the first night of the competitions, dressed in white as the Adoration of Hiroshima (Plate 10). Mr. Bernard carried a missile-styled scepter in one hand and a globe in the other as he paraded across the stage. With the power to destroy symbolized by the missile, this version of Hiroshima literally possessed the planet earth in one hand. This force of destruction must be adored lest she destroy. Perversion, Humming Bird of Blood, and Prince of Damnation were among the other individuals who acted out the clash of good and evil. Good and evil were also presented in band sections, including the Hawks and the Doves.

Peter Minshall's focus on the good and the bad in his Carnival bands has been guided by the nature of Carnival itself. Masquerade characters historically can be divided with respect to the moral–immoral, good–bad, fancy–fierce and other dichotomies that pit the good against the darker side of life. Clowns, sailors, and the old fancy-speaking Pierrot characters in tattered costumes make up the forces of good, whereas the Midnight Robbers, demons, bats, and devils represent the darker side. Most mas men of the past — and indeed today — design for one or the other, yet Minshall plays good against evil throughout this trilogy and has been doing so for most of his career.

In the Carnivals early in this century, Jab Molassie devils with horned headpieces and long tails with spiked tips paraded through the streets mostly naked and covered with molasses and later grease. These characters played mas in the early morning hours and threatened to smear their coatings on innocent victims. Later the bat costume, invented in the 1930s and inspired by a rabies scare, became a symbol of evil. The most terrifying representative of evil and the harbinger of death and destruction, however, was the Midnight Robber. These individual characters, armed with guns or knives, roamed the streets, confronting each other and the spectators with verbal challenges that announced their evil intentions. A typical Robber speech might be: "At the age of five, I, this dreaded monarch, was sent to school, but the schooling there was not drastic enough for me. . . . When it comes to snatching children's faces, ringing their ears, biting off pieces of their nose, I, King Korak, was always on the top. . . . At the age of two, I drowned my grandmother in a spoonful of water" (Crowley 1956:272).

Fascinated from childhood with such characters, Minshall synthesized all the elements of evil in his Mancrab. Robbers bragged of their ability to destroy cities, even the earth itself, defying the elements as they proclaimed themselves princes of darkness and criminal masters, mercilessly meting out destruction. In the last component of the trilogy, Minshall had several characters who were in fact called Princes of Darkness, a direct reference to the Robber characters. The Mancrab costume's skin-tight black bodysuit, crablike structure, and silk canopy resembled the Robbers' own. Robbers often wore baggy black pants, though some preferred skin-tight ones to increase their ability to draw their guns as rapidly as possible. Some Robbers prefer huge white hats to black ones. In this respect the white canopy represents an adaptation of that preference. The skulllike form of the crab and the mask are also closely tied to the Robber costume tradition. The crab carries its skeleton on the outside of the skin, so the creature is in a sense a walking skeleton. Similarly, Robbers often depict skulls and skeletons on their pants and capes or feature model skulls on their large and elaborate hats. The crab shape, moreover, is very similar to that of the spider with its multiple legs, and images of spiders commonly appear on Robber costumes, often on the headdress. Thus the skeletal and the insectlike features of Minshall's king derive from elements of older forms of Carnival costumes. Minshall incorporated Robber motifs again in his king of 1987, the Merry Monarch (Plate 11). The large skull and the emaciated treatment of the body of the costume directly relate to the Robber style.

Other sources for the crab include the Hollywood film *Star Wars*, in which the villainous character Darth Vader, dressed in black and with metallic parts, inspired Minshall in the metallic surfaces and the mechanical nature of the king. Like his *Star Wars* counterpart, Mancrab was part organic and part mechanical. Hindu gods of destruction such as Shiva and the kathakali dramas also influenced Minshall in rendering a creature with multiple arms and dancing to the music of the East Indian tassa drums.

As Daniel Crowley has said, "Any plodder can be authentic" (1956: 264). Trinidadians, however, have created a costumed character that is interpreted artistically in endless variations. Some Robbers wear ragged clothes, others Elizabethan dress, while some have even carried bomb- or torpedo-shaped accoutrements to amplify their destructive characters. In this regard, the daughter of Mancrab, Madame Hiroshima, displayed bomb-shaped breasts and a feathered headpiece in the shape of a mushroom cloud. Here the artist has again synthesized a number of old costume elements and motifs in his characters.

The King Callaloo of the 1984 band, the second in the trilogy, is also a synthesis of mas costumes of previous years. The winglike structures attached to the king's feet derive from the wings that appeared on the bats of the 1930s. In those early costumes the wings were made of bamboo ribs to which cloth was attached. The wings were then attached to the feet of the dancer, just as with the wings of an actual bat. This costume allowed the dancer great freedom of movement, with the motion of his feet being reflected in the motion of the wings. Many of the trilogy costumes incorporated this old mas technique (Minshall 1986:11). In addition to the bat source, Minshall included African-derived costume elements in the 1984 king, including the amulet packets on the bodysuit, which are related to African amulets, and the balsa-wood superstructure, patterned on the great Dogon *sigi* masks and funeral masking headpieces of the Mossi of Mali and Burkina Faso, respectively. In this respect Minshall has followed the example of Trinidad's most famous designer, George Bailey (1939–71), who created several bands with African themes which incorporated stylistic elements and motifs from the African costumes he had seen in photographs.

Except for the way the winglike forms are attached to the feet, the two queens of the trilogy, Washerwoman and the Bird of Paradise, show less influence by the older masking traditions. Washerwoman's skirt did seem to derive from the bele dance skirt of Trinidad. As the queen came upon the stage, she danced the bele while carrying a clothes basket with which at times she mimed washing clothes in a seated position. This "play" derives from the Ole Mas tradition, a masking competition that features a small band that acts out themes ranging from the scatological to stiff political satire. The red staining of the white silk of the Mancrab's costume and eventually the queen's, symbolizing pollution and dirtiness, is a preoccupation of Ole Mas. Even today, soiled cloth and clothing may represent the menstrual cycle or bed wetting.

Minshall also has been influenced by contemporary mainstream artists of the West, including Francis Bacon and Christo. The artist himself compares his artistic approach to that of Christo, who challenges his public with environmental works utilizing cloth on a massive scale. He once wrapped several islands near Miami, and he has covered various buildings. Minshall compares Christo with his creation of a half-mile-long "river" of cloth, which also closely resembles Christo's *Running Fence* in northern California. The riverlike canopy was also inspired by the ritual procession of members of the Brazilian Church of the Bonfin (the good end; Fig. 9.3). Indeed, Minshall has been inspired by many cultural traditions of Brazil, a country of many cultures and ethnic groups. The dress of Bonfin members and their cloth cover closely resemble costumes in "River" and the river cloth (Carybe 1980:240). Minshall has also been influenced by the paintings of Francis Bacon, which convey death, destruction, and bodily decay in a semi-abstract

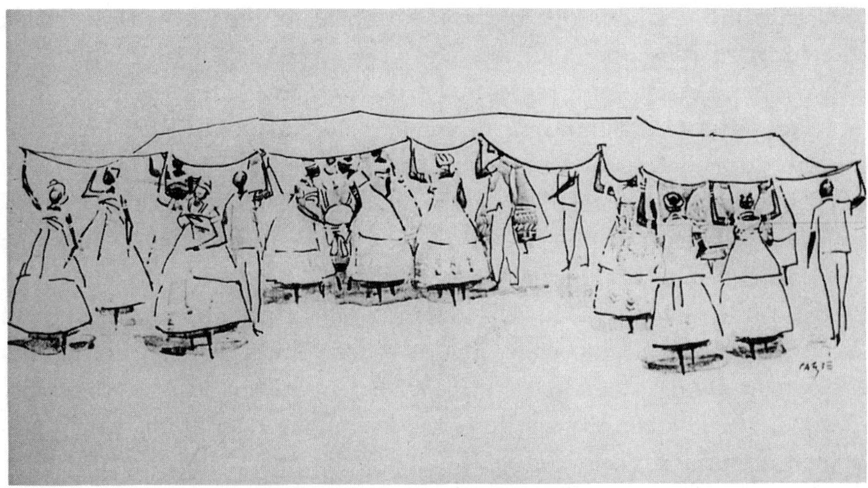

Fig. 9.3. From the ritual "do ala de Oaxal Carybe." This canopy and the participants illustrate a performance of the Church of the Bonfin, or good end, a religious cult in Brazil.

manner in which distorted figures are often placed in rigid architectural environments. Against these harsh backgrounds the contours of the figures are blurred by brushed color that appears to exude from the bodies as in the process of decay. The blurred effect is analogous to Minshall's stained cloth in his Trilogy bands, especially that of the Mancrab. Thus, in drawing on the historical repertory of Carnival, Western sources, and Hollywood films, Minshall demonstrates his talent for merging artistic movements into a unified style with a content concerned with the conflict of good and evil.

Minshall explores this conflict partly through his expression of the Christian doctrine of the trinity in a strongly Trinidadian fashion. King Callaloo, dressed in white, literally walks on water. The father of Callaloo, the invisible Papa Bois, who represents love, mates with the Washerwoman, the beautiful virgin of the pure waters, to produce a son in a way similar to that in which God impregnated Mary. Callaloo, like Christ, is exposed to lustful temptation, represented by Madame Hiroshima. The Bird of Paradise compares with the Holy Spirit, the dove that is the messenger of God. In a predominantly Catholic city such as Port of Spain, the Christian origin of the trinity of Papa Bois, Callaloo, and Bird of Paradise is certainly recognized, and by extension it represents Trinidad, named after the Trinity.

Yet there is a significant difference: the good and evil themes that concern the artist are not dualistic, as they are generally treated in Christian Theology. Instead, Minshall is ambivalent toward these black and white, good and bad forces that inspire his work. Callaloo, we are told, is all white, and his whiteness is the color of Everyman. When you see yourself reflected in the radiance of this character, he reflects whatever color you are (Minshall 1984:19). Thus white light is broken down prismatically into its component colors by reflection rather than refraction. Color, the artist states, is the symbol of pollution, as seen in the river cloth, which was stained the primary colors in 1983. Logically, Callaloo must be all bad as well as all good; he is both all white (good) and all colors in reflection (bad). Corruption and purity move in a dialectical dance in which one becomes the other. Remember that the soup called callaloo, the primary metaphor for this trilogy, contains the dasheen plant, which has a heart-shaped leaf that represents goodness. As well, this dish contains the crab himself. Hence good and bad, corruption and purity, are on the same side of the coin; one cannot exist without the other.

Unwittingly or otherwise, the artist has drawn on one of the primary attitudes concerning corruption and purity in the medieval institution of Carnival, which was introduced by the French settlers in Trinidad. According to Mikhail Bakhtin, Carnival before and during the time of Rabelais concerned itself primarily with renewal, and in that process corruption was a necessity. Feces, rotten flesh, mashed grapes, and dirt were all needed for the creation of new life. This view also held that all things were in the process of both disintegration and renewal. It was this knowledge which fed the laughter of the medieval Carnival, which, for Bakhtin, was personified by the fool or clown, the salient spirit of the medieval celebration. In writing about Carnival, Bakhtin concludes: "To degrade also means to concern oneself with the lower stratum of the body, the life of the belly and the reproductive organs; it therefore relates to acts of defecation and copulation, conception, pregnancy and birth. Degradation digs a bodily grave for a new birth; it has not only a destructive, negative aspect, but also a regenerating one" (Bakhtin 1984:21).

Carnival is, in a sense, a timeless state in which the past, the present, and the future become one experience. In this respect, the Mancrab represents the past because it is adapted from an old tale. It is also the future, as its style derives in part from futuristic Hollywood images. As a warning, it also portends the future. Most important, it represents the current state of the world and is the present embodiment of Trinidad. The descendants of East Indians, Europeans, and Africans all share in the pollution. It is a warning that the importation of too much Western technology, made possible by the 1970s oil boom, would render the Trinidadian economy totally dependent on the West. During those boom days the country imported canned fruit, meat, fish, and other goods rather than relying on its own resources simply because the oil dollars made these imports more affordable. As a result, bananas, for example, once sold at four to five dollars a pound during the boom because the local supply diminished as more processed fruits were imported. By selecting white, red, and black to represent the Crab, Minshall is referring to the colors of the national flag. Yet in the Crab the colors are fused in mad, unpredictable patterns, unlike the clean, straight-line contours of the actual flag. The Mancrab symbolizes the country in trouble.

Drawing on the interests of his band participants, who were nearly all Afro-descended, the artist has given his hero, Callaloo, a solidly African character despite the analogy with Christ. The story reads: "Callaloo had plenty sense. Callaloo sense did reach to de sky. Dat dasheen boy had brains! You could say Callaloo brains was tall as any skyscraper" (Minshall 1984:25). This skyscraper directly refers to the African-style plank headpiece Minshall had incorporated into the costume. Thus it is an African spirit that triumphs, and in Trinidadian terms that spirit also represents the African deity Shango, god of thunder, who has his own body of Shango worshippers and who is popular with the members of certain Baptist sects as well. Further, the dasheen plant is used in Afro-American religious ceremonies in Trinidad, thus its inclusion in the Callaloo image. By the same token, Washerwoman may represent a river spirit associated with the worship of Yemanja, a water spirit that came to the West Indies from Africa. In the West Indies, in fact, Yemanja is often considered the mother of Shango (Bascom 1972:16). Minshall refers to the dasheen as the magic leaf. The idea that the leaf has the power to keep the land pure is in part rooted in the physical property of the leaf itself, because its oil-like surface repels water. This in turn allows Callaloo to walk on the water just as oil skims across the water's surface (Minshall 1984:26).

The character Callaloo also has broader significance, as it incorporated many cultural motifs in the basic cosmology of the shamanic world, which divides the universe into Earth and Sky God, which are connected by the sacred tree or other symbols of the *axis mundi*. In Minshall's trilogy, Mother Earth is represented by Washerwoman and Sky God by Papa Bois. The *axis mundi* is the plant-shaped headpiece projection worn by Callaloo, the offspring of these two deities.

Madame Hiroshima explores another dimension of the Trinidadian character, one that would eagerly trade the purity of the land and its people for imported technology. This is represented by the panoply of color, sequins and beads, and various other fancy materials of the Hiroshima costume. The fact that she is the offspring of the Mancrab and his own technology makes her a product of incest, which in turn represents a violation of the natural order. The colors of Madame Hiroshima and her fancy materials also make reference to the materials used in what Minshall has referred to as "middle class Carnival." He views such materials and colors as decadent.

It is the play of symbols against one another in the mas and the combined good and evil of all things which preoccupy the artist. Drawing upon his Western artistic training at the Central School of Art and Design in London and his experience in that city as a stage designer, he has learned to synthesize Western art with the Trinidadian mas tradition in order to explore the good, the bad, and the old in his themes.

Minshall has challenged the tradition of mas with his extraordinary ability to synthesize styles and motifs and with his stinging political commentary, yet his use of materials and methods of costume construction may pose the bigger challenge to mas today. Prior to the performance of his trilogy, his masquerade band called Papillon featured large individual butterfly costumes with images of well-known people, such as Che Guevera, Marilyn Monroe, and Mohammed Ali. The Monroe costume featured the face of the movie star in an Andy Warhol pop image with a hairstyle adapted from Sandro Botticelli's *Birth of Venus* (Plate 12). The attention to detail and the use of expensive sequins, rhinestones, and other glittering materials required in this type of masquerade were already well accepted by other mas artists. Beginning with the trilogy, however, Minshall designed costumes with less expensive materials and that were larger in size, therefore requiring fewer man-hours in their construction. The hoop skirts of the Children of the Moon, the simple wing designs of King Callaloo, and the cloth cutouts of Washerwoman exemplify these new construction methods. Minshall's Jumbi band of 1988, moreover, utilized painted cardboard in simple shapes for the majority of the costumes.

Though influenced by contemporary art, the shift to these materials has also been influenced by economics and social change in Port of Spain. As the Trinidadian dollar has been devalued over the years, the cost of glittery materials, which are imported, has skyrocketed. The large mas bands are commercial ventures, and Minshall's are the epitome of this aspect of mas (Nunley and Bettelheim 1988:108). Moreover, the time required to add the detailing to these materials translates into money. In the 1950s and 1960s, bands depended on the voluntary efforts of their members to accomplish the intricate tasks of mas construction. Amid the faster pace of life today, however, such effort has been considerably reduced, though the volunteer spirit has by no means disappeared.

It remains to be seen whether Minshall's use of new technologies will shape the future of Carnival. Many critics have hailed his creations as the wave of the future, but his new approach to costume design has not escaped criticism. Ironically, one of the mas men to whom Minshall dedicated Calla-loo and de Crab, Irwin McWilliams, or "Mac," was most upset with the River band. When she was speaking for McWilliams while he was confined to a hospital with nervous strain in 1983, his wife said in a newspaper interview that "McWilliams was very upset at the fact that Peter Minshall's band, 'The River,' got so much acclaim and that his King 'Mancrab' won the coveted title, 'King of Carnival.' 'That will kill the whole spirit of carnival,' he commented bitterly. 'It will be no good. I have been playing carnival for 21 years and you look forward to things getting better, not worse.'"[2] Thus, even now Peter Minshall remains controversial, a condition upon which he thrives.

River was probably the most aesthetically successful of Minshall's bands because it raised participants and audiences to new ecstatic heights.

When the triumphant Mancrab entered the stage to the musical accompaniment of the tassa drums, the crowd roared. Then it suddenly quieted as the priestesses raised their calabashes above their heads. As if first inhaling in a mighty breath, the crowd received the Crab, and then in a mighty collective exhaling it quietly watched the blood ritual and then in an even louder exhalation responded to the mad spray of color polluting the river people on the stage. All were unified in a breath, a moment in time with no divisions. As Minshall stated:

> The artist touches the eternal infinite and relates it to the observer, who sees it, touches it himself, discovers himself in the midst of it. The human moment is evoked, infinitesimal, yet momentous and essential, the inevitable link between all that has been and all that will be. The moment is beyond time and yet continuous time. The vanity of us all, as well as our profundity, are plain in the moment, elucidated by art. Mas captures that moment inescapably. (Minshall 1984:6)

After the conclusion of this first band of the trilogy, I returned to my accommodations with my camera, hair, and clothes covered with the sprayed paint. In the shower, the colored water was funneled down the drain, carried by a sewer to a stream, and then to a river and out to sea. Conceptually, the point of the continuing process of pollution was made. Through the years the stains on my camera case have faded, and according to the artist himself such fading represents the unfulfilled promise of technology in the face of human worth and understanding. Yet it is faded technology, or built-in obsolescence, which out of the necessity for its own survival must invent new colors to replace the old, and in the pursuit of its goal must further pollute the land.

ACKNOWLEDGMENTS

The research for this paper was funded in part by the National Endowment for the Humanities, the National Endowment for the Arts, and the Rockefeller Foundation. I would also like to thank Roy Boyke, Christine Galt, and Peter Minshall, who in 1983 opened the way for this research.

NOTES

1. Unless otherwise noted, the photographs that accompany this essay are by John Nunley.

2. The exact date and the name of the newspaper in which this quotation appeared was not recorded on the clipping. It appeared, however, in February 1983.

REFERENCES CITED

Bakhtin, Mikhail
  1984   *Rabelais and His World*. Translated by Helene Iswolsky. Bloomington: Indiana University Press.

Bascom, William
  1972   *Shango in the New World*. Austin: African and Afro-American Research Institute.

Carr, Anthony M.
  1975   *Trinidad and Tobago*. London: Andre Deutsch.

Carybe
  1980   *Iconographia dos deuses Africanos no Candomble da Bahia*. São Paulo.

Crowley, Daniel.
  1956   The Midnight Robbers. *Caribbean Quarterly* 4:263–74.

Minshall, Peter
  1984   *Callaloo an de Crab*. Trinidad and Tobago: Privately printed.
  1986   *Callaloo*. London: Riverside Studios.

Nunley, John W., and Judith Bettelheim
  1988   *Caribbean Festival Arts: Each and Every Bit of Difference*. Seattle: University of Washington Press.

Pearse, Andrew
  1956   Carnival in Nineteenth Century Trinidad. *Caribbean Quarterly* 4:175–93.

Trinidad Carnival
  1983–   Edited by Roy Boyke. Port of Spain: Key Publications.
  85

10

Creativity and Continuity;
Communication and Clay

Dorothea S. Whitten and Norman E. Whitten, Jr.

Early European explorers of South America were impressed both by the aesthetic quality and by the mundane and festive uses of pottery in widely separated regions of Amazonia. Traveling down what is now known as the Napo River through the Upper and Middle Amazonian areas inhabited by Omagua Tupian speakers, Francisco de Orellana noted the quality of the ceramics produced by the very people his troops were raiding and plundering: "[T]his porcelain [is] of the best that has ever been seen in the world, for that of Málaga is not its equal. . . . [It] is all glazed and embellished with all colors, and so bright . . . that they astonish" (Carvajal 1934 [ca. 1541]: 200).[1]

Some thirty years later, Hans Staden (1944 [1557]; see, e.g., translations by Alexander [1976:106]; Tootal [Stade 1847 1:135–36]; Wernicke [Staden 1844:122–23]) wrote of how Tupinambá women of coastal Brazil knew how to make and paint clay vessels that glowed "like hot iron" when fired. They used manioc roots to make flour for thin cakes to be eaten with pounded dried fish and dried game. The women also made drinks by boiling manioc roots, which were masticated and put into special vessels half buried in the ground. These were tightly covered and the masticated manioc-water mixture left to ferment for two days to produce a strong, thick drink:

> Each hut makes its own drink. And when a village wants to make merry
> with it, which generally happens once a month, the men first go all
> together to one hut, and drink out there. This is so carried on in succes-
> sion, until they have drunk out the drink in all the huts. They sit around
> the vessels from which they drink. The women help them to the liquor
> in due order; some stand, sing and dance around the vessels. . . . The
> drinking lasts through the whole night; they also dance between the
> fires, shout and blow trumpets. (Stade [Staden] 1847 [1557]:135–36;
> see also Léry 1990 [1580]:69–77)

Beautiful ceramics are still being made today by indigenous people
living at the base of the Andes in Amazonian Ecuador. The potters there
produce polychrome and black wares quite reminiscent of Tupian traditions.
The origins of these fine, hand-coiled ceramics probably date back 4,500
years and are closely associated with manioc cultivation and utilization.
Such pottery developed from still earlier Amazonian traditions that could
be the earliest in the Western Hemisphere. According to Anna C. Roosevelt, an archaeologist, this "first pottery" is associated with settled fishing
communities:

> [T]hese fishing villages contain the earliest pottery in the Americas,
> about 1000 years earlier than northern lowland pottery and 3000 years
> earlier than that of the Andean and Mesoamerican areas. It is sometimes
> decorated with sinuous linear incised and punctate designs that continue
> to be popular in later lowland art styles and in the early pottery of the
> Andes and Mesoamerica. . . . Within about 2000 years of the appearance
> of the early pottery-age fishing villages, [a] shift in crafts and subsis-
> tence occurs in some areas of Greater Amazonia. (Roosevelt, in press a:
> mspp. 11–12; quoted by permission)

Roosevelt, who has undertaken extensive excavation in Greater Amazonia,
is explicit with regard to the ceramic tradition that probably gave rise to
Canelos Quichua pottery, and she draws a conclusion of considerable surprise to many specialists in New World prehistory, that tropical root crop-
ping had spread throughout the Amazon basin by 4,500 years ago in association with elaborate styles of pottery decorated with geometric and animal
designs (Roosevelt, in press a: msp. 2).

The florescence of superb pottery that occurred at the mouth of the
Amazon in association with manioc (and maize) horticulture and intensive

fishing endured for more than a thousand years on the 14,000-square-mile island called Marajó. Although Marajó Island was abandoned about 190 years before the European "discovery" and subsequent conquest of the New World (Roosevelt 1989a:74–83; Roosevelt, in press b), the pottery tradition spread throughout Amazonia and to the base of the Andes. This extended period from 4,500 B.P. to the mid sixteenth century was one of great expansion of the Amazonian peoples into many ecological niches through varied biomes. The conquistadors of the Caribbean and Amazonian regions encountered large-scale societies of indigenous people, some of them settled, some migrating. These societies had developed technologies that included the skills necessary to produce huge polychrome pottery jars, effigy (and even monumental) pottery statues, and probably delicate bowls and whimsical figurines.

Peoples migrating by 1492 included Tupian speakers who traveled from different parts of Amazonia westward all the way to the east Andean foothills. Searching for the "land without evil," these Tupians were led by powerful shamans who prophesied the location of the sacred land and made vast treks to find it (Brochado 1984; Lathrap 1970; Métraux 1927; Shapiro 1987; Whitehead, personal communication). In the early sixteenth century, a Spanish adventurer named Alejo García traveled with Tupian (Chiriguano) warriors to eastern Bolivia, where the Inca were mobilizing the Yura people to defend a sector of the east Andean slopes recently incorporated into their empire (Rasnake 1988; Rowe 1946:208). By the time Staden made his observations in coastal Brazil, thousands of Tupinambá had already traveled 4,000 miles or more to the edge of the Inca empire. "About 1540," Alfred Métraux noted, "several thousands of Tupinambá left the coast of Brazil in quest of the 'land-of-immortality-and-perpetual-rest' and, in 1549, arrived at Chachapoyas in Peru" (Métraux 1948:98).

On the basis of his field research in Upper Amazonia during 1916–19 and 1928–29 and additional museum research, Rafael Karsten (1935) identified the various ceramic styles of indigenous peoples of Upper Amazonian Peru and Ecuador. He noted the fragility of the clay and added that "certain magical or animistic ideas seem to be associated with the very material used." He thought that the Canelos people in particular brought their ceramic art "to a remarkable degree of perfection" (Karsten 1935:99–100). "Like the Achuares," he commented, "the Canelos Indians nearly always apply ornamental designs to their clay vessels, but their ornamental art is easily distinguished from that of the Achuares, and even the clay they use is different" (Karsten 1935:102).

The Quichua-speaking people now widely known as the Canelos Quichua still inhabit the Upper Amazonian territories of Ecuador visited by Karsten, and they still make a distinct type of fine pottery (Kelley and Orr 1976; D. S. Whitten 1981; N. Whitten 1976, 1985; D. Whitten and N. Whitten 1978, 1988, 1989) for storing and serving a manioc food beverage. Strikingly beautiful traditional ware today is flourishing in the most modern setting in this region. In this chapter we examine the "perfection of their ceramic art," first through the imagery of one potter and then more broadly through the imagery of other potters who work in the contemporary scene centered in and radiating from the town of Puyo, capital of Pastaza Province in Amazonian Ecuador.

Strong Visionary Woman

"Yachaj awashca," she said, picking up a piece of ancient thin-walled pottery with a smooth, shiny surface. "Mana yachaj awashca, mana sumaj," illustrating her description with a thick-walled, rough-textured sherd, a remnant of an old cooking pot. *Yachaj awashca* literally means something made by the most knowledgeable one, therefore master-crafted, well made and imbued with knowledge. *Mana* is negative, *sumaj* is beautiful. "Mana yachaj awashca, mana sumaj" refers to something not knowledgeably made and not beautiful; if it is not knowledgeably made, it lacks significance, and if it is insignificant, it lacks beauty.

Clara (Plate 13) had come to a point in her pottery making where some bowls and jars had to be air dried before she could paint them. Three monkeys and a couple of coiled snakes needed to dry awhile before their separate halves could be spliced together. It was time for a break, and she needed some nourishment from the manioc food beverage (*aswa*) and relief from sitting in a fixed position for hours. Before serving *aswa* in a decorated drinking bowl, she brought a small bundle from her treasure trove in the bedroom, put it on the dirt floor, and untied the corners of the cloth. Spreading it, she laid out an assortment of valuables collected mainly from the Copataza River region during visits to her husband's relatives and from the Upper Conambo and Curaray River regions during recent treks there to renew old bonds of friendship and kinship.

Her first concern was with her stones, some with explicit purposes, others with obscure functions. A smooth, flatish black *lumu rumi* (manioc stone) helps her manioc grow.[2] She does not need to talk to it, she just holds it against her body to make it work. She bought it from her son-in-law's mother, who lived in the Copataza River region. She sorted the stones into *warmi rumi* and *cari rumi* (female stones and male stones), then put aside only the manioc stone and an egg-shaped white alabaster one, a tourist item from the Cuenca area that had been given to her "for luck" by a North American to whom she sold pottery. She needed to keep her two female stones, but she indicated that she had no need for the polished black and red male stones, including a long, thin red one called a "tongue." Perhaps some tourist would like to buy these, she hoped.

Turning her attention back to her collection of sherds (Fig. 10.1), she explained that she had found all of them in one ravine off the edge of the small airstrip at Copataza during visits to her husband's relatives. Through her combination of Jivaroan, Quichua, and Spanish, she interpreted sherds as fragments of strange bowls made by outside or foreign women of ancient times. She singled out the sherds that she associated with drinking bowls as *yachaj awashca, sumaj,* because the inside surfaces were well scraped and burnished, and the rims were clean and smooth. Some had punctate designs, "painted or decorated with a stick"; others bore traces of painted designs, said to be *sumaj pintashca* (beautifully painted). The *sumaj* sherds were quite distinct both from those identified as eating bowls by their folded-over rims, and from cooking pots, which were thick walled, coarser grained, unpainted or undecorated, and not beautiful.

A round, chunky object that at one time might have been a rudimentary anthropomorphic figurine had been given to her by a relative, and she did not know much about it, except that it was ancient. She identified a small spindle whorl with punctate marks as *algudunta tisana*, literally cotton disentangler, a spindle whorl used for working cotton.[3] She was more interested, however, in the punctate designs on the *sumaj* sherds: she interpreted diamond shapes as *amarun* (anaconda), zigzag lines as a twisting river or the skyline silhouette of the Andes, a pattern of linked Us as *shiwai cara* (centipede shell), and a flattened diamond form as an anaconda skin

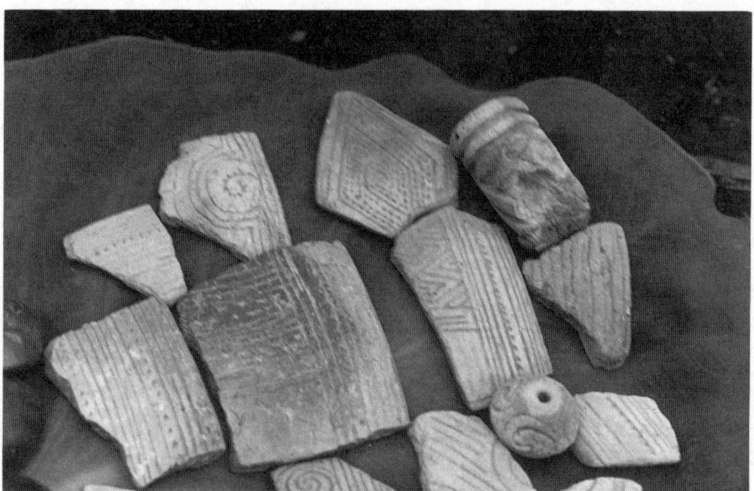

Figure 10.1. The sherds Clara Santi Simbaña collected in Copataza.

shed during molting. Some circular punctate designs puzzled her; she sighed and said, "We don't know these designs now," and went on to add that she would like to learn them, but they were made by "the other women long ago."

The contents of the plank shelves in her small pottery-making shed revealed the extent of her knowledge and skill. A row of toucan jars (*si-cuanga manga*s) and drinking bowls (*mucawa*s) lay in various stages of completion. Their thin walls were slipped in cream, red, and rose tones and burnished to a soft sheen with a special water-polished stone. Brown, black, and white line drawings on some vessels took the shape of diamonds, zig-zags, or five- and six-sided geometric designs. After the monkey- and snake-halves had been joined into whole figurines, and after the array had been slipped, air dried, burnished, and painted, each piece would be fired and then covered with resin to fix the colors and decorations under a bril-liant lacquerlike coating to make the piece waterproof. The final results bore an eerie resemblance to the *yachaj awashca* fragments of antiquity in Clara's collection.

She attributed much of her knowledge to her mother and grand-mother, and to the mother of a close sister-in-law. As a child, she would hang around while her mother made pottery, watching closely and then practicing rolling out coils of clay on a flat board, just as her granddaughter was now doing at her side. Through continued observation and practice, she gradually became more adept at handling clay and turning it into little animal figurines and small bowls. She had long worked the plastic clay intuitively. Now, as she held a bowl on her lap to scrape its walls thin, it changed from round to oval; when she put it down on her flat board, the slight, sure pressure of her hands restored its roundness.

Her horizons constantly expanded as she accompanied her parents on periodic treks (*purina*) from their home in the village of Puyo to the dispersed settlements of the Conambo, Curaray, and sometimes Copataza River regions. Strangers seeking cures for their ailments from her shaman father came from other parts of Amazonian Ecuador, as well as from the Andes to the west. Her father also traveled to these areas, gleaning knowledge of the worlds of other people, diagnosing the causes of their illnesses, and bringing home reports of his travels and, sometimes, special gifts from his patients. One prized gift was a violin from the dispersed settlement of Chapana near the headwaters of the Curaray River on the very edge of Waorani territory. It was hand carved and was fastened together with palmwood nails. She remembered listening to him play shamanic tunes and sing his special shamanic songs, communicating with the world of spirits and distant and foreign others. Through his music and the telling of mythic and historical episodes, she came to understand the meaning of *unai* (mythic time-space) and *callarirucuguna* (beginning times-places). She incorporated this knowledge of distant worlds into her increasing familiarity with her rain-forest environment and with the customs, histories, and myths of her people.[4]

When Quillara (this is Clara's indigenous name) was fifteen, her father contracted her marriage to Paushi (Paukich in Achuar), a youth from Capahuari, a dispersed Achuar settlement midway between the headwaters and the mouth of the Capahuari River. Living among his wife's kindred in her father's territory, he mastered the Quichua language while retaining his own native Achuar. Clara's experience deepened as she learned more of her husband's language, customs, and myths (which, not accidentally, were originally those of her father, who came from the Copataza River region). Through visits with Paushi's female relatives, she became familiar with their distinct pottery styles. She admired their skill in making very large drinking bowls and considered beautiful the cooking pot for Ilex (*huayusa*) tea, with its dramatically flared rim and gleaming black inside, but she preferred her more elaborate polychrome pottery to theirs.

During her childhood, Clara witnessed the transformation of Puyo from a largely indigenous village with some mestizo settlers into a frontier town swelled by waves of Andean colonists. About the time her father was arranging her marriage, he also was moving his family into the Comuna San Jacinto del Pindo, the newly established indigenous territory ranging from just south of Puyo to the Pastaza River.[5] The young couple started their married life in this territory and continued to live there as they reared their ten children over the course of a number of difficult years. Being an outsider brought inside to help his father-in-law, Paushi had tentative control of some land because the oldest daughter has permanent rights to swidden garden territory, and this becomes part of her husband's right as well. But in practice such rights of usufruct depend on sustained alliances with recognized kin. The couple moved periodically as alliances shifted in the face of ecological factors, on the one hand, and national and international pressures, regionally defined, on the other. Eventually it became necessary for Paushi to accept sporadic contract labor for petroleum exploration companies.

Paushi was not alone in seeking outside work, for practically all the *comuneros* were being thrust into the booming capitalist economy as it became more and more difficult to balance subsistence work, trade, and religious and commercial patronage. During the early forays of foreign petroleum companies into the eastern rain forests of Ecuador, Paushi worked alongside some of his wife's brothers and cousins. In later explorations, many of the same men and their older sons and/or sons-in-law were hired for the labor force that cleared passages through the forest, strung dynamite wire, built base camps, and cooked for the crews. By the 1970s the men were being flown to work sites that earlier could be reached only by foot and canoe, near land that Clara's father had cleared during the 1930s in anticipation of the grand scheme to build a railroad from Andean Ambato to Amazonian Curaray to connect with the lines running between the Andes and the coast.

The nation's early-twentieth-century dream, shared with Brazil, was to link the Pacific and Atlantic Oceans. The Amazonian, Andean, and coastal railroads would be coupled with the Amazon and tributary ports to serve both nations. The Ecuadorian and Brazilian vision was shattered in 1941 when Peru invaded Ecuador during what Jaime Galarza (1972) called "the Petroleum War" (between Royal Dutch Shell in Ecuador and Standard Oil of New Jersey in Peru). Peru seized half of Ecuador's Amazonian territory and carved out a sovereign swath across the region of imagined collaboration. Ecuador's desire to link its coast with its eastern forest was renewed in the 1970s, this time by an oil pipeline that would fuel an anticipated epoch of new industrial expansion and wealth.

Once oil was flowing from the northern Amazonian region, petroleum interests temporarily abandoned the central and southern sections and shifted their exploration to the coastal side of the Andes. In July 1980 a labor recruiter held interviews at a local hotel in Puyo (on the site where Clara's father had sold land to a German colonist and his Ecuadorian wife), and Comuna men flocked in, hoping to be part of the thirty or so chosen. While waiting their turn for an interview, they talked to some of the hotel guests, including an ethnobotanist from Harvard and two herpetologists from the University of Kansas. On the Fourth of July they were treated to a North American–style barbecue and picnic, stayed around awhile to watch the assembled gringos gyrate to thunderous disco music, and then took bags of leftover hamburgers and hot dogs home to their families. They were back the next morning for the final selection, and at 6:00 P.M. a busload set out for the area near Santo Domingo de los Colorados, where they would run dynamite lines through a region dominated by African palm and sugar-cane plantations. Paushi and one son signed on with the recruiter. Another son wanted to go but decided to stay home to complete his paramedical training, tend his twenty or more cattle, and help his wife through the impending birth of their sixth child.

Watching the excitement of the busy hiring scene, Clara's older brother reminisced about his experiences in the Ecuadorian-Peruvian War of 1941, when he was about sixteen years old, and about his subsequent work trips for petroleum companies. He was eager to join this group but lacked some necessary permits. His wife was not well and wanted him to stay home anyway. He said his good-byes to several nephews who were leaving on the bus and returned home to the Comuna. The next evening he was back in Puyo, this time to report that he had just taken his next-to-youngest son to a nearby hospital. The sixteen-year-old youth had fallen from a tree while hunting, and his gun had discharged, sending two small shot into his head. They penetrated the upper eyelid, moved into the brain through the eye socket, and continued all the way to the back of the skull, leaving massive damage. Death came to him in thirty-six hours. During the following days, the wake and funeral were crushing for the immediate family and close kin.

Unable to provide the required military release forms, Paushi returned from Santo Domingo the next day in time to help his brother-in-law with wake and funeral arrangements. The occasion was triply sad for Clara and him, for they mourned not only the loss of their nephew but also of their last-born child, who had died before he turned two, and of their eighteen-year-old daughter, who had died just a few years ago. During the wake, the mothers cried out their stylized death wails, male relatives of the deceased's father served alcohol, and guests not related to the deceased's immediate kindred played traditional funeral games (see N. Whitten 1976:136–37) through which the opposite of grief—uproarious humor—is expressed. Clara's daughters continuously served manioc food beverage from delicate ceramic bowls that they and their mother had made.

While Clara, like other Canelos Quichua women, makes ceramics for the basic purposes of producing, storing, and serving *aswa*, the quality and variety of vessels far exceeds the demands of necessity. Her own store of knowledge and ability to integrate this with her participatory and visionary experiences are the sources of her creative expressions in pottery and in songs. Because these expressions reflect her control of powerful imagery, she is widely regarded as a strong visionary woman (*sinchi muscuj warmi*). This figure of speech is one of respect and admiration, but it is also tinged with envy when used by some of her fellow master potters. When Clara sings the song *Sacha Allcu Warmi Mani* (I am a bush dog woman), which she learned by listening to her grandmother, she takes the role of the little bush dog, wandering around through a palm thicket in the forest, seemingly lost but trying to return, looking very sad and barking "how how

how" as she walks, stands up, then walks some more. Clara's small *sacha allcu* figurine has small, rounded ears and a short snout. To an outsider, the song and the figurine are unremarkable depictions of an animal that exists deep in the forest but that is seldom seen. To Canelos Quichua people, they evoke the image of Amasanga, master spirit of rain-forest dynamics, for *sacha allcu* is his mascot; it accompanies him on his travels, barking "how how how" at any sign of danger.

Included in her repertoire are songs about other animals and birds, nuts and trees of the forest, and mythical figures such as the Toucan person, a symbol of liberation "who doesn't kill in eating nuts." Some of her songs tell of personal experiences in going to Quito, capital of the Republic of Ecuador, where her mother had never gone, and walking the streets in black, black shoes. Other songs draw on imagery and events from mythic time-space and apply them to present circumstances, as in *Jatun Machinmi* (Big monkey):

> Big monkey, big monkey, big monkey, from just here he will call,
> from just here he will call.
> They say if the big monkey comes, he will stay, dying in a big trap,
> he will stay, dying.
> If the big, big monkey just comes, he just stays, remains, dead.
> What are you saying to me, little sister,
> what do you say to me?
> Perhaps he didn't die, perhaps he will come — we'll just see, little
> sister.
> Perhaps the monkey person isn't dead.
> My dear husband, my dear husband was a monkey person,
> perhaps in vain he became dead.
> He will come, little sister, we shall see, little sister,
> we shall see his face, little sister.

Two pieces of Clara's pottery reflect the dual meaning of the word *machin* and the essence of her song. One figurine is a straightforward representation of a woolly monkey, with his face blackened and his tail casually resting on his shoulder. A spout protrudes from his back, for this *machin* was designed to serve *aswa* at a traditional kinship festival. The other figure has a round head placed on a body shaped like an edible gourd. One hand is raised to the baseball cap shoved back on his head, and the mouth is wide open. This monkey is the epitome of *machin* as stranger, or *machin runa*, a foreign person. He is the oil boss shouting orders to his indigenous workers, orders that they must understand emotionally if not literally. In mythic time-space, *machin runa* tried to ensnare two beautiful women, but they were liberated by the forest-dwelling *sicuanga runa*, toucan person. Clara's husband was an outsider brought into a system where he was nearly trapped by another external system, the capitalist economy. The oil boss was seen as a figure of entrapment, and the ceramic image of entrapment was made to sell to tourists for much-needed money.

Imagery and Art Worlds

In historical times, nonindigenous middlemen traded Canelos Quichua ceramics eastward toward central Amazonian markets at Iquitos and Manaus, and westward toward Andean markets. Within their own region, Canelos Quichua people themselves exchanged ceramics for favors from patrons, offered them as gifts to prestigious visitors, and sporadically sold them for extra cash. Some pieces found their way to exclusive shops in Quito, in North America, and in Europe. A few were included in a batch of largely lowland Peruvian ethnographic art auctioned by the Parke-Bernet Galleries in 1970.[6] The catalogue for this sale included notes provided by the North American collectors about when and where pieces were collected; use of the item; from whom the item was acquired, meaning the "tribal name" and previous Western owner, if any; and the condition of the "tribe" — for example, "completely assimilated," "impoverished" with no tribal tradition, or "entirely Christianized." The lack of complete information about every item did not distract from the lure of exotica created by this and many other galleries and shops.

The message of salvaging the last examples of the art of destabilized, and preferably savage, "tribes" suggests an ancient heritage lost to the consciousness of fast-disappearing peoples of dark, alien worlds. After cloaking the art of indigenous others in mystery, dealers then situate it within the framework of contemporary Western art worlds:

"the ideas and shapes of primitive art fit well with modern design." Alas, "original Tribal Art came to an end around the turn of the century in Oceania, and in Africa a few decades later. . . . Because the usual medium of primitive art was perishable, little exists from previous centuries, so a time shutter before and after the 19th Century limits supply. Collectors can now buy beautiful craftsmanship cheaply in a market that is likely to appreciate the art over the next few years. (*Anthropology Today* 1989:26, quoting from Bonham's Auction Guide No. 10)

Pressures toward exclusivity in the art world are countered by efforts to promote mass production. During the 1970s, some Peace Corps volunteers, in trying to increase the cash flow to Canelos Quichua peoples, encouraged potters to produce ashtrays, coffee cups, saucers, and plates in large quantities. When enough stock could be accumulated, they said, a full-page advertisement in the Sears catalog would be purchased, and successful sales of "Indian pottery" would allow the potters to purchase "good" commercial clays, paints, glazes, wheels, and kilns. Potters could transform their traditional art into a growth industry and become prosperous, if only the Sears venture were to succeed. It did not. The few potters who experimented with the new forms tested local and national markets and soon learned that there is such a thing as aesthetic appreciation for a beautiful, knowledgeably made object. The manufacture of Canelos Quichua ceramics has thus far survived pressures toward the two extremes of exclusivity and mass production, and it continues in the face of rapid modernization.

For more than two decades, external development forces have contributed heavily to the growth of infrastructure within Ecuador, with consequences reaching from the national political economy right down to the basis of local indigenous livelihood. Near the headwaters of the Pastaza River, in an eastern Andean gorge, a huge dam, financed by an international consortium, is the source of electricity for the Amazonian Pastaza Province. Old roads are constantly being improved, and heavy machinery is used to decimate forests and construct new roads through the heart of indigenous terrain. New schools, springing up alongside the roads, serve as meeting halls for assemblies organized by anyone wishing contact with local community members. On the edge of indigenous territory, a complex of large wooden buildings has been constructed by another international consortium and given to the indigenous confederation of the Amazonian region to conduct various training courses and eventually to house a high school. One indigenous organization now has its own airplane and a foreign pilot to fly leaders to outlying areas, and perhaps to train them to fly. Puyo, the capital of Pastaza Province, had an official population of 18,000 in 1989 and according to its mayor "is a city in permanent growth" (*El Comercio, Crónicas* sec., Dec. 29, 1989).

In the face of this constantly modernizing situation, Canelos Quichua women continue to make pottery for their own everyday household use, for ceremonial occasions, and for sale. As indicated earlier, sales of ceramics have evolved from local to national and international markets. During the late 1970s and early 1980s, the sporadic but pervasive commoditization of ceramics was surpassed by the rampant commoditization of a newly introduced art form: balsa wood carving and painting. This strictly commercial enterprise fulfilled a consumptive urge of the outside world and an economic need of the indigenous world. Completely externally directed, this new art form could not have become successful without the woodworking skills and ecological knowledge of the indigenous carvers, primarily men, and the technical input of a North American artist-entrepreneur. The manufacture and sale of wood and pottery art have become important sources of income for many Canelos Quichua people and have involved them in a myriad of collaborative, sometimes hostile, and cross-cutting relationships and negotiations that are both intracultural and intercultural.[7]

While the wood carvings caught on very quickly in the tourist-oriented ethnic-art market, the ceramics limped along, frequently under the misnomer of "Jívaro pottery." Finally, however, these ceramics have gained national and international recognition, in part through publications about them, and the appreciation of them in their own right has enhanced sales far more than did the earlier promotion of them as objects made by "pristine savages" best known for their head-shrinking skills.[8]

Recognition and appreciation of the ceramics by participants in the art worlds of others eventually led to exhibitions, which in turn triggered another kind of feedback. When potters looked at photographs of their works on display and heard the words of praise from others, they responded by creating pottery for a new purpose: to be exhibited in order to educate outsiders about Canelos Quichua culture. Forerunners, or pioneers, of this movement to create in order to educate were Juana Catalina Chango and

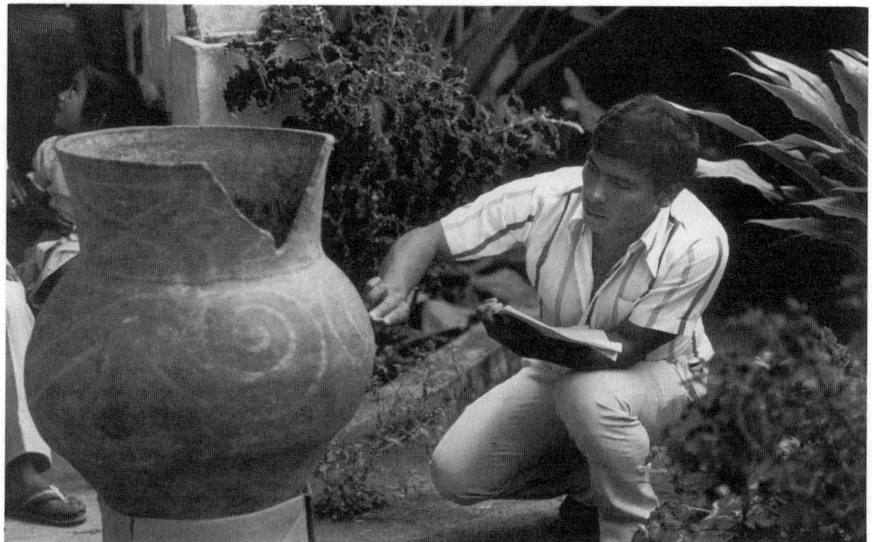

Figure 10.2. Alfonso Chango making an initial sketch of an archaeological urn from Charapa Cocha.

her brother, Alfonso Chango. In 1975 Juana made a large ceramic tapir with thick walls and no serving spout. It was unlike festival figurines but realistic enough for North American audiences to visualize this tropical rain-forest animal. Alfonso works with paper, pens, and paints to portray the cosmology of the Canelos Quichua (Fig. 10.2). His drawings and descriptions of shamanic practices have been published and distributed in Ecuador and the United States. In Amazonian Ecuador, his booklet *Yachaj Sami Yachachina* (Shaman-class teachings; Chango Santi 1984), has been used in a course for training medical auxiliaries. Eventually, through drawings and explanations based on songs and tales of his mother and father, he clarified the picture of the mythical origin of pottery clay that had been emerging from many people over a number of years.[9]

Prelude to a Myth

Two exhibitions in 1987 framed an outpouring of lore, including the mythical origin of pottery clay, conveyed through songs, stories, and ceramic figurines. The exhibitions took place during our residence in Ecuador in 1986–87. The first was invited by the director of the Museum of the Central Bank of Ecuador, to be held in Quito to commemorate February 12, 1542, the day that Francisco de Orellana purportedly discovered the Amazon. The second was invited by the mayor of Puyo and was to be held in that city in conjunction with the annual celebration of its legendary founding on May 12, 1899, by Friar Alvaro Vallardares. Four hundred and ninety-five years after its "discovery" by Europeans, the Amazonian region — itself declared a myth by President Galo Plaza Lasso in 1948 and revived as a nationalist emblem by President Velasco Ibarra in the early 1960s ("Ecuador has been, is, and will be, an Amazonian Nation!") — was receiving national and local recognition through the artwork of its indigenous people. The title of both exhibitions was ¡*Causaunchimi!* — We are living!

Initially the Quito exhibition was intended to display ceramics from the museum's own collection, to be complemented by some new acquisitions. As planning progressed, it became clear that the museum's holdings did not include representations of important facets of Canelos Quichua culture revealed to us after we made the collections in the early and mid 1970s, and the director authorized us to acquire new items. Even before a date was confirmed, we began to spread the word of a probable exhibition later in the year, in Quito. Both the time and the place seemed remote, and responses were fairly casual except for the intense interest of a few potters. One of these was Esthela Dagua (Plate 14), who had been living in urban Puyo for several years and who was dedicating herself to pottery making full-time in order to support her eight children. Before long she had turned out a series of large-scale animals and birds, smaller figurines, intricately painted storage jars, and a blackware cooking pot so big that she had to have help from her teenage son when she fired it. Between the sequences of coiling, drying, decorating, and firing large pieces, she found time to make a number of significant small items. Among these were figures of edible palm larvae, edible flying ants, turtles, and turtle eggs, all of which were indicative of human dependence on a tropical ecosystem for protein to supplement the basic carbohydrates from cultivated crops. She also made figures of inedible bracket fungi with faces painted on one side, symbolic of mythic transformation and regeneration, and realistic wild cacao nuts, representative of the natural festival drinking bowls of humanlike monkeys in mythic time-space. She gave special attention to a pair of ceramic trumpets to be presented to two important men to blow during festival activity. In addition to rounding out the museum's collections with her own work, she helped to obtain pottery from women who were visiting Puyo from outlying areas of Pastaza Province, and she brought to our attention another Puyo household of potters who were producing ceramic art for the national and international ethnic-art market.

Little new information about myths and mythic beings was generated during the period of collecting in the fall of 1986, with two exceptions. Soon after we began work in Puyo in 1986 we accompanied Esthela and her son to cut and gather bamboo firewood for her pottery making. The next day, as she was working her clay, Esthela asked if I (Sibby) saw something and became frightened while in the bamboo thicket. Not knowing that I had stepped on a bamboo thorn, she became frightened after seeing me leave hurriedly but said nothing at the time. She now said she thought I had seen the bamboo spirit (Wamaj supai), a fierce female spirit that lives in the thicket and that jealously guards it from those who come to steal from her. After Esthela confided that she cuts in that thicket only when the owner is in Quito, she showed us a pair of bamboo spirits (male and female) that she was fashioning. This was her first movement into the rare potter's universe of actually creating representations of dangerous spirits. She was becoming *sinchi muscuj warmi*, a strong visionary woman.

A few weeks later, during a trip to mine pottery clay, Esthela and several friends explained to us, as had other potters in the past, the different qualities of clay needed to make fine bowls, large storage jars, and cookware, and where these clays could be found at distant mine sites. The mine near the Shuar Jivaroan settlement of Pitarishca on the Sigüín road, for example, yields the smooth gray plastic clay (similar to Kentucky Blue in the United States) with evenly distributed fine, sandy granules that is ideal for making thin-walled drinking bowls. The mine near the colonist settlement of San Pedro on the road to the headwaters of the Bobonaza River contains the heavier grade yellowish clay with more grit and minute pebbles, suitable for the pots that have to withstand high cooking temperatures.

Storage jars must have strong walls to endure the heavy bulk of fermenting manioc pulp, but their exterior surface should be beautiful, smoothly burnished, and decorated. If an ideal clay is not found, a mixture

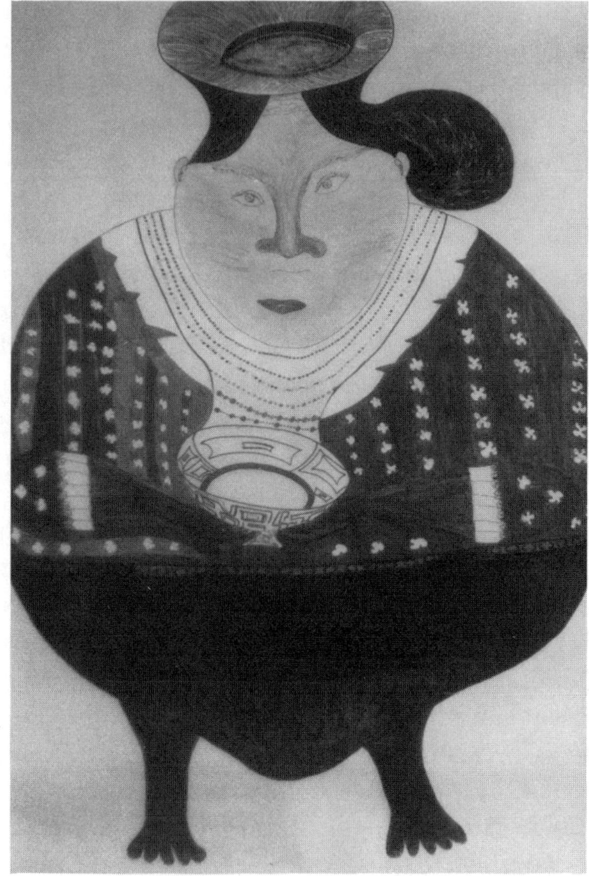

Figure 10.3. Manga allpa mama (Master spirit of pottery clay), as rendered by Alfonso Chango.

is made from the gray and yellow clays to produce a sturdy paste with a balance of grittiness and tiny pebbles that feels right to the potter's touch. Although they know about the use of sand, ash, and ground-up sherds for temper, they prefer naturally tempered secondary clays to which they add nothing. As the women discussed clays and mines, they repeatedly mentioned "Manga allpa mama" (Fig. 10.3) without explaining what this meant. We knew from previous remarks by other potters that the name referred to a master spirit of pottery clay, but at this time we had little understanding of it other than that it was a transformation of the spirit master of garden soil and pottery clay, Nungwi (see, e.g., D. Whitten 1981; N. Whitten 1976, 1985; D. Whitten and N. Whitten 1988).

Activities escalated in the spring of 1987, with a concomitant flow of information. *¡Causaunchimi!* opened in Quito on March 10 (about a month later than originally planned), and several weeks later we returned to see it with a busload of the artists who had contributed to it. After first checking their own individual works on display, the thirty-one people went systematically through the entire exhibition, commenting on every concept and component, going over the myths that were represented, and explaining all of this to a Quichua-speaking guide from Otavalo. She could read the Spanish labels and texts, but many of the artists could not. Later, when she took them through the archaeological museum in the same building, her explanations and the lively questions and discussions were again in Quichua.

Shortly after this trip, city counselor César Abad informally invited us to "bring the Quito exhibition to Puyo." When this turned out to be impossible, because the Quito exhibition was scheduled to run through June, we immediately set out to re-create *¡Causaunchimi!* with new materials. The artists who went to Quito, having interpreted and absorbed two professionally mounted exhibitions, were well prepared to help, and enthusiastically spread the news that *ñucanchi yachai*, "our cultural knowledge," would be displayed in Puyo. Suddenly preparations were underway for an exhibition that would feature an array of significant indigenous ceramic portrayals of myth, history, and modernity. Everything had to be produced in a very brief span of time.

Pottery making was especially intensive and expansive in the household that specialized in fine pottery for the market.[10] Rebeca Hualinga, originally from Sarayacu, seemed to attract other potters from that Bobonaza River settlement — noted for its exquisite ceramics — to her Puyo home, where she had lived for years. She was working collectively with two other potters from Sarayacu, Amadora Aranda Canelos and Santa Hualinga, whom we had known since 1971. We had visited Rebeca's home several times in recent months to see the women's pottery, usually finely decorated drinking bowls and shiny black eating bowls. To this point, most of their products had been sent to Quito with indigenous and nonindigenous entrepreneurs as a strictly commercial venture. Now, a week after the Quito trip, Santa had two figurines to sell for the exhibition; one was Indi, the sun, and the other portrayed Nungwi, the master spirit of garden soil and pottery clay. Rebeca, holding Santa's Nungwi in her hands, spontaneously rendered the Manga allpa mama myth and then asked if she and the others could see "the video" we had previously invited them to watch.[11]

A few days later, the three women and Esthela came to our house, and after being served cokes and cookies, settled down to watch *Our Knowledge, Our Beauty*. The festive atmosphere and initial joking and giggling quickly turned into intense concentration as they watched the unfolding of scenes of familiar places and people, listened to the songs, and commented under their breath about the juxtapositions of ceramics and wood carvings. Santa squealed with pleasure as she saw her Black woman figurine, made in 1975, blow her magical breath on Toucan person (made by Alicia Canelos, Amadora's mother, for a kinship ceremony in Sarayacu in 1976) to transform him into the long-billed bird we know today. Esthela beamed when she was shown making pottery, and they all commented on whatever concept was being portrayed even though the narration was in English. Before long, another master potter, Apacha Vargas, and her husband joined the group to watch a tape made earlier that morning of the final burning of a dugout canoe — to make it buoyant and impervious to water — and to see portions of the video of the indigenous artists going through their exhibition in Quito. Among those artists was a man affectionately nicknamed Rucu, "The Elder," who was now completing this canoe for the Puyo exhibition, and his wife, a well-known potter.

During the same week we acquired more ceramic figurines, bowls, and hardwood carvings, accepted the formal invitation for the exhibition from the mayor, and submitted a brief article about the vitality of the indigenous people to the municipal review (*Pastaza: Un municipio al servicio del Pueblo*; N. Whitten and D. Whitten 1987) to be distributed on May 12. We were shown the city architect's plans for a huge concrete *mucawa* already under construction in the center of town, and then the delicate bowl from Sarayacu with a striking anaconda motif that was his model for the monument. The bowl itself was for sale in a music and ethnic-art store in Puyo.

An interlude followed in the form of a short business trip to Quito, during which we arranged for the Abya-Yala Press to set up a book exhibit in the forthcoming exhibition and saw the Quito version of ¡*Causaunchimi!* dismantled two months early. Back in Puyo by May 1, we found the bases for the exhibition nearly finished and the women potters with a bevy of new creations. Esthela had completed a large standing anteater, other animal figurines, and a very large cooking pot covered with thumbnail impressions that simulated an armadillo's skin. At Rebeca's house, the women brought out an astounding array of figurines: Amasanga, master spirit of the rain forest; an iguanid, his seat of power; a jaguar, his corporeal representation; Hurihuri supai, a dangerous spirit master transformed from the Amasanga associated with "our rain forest" into an underearth spirit of others, the *machin runa*, monkey people; and two representations of Nungwi, one as spirit master of garden soil and the other as spirit master of pottery clay. Seemingly inspired by all of this, Rebeca held Santa's Hurihuri figurine before our video camera and told about this peculiar creature, with his doglike feet and with teeth in the back of his head, then went on to repeat the myth of Manga allpa mama, illustrating with her own Nungwi-pottery clay figurine, and finally sang a song about Ayambi, an iguanid, while demonstrating its undulating movements with the ceramic likeness she had made.

Wedged in between the opening of ¡*Causaunchimi!* in Quito and the return to see it with indigenous artists was a full day's video "studio" work with Alfonso and his mother, Clara, documenting various segments of the Manga allpa mama myth: the moon, the Squash woman, Potoo bird (a member of the Nightjar family), and different manifestations of the spirit of pottery clay and garden soil. In the past, Clara and her daughter Juana, among many others, had rendered myth segments as both encapsulated and continuing parts of a larger emerging story about these transformational beings. Alfonso was now drawing graphic representations of his mother's stories, while she explained his drawings through song and narration. The day yielded volumes of songs and tales to be transcribed and translated at some future date and two large, colorful paintings — soon put to use — of the spirit of pottery clay and an affiliate, the spirit of drinking bowls.

As Alfonso's paintings were being hung in the Puyo gallery (the converted municipal library), César Abad became fascinated with the interplay of ceramic and painted images. He rushed home and returned with his contribution to the exhibition: two intact archaeological urns. They were about 2.5 feet high and were painted with deep-red and white diamond and circular designs. They appeared to be transitional between Marajó pottery, various manifestations of Tupian pottery, and contemporary Canelos Quichua pottery. They had been found recently by residents of Charapa Cocha (Turtle Lake), a settlement on the Pastaza River near the Peruvian border, forty-five minutes flying time southeast of Puyo. This territory had been settled in 1980 by an extended kindred group of Achuar Jivaroan people seeking refuge from escalating feuds in their former home, Capahuari, which was the original home of Paushi, husband of Clara and father of Alfonso.[12]

By 1985, Charapa Cocha had an airstrip, a school, and a meetinghouse for the rapidly growing population of about a hundred. César Abad had worked unstintingly to bring the school and bilingual education to the settlement, and for this he was presented with the first two urns discovered in a section of riverbank that had fallen after floodwaters receded (Plate 15). They were given not only to express appreciation, and for safekeeping from would-be looters, but also because they did not fit the self-identified cultural heritage of the Achuar, who wanted to know what outsiders thought about the urns they regarded as inherently beautiful and powerful, but "of others," not "theirs."

The *¡Causaunchimi!* exhibition opened on schedule the evening of May 8 after two final days of putting up texts and maps, securing objects to bases with monofilament fishing line, moving in the full-size canoe, fetching newly made wooden items from outlying hamlets, escorting a local photographer through his video coverage, and setting up television and audio systems. The activity and mood of excitement approached the frenzy of final preparations for an indigenous festival. Space had to be found for last-minute spontaneous contributions, including large storage jars and cooking pots and a small-scale pottery canoe Rebeca had made after she saw the real one on video at our house. Impressed by the beauty and significance of the ceramics (which represented virtually all major myths and mythical beings), a crowd of indigenous and nonindigenous people alike lingered over displays, the former frequently becoming enthusiastic interpreters for the latter. Indigenous appreciation was reflected by

Rucu, the canoe maker, a long-time friend who strode around the room, looking carefully at everything, apparently reliving memories. Rubbing his palms, he repeatedly said "I like it, I like it."

Drawn to the urns, a cluster of indigenous women gathered around Abad for a serious discussion. They were fascinated with the designs and with the idea of beautiful antiquity extending from beginning times-places, perhaps from mythic time-space, down through the times of destruction to the times of the ancestors and into the present. Compared to their own delicate, thin-walled pottery, the thick walls of the urns were "like cement," but they were beautiful in their near indestructibility. The women wondered where the ancient potters got their clay and what kind of clay it was. Abad admitted that this also puzzled the women and men of Charapa Cocha. They had no source of clay as strong as cement, and they were sure the urns were not made by their ancestors.

The Achuar relegated the urns to the domain of Tsunki, their master spirit of the water world and first shaman, whose power is often related to outsiders.[13] The Canelos Quichua discussed whether these giant vessels had been made to store *aswa* or to hold the bones of deceased humans (some are found with human bones in them), a practice several women had heard of from their grandparents. There was no doubt in the potters' minds that the diamond-patterned mazeway painted on one urn represented the anaconda, but the swirling circular motif of the other could not be clearly interpreted, though it evoked a great deal of speculation about the Charapa runa, the mythical spirit person who is believed to inhabit the area around Charapa Cocha and to steal Achuar women. The Charapa runa is said to have special relationships with the Canelos Quichua people of the Bobonaza River region. The design itself was unknown in the contemporary potters' iconography but was obviously important to the ancient ones who made the urn. By the time the exhibition ended ten days later, it was generally conceded that those ancient pottery makers could safely be claimed as ancestors of the contemporary Canelos Quichua people but not of the Achuar Jivaroan people, with whom they intermarry. The source of the clay, however, remained a deep mystery, as did the meaning of the spiral designs.

The sad, empty feeling that comes with dismantling an exhibition was not only shared but poignantly expressed by two friends. Rebeca and Rucu stopped by at different times to take a last look and to offer assistance in packing. When we arrived home to unload, Rucu was waiting, and he stayed to watch, commenting in a melancholy way on each item — who made it, where it came from, and where it was in the exhibition. We stopped by Rebeca's house later to purchase her pottery canoe and to say good-bye to Amadora, who was to return to Sarayacu the next day. Suddenly Rebeca was telling us how sad the big kinship ceremonies used to be. Hundreds of people would come, they would have a wonderful festival, then everybody would go away, leaving only three or four families in the place where all had been together — very, very sad. To some, at least, the massed spirits in the exhibition evoked the expansive sentience of a festive ceremony, with its merger of intrusive outside forces and inside, indigenous knowledge and power. The end of the exhibition signaled a return to the reality of the mundane world.

A new outside force soon appeared in the hubbub of everyday life in Puyo in the form of the United States Army. Through an agreement between President León Febres Cordero and Vice-President George Bush, the troops were sent to Ecuador to build a new road between Archidona and the Agua Rico River. Construction began only fifty miles north of Puyo in the area of Napo Province that had been very badly damaged by an earthquake on March 5. In Quito the National Congress refused to allow the United States armed forces to land on sovereign territory, but after heated debate among Ecuadorian military leaders and legislators, the agreement with Bush prevailed and the troops moved in. The airport at Shell, eight miles west of Puyo, was readied as a staging area for Hercules fixed-wing aircraft and Blackhawk helicopters. United States army pilots, officers, and key personnel were housed in Puyo hotels, while field troops set up camp on the outskirts of Archidona. Almost overnight, prostitutes driving late-model Troopers appeared on the streets of Puyo, and cases of Bacardi rum were stocked by enterprising store owners. In Archidona, a reported thirty booths were set up by artisans from Otavalo to sell their famous hand-woven woolens as souvenirs, and thousands of cases of Budweiser beer were airlifted from the United States and stocked in the temporary PX.

While the military was becoming entrenched amidst continuing national debates on the question of sovereignty and on the danger of the introduction of AIDS by U.S. troops, Esthela's world was shattered when her landlady decided to bulldoze her house into the abutting creek with only a few hours' abrupt notice. Esthela kept working on her pottery until the very last minute, trying to fire one large, incompletely dried storage jar in the rain as the roaring bulldozer approached. Inside her house, the opening strains of the *Ode to Joy* poured forth from her radio. After the house was razed, she stated quite simply that "when the house died, Esthela died." Within a few days, however, she had relocated her family to a new site where her husband was building their house with materials bought with her earnings from pottery sales, and she was once again busy at work. Within a month she had assembled her first pottery shaman group, made figurines based on one she had seen in the archaeological museum in Quito, and created a representation of Cachi amu, spirit master of salt.

During this same period, Alfonso volunteered to translate into Quichua the Spanish version of the script of *Our Knowledge, Our Beauty*. Before he tackled that job, however, he decided it was time to review some of the abundant materials we now had.

It was important, he carefully pointed out, for him to *interpret* what had been given to us so that we and others might better understand the nature of the indigenous incorporation of thought and knowledge. In Spanish he used the exact cognate, *interpretación*, that one would expect. In Quichua, he explained, "we call this *cuintaushcata ricuchina quillcaushcata*." *Cuintaushcata* means spoken or told; *ricuchina* means to show, teach, or explain; *quillcaushcata* means written or inscribed. His phrase for interpretation, then, means "narrative written to explain." Specifically, he wanted to interpret the myths recently written, drawn, sung, and narrated by his mother and him. Part of the process of interpretation must involve full explication (*explicación*) of the text. That which is obviously implicit among sharers of indigenous knowledge must be made explicit in an interpretation to outsiders. The prelude had ended, the myths were recorded, but only through indigenous interpretation based on reflexivity could others, such as us, understand something embedded in Canelos Quichua mythology that is usually left unsaid.

Explication of a Myth

From the extensive, expansive, on-going mythology of the Canelos Quichua presented to us over a number of years, we extract here only those segments that have immediate relevance to Alfonso's interpretation. His reflexive explication is based on his deep cultural knowledge and his awareness that others do not share that knowledge.

In the transition from the earlier mythic time-space into beginning times-places, Hilucu was a beautiful woman whose handsome lover came to her only at night. After becoming pregnant she wanted to see the father of her child, so one night before his arrival she cooked a seed from the *Genipa americana* tree and later painted her lover's face and body with beautiful designs, telling him that it would make him feel "fresh" (*Genipa americana* is an astringent). Much later, in the predawn hours after he had left, she looked at the sky and saw the full ("ripe") Quilla (Moon man) in his complete masculinity. Clearly, he was her brother, and his face and body were covered with the lovely black designs she had painted on him.

She knew then that she had committed incest, that her children would inherit male and female soul substances from the same consanguine source. Her sisters, including Red woman (*Bixa orellana*) and Black woman (*Genipa americana*) were also living in the sky at this time. Seeing that their brother, moon, and their sister had enjoyed an incestuous union, they painted their faces black with the same paint, and they cried and cried. Their tears fell to earth and seeded the *Genipa americana* tree in all of the areas where the contemporary people now live and where their ancestors lived.

All the stars cried too, producing the dreaded merger of rain, earthquake, and flood. The rivers swelled, volcanoes erupted, high new hills appeared, and the earth shook and shuddered. The earth people, descendants of Hilucu and Quilla, were caught up in a great river that swept them eastward into the (Amazonian) sea. Out of this river came Indi, the sun, who had been living in a cave at the base of the Andes. He ascended to the sky to begin his regular course and to bring the orderly east-west axis to the earth world. As Indi exploded out of the Amazon, thousands of tiny colored bubbles flew outward, as did thousands of white ones. The colored bubbles became seed beads, to be found later by deep Amazonian peoples such as the Achuar Jivaroans and Cocama Tupians, who traded them westward to the contemporary people.

The white bubbles became salt that lodged in eastern mines to which the indigenous people would trek for this desirable flavoring for their native foods. Some would travel for a year or more to the Marañón River area, where, many say, they had to appease not only Jivaroan, Cocama, Candoshi, and other residents but also the Cachi amu. Cachi amu is an undulating, sentient overseer of salt. Many women, especially master potters, say that Cachi amu is strictly feminine, but men, whose fathers made the trips to collect salt, say that Cachi amu is androgynous.

While humans and animals were becoming what they are today in the transformations occurring from mythic time-space to beginning times-places, spirit masters, too, were transforming.

Nungwi, a beautiful spirit woman dressed in shimmering blue-black, was a sister of Manduru warmi (Red woman) and Widuj warmi (Black woman). As Nungwi walked in the forest with her daughter, Hunculu (who in some variants of this myth may also be her sister), three men — Quindi (hummingbird), Acanga (hawk), and Sicuanga (toucan) — competed for Hunculu's hand in marriage by trying to clear trees for a garden plot.

Eventually the women came to an area that Hummingbird had cleared, where sunlight warmed the leaf litter. They decided to plant manioc and got lots of manioc sticks, piles of them. Nungwi painted them red with *Bixa orellana* and then painted her own face with the color of her red sister, and in that way the manioc and Nungwi "knew" each other. Without this relationship of knowledge, the manioc would suck the blood of anyone who tried to control the plant's growth. Nungwi began to dig with a palm-wood stick. She dug and dug, working steadily in the leaf litter and upper soil until she became very tired. Hunculu said, "I'll dig for you," and she dug half a garden, becoming so tired that she could not continue. Soon she regained her strength and attacked the soil with her digging stick, going deeper and deeper into the unproductive base of the forest rather than remaining in the litter and rich upper soil. Whack, whack — she dug a great hole. Down went Hunculu into this hole, down into the base of the forest roots, digging and digging.

Nungwi looked down into the hole at her daughter and blew on her with her magical breath, saying, "Stay that way," and changed Hunculu into a large frog. And so Hunculu remained, and so she is today, a sentient, feminine being deep within the roots of the garden and forest. Hunculu then looked up at Nungwi and said, "Suuuuuuuu, Nungwi mama, saquiringui (You stay that way)." And Nungwi stayed as she is today, a harmless white-throated black coral snake with a mouth too small to bite even the little finger of a human. Nungwi then blew on Quindi and created him as the hummingbird. Thus began the manioc garden, from which comes the fundamental food energy of Amazonian peoples, their source of life-sustaining *aswa*. Nungwi remained in the leaf litter as "upper Nungwi" and in the soil as "lower Nungwi," where she could control the growth of roots, pushing up the precious stems in the cool of the night and being sure that the soul substance "within" was imbued with her totally feminine power of fecundity. Hunculu stayed "within," too, in deep holes in the garden and in the forest, a domesticated female link to the encompassing rain forest. Nungwi today is regarded as the master spirit of women's agriculture and is manifest in garden soil and special growth-promoting stones.

In beginning times-places there was a voluptuous unmarried Squash woman (Sapallu warmi) who was having an affair with Moon man (Quilla). The woman planted a swidden garden with squash, and in the middle of it she lived with Moon man in a huge oval house with a thatched roof. Before the squash matured the only food in the house was that captured by Moon man from the forest with his blowgun. When the squash ripened, Squash woman wished to deceive Moon man, so she stitched up her mouth, saying that she did not like squash. The stitches were to show that the squash was reserved just for Moon man.

One day when he came home from the forest Moon man found that Squash woman had "prepared" raw green squash for him to eat instead of the ripe squash she had previously served. He demanded cooked ripe squash. The woman mumbled through her closed mouth, "There are no ripe ones in the garden." And then, implying that he had accused her of eating the ripe squash, she asked: "How do you think I can eat with this closed mouth?"

The next day, without saying anything, Moon man went to the garden and found nice ripe squash there. He brought them back to Squash woman and said "Please cook these for me and have them ready when I return." He pretended to go off to the forest, but after his woman went to her garden he returned secretly to hide on the roof. Soon, Squash woman brought ripe squash to the house and cooked them. Opening her stitched mouth wide, she ate all of them and began to prepare green squash for her man. When she left to fetch water for cooking, he came down from the roof and left. Later he came back from the forest and was served cooked green squash. He said, "The squash is green." He became angry and vexed and told the truth: "You say that you don't like to eat squash, and you say that you don't eat ripe squash in order to deceive me. All right, then," he said, "I am going back to the sky where I belong."

Playing sad songs on his three-hole flute, he moved away toward a vine ladder he had left when he descended to visit Hilucu earlier. He now climbed the ladder linking sky and earth. Hearing and seeing this, Squash woman believed that they both would go live in the sky. She tarried in gathering all of her things, including everything needed to make pottery, but then she filled her basket and set out for where her man had gone. When she arrived at the ladder she could see that he was halfway up it, and she began to climb. When she got halfway up she could see that her man was now in the sky. Moon man turned back to see that she was now halfway up the ladder, and he said, "You defamed me when you tried to deceive me." He cut the rope holding the ladder and she and all of her household and garden belongings fell to earth. Then Quilla blew on the woman with his magical breath, "Suuuuuuuu Hilucu," and said, "You become Hilucu [the Common Potoo bird], and your shit will become special pottery clay!"[14]

Hilucu today is regarded as Manga allpa mama, a transformation of Squash woman; she is the master spirit of pottery clays for eating, drinking, cooking, and storage vessels. The final part of the story of Squash woman, to the best of our knowledge, had always been implicit in previous tellings but was made quite explicit at this time by people stimulated by the festive atmosphere of the exhibitions, the melancholy letdown after the Puyo exhibition, and their reflexive interest in communicating to others their own indigenous interpretation of imagery portrayed through narration and ceramic art. Clara, Alfonso, Rebeca, and others self-consciously told us complete stories so well known among themselves that customarily they are told casually, in segments, and their content expressed by allusion.

Aesthetic Forces

Through indigenous peoples' explication of their imagery, we came to appreciate the aesthetic force of mythology as a sort of transformational tunnel through which lore and history are projected into contemporary life. For example, at one point in the tunnel, Hilucu and Quilla were the mythic ancestral mother and father, and the seed beads that were eventual transformational consequences of their incestuous relation became a medium of exchange connecting early to contemporary Amazonian peoples. In a series of transformations, Hilucu became the master spirit of pottery clay (which needs no temper) for contemporary women potters and presumably for their ancestors. As such, she is a counterpart of Nungwi, the master spirit of women's agriculture.

The strictly feminine force of domestication, seen in the pottery clay–garden soil spirits of Hilucu-Nungwi, is complemented by the master spirit of the rain forest, Amasanga, an androgynous, predatory force who controls the ultimate power of the hydrosphere, Sungui (Tsungui). Amasanga's counterpart, Hurihuri, went through a series of transformations to become the underearth spirit of other people, known as the *machin runa*, monkey people. Mythological beginning times-places are brought into contemporary life in Canelos Quichua festive activity, which plays out the contrast between fully human territory, overseen by Amasanga, and other peoples' territories, associated with monkey abundance and overseen by Hurihuri.

Nowhere is the contrast between the self and the other in mythic and experiential realms more apparent than in the human enactment of kinship festivals. This is a time of expansion, merger, and transformation signaled by the rich integration of performance, narration, and ceramic representations.

The festival has been described in detail elsewhere (Reeve 1985, 1988; N. Whitten 1976, 1985; D. Whitten and N. Whitten 1988). Here it is important to note that the *ayllu jista* (kinship festival), partially embedded in the history of Roman Catholic dominance over indigenous people, continues to be held once or twice a year in every Canelos Quichua hamlet where there is a tangible manifestation of Catholic control, such as a chapel or a niche with a saint. This festival is held whether or not a priest or friar is present, often at a time and place selected without consultation with church officials.[15]

Preparations begin with residents deciding on a division of the hamlet into female and male halves, which represent Hilucu (Potoo bird woman) and Quilla (Moon man), respectively, and then designating a couple to host or be responsible for each division. Each "festival woman" hostess plants a huge manioc garden a year in advance to assure that she will be able to make vast quantities of *aswa*. As the festival approaches, she mines sacks of clays from which she produces, with the help of female relatives and in-laws, a large array of pottery storage jars, several sizes of serving bowls, and fanciful effigy and serving jars. Festival pottery may refer to mythical beings, events, or episodes, or to life at home or in distant places. A few pottery trumpets are usually made for presentation to indigenous authorities. The vivid imagery seen in each potter's distinctive creations expresses the dynamics of her cosmos.

Each division must have its own large festival house to represent Hilucu and Quilla. The men responsible for each festival house select several close male relatives to accompany them on a hunt. A week or so before the actual festival, they trek to distant territories of other people and return on the eve of the event with large quantities of smoked meat and fish.

When the hunters return, the festival begins as controlled chaos. Men don the plumage and animal skins of their game and circle and circle, first counterclockwise, then clockwise, then back again, all the time beating snare drums they have made. The pulse-tremolo of their synchronized drumbeats represents the thunder of the forest spirit master, Amasanga, just as the snares signify the buzz that bees make as they come to the shaman entering seance. Women dance back and forth, their steps like the hop of the toucan-liberator. They throw their hair from side to side, simulating the dance that Nungwi performs before dawn to help the manioc grow. The movement of a woman's head from side to side and the throwing of her unbound hair back and forth signal that *unai* (mythic time-space) has been entered by festival participants. Women constantly serve *aswa* to men and other women (Fig. 10.4), and when strong men become boisterous, women throw *aswa* on them, saying, "If you walk like thunder you must expect to get rained on."

Periodically, the festival crowd forms a ragged procession to move en masse from one house to the other, drumming, playing flutes, and blowing pottery trumpets as they go, and the reciprocal visits continue throughout the ceremony, which lasts about three days. (Fig. 10.5)

During the entire festival period, people tell myths and sing songs, sometimes silently to themselves, to communicate with the spirit world.[16] Clara Santi tells of how they *like* to sing, that it is the "custom" to exchange songs (literally, "to catch each other's songs"). These include the beginning

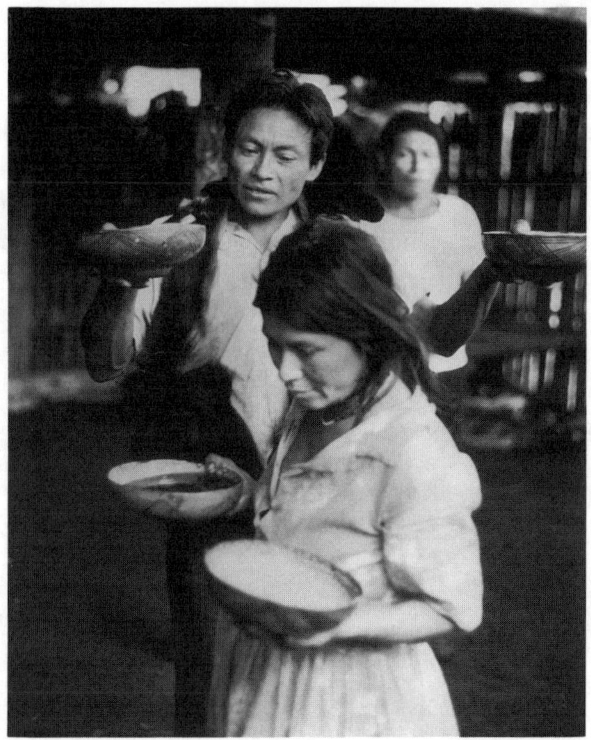

Figure 10.4. Bowl after bowl of *aswa* is served to invited guests.

times-places' song, our mothers' song, and our grandmothers' song. They sing songs for each other, and their hearts become sad. As they sing and tell myths, imagery of the past and present is evoked by the forms and motifs of pottery from which women serve, drink, and play with *aswa*.

The final phase of festival activity is called the *dominario*, from the Spanish word *dominar*, to dominate or control. The *dominario* begins with the men and women dancing through palm arches, like good Christians approaching the chapel. It ends when the greatest force of all, the mighty anaconda, is brought from the river or stream and made to "go out of control." This is represented by a bamboo pole containing four copal torches and borne by four "jaguar men." First it disrupts all the dancers by knocking down the arches. Then it lurches around the central plaza and eventually crashes into the Catholic chapel, symbolically ending external domination. At this point indigenous people say they fear that volcanoes will erupt, floods will come, the sky will turn dark, and everyone will be swept eastward into the Amazon River sea. In mythic times-places, the regeneration and restoration of souls occurred when humans struggled homeward from their ordeals in the interior of Greater Amazonia. People separated by chaos were gradually reunited with their own kind through a wonderful transformation and a shared knowledge of their cosmos.

Aesthetic Conjunctures

The indigenous cosmology signaled by the Canelos Quichua kinship ceremony shows remarkable commonalities with other Amazonian societies

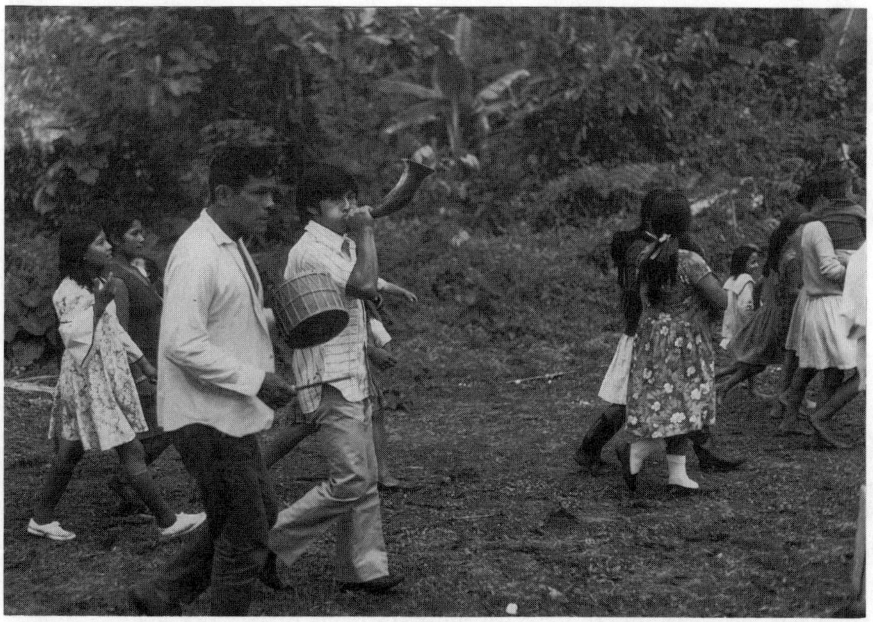

Figure 10.5. While drumming and blowing ceramic trumpets, men and women from the Potoo bird (female) house go en masse to the Moon (male) house during a festival near Puyo.

past and present, as analyzed recently by Lawrence Sullivan (1988). We are tempted to compare this contemporary festival with activities of the Tupinambá described 450 years ago by a European 4,500 miles east of Canelos Quichua territory. But we are restrained from this by the knowledge that contemporary Canelos Quichua perform their richly lived and deeply felt traditional festivals *only* where there is a manifestation of imposed Catholic order. Their ritual performances clearly reflect this tradition as it is now embedded in the historical and contemporary structure of domination and as it expresses contrahegemony in its final, dramatic phase, the *dominario* (see, e.g., D. Whitten and N. Whitten 1988:38–40; N. Whitten 1976:165–202).

When large numbers of people are gathered for a kinship festival, a priest has an opportunity to celebrate mass and perhaps perform marriages. Before a priest's scheduled visit, whether or not he actually arrives, wives and female relatives of the hosts place pottery chalices and candlesticks on the crude split-bamboo altar in the chapel, and visitors present these women with candles just as they do during a wake. On the final afternoon, the priest and his entourage are served a special dinner at tables set in each festival house. Otherwise, the structure and enactment of the festival is entirely indigenous, though Christian symbols are embedded in pottery decorations derived from powerful indigenous images. In addition to chalices or candlesticks, women may shape small pottery chapels or decorate bowls with a cross motif. Explication of the cross is difficult to elicit (though people commonly use the Spanish word *cruz*), but one woman finally and firmly identified her striking design on several bowls as the *cura cruzashca*, the symbol of the priest's blessing as he makes the sign of the Christian cross.

After the hordes of guests depart, quotidian life begins anew before dawn the next day, often with women using up their supply of clay by making more jars and bowls for their home and increasingly, today, for the growing ethnic-art market and for exhibitions. A number of women had quite a large stock of pottery ready and waiting for the annual May 12 celebration in Puyo in 1989. Several of these had a copy of the book *From Myth to Creation: Art from Amazonian Ecuador* opened to a page showing their earlier creations, to validate their status as master potters.

Among them was Esthela Dagua. Because of her urban residence in Puyo, she is removed from the everyday routine of indigenous life, but she nevertheless keeps track of activities (including festivals) through a stream of kith and kin to her home. They, as well as other indigenous cultural resources, past and present, provide inspiration for her continuing creative production of pottery for sale and for exhibit. After her ceramic portrayal of a series of master spirit beings — of salt, fire, and bamboo, among others — she created several Banco Central men, based on her memory of an Andean archaeological figurine she had seen during the museum excursion to Quito. Her little figurines, however, were rendered as lowland people carrying deer and other rain-forest game animals with tumplines. She then turned her attention to making several sets of figurines portraying shamanic practice. The sets include the shaman, his patient, the person who negotiates treatment for the patient, the shaman's special curing stones, and even the canoe used to transport the patient to the shaman. Every set is complete with the names of the shaman and the patient, and each of the stones is named.

Some of her more recent innovations are drawn from the imagery of indigenous architecture. She has produced her version of the Curaray chapel pictured in her copy of *From Myth to Creation* and a portrayal of a festival house from Sarayacu, where she grew up. Her most elaborate and beautiful construction to date is her Charapa Cocha *wasi,* Turtle Lagoon house (Plate 16), made after seeing a photograph of the traditional oval house with thatched roof and open sides built by the Achuar elders and founders (*uunt*) who live today in Charapa Cocha (Fig. 10.6). The geometric turtle designs she painted on her roof do suggest thatch, and they represent the seat of power of forest spirit-master Amasanga. She enclosed her house with walls decorated with the powerful anaconda-embedded-in-water-turtle motif, symbolic of the first shaman, Sungui (as anaconda), and his seat of power (Amazon water turtle). As she did with her Central Bank people, she appropriated a theme of another indigenous culture but embellished her creation aesthetically through the imagery of her own culture.

The arts of the Canelos Quichua demonstrate, we think, that reflexivity enters and reenters the creative process to incorporate and integrate imagery projected in multiple ways. As artistic representations by native peoples are introduced to and accepted by participants in the outside art worlds, the artists seek to explicate their sense of meaning, and their expli-

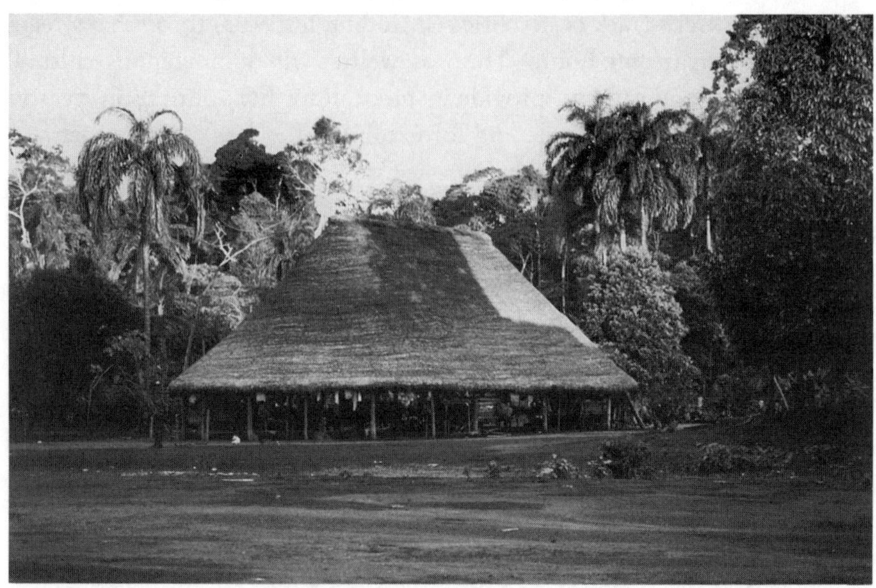

Figure 10.6. The house of an Achuar *uunt* (great man) at Charapa Cocha.

cation is capable of influencing the tastes of those strangers who come increasingly to their territory to learn about or to purchase something inherently beautiful and knowledgeably made.

Each New World art form represented in this book has a vitality and aesthetic force that forms a distinct affecting presence:

> The complete, total affecting presence is a web of tension — tension between form and formlessness, intension and extension, continuity and discontinuity, physical conformation (spatial or temporal) and emotion, media and metaphor, and the ordinary and the extraordinary. Further, it is a complex of metaphoric levels, all coming simultaneously to focus in the work — the universal metaphor, the cultural metaphoric base, the space/time metaphor, the objective metaphor, the formal metaphor, and the objective correlative. It is a wonder, but no surprise, that the affecting work may be described as a presence, an entity which though it is native to a time and place, is not the prisoner of either. At the same time, however, the affecting presence is as subject to misunderstand-

ing — or, indeed, understanding — out of its own culture as its creator himself [or herself] might be. (Armstrong 1971:196)

Native arts "speak," as the authors of these chapters demonstrate. The heritage of anonymous artists of ancient Mesoamerica and the Central Andes has left its messages. The contemporary voices of Carl Beam and Frieda Deesing, of Helen Cordero, of Alfonso Chango, Esthela Dagua, and Clara Santi, of Kasólu and Akóbo, and of Peter Minshall, among so many others, speak for a multitude of artists of the Americas who continue to create beauty amidst ceaseless and relentless change. Neither they nor their works are "prisoners" to time, place, or encounters with the art worlds of others. Their interactions *on their own terms* with representatives of these art worlds suggest that their creativity may be enhanced by reexamining tradition against a backdrop of change, to produce aesthetic expressions that transcend time, space, and cultural barriers.

ACKNOWLEDGMENTS

We greatly appreciate the help given us over many years by all of the indigenous people who have been named in various publications, and countless others who have not been so named. For their collaboration and colleagueship in specific projects from 1986 to the present, we must thank Clara Santi Simbaña (Quillara), Abraham Chango (Paushi), Faviola Vargas Aranda, Marcelo Santi Simbaña, Alfonso Chango, Luzmila Salazar, Segundo Vargas, Balvina Santi, Apacha Vargas, Esthela Dagua, Rebeca Hualinga, and Amadora Aranda. Everything "ethnoaesthetic" in this and other recent works is a consequence of their indefatigable efforts to inform a Western world of the values and beauty inherent in their lifeways and thought processes.

In Puyo a group of dedicated educators has been most supportive of recent indigenous endeavors to conjoin the ethnoaesthetics of Canelos Quichua traditions with the art worlds emerging in Upper Amazonia and the adjacent Andes. Here we must single out Absalón Guevara, César Abad, Carlos Duche, Jenny Liscano, and Esthela Vallejo for special mention, and from the standpoint of our studies, for special thanks.

Funds contributing directly and indirectly to this study were allocated by the University of Illinois at Urbana-Champaign through the Research Board, College of Liberal Arts and Sciences, and the Center for Latin American and Caribbean Studies, and by the Museos del Banco Central and the Municipal Council of Pastaza Province in Ecuador. Three grants by the Wenner-Gren Foundation for Anthropological Research (numbers 3287, 4405, and 5232) supported research on ceramic symbolism and indigenous reflexivity and interpretation.

We thank Dee Robbins for coordinating activities between the University of Illinois and our work in Quito and Puyo from the fall of 1986 through the summer of 1992. We are grateful to the Director of the Museos del Banco Central from 1986 to 1988, María del Carmen Molestina (now Director of International Studies at the Universidad San Francisco de Quito) for sustained collegiality, technical help, and unflagging encouragement. Her successor as Director of the Museos del Banco Central, Rodrigo Pallares Zaldumbide, has facilitated our work in many ways.

NOTES

1. We use the terms *pottery* and *ceramics* interchangeably. In the southwestern United States *pottery* or *potteries* denotes traditional hand-made ware, and *ceramics* means commercial ware painted by indigenous or nonindigenous people. Canelos Quichua pottery, made exclusively by women, is hand coiled and hand painted (with all paints and slips being made from natural rocks and clays), and fired without a kiln. Indeed, there are great similarities between the "potteries" of the Southwest and Canelos Quichua pottery, or ceramics. We use *ceramics* in the South American sense as a cognate for *alfarería* (pottery) and *cerámica* (fine pottery). For cognate Upper Amazonian pottery, see Gebhart-Sayer 1984. For an ethnoarchaeological approach to Achuar Jivaroan pottery, see Zeidler 1983.

2. For a fascinating discussion of magical gardening stones, see Brown and Van Bolt 1980. Information about the significance of stones in shamanism and cosmology is given in N. Whitten 1976 and 1985.

3. In a letter written in 1857, Richard Spruce noted that the woven "cushmas" of the "Jibaros" of the Upper Pastaza were stronger than the stoutest unbleached cotton he had seen in England and that another species planted on the banks of the Bombonasa (Bobonaza) near Pacayacu yielded as strong a cotton fiber as he had ever seen anywhere in the world (Schultes 1978:135). The stylized woven patterns of what Spruce called the "Jibaro" were characteristic of Zaparoan and

Canelos Quichua of this area, as well as, perhaps, Jivaroans there. The patterns, together with the techniques used to spin, dye, and weave them, are described ethnographically in Karsten 1935:104–6.

4. For parallels between female master potters and male shamans, see Gebhart-Sayer 1984, N. Whitten 1985, and D. Whitten and N. Whitten 1988. For more information about the relation of shamanism and art, see Flaherty 1992; Furst 1977; Guss 1989; Reichel-Dolmatoff 1971, 1987, 1988; Serov 1988; and Wilbert 1975. For more information about shamanism in South America, see Campbell 1989, Crocker 1985, and Wilbert 1987.

5. Richard Spruce (1817–1893), a Yorkshireman, made extensive botanical studies and collections throughout Amazonia. In 1857, while residing in Tarapoto in eastern Peru, he received a request from Her Majesty's Secretary of State for India to "proceed" to Ecuador to procure seeds and plants of the Red Bark Tree, the source of quinine. He traveled northward via the Pastaza and Bobonaza rivers and then trekked through the heart of Canelos Quichua territory. Stopped by swollen rivers at the tributary called Puyu, or Puyo, Spruce found himself in the mossiest place he had ever seen. "Even the topmost twigs and the very leaves were shaggy with mosses," he wrote, "and from the branches overhanging the river were suspended festoons of several feet in length composed chiefly of *Bryopteris* and *Phyllogonium fulgens* in beautiful fruit." His studies here, on the edge of what is now the Comuna San Jacinto del Pindo, contributed greatly to his noted six-hundred-page *Hepaticae Amazonicae et Andinae* (Spruce 1908, 2:140).

6. Charles W. Smith notes that "auctions tend to be used extensively and primarily with highly perishable goods, used goods, goods of questionable origin, and goods seen to possess certain artistic merit. . . . There is a relatively high degree of value ambiguity because the goods can't be related easily to a standard market or a standard accepted formula for evaluation" (Smith 1989:164). For specifically ethnographic auctions, see Benthall 1987:9–13.

7. These relationships and the processes of commoditization that define them are elaborated in a paper prepared for a 1989 symposium at the University of Iowa on "Redefining the Artisan in Traditional and Modern Societies" (D. Whitten and N. Whitten 1992). For examinations of the controversies surrounding the imagery and commercialization of Southwestern native arts, see Babcock, in press, and Wade 1986. The impact of factionalism on the design and sale of Hopi Third Mesa pottery is discussed in Wycoff 1990.

8. See especially Flornoy 1953, Zikmund and Hanzelka 1963, and Harner 1972; for balance, see Taylor 1981, Brown 1985, and Descola 1986.

9. Since 1968 we have collected a great deal of mythology using traditional ethnographic methods, including audio tape recording, in indigenous hamlets and

dispersed settlements. In 1986–87, however, we were specifically working in urban Puyo, with great interest in the ways by which indigenous people reflected on and discussed cultural consciousness and continuity. To further our understanding and provide native people with immediate visions of their own presentations, we developed a modest studio complete with VHS camcorder, VHS VCR, Beta VCR, and two color monitors. This "studio" work continued in urban Puyo during the summers of 1988, 1989, and 1990.

10. While we had become very close to most of the native people working with us in our studio setup in Puyo, we had never known the Hualinga family well, and we visited their residence only occasionally, because of the high degree of commoditization manifest there. We did not want to appear overly interested in an urban endeavor to produce fine artwork for the ethnic-art market for profit. However, through the overlapping networks of people who had worked with us for years, we were drawn into the lively discussions of myth and its relationship to ceramic design and form in the Hualinga household.

11. See D. Whitten and N. Whitten 1985.

12. Conflict between the "great men" (*uunt*) of Capahuari had been growing for many years and had ramified to include shamans and assassins up and down that river system. In 1978 one great man with a few kin and affines explored the hunting and fishing territory of Charapa Cocha, noting the richness of the gardening, fishing, and hunting habitats that had long been a buffer zone between Achuar territories on either side of the Pastaza River. Several mystical and real dimensions of life there could pose serious problems to congenial cohabitation of the migrating people. Nonetheless, in 1980 members of the extended kindred radiating from two cooperating great men were ready to confront what they must to escape the escalating conflict at Capahuari. They founded the territory of Charapa Cocha. As they began to clear land for swidden gardens, they found not only thousands of sherds but also entire urns and drinking bowls associated with "other pasts, other people."

13. *Uunt* in Achuar refers to "great man." This status entitles — indeed it obliges — the *uunt* to process publicly the mystical and allusive imagery of the shaman and also to reflect publicly on the workings of the powerful assassins, because these affect life in his territory. Unlike the shaman and the assassin, who work in relative secrecy with powers outside of the territory and whose existence in an Achuar territory is usually initially denied, the knowledgeable one is supposed to be prominent and to represent Achuar images of the self and the other internally to the growing settlement and externally to increasing numbers of visitors.

The collaborating great men at Charapa Cocha immediately petitioned the Protestant missionaries to convert members of their settlements to Christianity and, among other things, to build an airstrip and bring them cattle. Working with the evangelical Protestants, members of the Ministry of Education quickly provided bilingual (Achuar-Spanish) schoolteachers, and within three years one of the most traditional groupings of Achuar had one of the most modern infrastructures.

During the early years of settlement, large urns began to turn up, which, in shamanic seances, most Achuar interpreted as being from (in) the realm of Tsunki, master spirit of the water, all-powerful one, outsider, and first shaman. Later dreams of the Charapa runa, Amazon Turtle person, were told from one Achuar to another, and a body of lore about a fearsome Turtle person linked to the area and to the Canelos Quichua developed. The principal Charapa runa motif is that of the spiral design, yet to be explained by indigenous people. We are currently studying this phenomenon. Norman Whitten has now visited Charapa Cocha on two occasions and has photographed a number of archaeological sites there, as well as the urns, figurines, drinking bowls, and other manifestations of what looks like a tremendous series of occupation sites.

14. The Achuar, however, do tell this segment of the same myth; see, e.g., Descola 1986:104). For more information on the Common Potoo (*Nyctibus griseus*) see Skutch 1970.

15. For centuries the Catholic church has endeavored to dominate the Canelos Quichua people (e.g., Reeve 1985, 1988). Its primary technique, the nucleation (*reducción*) of dispersed populations, was tangibly signaled by its constructing a crude chapel, hanging an iron bell at the entrance to the chapel, and establishing a shrine to a patron saint. Church officials, who lived far from the indigenous hamlet, made occasional visits to designate indigenous authorities for the hamlet and the surrounding territory. Such designates were given a staff of authority, *vara*, and were known in Quichua as *varayuj* Runa, people who possessed the staff. The church also required one or two indigenous festivals to be held each year on the plaza of the hamlet and selected a *prioste*, a steward of a brotherhood or confraternity, to be responsible for the next year's festival. The Canelos called this person *chayuj* Runa, host. The hosts were chosen by a visiting friar at the end of one year's ceremony, and they were required to consult with the friar or curate during the year to determine the exact date for the next festival.

16. The transcendence of music in other Amazonian cultures is analyzed in Basso 1985, Hill 1985, and Seeger 1987.

REFERENCES CITED

Alexander, Michael, ed.
  1976   *Discovering the New World: Based on the Works of Theodore de Bry.* London: London Editions.

Anthropology Today
1989 News: Auction Houses. 5 (5): 26.

Armstrong, Robert Plant
1971 *The Affecting Presence: An Essay in Humanistic Anthropology.* Urbana: University of Illinois Press.

Babcock, Barbara A.
in press Mudwomen and Whiteman: A Meditation on Pueblo Potteries and the Politics of Representation. In *The Material Culture of Gender / The Gender of Material Culture*, edited by Kenneth Ames and Katharine Martinez. New York: W. W. Norton and Company.

Basso, Ellen B.
1985 *A Musical View of the Universe.* Philadelphia: University of Pennsylvania Press.

Benthall, Jonathan
1987 Ethnographic Museums and the Art Trade. *Anthropology Today* 3 (3): 9–13.

Brochado, José P.
1984 An Ecological Model of the Spread of Pottery and Agriculture into Eastern South America. Ph.D. diss., Department of Anthropology, University of Illinois at Urbana-Champaign. Ann Arbor: University Microfilms.

Brown, Michael F.
1985 *Tsewa's Gift: Magic and Meaning in an Amazonian Society.* Washington, D.C.: Smithsonian Institution Press.

Brown, Michael F., and Margaret L. Van Bolt
1980 Aguaruna Jívaro Gardening Magic in the Alto Río Mayo, Peru. *Ethnology* 19:169–90.

Campbell, Alan Tormaid
1989 *To Square with Genesis: Causal Statements and Shamanic Ideas in Wayïbi.* Iowa City: University of Iowa Press.

Carvajal, Gaspar de
1934 *The Discovery of the Amazon, According to the Account of Friar Gaspar de Carvajal and Other Documents.* Compiled by José Toribio
[ca. Medina. Edited by H. C. Heaton. Special Publication 17. New York:
1541] American Geographic Society.

Chango Santi, Alfonso
1984 *Yachaj Sami Yachachina.* Quito: Abya-Yala.

1989   *Jatun Tandarishca Causaj Runa.* Oaxaca, Mex.: Centro Editorial en Lenguas Indígenas Latinoamericano (CELIL).

Crocker, Jon Christopher

1985   *Vital Souls: Bororo Cosmology, Natural Symbolism, and Shamanism.* Tucson: University of Arizona Press.

Descola, Philippe

1986   *La Nature domestique: Symbolisme et praxis dans l' écologie des Achuar.* Paris: Editions de la Maison des Sciences de l'Homme

Ferguson, R. Brian

1990   Blood of the Leviathan: Western Contact and Warfare in Amazonia. *American Ethnologist* 17:237–57.

Flaherty, Gloria

1992   *Shamanism and the Eighteenth Century.* Princeton, N.J.: Princeton University Press.

Flornoy, Bertrand

1953   *Jivaro: Among the Headshrinkers of the Amazon.* London: Elek.

Furst, Peter T.

1977   The Roots and Continuities of Shamanism. In *Stones, Bones and Skin,* edited by Anne Trueblood Brodzky, Rose Danesewich, and Nick Johnson, 1–28. Toronto: Society for Art Publication.

Galarza Zavala, Jaime

1972   *El Festín del Petroleo.* 2d ed. Quito: "Cicetronica Cía Ltda." de Papelería Moderna.

Gebhart-Sayer, Angelika

1984   *The Cosmos Encoiled: Indian Art of the Peruvian Amazon.* New York: Center for Inter-American Relations.

Guss, David M.

1989   *To Weave and Sing: Art, Symbol, and Narrative in the South American Rain Forest.* Berkeley: University of California Press.

Harner, Michael J.

1972   *The Jívaro: People of the Sacred Waterfalls.* Garden City, N.J.: Natural History Press.

Hill, Jonathan

1985   Myth, Spirit-Naming, and the Art of Microtonal Rising: Childbirth Rituals of the Arawakan Wakuénai of Venezuela. *Latin American Music Review* 6 (1): 1–30.

Karsten, Rafael

1935   *The Head-Hunters of Western Amazonas: The Life and Culture of the Jibaro Indians of Eastern Ecuador and Peru.* Helsinki: Societas Scientiarum Fennica, Commentationes Humanarum Litterarum, vol. 2, no. 1.

Kelley, Patricia, and Carolyn Orr

1976   *Sarayacu Quichua Pottery.* SIL Museum of Anthropology, Publication 1. Dallas: Summer Institute of Linguistics.

Lathrap, Donald W.

1970   *The Upper Amazon.* New York: Praeger.

Lathrap, Donald W., and José R. Oliver

1987   Agüerito: El Complejo polícromo más antiguo de América en la confluencia del Apuré y el Orinoco (Venezuela). *Interciencia* 12:274–89.

Léry, Jean de

1990   *History of a Voyage to the Land of Brazil, Otherwise Called America.*
[1580]   Translated by Janet Whatley. Berkeley: University of California Press.

Lévi-Strauss, Claude

1988   *The Jealous Potter.* Translated by Bénédicte Chorier. Chicago: University of Chicago Press.

Métraux, Alfred

1927   Migrations Historiques des Tupi-Guaraní. *Journal de la Société des Américanistes* 19:1–45.

1948   The Tupinambá. In *Handbook of South American Indians*, vol. 3: *The Tropical Forest Tribes*, edited by Julian H. Steward, 95–133. Smithsonian Institution, Bureau of American Ethnology, Bulletin 143. Washington, D.C.

Parke-Bernet Galleries

1970   *Ethnographical Art: North and South America, Oceania.* New York.

Rasnake, Roger

1988   *Domination and Cultural Resistance: Authority and Power Among an Andean People.* Durham, N.C.: Duke University Press.

Reeve, Mary-Elizabeth

1985   Identity as Process: The Meaning of "Runapura" for Quichua Speakers of the Curaray River, Eastern Ecuador. Ph.D. diss., Department of Anthropology, University of Illinois at Urbana-Champaign. Ann Arbor: University Microfilms.

1988   *Cauchu Uras*: Lowland Quichua Histories of the Amazon Rubber Boom. In *Rethinking History and Myth: Indigenous South American*

Perspectives on the Past, edited by Jonathan D. Hill, 19–34. Urbana: University of Illinois Press.

Reichel-Dolmatoff, Gerardo

1971   *Amazonian Cosmos: The Sexual and Religious Symbolism of the Tukano Indians.* Chicago: University of Chicago Press.

1987   *Shamanism and Art of the Eastern Tukanoan Indians.* Iconography of Religions. Institute of Religious Iconography, State University Gronigen, Section IX, South America. Leiden: E. J. Brill.

1988   *Goldwork and Shamanism.* Medellín, Colombia: Editorial Colina.

Roosevelt, Anna C.

1989a   Lost Civilizations of the Lower Amazon. *Natural History*, February, 74–83.

1989b   Resource Management in Amazonia Before the Conquest: Beyond Ethnographic Projection. In *Resource Management in Amazonina: Indigenous and Folk Strategies*, edited by Daryl A. Posey and W. Balée, 30–62. Advances in Economic Botany, vol. 7. New York: New York Botanical Gardens.

1991   *Moundbuilders of the Amazon: Geophysical Archaeology on Marajó Island, Brazil.* New York: Academic Press.

in press a   Methodological Problems in Amazonian Research. In *Amazonia: A Dynamic Habitat — Past, Present, and Future*, edited by Anna C. Roosevelt and Archibald O. Haller. Washington, D.C.: AAAS Press.

in press b   Twelve Thousand Years of Indigenous Occupation in Amazonia. In *Amazonia: A Dynamic Habitat — Past, Present, and Future*, edited by Anna C. Roosevelt and Archibald O. Haller. Washington, D.C.: AAAS Press.

Rowe, John Howeland

1946   Inca Culture at the Time of the Spanish Conquest. In *Handbook of South American Indians*, vol. 2: *The Andean Civilizations*, edited by Julian H. Steward, 183–330. Smithsonian Institution, Bureau of American Ethnology, Bulletin 143. Washington, D.C.

Schultes, Richard E.

1978   Richard Spruce and the Potential for European Settlement of the Amazon: An Unpublished Letter. *Botanical Journal of the Linnean Society* 77:131–39.

Scott, Raymond J.

1988   A View from the Tropical Rain Forest. In *Peruvian Prehistory*, edited by Richard W. Keatinge, 279–300. New York: Cambridge University Press.

Seeger, Anthony
 1987   *Why Suyá Sing: A Musical Anthropology of an Amazonian People.*
         Cambridge: Cambridge University Press.

Serov, Serguei Ia.
 1988   Guardians and Spirit-Masters of Siberia. In *Crossroads of Continents:
         Cultures of Siberia and Alaska,* edited by William W. Fitzhugh and
         Aron Crowell, 241–55. Washington: Smithsonian Institution Press.

Shapiro, Judith
 1987   From Tupí to the Land Without Evil: The Christianization of the Tupí-
         Guaraní Cosmology. *American Ethnologist* 14:126–39.

Skutch, Alexander F.
 1970   Life History of the Common Potoo. *The Living Bird* 9:265–80.

Smith, Charles W.
 1989   *Auctions: The Social Construction of Value.* New York: Free Press.

Spruce, Richard
 1908   *Notes of a Botanist on the Amazon and Andes.* Edited by Alfred Russel
         Wallace. London: Macmillan and Company.

Stade [Staden], Hans
 1847   *The Captivity of Hans Stade of Hesse, in A.D. 1547–1555, Among the*
 [1557] *Wild Tribes of Eastern Brazil.* Translated by Albert Tootal, Esq. London:
         Hakluyt Society.

Staden, Juan [Hans]
 1944   *Vera historia y descripción de un pais de las salvages desnudas feroces*
 [1557] *gentes devoradoras de hombre situado en el nuevo mundo América.*
         Edited and translated by Edmundo Wernicke. Biblioteca de Fuentes, vol.
         1. Buenos Aires: Universidad de Buenos Aires, Museo Etnográfico.

Sullivan, Lawrence E.
 1988   *Icanchu's Drum: An Orientation to Meaning in South American Reli-*
         gions. New York: MacMillan.

Taylor, Anne-Christine
 1981   God-Wealth: The Achuar and the Missions. In *Cultural Transforma-*
         tions and Ethnicity in Modern Ecuador, edited by Norman E. Whitten,
         Jr., 647–76. Urbana: University of Illinois Press.

Wade, Edwin L.
 1986   Straddling the Cultural Fence: The Conflict for Ethnic Artists Within
         Pueblo Societies. In *The Arts of the North American Indian: Native
         Traditions in Evolution,* edited by Edwin L. Wade, 243–54. New York:

Hudson Hills Press in association with the Philbrook Center, Tulsa, Okla.

Whitten, Dorothea S.

1981   Ancient Tradition in a Contemporary Context: Canelos Quichua Ceramics and Symbolism. In *Cultural Transformations and Ethnicity in Modern Ecuador,* edited by Norman E. Whitten, Jr., 749–75. Urbana: University of Illinois Press.

Whitten, Dorothea S., and Norman E. Whitten, Jr.

1978   Ceramics of the Canelos Quichua. *Natural History,* October, pp. 90–99, 152.

1985   *Our Knowledge, Our Beauty: Expressive Culture of the Canelos Quichua of Ecuador.* Urbana: Film Center of the University of Illinois at Urbana-Champaign. Videotape.

1988   *From Myth to Creation: Art from Amazonian Ecuador.* Urbana: University of Illinois Press.

1989   Potters of the Upper Amazon. *Ceramics Monthly,* December, pp. 53–56.

1992   Development and the Competitive Edge: Canelos Quichua Arts and Artisans in a Modern World. In *Redefining the Artisan in Traditional and Modern Societies,* edited by Karen Chappell, Paul Greenough, and Douglas Midgett. Iowa City: University of Iowa Press.

Whitten, Norman E., Jr.

1985   *Sicuanga Runa: The Other Side of Development in Amazonian Ecuador.* Urbana: University of Illinois Press.

1988   Commentary: Historical and Mythic Evocations of Chthonic Power in South America. In *Rethinking History and Myth: Indigenous South American Perspectives on the Past,* edited by Jonathan D. Hill, 282–329. Urbana: University of Illinois Press.

Whitten, Norman E., Jr., with the assistance of Marcelo Naranjo, Marcelo Santi Simbaña, and Dorothea S. Whitten

1976   *Sacha Runa: Ethnicity and Adaptation of Ecuadorian Jungle Quichua.* Urbana: University of Illinois Press.

Whitten, Norman E., Jr., and Dorothea S. Whitten

1987   Una Presencia dinámica indígena en la vida moderna de Pastaza. In *Pastaza: Un Municipio al Servicio del Pueblo; Informe de Labores, 1984–1987,* 22–25. Puyo, Ecuador: Revista Municipal.

Wilbert, Johannes

1975   *Warao Basketry: Form and Function.* University of California, Museum of Cultural History, Occasional Papers, no. 3. Los Angeles.

1987   *Tobacco and Shamanism in South America.* New Haven, Conn.: Yale
        University Press.

Wycoff, Lydia L.

1990   *Designs and Factions: Politics, Religion and Ceramics on the Hopi Third
        Mesa.* Albuquerque: University of New Mexico Press.

Zeidler, James A.

1983   *La etnoarqueología de una vivienda achuar y sus implicaciones arque-
        ológicas.* Miscelánea Antropológica Ecuatoriana, no. 3, 155–93.

Zikmund, Miroslav, and Jirí Hanzelka

1963   *Amazon Headhunters.* Translated by Olga Kuthanová. Prague: Artia.

ABOUT THE CONTRIBUTORS

BARBARA A. BABCOCK   is Professor of English and Comparative Cultural and Literary Values at the University of Arizona. She has been working on subjects pertaining to pottery of the Southwest since 1978. Among her many publications are the books *The Reversible World* and (with Guy and Doris Monthan) *The Pueblo Storyteller: Development of a Figurative Ceramic Tradition.*

SUSAN D. GILLESPIE,   an archaeologist and ethnohistorian, specializes in Middle American cosmology and iconography. A Research Associate in the Department of Anthropology at the University of Illinois, Urbana-Champaign, she has published the prizewinning book *The Aztec Kings* and is working on a second, related book.

NELSON H. H. GRABURN's   many books include his edited volume *Ethnic and Tourist Arts* and, with Molly Lee, *Alaska Commercial Company: Commerce and Curios, 1868–1904,* a companion book for an exhibition that he curated. He is Professor of Anthropology and Curator of North American Ethnology of the Lowie Museum at the University of California, Berkeley.

JOHN W. NUNLEY is Curator of Arts of Africa, Oceania, and the Americas at the St. Louis Art Museum. He is the author of *Moving with the Face of the Devil: Art and Politics in Urban West Africa* and, with Judith Bettelheim, *Caribbean Festival Arts: Each and Every Bit of Difference*. The latter was written in association with an exhibition of the same name.

RICHARD PRICE'S numerous publications about the Saramaka of Suriname include the recent prizewinning books *First Time: The Historical Vision of an Afro-American People* and *Alabi's World*. His books written with Sally Price include *Stedman's Suriname* and *Equatoria*. Sally Price and he live in Martinique.

SALLY PRICE is the author of the prizewinning book *Co-Wives and Calabashes* and of *Primitive Art in Civilized Places*. Richard Price and she mounted the exhibition *Afro-American Arts of the Suriname Rain Forest*, and they wrote the accompanying book of the same title and the recent *Two Evenings in Saramaka*.

HELAINE SILVERMAN is Assistant Professor of Anthropology at the University of Illinois, Urbana-Champaign. She is the author of the forthcoming book *Cahuachi in the Ancient Nasca World*, based on her archaeological field research and analyses of ancient cultural materials from the south coast of Peru.

J. EDSON WAY has served as Director of the Logan Museum, Beloit College, and the Wheelwright Museum of the American Indian, Santa Fe. He is currently Executive Director of the Space Center at Alamogordo, New Mexico. He has mounted many exhibitions of Native American art, culture, and aesthetics.

DOROTHEA S. WHITTEN, a sociologist, is Research Associate in the Center for Latin American and Caribbean Studies, University of Illinois, Urbana-Champaign. Recent exhibitions and related books about Canelos Quichua art by Norman E. Whitten, Jr., and her include *¡Causaunchimi!* [We are living!] and *From Myth to Creation: Art from Amazonian Ecuador*.

ABOUT THE CONTRIBUTORS

NORMAN E. WHITTEN, JR., Professor of Anthropology and Latin American Studies at the University of Illinois, Urbana-Champaign, has published *Sicuanga Runa: The Other Side of Development in Amazonian Ecuador, Cultural Transformations and Ethnicity in Modern Ecuador,* and many other works based on long-term ethnography in Ecuador.

INDEX

References to figures are in italics. References to plates are preceded by
"pl." or "pls."